W9-CMF-412

THE LOEB CLASSICAL LIBRARY

FOUNDED BY JAMES LOEB

CICERO

I

LCL 403

[CICERO]

RHETORICA AD HERENNIUM

WITH AN ENGLISH TRANSLATION BY

HARRY CAPLAN

HARVARD UNIVERSITY PRESS
CAMBRIDGE, MASSACHUSETTS
LONDON, ENGLAND

First published 1954
Reprinted 1964, 1968, 1977, 1981, 1989, 1999

LOEB CLASSICAL LIBRARY® is a registered trademark
of the President and Fellows of Harvard College

ISBN 0-674-99444-2

Printed in Great Britain by St Edmundsbury Press Ltd,
Bury St Edmunds, Suffolk, on acid-free paper.
Bound by Hunter & Foulis Ltd, Edinburgh, Scotland.

CONTENTS

INTRODUCTION

The Greek art of rhetoric was first naturalized at Rome in the time of the younger Scipio, and Latin treatises on the subject were in circulation from the time of the Gracchi. But the books by Cato, Antonius, and the other Roman writers have not come down to us, and it is from the second decade of the first century B.C. that we have, in the treatise addressed to Gaius Herennius, the oldest Latin Art preserved entire. Like Cicero's incomplete *De Inventione*, which belongs close to it in time, this work reflects Hellenistic rhetorical teaching. Our author, however, gives us a Greek art in Latin dress, combining a Roman spirit with Greek doctrine. It is a technical manual, systematic and formal in arrangement; its exposition is bald, but in greatest part clear and precise. Indeed the writer's specific aims are to achieve clarity and conciseness, and to complete the exposition of his subject with reasonable speed. He seeks clarity through the use of Roman terms, and of specially selected examples; he seeks conciseness by keeping practical needs always in view, by scrupulously avoiding irrelevant matter, and by presenting methods and principles, not a host of particular illustrations of a given point.[a]

The fact that the treatise appeared, from Jerome's

---

[a] See Schanz, ed. 1909, p. 466.

time on, as a work by Cicero [a] gave it a prestige which it enjoyed for over a thousand years. Because of its position in the MSS. following *De Inventione* it was in the twelfth century called *Rhetorica Secunda*; perhaps because of a belief that Cicero wrote the treatise to replace his juvenile *De Inventione*, it was later called *Rhetorica Nova*.[b] But Cicero never refers to any work of his which might be identified with our treatise; the disparaging reference in *De Oratore* 1. 2. 5 to those " crude and incomplete " essays of his youth is obviously to the two books *De Inventione*. The picture we draw of our author does not fit the early Cicero, and his doctrines in many crucial instances, as will be seen later, are in sharp contrast with those of *De Inventione*. Furthermore, the thought and style of the work are unworthy of the mature Cicero. Finally Quintilian [c] (who often cites *De Inventione*),[d]

[a] The uncritical editor who, before Jerome's time, made this ascription may also have been responsible for the division of the work into six books. He may have thought the un-titled work Cicero's because of its resemblance to *De Inventione*, and may have interpreted the *inchoata ac rudia* of *De Oratore* 1. 2. 5 as referring to two distinct works. An interesting interpolation, based on the belief in Ciceronian authorship, appears in the MSS. at 1. xii. 20: [*Tullius*] *heres meus* [*Terentiae*] *uxori meae*.

[b] For like parallel designations of literary works in the Middle Ages, see E. R. Curtius, *Europäische Literatur und lateinisches Mittelalter*, Bern, 1948, p. 161.

[c] It is argued, for example, that if Quintilian at 4. 5. 3, where he considers the view that the propositions in a Partition should not exceed three (cf. the like principle for the Enumeration in our treatise, 1. x. 17), or at 3. 6. 45, where he deals with the three Types of Issue (cf. our treatise, 1. x. 18), had known that these were identical with, or akin to, Ciceronian notions, he would not have kept silent on the point.

[d] Usually under the title *Libri Rhetorici*.

INTRODUCTION

and similarly Gellius,[a] Marius Victorinus, Servius, and Cassiodorus show no acquaintance with any Ciceronian work of this nature. Although the belief in Ciceronian authorship has still not entirely disappeared, all the recent editors agree that the attribution is erroneous.

The first to doubt that the treatise was worthy of Ciceronian authorship was Lorenzo Valla (middle *saec.* xv). Then Raphael Regius in 1491 positively divorced the work from Cicero's name. The question of authorship has occupied the attention of scholars at intervals ever since, but has never been settled to the satisfaction of all. It is wisest, I believe, to ascribe the work to an unknown author, although a good many reputable scholars have made out a case, at first glance attractive, for assigning it to a rhetorician named Cornificius.[b] These rely on citations in Quintilian which correspond with passages in Book 4 of our treatise. Cornificius is mentioned, and always with disapproval, in the following places:

In 5. 10. 2 Quintilian, discussing *arguments*, criticizes Cornificius for calling a Conclusion from Incompatibles *contrarium* ; *contrarium* appears in our treatise as a *figure* (of diction).

In 9. 2. 27 Quintilian tells us that *oratio libera*— which he would allow to be called a figure only if it is

---

[a] Gellius, 13. 6. 4, says that he has been unable to discover whether the term *barbarismus* was used before the Augustan age; *cf.* our treatise, 4. xii. 17.

[b] The first to ascribe the work with assurance to Cornificius was Petrus Victorius in 1582; Regius had vacillated, assigning it variously to Cornificius, Verginius Flavus, and Timolaüs. Recent scholars who have upheld the theory of Cornifician authorship are Johannes Tolkiehn, *Jahresb. des philol. Vereins zu Berlin* 45 (1919). 73, and Wilhelm Kroll, *Glotta* 22 (1934). 24, and *Philologus* 89 (1934). 63.

simulated and artfully designed—is by Cornificius called *licentia*; *licentia* is the term used by our author (4. xxxvi. 48) for a figure which, in one form, fulfils Quintilian's requirements.

In 9. 3. 69–71 Quintilian, dealing with *adnominatio*, gives three examples of flat punning to be avoided, not imitated; Cornificius, he says, calls this word-play *traductio*. Two of these examples are used by our author, one to illustrate *traductio* (4. xiv. 21), but the other to illustrate *adnominatio* (4. xxi. 29). To meet this real difficulty, the advocates of Cornician authorship maintain that *adnominatio* and *traductio* are brought together by Quintilian because they are indeed kindred figures, but these scholars are forced also to blame Quintilian for casual excerpting at this point, or for drawing upon his memory—a charge hard to prove against so careful a workman.

In 9. 3. 91 Quintilian criticizes Cornificius and Rutilius for regarding *finitio*, which is no figure at all, as a figure of diction; *definitio*, somewhat differently characterized, appears as a figure of diction in our treatise (4. xxv. 35).

In 9. 3. 98 Quintilian tells us that Cornificius lists ten figures of diction of which the first five must be regarded as figures of thought: *interrogatio* (cf. 4. xv. 22), *ratiocinatio* (4. xvi. 23), *subiectio* (4. xxiii. 33), *transitio* (4. xxvi. 35), *occultatio* (4. xxvii. 37), and the other five as not figures at all: *sententia* (4. xvii. 24), *membrum* (4. xix. 26), *articuli* (*articulus* = 4. xix. 26), *interpretatio* (4. xxviii. 38), *conclusio* (4. xxx. 41).[a] These all appear in our treatise, in the places indicated in parentheses.

---

[a] Georg Thiele, *Gött. gel. Anz.*, 1892 (2). 725 ff., compares the order of the figures in this passage with that which they

x

INTRODUCTION

Quintilian mentions Cornificius in two other places. In 3. 1. 21, sketching the history of writers on rhetoric, he says: " Cornificius wrote a great deal (*non pauca*) on the same subject (rhetoric), Stertinius something, and the elder Gallio [a] a little. But the predecessors of Gallio, Celsus and Laenas,[b] and in our own day Verginius,[c] Pliny,[d] and Tutilius wrote with greater care. And even today there are distinguished authors. . . ." To this passage may be joined 9. 3. 89, where Cornificius appears in a list of authors who devoted whole books (*non partem operis . . . sed proprie libros*) to the discussion of figures: " Caecilius, Dionysius,[e] Rutilius,[f] Cornificius, Visellius, and a number of others, although there are living authors whose glory will match theirs." [g]

---

follow in our treatise, and sees in the comparison an argument for Cornifician authorship; Curtius Koehler, *De Rhetoricis ad Herennium*, Berlin, 1909, pp. 8 ff., presents the refutation.

[a] Long survived the elder Seneca, who died *c.* A.D. 39.

[b] Both A. Cornelius Celsus and Popilius Laenas fl. under Tiberius.

[c] Verginius Flavus fl. under Nero.

[d] The Elder (A.D. 23/4–79).

[e] Both Caecilius and Dionysius fl. under Augustus.

[f] P. Rutilius Lupus fl. in the late Augustan period.

[g] In five other places Quintilian gives examples which, with greater or less completeness, appear also in our treatise : 9. 3. 31 (*complexio*, 4. xiv. 20); 9. 3. 56 (*gradatio*, 4. xxv. 34); two examples in 9. 3. 72 (*adnominatio*, 4. xxii. 30 and 4.xxi. 29), the wording of one differing slightly, that of the other a great deal, from that in our treatise; 9. 3. 85 (ἀντιμεταβολή = *commutatio*, 4. xxviii. 39); 9. 3. 88 (*dubitatio*, 4. xxix. 40). None of these examples is assigned by Quintilian to Cornificius or to any other author; whether they appeared in Cornificius' book and were from there borrowed by Quintilian we cannot know. Some or all of these examples may have been common to a number of manuals. The well-known remark attributed to Socrates (" I do not live to eat, but eat to live "), which

INTRODUCTION

An examination of these passages, especially in their context, leads us to several conclusions. First, Cornificius lived after the time of Cicero and near (but before) Quintilian's own day. In 3. 1. 8 ff. Quintilian is obviously preserving a chronological order: Cornificius appears after Cicero (rather than immediately after Antonius) and before the writers *aetatis nostrae*. Again, in 9. 3. 91 and 9. 3. 98–9 Cornificius, Caecilius, and Rutilius are mentioned following discussions of Cicero. Finally, in 9. 3. 89 Cornificius is listed with writers of the Augustan age, and we assume that he was contemporary with them or flourished soon after them.[a] It would seem preposterous to place a writer of Marian times in this group.

We further conclude that Cornificius was the author of a special book on figures,[b] and that this is

---

Quintilian uses as an example in 9. 3. 85, he may have found in a Greek source.

[a] The efforts that have been made to identify Cornificius with any one of that name who lived at this time have come to nought. Nor have the many scholars who have ascribed our treatise to a Cornificius, and so sought to identify him with an earlier bearer of that name, agreed in their identification. C. L. Kayser's choice, the Q. Cornificius who with Cicero was candidate for the consulship in 64 B.C. was favoured for a time.

[b] It is likely that this work did not contain a section on tropes. Quintilian (8. 6. 1 ff.) never cites Cornificius on this subject, nor refers to any of the several resemblances, in rules and examples, that exist between his treatment and our author's. In large part, however, his treatment differs from our author's. If Cornificius had discussed tropes, it is perhaps safe to assume that passages from his book would have been excerpted by Quintilian. Again, in 9. 1. 2 Quintilian mentions Proculus as among the writers who call tropes "figures"; our author, too, attaches the tropes to the
xii

the source from which Quintilian makes his citations in Book 9. That Cornificius produced additional work in the field of rhetoric is possible; [a] the phrase *non pauca* in 3. i. 21, however, does not permit us to be certain whether this was in the form of a complete Art of rhetoric,[b] or of several works on single parts of the subject.

---

figures in this way (4. xxxi. 42), but Quintilian does not name Cornificius along with Proculus.

The separation of tropes from figures was first made, we think, in the Augustan age. If Cornificius dealt only with figures, that fact, too, might be evidence for placing him at a time not earlier than that period.

[a] Marx, however, believes that Cornificius wrote only the special work on figures.

[b] Thiele (*Gött. gel. Anz.*) and Ammon believe that it was such a complete Art of rhetoric. Thiele identifies it with our treatise; the special book on figures was a portion (= Bk. 4) of this Art. Ammon (*Blätter*, pp. 409 ff.) argues as follows: The division, in the MSS., of Book 4 (which is especially large) into three books indicates that we have in our treatise a contamination of Cornificius' complete Art and his special work on figures. The " Art " extends to 4. xiii. 18, at the end of which there is a lacuna; 4. i. 1 to 4. xiii. 18 corresponds to " Book iv " of the MSS. The special book on figures also perhaps included two books; " Book v," dealing with figures of diction, extends from 4. xiii. 19 to 4. xxxiv. 46, and " Book vi," treating figures of thought, extends from 4. xxxv. 47 to the end. In the union a portion of the complete Art of rhetoric was lost—a short exposition of the two types of figures, and the beginning of their treatment. That Cornificius' attitude towards the use of one's own examples differed in the two works Ammon thinks is not significant. But Ammon's hypothesis is not acceptable, since the division into four books follows from the author's own words; the lacuna at 4. xiii. 18 is brief (only a transition is indicated); neither are the first three books of uniform length; and the author's special interest in *ornatus* justifies the length of Book 4, which in any event may as it stands lay claim to unity.

Cornificius, then, lived in a later period than our author, and so cannot have written the *Rhetorica ad Herennium*. The book by Cornificius which Quintilian cites is not the *Rhetorica ad Herennium*, and there is no evidence that Quintilian knew or made use of our treatise.[a] The agreements between Cornificius' work and our author's we explain by assuming a common source,[b] and we should remember, too, that some of the matter, especially some of the examples, shared by both can be classed among the commonplaces of the subject.

Who, finally, was the real author? We have no evidence to determine that question, and so must assign the work to an *auctor incertus*.[c]

[a] Further arguments (see Koehler) rest frankly on the *argumentum e silentio*. For example, Quintilian often refers to Cicero's *De Inventione* but never mentions the agreements between that work and " Cornificius." Again, in 9. 2. 54 he lists four terms used for the figure Aposiopesis, but not the term used by our author (*praecisio*, 4. xxx. 41); this silence leads some to question whether, had he known our treatise, he would not in such cases as this have referred to the terms our author employs. Or again, in 9. 3. 99 ἠθοποιία and χαρακτηρισμός are cited from Rutilius among figures supplementary to those found in other authors. Since Cornificius has just been mentioned, it is inferred that his book lacked these figures; but they appear in our treatise as *notatio* (4. 1. 63) and *effictio* (4. xlix. 62). Or again, in 3. 6. 45, where Verginius Flavus is referred to as favouring the Antonian classification of the Types of Issue (*cf.* our treatise 1. x. 18), Cornificius is not mentioned—but as I should remind the reader, the advocates of Cornician authorship believe that Quintilian was not interested in the first three books of our work, or in 4. i. 1–xii. 18, because on the subjects there treated he had recourse to better material elsewhere.

[b] Teuffel-Kroll and others, however, believe that Cornificius probably used our treatise directly.

[c] Other attributions, none of them seriously pressed to-day, have in the course of time since the fifteenth century been made

INTRODUCTION

The original title is as unknown to us as the name of the author. Marx, on the basis of the introductory remarks in Book 1, suggests, with plausibility, that this might have been *De Ratione Dicendi*, which was also the title of Antonius' treatise on rhetoric.

Our author dedicates his work to Gaius Herennius; we know several Herennii [a] of this period, but no one definitely identifiable with the addressee. Marx, influenced by the apparent fact that the work remained unnoticed for five hundred years, believed that it was intended only for private use, and not for publication, but this hypothesis does not receive universal acceptance.

As we have said, the treatise is altogether Greek in doctrine. The Rhodian [b] rhetor who represents its original source sought to bind rhetoric to philosophy, and the book as it stands is a synthesis of various teachings: pre-Aristotelian (Isocratean and " Anaximenean "), Aristotelian and Peripatetic, Stoic, Hermagorean, and possibly Epicurean. Hellenistic theorists selected from all schools what they needed, and indeed some of the precepts were by then a common possession.[c] We must remark, too, in our

---

to : Verginius Flavus (time of Nero), Timolaüs (time of Aurelian), M. Tullius Tiro and M. Tullius Laurea (freedmen of Cicero), the rhetor Junius Gallio (friend of the elder Seneca), M. Antonius Gnipho and L. Aelius Stilo (teachers of Cicero), M. T. Cicero (son of the great orator), L. Ateius Praetextatus (d. after 29 B.C.), and Papirius Fabianus (time of Tiberius).

[a] They were of plebeian stock, and were allied to the family of Marius.

[b] Many Romans came to Rhodes, a great centre of rhetorical studies, and in 87 B.C. Apollonius Molo visited Rome. The notes indicate a number of echoes of Rhodian life and thought.

[c] *Cf.* Cicero, *De Inv.* 2. iii. 8 : " [Isocratean theory and Aristotelian theory] were fused into one by their successors."

author's case the thoroughly practical motives to which he constantly gives expression. The notes in the present volume attempt in many instances to indicate the ties by which he is bound to the traditions of different schools. To illustrate briefly, and almost at random: the threefold purpose of the Direct Opening is pre-Aristotelian doctrine; the concept of the *officia oratoris* is Aristotelian; the " virtues " of Style go back to Theophrastus; the detailed treatment of Delivery belongs probably to post-Theophrastan theory; the discussion of Solecism and Barbarism shows a debt to Stoicism; the definition of rhetoric is Hermagorean, and so too, though in modified form, is our author's *status* system—indeed every art which had a *status* system was beholden to Hermagoras; the opposition to amphibolies may be Epicurean; and in the case of some principles the Sophists and Plato play an originating or participating rôle.

The precepts are often illustrated by excellent examples, many of them allusions to the recent and the contemporary political scene, especially the Marsic and Marian Wars, and many bringing back to life the older Roman eloquence. Of the older Latin orators, our author shows special admiration for Gaius Gracchus and Crassus (4. i. 2, 4. ii. 2), but he tells us that Cato, Tiberius Gracchus, Laelius, Scipio, Porcina, and Antonius also commonly serve as models in the field of style. Poets and historians, too, may be models (4. v. 7); he has praise for Ennius and Pacuvius (4. iv. 7), but he does not

Interdependence is often hard to trace definitely even in the earlier periods.

hesitate to use these poets and Plautus [a] and the historian Coelius Antipater in illustration of faults of argumentation or of style. Examples of figures of speech (whose sources he does not name) are drawn from Greek authors as well; the speeches of Demosthenes (especially *De Corona*) and Aeschines are special favourites, but sayings originated by Homer, Simonides, Pythagoras, Isocrates, Socrates, Theophrastus, Aristarchus, Apollonius ὁ μαλακός, and others also appear, as do references to Greek mythology. The author's experience and mastery of Greek literature, however, do not seem to have been great; this Greek lore was transmitted to him from the schools.

The schools emphasized declamation and the study of models, and the treatise is in this respect an image of school practice. Declamatory exercises—the author again and again stresses the importance of exercise [b]—are represented in the form of *progymnasmata* of various types (including training in epideictic), of deliberative questions (*deliberationes, suasoriae*), and of judicial cases (*causae, controversiae*). The deliberative questions are all taken from events of Roman history, none of them antedating the war with Hannibal.[c] Of the judicial cases drawn from Roman history, almost all date from the end of the Jugurthine War to the end of the Marian War; a number are also Greek in origin, and occasionally are

[a] And probably also Accius; see 2. xxvi. 42.

[b] But never a word about declaiming in Greek; *cf.* on the other hand the custom followed by Cicero (*Brutus* 90. 310).

[c] For events connected with the Hannibalic war Coelius Antipater may have served as a source, for the subsequent period the orators, and perhaps also Cato's *Origines*; see Bochmann.

altered to fit Roman conditions. Our author doubtless used collections of declamations current in his day.

The organization of the treatise is rather complicated.[a] The author is heir to two structural schemes—the pre-Aristotelian, based on the *partes* of the discourse (μόρια λόγου), and the Peripatetic, based on the five *officia* (ἔργα) of rhetoric. In his discussion of judicial oratory—which held the foreground in Hellenistic rhetoric, and claims most of his attention—both schemes are fused, " in order to make the subject easier to understand " (1. iii. 4), and with interesting results. The *partes* are treated under Invention, and not, as in the Peripatetic system, under Disposition. Disposition, which is therefore narrow in scope and rather sterile, becomes an adjunct of Invention [b] (3. ix. 16), and is treated directly after it, where in the Peripatetic structure we should expect a discussion of Style. The Types of Issue are subjoined to Proof, which is one of the *partes*, and not as in Aristotle a primary and central function of the whole art. The discussion of the deliberative and epideictic kinds, on the other hand, is more in line with the Peripatetic method : in both cases

[a] See Karl Barwick, *Hermes* 57 (1922). 1 ff.; Thiele, *Quaestiones,* pp. 96 ff.; Ioannes Radtke, *Observationes crit. in Cornifici libros de arte rhetorica,* Koenigsberg, 1892, pp. 22 ff.; Friedrich Solmsen, *Amer. Journ. Philol.* 62 (1941). 35–50, 169–190.

[b] The conflation results in certain inconsistencies; see, *e.g.,* the reference to Invention at 1. x. 16, and the note on 3. x. 17. Certain other inconsistencies in the order are, however, not the result of conflation; the author at times in his treatment transposes his original order of topics (*e.g.,* in 1. xiv. 24 and 2. xvi. 23; and *cf.* 1. xiv. 24 ff. with 2. xiv. 21 ff.).

INTRODUCTION

Invention receives first consideration, and then comes the Development of the cause based on the parts of the discourse.

Each book has a Preface and a Conclusion, which, by brief summaries and transitions characteristic of lecture or text-book style, serve to tie the parts together, and to keep the plan of the work clear in the reader's mind.

The first two books deal with Invention in judicial causes; Invention in deliberative and epideictic speaking is discussed much more briefly in a part of Book 3. Disposition is also accorded little space for the reasons set forth above. But the treatment of Delivery, Memory, and Style is of special interest and importance.

The doctrine of Delivery had been developed in post-Aristotelian times, and our author is familiar with books on the subject. He is dissatisfied with these and wishes to treat the subject with greater care and completeness than had characterized the work of his predecessors (3. xi. 19). In the section which he devotes to Delivery two observations will present themselves to the modern student of public speaking. The rules are for the most part prescriptive; the speaker is told precisely what use of voice, pause, and gesture he ought consciously to make in a variety of situations. And secondly, the doctrine represents a salutary reaction against Asianism; piercing exclamations and the continual use of the full voice are more than once reprehended (3. xii. 21 ff.), and the speaker is more than once warned against imitating the delivery of the stage-actor (3. xiv. 24, xv. 26).

The section on Memory is our oldest surviving

treatment of the subject. Based on visual images and " backgrounds," the mnemotechnical system which it presents exerted an influence traceable to modern times. Here too the author refers to previous writers on the subject in order to combat their theory; he specifies that these are Greek, but he does not mention any of them by name.

In Book 4 we have the oldest systematic treatment of Style in Latin, indeed the oldest extant inquiry into the subject after Aristotle. It offers, furthermore, the oldest extant division of the kinds of Style into three, and the oldest extant formal study of figures. Our author gives more space to Style than to any other of the departments of rhetoric, and much more to *ornatus*—which is limited to the figures —than to the other aspects of Style. The exceptionally large enumeration of figures is of course more in accord with Isocratean than with Aristotelian doctrine; our author, together with the younger Gorgias (through the translation by Rutilius), provides us with an important source for our knowledge of Hellenistic theory in this field. The treatment of the figures is not always bald and jejune, despite their formal array. Occasionally our author writes good literary criticism; read for example the advice, anti-Asian in character, which he gives on the use of the Gorgianic figures (4. xxi. 32). He is often sensitive to the effect which a figure of speech, well-used, can work upon the hearer. He never advocates the tricky cunning which would have justified the scorn that Longinus (*De Sublim.*, ch. 17) expressed for the " petty figures (σχημάτια) of the rhetorical craftsman." His counsel is for moderation and the consideration of propriety—in the use of Apostrophe

(4. xv. 22), Maxims (4. xvii. 25), Disjunction (4. xxvii. 38), Onomatopoeia (4. xxxi. 42), Metaphor (4. xxxiv. 45), and Comparison (4. xlviii. 61). The author is not always at ease among technical terms (see 4. vii. 10, and also 4. x. 15 and 4. xi. 16), since not all of these had yet become stable in Latin. Inasmuch as a like difficulty attends the translation of his terms into English, I have thought it my duty to readers to use the terms most familiar to them; accordingly in rendering the names for the figures I have, abandoning strict consistency, used the English derivatives of the author's terms wherever possible, or the accepted English equivalents, and have employed terms of Greek origin where their use was indicated.

A number of questions concerning the treatise are vigorously debated. How old was the author when the work was composed? Is the treatise nothing but the notes of lectures delivered by his Latin teacher? Does our author favour the *populares*? What is his philosophical bias, if any? And most baffling, what relation does the treatise bear to Cicero's *De Inventione*?

Whereas in the nineteenth century it was customary to praise our author for " manly independence of thought," it is now, especially since Marx' work [a] appeared, common to make him out an uncritical and very young man, or a boy, who copied down, virtually word for word, the lectures of his Latin teacher, and worked these up with only slight additions, mostly represented by the Introductions and Conclusions to the several Books. The style does show puerilities, and signs of immaturity are sought and found here and there in the thought. But not

[a] See p. xxxvii.

INTRODUCTION

everything labelled as puerile by some critics justifies
the label, and in some degree the charge would have
to be shared by the teacher.   The confusion between
student and teacher arises necessarily from the theory
that we have here only a student's notebook.[a]
Actually our author seems old enough to have spent
(*consuevimus*, 1. i. 1) time in philosophical studies,[b]
older enough than his kinsman Herennius to have
composed the book for his use, and to encourage him
in industry (1. i. 1; 2. xxxi. 50; 3. xxxiv. 40; 4. lvi.
69), young enough still to practise with him (3. i. 1;
4. lvi. 69), and to make plans for the future—he
expects to write on Grammar (4. xii. 17), on
Military Science and State Administration (3. ii. 3),
on Memory (3. xvi. 28), and (if encouraged) against
the dialecticians (2. xi. 16).   We have no reason to
believe that when he speaks of the pressure of private
affairs (1. i. 1) and the demands of his occupations
(1. xvii. 27) he is merely following a literary con-
vention or indulging in rhetorical fiction.   He charges
Greek writers with childish argumentation in respect
to the use of examples (4. iii. 4), warns against
puerilities in the use of Isocolon and Paronomasia
(4. xx. 27, xxiii. 32), and finds recourse to amphibolies silly (2. xi. 16).   His apologies for slow
progress and references to the magnitude of his task
and the care he has devoted to it (*e.g.*, 1. xvii. 27;
2. xxxi. 50) are inconsistent with the picture of one
who is merely working over dictated material.   He

[a] *Cf.* Quintilian, 3. 6. 59, on Cicero, *De Inv.*: " Such
faults as [this collection of school-notes] has are assignable to
his teacher."
[b] Which he thinks conduce more to the good life than does
the study of rhetoric; he is not a professional rhetorician.

professes to have taken pains in assembling his material (*conquisite conscripsimus*, 1. xxxi. 50, and *studiose collegimus*, 4. lvi. 69), and this seems to imply the use of sources, although we cannot know how wide this use or how comprehensive his study of them may have been.

Lecture notes doubtless form the core of the treatise, but the author probably made use of other sources as well, and worked the matter over with some degree of independence. Some of the very incongruities that we find in the treatise may derive precisely from this weaving together of material drawn from a number of places. Dependence on his teacher is explicit only in connection with a disputed point, on the number of Types of Issue [a] (1. x. 18). We go too far if we assume that the precepts all belong to the teacher and very little more than the Introductions and Conclusions to the author. And one wonders how the teacher would have regarded the release of his own work, even if only for private use, as the work of his pupil.[b]

Does our author favour the Popular party? It is believed that his teacher may have belonged to the school of L. Plotius Gallus and the *rhetores Latini*. These teachers of public speaking, whose identity and innovations remain obscure to us, apparently as a matter of principle taught their subject in Latin, rigidly suppressing the Greek language; they prob-

---

[a] Who the teacher (*noster doctor*) here referred to was we do not know.

[b] See Schanz, ed. 1909, p. 470. Quintilian, 1. Pr. 7, regrets that two books of lecture notes, taken down by pupils, and by them published under his name, but without his consent, are in circulation. Marx, of course, maintains that our treatise was never intended for circulation.

INTRODUCTION

ably were Marian in sympathy and had as students only the sons of the *populares*.[a] Our author can indeed in his examples praise or sympathize with the Gracchi, Saturninus, Drusus, and Sulpicius (2. xxviii. 45; 4. xxii. 31; 4. lv. 68; 4. xv. 22), and advise us to bring our adversaries into contempt by revealing their high birth (1. v. 8), but he can likewise accuse Gaius Gracchus of promoting panics (4. xxviii. 38), praise Caepio's attack on Saturninus as patriotic conduct (1. xii. 21; 2. xii. 17), warn Saturninus against the excesses of the popular mob (4. liv. 67), attribute the future revival of prosperity to the Conservatives (4. xxxiv. 45), and regard their slaughter as a disaster (4. viii. 12). The themes of the *causae* are variously Popular and Conservative in spirit, and we must infer that our author took his material where he found it and used it to suit his primary purpose—technical instruction in the art of rhetoric. If he really belonged to the Popular party, then he still must have believed in giving the Conservative cause a hearing.

Nor again should our author's attitude to the Greeks be represented as an antagonism approaching hatred. True, he deliberately takes most of his historical *exempla* from Roman history, repeatedly finds fault with the methods of Greek rhetoricians (1. i. 1; 3. xxiii. 38; 4. i. 1), and suppresses the names of Greek writers whose examples he uses in Book 4. But he also omits the names of Roman authors whose examples he uses in that Book. Furthermore, he professes to know Greek books, occasionally uses Greek technical terms and other

[a] See Marx, *Proleg.*, pp. 141 ff., and Aubrey Gwynn, *Roman Education from Cicero to Quintilian*, Oxford 1926, pp. 58–69.

Greek words, and praises the Greeks for their invention of the art of rhetoric (4. vii. 10).

A few traces of Epicureanism in the work have given rise to the notion that our author was an adherent of that school of philosophy. A maxim of Epicurus, in altered form, is quoted without attribution (4. xvii. 24); in another example, religion and the fear of death are listed among the motives that impel men to crime (2. xxi. 34); and the dialecticians are censured for their love of ambiguities (2. xi. 16). But, as the notes in the present volume illustrate, the examples are drawn from the literature of various philosophical schools—a condition one would expect, inasmuch as manuals of rhetoric reflecting diverse schools were then extant, and these manuals may well have had much material in common.

But the most vexing problem—and, as Norden [a] says, one of the most interesting in the history of Roman literature—concerns the relations between our treatise and *De Inventione*.[b] We are not even sure of the respective dates of composition. The reference in *De Oratore* 1. 2. 5 to the " essays . . . which slipped out of the notebooks of my boyhood, or rather of my youth " [c] does not enable us to fix upon a particular year for the composition of *De Inventione*, but internal evidence points to *c*. 91 B.C. By this we mean only that the work contains no reference to any event that took place during or after the Marsic War.[d] Cicero may, of course, have

[a] Gercke-Norden, *Einleitung in die Altertumswissenschaft*, Leipzig–Berlin, 1910, 1. 471.
[b] Relevant passages of *De Inventione* have been indicated in the notes.
[c] *Cf*. Quintilian, 3. 6. 59 and 3. 1. 20.
[d] See Marx, *Proleg.*, pp. 76 ff.

worked the material into its final form later. When he published the book remains uncertain; allowing even for the possibility that in the passage above Cicero understated his years with ironic intent, we may not suppose a date much after 86 B.C. Likewise on internal evidence we assign our treatise to *c.* 86–82 B.C. The reference in 1. xv. 25 to the death of Sulpicius, which took place in the year 88, supplies us with a *terminus post quem* for the composition of Book 1.[a] 4. liv. 68 contains a reference to Marius' seventh consulship, which he held in the year 86. And since nothing in the work mirrors the conditions which obtained in the state under Sulla—for instance, the first illustration in 4. xxxv. 47 reflects a jury system still comprising both senators and *equites*— we may set the year 82 as the *terminus ante quem.* But again these dates regard only the contents; our author could have collected his examples by the year 82 and have composed the treatise later—not much later, probably, for he is eager to complete the work and send it to Herennius. It seems then likely, though not certain, that *De Inventione* was composed before our treatise.

Agreements are so frequent that obviously there is a close tie between the two works. Some precepts are set forth in virtually the same language, and some of the illustrations are identical. This is not the place to enumerate these likenesses, nor the differences,[b] which are even more striking; the treatises

[a] In 3. i. 1 it is implied that separate books were sent to Herennius.

[b] See Marx, *Proleg.*, pp. 129 ff. Our author differs from Cicero in the method of presenting his material, in organization, and in spirit; for example, in many technical terms; in the doctrine of Proof, of the Types of Issue, of the sources

have been compared in several studies, but the last word on the subject has not yet been said. I may here only review recent opinion.[a] No one now believes that our author used *De Inventione*. On the other hand, the belief that Cicero used the *Rhetorica ad Herennium* still finds adherents; but since it is probable that Cicero's work antedates our treatise, we hesitate to accept this notion. Other critics postulate a common source. That both authors had a single Greek original in common is not acceptable, for it would be unbelievable that two independent translators should have rendered their text in precisely the same words; furthermore, the illustrations from Roman writers shared by both make such a solution impossible.[b]

Or did both make direct use of the same Latin source? This view is popular, and takes two forms: (1) that both had the same Latin teacher, the differences being explained by the assumption that they heard this teacher at different times—our author later, and when the teacher had changed his mind on a number of points; and that Cicero used

---

of Law; in the number of *genera causarum*; in his emphasis upon the judicial kind of discourse as against Cicero's full treatment of all three kinds; in his much briefer discussion of many topics; in his less accurate quotations; in the more limited scope of his historical references (Cicero uses events in Roman history that antedate Hannibal); in his thoroughly Latin spirit—Marx' analogy is telling: our author is to the *togata* as Cicero, who is much more learned in Greek literature, is to the *palliata*.

[a] I have not seen M. Medved, *Das Verhältnis von Ciceros libri rhetorici zum Auctor ad Herennium*, unpublished Vienna dissertation, 1940.

[b] See William Ramsay in Smith's *Dict. of Greek and Roman Biography and Mythology* (London, 1880), 1. 727.

other sources in addition;[a] (2) that both used the same Latin manual,[b] our author only this manual, and without many changes—except for certain transpositions and abridgements, some omission of examples, and slight additions (*e.g.*, the Introductions and Conclusions)—and Cicero with greater alterations; and that Cicero further used Hermagoras.[c] Marx, on the other hand, finds that the contrast between the two works is too sharp to permit a theory either of direct dependence or of a single immediate common source, whether teacher or manual; he posits two Latin teachers, and behind these, two Rhodian masters who advocated opposing doctrines, our author inheriting the older theory and Cicero a fuller and more recent system.

Without accepting Marx' thesis that the treatise is entirely a set of lecture notes—for I would assign more of the work to the author than Marx allows—I believe that something like his hypothesis is required. The differences between the two works seem to rule out a single immediate common source; the likenesses we may best refer to the use by both authors (or by their teachers) of Latin treatises like the *De Ratione Dicendi* of Antonius.[d] We cannot appraise the

---

[a] In *De Inv.* 2. ii. 4 he professes an eclectic method of excerpting from his sources.

[b] This second view is that of Herbolzheimer.

[c] Whether directly or through an intermediate source; the point is debated.

[d] Most now believe that the influence of Antonius' book (*cf.* Cicero, *Brutus* 44. 163, *De Oratore* 1. 21. 94, Quintilian, 3. 1. 19) is apparent in our treatise; see Kroehnert, pp. 23 ff. (but he thinks that Antonius was our author's Latin teacher), Marx, *Proleg.*, p. 131, and Koehler, pp. 35–8, but also Weber, pp. 22 ff., and Thiele, *Quaest.*, p. 94. Antonius' book appeared sometime before 91 B.C.

influence of these older Latin arts of rhetoric which
are lost to us, but it may well have been considerable.

Our main difficulty when we compare the two
works is in explaining the following coincidence. In
1. vi. 9 our author distinguishes three occasions
(*tempora*) for the use of the Subtle Approach, and in
1. ix. 16 maintains that this is his own innovation;
in *De Inventione* 1. xvii. 23, however, a like threefold
classification occurs, but instead of occasions we have
" motives " (*causae*). Again diverse explanations are
offered, but in the end we are, I believe, forced either
to accept Marx' view that the classification is of
Greek origin or to take the author's words at their
face value. Marx finds the context here thoroughly
Greek, even though we do not know any specific
Greek source for the threefold classification, and
hurls the charge of fraud and impudence at our
author; the principle, he is sure, originated with the
Rhodian rhetor whose doctrines our author followed,
and Cicero in his turn received it from his own teacher
in a modified form. Some of those who, like Marx,
consider our treatise merely lecture notes, and yet
wish to absolve the writer of the charge of fraud,
make the point that he may not have known that
his teacher had borrowed the precept from a Greek
source; but the notion that the author did not know
Greek well enough for his purposes would require
proof. Schanz and others believe that Cicero
borrowed the principle from our treatise, but that
hypothesis would be more acceptable if we could be
certain that the *Rhetorica ad Herennium* was actually
published and available to Cicero before his publication of *De Inventione*. As a matter of fact, the
precept appears in a somewhat different setting in *De*

Inventione, where its use is confined to the *admirabile* kind of cause. Our author doubtless depends on a Greek source for his general treatment of the doctrine of the Subtle Approach. Yet he always writes with practical motives, and on this particular point specifically says that his purpose is to provide a sure and lucid theory. When, therefore, he claims as an innovation the slight distinction between *tempora* and *causae,* we find him guilty, not of fraud, but of the exaggerated self-esteem which is also elsewhere characteristic of him.[a]

The chief basis of Marx' charge of deceit is provided by the Introduction to Book 4, considered in relation to the examples used in that Book. This Proem, organized and developed like a *chria* [b] according to the rules of the classroom, is rather graceful and learned; in language, too, it is smoother than the purely technical parts of the treatise; and its contents are Greek in character. Marx and others contend that it did not belong in this place originally, but was in its main outlines taken from a Greek source, inserted here, and made over to seem a Latin product. In this Preface our author presents a long argument against a theory, which he labels as Greek, of using borrowed examples, and promises to give only those of his own creation (except in the case of faulty ones). But the execution does not fulfil the promise, for he then proceeds actually to use borrowed

[a] He has not been moved to write by hope of gain or glory, " as others have been " (1. i. 1); " no one else " has written with sufficient care on Delivery (3. xi. 19); he " alone, in contrast with all other writers," has distinguished three occasions for the use of the Subtle Approach (1. ix. 16); *cf.* also 1. vi. 10, 3. vii. 14, 3. xxiv. 40, and 4. lvi. 69.

[b] See the figure, Refining, 4. xlii. 54 ff.

examples, and without naming his sources, many of
which are Greek. The author (or rather his teacher)
thus got into trouble when, having used a Greek art
which employed borrowed examples, he tried to
adjust to it the contrary precepts of another Greek
author who created his own examples. This is the
person, say his critics, who in 1. i. 1 accuses Greek
writers of futile self-assertion.

According to another interpretation, which is
intended to save the honour of both student and
teacher, the young student here put down the notes
of a lecture once delivered by his teacher, thinking
this to be an appropriate place, but being no master
of Greek, he was unaware that his teacher had in the
rest of what comprises his Book 4 taken so many
examples from Greek sources.

It seems best, however, to grant the author some
degree of literary individuality, and to regard his
claim to the use of his " own " examples as at least
an honest one. The notion that he did not know
Greek well enough for his purpose is gratuitous. To
be sure, one cannot deny the contradiction between
promise and fulfilment, nor assign to the author more
than a relatively small share in the fashioning of the
Proem, the Greek origin of which is obvious. But he
made good use of this Proem, which as it stands
coheres well enough with the text that follows it;
he would naturally use material that he had heard or
read, perhaps not always knowing where he had
picked it up; [a] and what is most likely, he may have

---

[a] Crassus in Cicero, *De Oratore* 1. 34. 154, tells how in his
practice declamations, trying to choose diction different from
that of the poetic passage by Ennius or speech by Gracchus
on which he was practising, he would discover that the best
words had already been used by his author.

considered his free translation of the Greek examples
and alteration of the Latin a large enough task to
justify his feeling that they were now his own. He
is sometimes adroit in transposing the original
examples and adjusting them to Roman conditions.[a]
The claim to originality becomes then a pardonable,
or at least an understandable, exaggeration, rather
than evidence of misrepresentation.

Since the treatise stands near the beginnings of
Latin prose,[b] its style has been the subject of close
study. The faults have received special attention,
especially those resulting from the author's quest for
variety and for refinements in forms and constructions
—for example, *abundantia*, artificially balanced
clauses, the love of synonyms, of word-play, hyper-
bata, and asyndeta, the inflated language of the
Conclusions to each Book, and other extravagances
of rhetorical style; also the awkward transitions and
the author's tendency merely to reiterate, under the
guise of remarks concluding the treatment of a
precept, what he has already said. Further pecu-
liarities are the arbitrary use of pronouns, the omission
of subjects of verbs in the infinitive, the mixture of
present and future in the sequence of tenses, the
frequent employment of the first person future
active indicative, of substantives in *-io*, of the *ut . . .
ne . . .* construction, and of the indicative in indirect
questions. The dry style of the precepts usually
contrasts with the lively and smooth style of the

---

[a] See, *e.g.*, in 4. xxix. 40, how the example of the figure
Indecision from Demosthenes, *De Corona* 20, receives a Roman
character.
[b] Of extant complete prose works only Cato's *De Agri Cultura*
is older.

examples. Although the style is in general not highly developed nor fluent, and there are several passages of which the meaning is obscure, our author in greatest part achieves, as I have said, his aim of clarity. It would not be fair to class his treatise with the crude textbooks (*libri agrestes*) disparaged in *De Oratore* 2. 3. 10. The language is up to a point " plebeian " and there are puerilities, but some of the qualities thus designated are rather to be assigned to what we may call the schoolmaster's manner and to the nature of technical, textbook style. Some of the irregularities perhaps also derive from the author's desire to make haste and to be brief, and from the process of translation; here and there the language betrays a Greek origin.

Our author is fond of periods formed with rhythmic clausulae. It is another echo of the school practice of his time that the dichoree, favourite of Asianic style, plays the chief rôle,[a] but other cadences are also frequent. In the examples illustrating the three types of style in Book 4, rhythms are chosen with a fair degree of taste so as to correspond to the character of the different types.

We may say that the style is within limits archaic, and sometimes reminiscent of Roman comedy; yet today it is no longer set in such sharp contrast as formerly to Ciceronian style. Kroll[b] looks upon it as having been formed on the same principles as those of the Roman orators whom Cicero regarded as his own forerunners.

In the present century it has been customary to undervalue the treatise because of its shortcomings—

[a] See notes on 4. viii. 12, 4. xix. 26, and 4. xxxii. 44.
[b] *Glotta*, 22 (1934). 24 ff.

which in large part are those inherent in the nature of a textbook—even as its virtues were often exaggerated in the nineteenth century, when more than one critic (*e.g.*, Chaignet) held the work up as superior to Quintilian's *Training of an Orator*. Regarded from a historical point of view, the treatise presents no strikingly novel system; for us, however, it has literary importance because it is our only complete representative of the system it teaches. We may further readily admit that the work lacks the larger philosophical insight of Aristotle's *Rhetoric*, but that is not to deny its excellence as a practical treatise of the kind doubtless used by Roman orators. It is, moreover, itself not without usefulness for the modern student of the art. We ought now to redress the balance, to recognize that, though Greek in origin and inspiration, it marks a significant stage in Roman rhetorical theory, to assign due value especially to Book 4, and to bear in mind that the work exerted a beneficent influence for hundreds of years. One of the distinguished modern students of rhetoric, Spengel, called it " a book more precious than gold."

LATER HISTORY

Interpreting a *subscriptio* in MS. H, Marx assumed that the book first came to light in Africa in the middle of the fourth century and was soon thereafter brought to Lombardy.[a] Therefore the first references to it appear late—in Jerome (in works written in the years A.D. 395 and 402), Rufinus (late fifth

---

[a] See *Proleg.*, pp. 1 ff. Not all believe that the work could have lain so long in oblivion; some think that it was used by Cornificius (see p. xiv, note *b*, and p. xv above).

century), Grillius [a] (late fifth century), and Priscian
(early sixth century). MSS. of the M class were
known to Servatus Lupus, as we learn from a letter
he wrote in 829 or 830, and indeed our oldest extant
MSS., which belong to that class, date from the ninth
and tenth centuries. Later the treatise was much
used, abstracted, annotated, and interpolated; it
shared favour with Cicero's *De Inventione*, which, as
against modern taste, seems to have been preferred
to his *De Oratore*. The great number of MSS. of the
Ad Herennium—we have more than a hundred—is in
itself an index of its popularity. Complete commentaries began to appear as early, perhaps, as the twelfth
century, translations as early as the thirteenth. The
full story, however, of the influence which the treatise
enjoyed in education and in the poetry and prose of
the Middle Ages and Renaissance has yet to be
worked out.

TRANSLATIONS

The MSS. containing mediaeval translations of the
treatise have not yet been adequately studied;
several versions in Western vernaculars doubtless
remain to be brought to light. We may, however,
mention the compendium in Italian that is associated
with the names of both Guidotto da Bologna and Bono
Giamboni (*Fiore di rettorica* or *Rettorica nuova di Tullio*),
which in its original form was composed before 1266,
and the French rendering (of both our treatise and
Cicero's *De Inventione*) made by Jean d'Antioche de
Harens in 1282. Enrique de Villena translated the
work into Castilian in 1427. And the Greek version

---

[a] See Josef Martin, *Grillius : Ein Beitrag zur Geschichte
der Rhetorik*, Paderborn 1927, p. 156 (48. 15).

of the section on Memory in Book 3 (reprinted in Marx, *ed. maior*, pp. 54–59) has been assigned, without strong evidence in either case, to Maximus Planudes (early *saec.* 14) or Theodore Gaza (*saec.* 15).

The following translations belong to modern times:

French : Paul Jacob, Paris 1652, 1670 (*Les Oeuvres de Cicéron*, tr. by Pierre du Ryer *et al.*, vol. 1).

J. N. Demeunier, Paris 1783 (*Oeuvres de Cicéron, trad. nouvelle*, vol. 1).

J. B. Levée, Paris 1816 (*Oeuvres Complètes de Cicéron, trad. en Français*, vol. 1).

J. V. LeClerc, Paris 1821, 1827 (*Oeuvres Complètes de Cicéron*, vol. 1, Pt. 2, 2nd ed.), and later eds.

L. Delcasso, Paris 1826 (in *Bibliothèque Latine-Française*, ed. C. L Panckoucke, vol. 1), and later eds.

Thibaut, Paris 1881 (*Oeuvres Complètes de Cicéron*, ed. J. M. N. D. Nisard, vol. 1).

Henri Bornecque, Paris [1932].

German : Christian Walz, Stuttgart 1842 (in *Römische Prosaiker in neuen Übersetzungen* 22. 3354–3532).

Karl Kuchtner, Munich 1911.

So far as the present translator knows, the treatise has not hitherto been completely translated into English; a rendering by Ray Nadeau of Book 1, based on Kayser's edition of 1854, appears in *Speech Monographs* 16 (1949). 57–68.

INTRODUCTION

EDITIONS

The *editio princeps* was issued in Venice in 1470 by Nicolaus Jenson, under the editorship of Omnibonus Leonicenus. At least twenty-eight other editions appeared in the fifteenth century, several with commentaries. For the long list of editions that followed until the year 1834 the reader may be referred to J. C. Orelli's *Onomasticon Tullianum* in the Orelli-Baiter edition of Cicero's Works (Zurich 1836), vol. 6, pp. 197, 215, 218, and 223. Of the nineteenth-century editions that appeared thereafter, we must list C. L. Kayser's separate edition, Leipzig (Teubner) 1854, and his Tauchnitz edition (among Cicero's Works), Leipzig 1860; G. F. Friedrich's edition, Leipzig (Teubner) 1884; and especially the excellent *editio maior* by Friedrich Marx, Leipzig (Teubner) 1894. This last, together with Marx' *editio minor*, Leipzig (Teubner) 1923, forms the basis of the text used by the present translator, who acknowledges also the profit derived from the critical notes in both editions and from the Prolegomena and Index in the *editio maior*—a debt which will be obvious in many places. Marx' work represents a great advance in the study of our treatise, and on it all students, even when they reject his conclusions on certain points, now base their investigations.

THE TEXT

The text depends on two groups of MSS.—an older group, M(utili), whose archetype contained lacunae and corruptions, and a younger, E(xpleti). The lacunae in M are filled out in E in part from another tradition. The Expleti derive from an archetype of perhaps the twelfth century; for that recension three aids were used: a MS. of class M, a lost *integer*,[a] and the recensionist's own conjectures and emendations.

In a number of places the text cannot be restored with certainty. At times the readings of M, especially when the text is corrupt and cannot otherwise be filled out, must give way to those of E. Neither M nor E can be followed alone throughout, and often the decision between the two is hard to make. As Marx says, each reading must be examined in accordance with the editor's conception of the author's habits of writing. To be sure E, which contains many conjectures made in the Middle Ages, must be used with caution, but even Marx, an editor of praiseworthy conservatism, adopts many of its readings. I have found it advisable to follow M in a number of cases where Marx followed E, but most of my changes from Marx have favoured E. The text in the present edition rests on that of Marx, *editio minor*; an apparatus is supplied only for those places where I deviate from the text of that edition.

In the apparatus *Mx* stands for Marx, *ed. minor*, 1923; *Mx ed. mai.* for his edition of 1894.

Marx constructed his text on the basis of the following MSS.:

[a] A MS. of a fourth or fifth century edition of five works of Cicero (including our treatise) was found again in the twelfth century, and was used in forming the archetype of E. The Laudensis, discovered in Lodi by Landriani in 1421, and again lost some four years later without any copies of our treatise having been made from it, stems from this old edition of Cicero's works.

INTRODUCTION

M(utili) : lacking Bk. I, chaps. 1–5

H	Herbipolitanus (*saec.* 9/10)
P	Parisinus 7714 (9)
B	Bernensis (9/10)
C	Corbeiensis (or Leninopolitanus) (9/10)
Π	Parisinus 7231 (12)
M	consensus of H P B C Π

E(xpleti)

b	Bambergensis (12/13)
l	Leidensis (12)
d	Darmstadiensis (12/13)
v	Vossianus (12/13)
p	Parisinus 7696 (12)
E	consensus of b l d

The reader is referred to Marx, *ed. maior*, pp. 10 ff., and the Preface to the *ed. minor*, for a description of the MSS. The stemma that appears on the next page is taken from p. xxiv of the *ed. minor*.

The spelling in the present text differs in a number of places from that of Marx' editions. As some critics have charged, Marx at times went out of his way to set up archaic or unusual spellings (some of which he formed from *corruptelae*). My changes—not as a rule noted in the apparatus—have, I believe, sound support in the MSS.; and in several instances —which are noted—I have felt that the MSS. should not be allowed to determine forms regarded as incorrect. A completely uniform orthography, for example in the assimilation of prepositions, has not been sought.

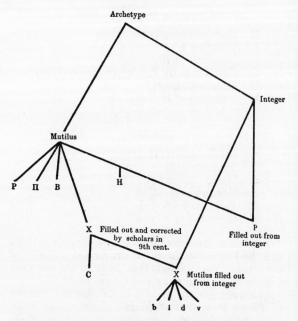

Archetype

Integer

Mutilus

P Π B H

X Filled out and corrected
by scholars in
9th cent.

P
Filled out from
integer

C

X Mutilus filled out
from integer

b l d v

In closing this Introduction, I wish to express the thanks I owe to a number of friends at Cornell University for generous assistance. To Professor Ernst Levy of the University of Washington I am indebted for his kindness in answering several questions on Roman Law.

BIBLIOGRAPHY

Georg Ammon, rev. of Marx, *ed. maior*, *Blätter für das Bayer. Gymn.-Schulwesen* 33 (1897). 407–415.

Georg Ammon, rev. of Marx, *ed. minor*, *Bursians Jahresbericht* 204 (1925). 10–16.

Otto Angermann, *De Aristotele rhetorum auctore*, Leipzig, 1904.

Karl Aulitzky, " Apsines περὶ ἐλέου," *Wiener Studien* 39 (1917). 26–49.

C. Bione, *I piu antichi trattati di arte retorica in lingua latina*, Pisa, 1910.

H. E. Bochmann, *De Cornifici auctoris ad Herennium qui vocatur rerum Romanarum scientia*, Zwickau, 1875.

J. Brzoska, art. " Cornificius," in P.-W. 4. 1605–1623.

Georg Golla, *Sprachliche Beobachtungen zum auctor ad Herennium*, Breslau, 1935.

Georg Herbolzheimer, " Ciceros rhetorici libri und die Lehrschrift des Auctor ad Herennium," *Philologus* 81 (1926). 391–426.

Carolus Hoffmann, *De verborum transpositionibus in Cornifici rhetoricorum ad Herennium libris*, Munich, 1879.

Curtius Koehler, *De rhetoricis ad Herennium*, Berlin, 1909.

Rudolfus Kroehnert, *De rhetoricis ad Herennium*, diss. Koenigsberg, 1873.

BIBLIOGRAPHY

Wilhelm Kroll, " Die Entwicklung der lateinischen Sprache," *Glotta* 22 (1934). 24–27.

Wilhelm Kroll, " Cornificianum," *Mélanges Bidez* 2. 555–561, Brussels, 1934.

Wilhelm Kroll, " Der Text des Cornificius," *Philologus* 89 (1934). 63–84.

Wilhelm Kroll, " Rhetorica V," *Philologus* 90 (1935). 206–215.

Wilhelm Kroll, " Rhetorik," in P.-W., *Suppl.* VII (1940). 1039–1138.

Friedrich Marx, *Prolegomena* in *editio maior*.

Claus Peters, *De rationibus inter artem rhetoricam quarti et primi saeculi intercedentibus*, Kiel, 1907.

Robert Philippson, rev. of Marx, *ed. minor, Berl. Philol. Wochenschrift* 44 (1924). 1181–1186.

Schanz-Hosius, *Geschichte der römischen Literatur*, Part 1, pp. 586–90, Munich, 1927; Martin Schanz, ed. 1909, Part 1, pp. 466–473.

Eduard Stroebel, " Cornificiana," *Blätter für das Bayer. Gymn.–Schulwesen* 38 (1902). 71–83.

Eduard Stroebel, *Tulliana*, Munich, 1908.

W. S. Teuffel, *Geschichte der römischen Literatur*, 6th ed., Berlin, 1916, 1. 305–309 (revised by Wilhelm Kroll).

Georg Thiele, *Quaestiones de Cornifici et Ciceronis artibus rhetoricis*, Greifswald, 1889.

Georg Thiele, rev. of Marx, *ed. maior, Göttingische gelehrte Anzeigen* 1895 (2). 717–735.

Georg Thiele, *Hermagoras*, Strassburg, 1893.

Philippus Thielmann, *De sermonis proprietatibus quae leguntur apud Cornificium et in primis Ciceronis libris*, Strassburg, 1879.

Heinrich Weber, *Über die Quellen der Rhetorica ad Herennium des Cornificius*, Zurich, 1886.

xlii

BIBLIOGRAPHY

Richard Weidner, *Ciceros Verhältnis zur griechischen und römischen Schulrhetorik seiner Zeit*, Erlangen, 1925.

Julius Werner, *Zur Frage nach dem Verfasser der Herenniusrhetorik*, Bielitz, 1906.

References in the Notes to the following works, and to a number of those in the Bibliography above, appear in abbreviated form:

Halm: Carolus Halm, *Rhetores Latini Minores*, Leipzig, 1863.

Mommsen: Theodor Mommsen, *Römisches Strafrecht*, Leipzig, 1899.

Otto: A. Otto, *Die Sprichwörter . . . der Römer*, Leipzig, 1890.

P.-W.: Pauly - Wissowa - Kroll, *Real - Encyclopädie der classischen Altertumswissenschaft*, Stuttgart, 1894 ff.

Ribbeck: Otto Ribbeck, *Scaenicae Romanorum Poesis Fragmenta*, vol. 1: *Tragicorum Fragmenta*, 3rd ed., Leipzig, 1897; vol. 2: *Comicorum Fragmenta*, 3rd ed., Leipzig, 1898.

Sav. Zeitschr.: *Zeitschrift, Savigny-Stiftung für Rechtsgeschichte: Romanistische Abteilung*, Weimar, 1880 ff.

Schmalz-Hofmann: J. H. Schmalz and J. B. Hofmann, *Syntax und Stilistik*, in Stolz-Schmalz, *Lat. Grammatik*, 5th ed., Munich, 1928 (revised by Manu Leumann and J. B. Hofmann).

Spengel: Leonardus Spengel, *Rhetores Graeci*, vols. 2 and 3, Leipzig, 1854 and 1856.

Spengel-Hammer: L. Spengel and C. Hammer, *Rhetores Graeci*, vol. 1, Part 2, Leipzig, 1894.

BIBLIOGRAPHY

Vahlen: Iohannes Vahlen, *Ennianae Poesis Reliquiae*, 2nd ed., Leipzig, 1903.

Volkmann: Richard Volkmann, *Die Rhetorik der Griechen und Römer*, 2nd ed., Leipzig, 1885.

Walz: Christianus Walz, *Rhetores Graeci*, Stuttgart, Tübingen, London, and Paris, 1832-6. 9 vols.

Warmington: E. H. Warmington, *Remains of Old Latin*, Cambridge, Mass., and London, 1935-8. 4 vols., Loeb Classical Library.

Addendum (1981)

G. M. A. Grube, *The Greek and Roman Critics*, Toronto, 1965.

G. A. Kennedy, *The Art of Rhetoric in the Roman World*, 300 B.C.–A.D. 300, Princeton, 1972.

ANALYSIS

Book I

(1) In a short Preface the author dedicates the treatise to Herennius, disclaims the intention of treating material irrelevant to the art of rhetoric, and stresses the need to apply in practice the rules he will set forth. (2) The task of the public speaker is to discuss capably those matters which law and custom have fixed for the uses of citizenship, and to secure as far as possible the agreement of his hearers. The kinds of causes are three: (*a*) Epideictic, (*b*) Deliberative, and (*c*) Judicial. (3) The speaker should be competent in (*a*) Invention, (*b*) Arrangement, (*c*) Style, (*d*) Memory, and (*e*) Delivery, and the means of acquiring these kinds of competence are three: (*a*) Theory, (*b*) Imitation, and (*c*) Practice. (4) In showing how to adapt the discourse to the theory of the speaker's function, the author gives primary consideration to Invention as used in each of the parts of a discourse in a Judicial cause: (*a*) Introduction, (*b*) Statement of Facts, (*c*) Division, (*d*) Proof, (*e*) Refutation, and (*f*) Conclusion. Each part of the discourse is defined before receiving special treatment in detail.

(5) To make an appropriate Introduction we must consider whether the cause is (*a*) honourable, (*b*) discreditable, (*c*) of doubtful creditableness, or (*d*) petty. (6) The nature of the cause thus viewed from a moral standpoint determines whether the Introduction shall take the form of (*a*) a Direct Opening, or

(*b*) a Subtle Approach. (7) Since the aim of the Introduction is to make the hearer (*a*) attentive, (*b*) receptive, and (*c*) well-disposed, the means whereby these states can be brought about is next discussed, (8) extended consideration being given to the four methods of making the hearer well-disposed: by discussing (*a*) our own person, (*b*) our adversaries, (*c*) our hearers, and (*d*) the facts themselves. (9) The Subtle Approach is reserved for three occasions: (*a*) when the cause is discreditable, (*b*) when the hearer has been won over, or (*c*) wearied, by the previous speakers of the opposition; and (9–10) the topics to be used in each of these situations are subjoined. (11) The Subtle Approach differs from the Direct Opening in achieving its results less obviously. Various kinds of Faulty Introductions are next listed.

(12–13) There are three kinds of Statement of Facts: (*a*) narrative directed towards victory in causes in which a decision is to be rendered; (*b*) Incidental Narrative, introduced to gain credit, incriminate the opponent, or the like; (*c*) narrative used in practice exercises, whether based on (*a*) the exposition of facts, which presents three forms: (*a*) legendary narrative, (*β*) historical, and (*γ*) realistic, or based on (*b*) persons, which emphasizes diverse traits of character and reversal of fortune. (14) The Statement of Facts in an actual cause should have three qualities: (*a*) brevity, (*b*) clarity, and (*c*) plausibility; (14–16) how these may be achieved is next explained.

(17) The Division sets forth what points we and our opponents agree upon, and what points remain contested, and then makes use of the Distribution, subheads under which are (*a*) the Enumeration, and (*b*) the Exposition, of the points we intend to discuss.

ANALYSIS

(18–25) We next pass to Proof and Refutation, the most important divisions of the discourse. In order to develop these we must know the Types of Issue presented by the cause. These types are three, and can be charted as follows:

1. Conjectural
(question of fact)
|
(For scheme, see Analysis
of Book II)

2. Legal
(question concerns inter-
pretation of a text)

(*a*) Letter and Spirit
(*b*) Conflicting Statutes
(*c*) Ambiguity
(*d*) Definition
(*e*) Transference
(*f*) Reasoning from Analogy

3. Juridical
(act admitted, but right or wrong of act is in question)

Absolute
(defence contends that
act in and of itself
is right)

Assumptive
(defence draws on extraneous
considerations)
|
(*a*) Acknowledgement of Charge

Exculpation
(*a*) Ignorance
(*β*) Accident
(*γ*) Necessity

Plea for Mercy

(*b*) Shifting of the Responsibility to

Some other
Person

Some Circumstance
(Enactment)

(*c*) Shifting of the Question of Guilt

(*d*) Comparison with Alternative
Act

ANALYSIS

(26) Before explaining how causes representing these Types of Issue should be developed, our author discusses the Justifying Motive of the defence, and the Central Point of the accusation, from the meeting of which in juridical and legal causes arises the Point to Adjudicate; (27) in a conjectural cause the Point to Adjudicate is established rather from the meeting of the Accusation and the Denial.

Book II

(1) Like Book I, this Book will be devoted to the most difficult kind of cause, the Judicial, and to the most important and difficult of the speaker's tasks, Invention. (2) Three subjects now demand attention: under Proof and Refutation, (a) how to apply the means of invention to each Type or Subtype of Issue, and (b) what sort of epicheiremes to seek or avoid; (c) under the divisions of the discourse, the Conclusion. The most important and difficult of the Types of Issue, the Conjectural, will be studied first. (3–12) After the contents appropriate to the Statement of Facts of both prosecutor and defendant's counsel have been set forth, the scheme of the Conjectural Issue is shown to include six divisions which can be charted as follows:

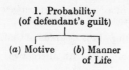

1. Probability
(of defendant's guilt)

(a) Motive   (b) Manner
of Life

2. Comparison
(no one else likely
to be guilty)

ANALYSIS

3. Signs
(pointing to guilt)

(a) Place
(b) Point of Time
(c) Duration of Time
(d) Occasion
(e) Hope of Success
(f) Hope of Escaping Detection

4. Presumptive Proof

(a) Preceding the crime
(b) Contemporaneous with the crime
(c) Following the crime

5. Subsequent Behaviour

6. Confirmatory Proof

Special topics

Common topics
(a) For and against witnesses
(b) For and against testimony given under torture
(c) For and against presumptive proof
(d) For and against rumours

Under the above rubrics the topics to be used by both prosecutor and defendant's counsel are indicated.

(13–18) We now turn to the procedure to be followed in the various types of Legal Issue, rules for both sides being supplied to meet the situation in which (a) the intention of the framer appears to be at variance with the letter of the text (13–14); (b) two statutes conflict (15); (c) a text is regarded as ambiguous (16); (d) we must define a legal offence in order to decide whether an admitted act comes within the definition (17); (e) the procedural principle of Transference is involved (18); or it is argued, by analogy with other laws, that (*f*) a matter not provided for by any special law comes within the spirit of other existing laws (18).

(19–20) The Juridical Issue: In developing an Absolute Juridical cause, we must first know whether the act was in accord with the Law, which derives from six sources: (*a*) The Law of Nature, (*b*) Statute Law, (*c*) Legal Custom, (*d*) Previous Judgements, (*e*) Equity, (*f*) Agreement; each is defined and illustrated. (21–22) The development of the Sub-types of an Assumptive Juridical cause is discussed in the following order: (*a*) Comparison with the Alternative to show that the admitted act was less evil; (*b*) Shifting of the Question of Guilt (22); (*c*) Acknowledgement of the Charge (23–25); and (*d*) Rejection of the Responsibility (26).

(27) Having shown what arguments to use in a judicial cause, the author now studies the artistic Development of an argument. The five parts of a complete argument are (28–30) defined and illustrated: (*a*) the Proposition, (*b*) the Reason, (*c*) the Proof of the Reason, (*d*) the Embellishment, (*e*) the Résumé, provision being made for situations in which not all the five parts are to be used. (31) He next investigates defective arguments, illustrating (32–46) faults for each of the parts, and treating (46), under Embellishment, (α) similes, (β) examples, (γ) amplifications, and (δ) previous judgements.

(47) The Conclusion of a speech is tripartite, including: (*a*) the Summing Up; (*b*) the Amplification, which draws commonplaces from ten formulae, and (*c*) the Appeal to Pity.

ANALYSIS

Book III

(1) will deal with Deliberative and Epideictic causes, and, of the departments of rhetoric, with Arrangement, Delivery, and Memory.

(2) A Deliberative speech concerns a choice among two or more courses of action; the question may be examined either on its own account or on account of a motive extraneous to the question itself. (3) The aim in a deliberative speech is Advantage, to be studied in accordance with the following topics:

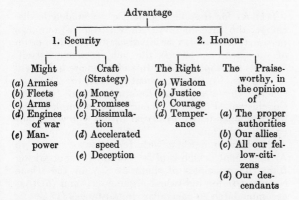

Advantage

1. Security

Might
(a) Armies
(b) Fleets
(c) Arms
(d) Engines of war
(e) Man-power

Craft (Strategy)
(a) Money
(b) Promises
(c) Dissimula-tion
(d) Accelerated speed
(e) Deception

2. Honour

The Right
(a) Wisdom
(b) Justice
(c) Courage
(d) Temper-ance

The Praise-worthy, in the opinion of
(a) The proper authorities
(b) Our allies
(c) All our fel-low-citi-zens
(d) Our des-cendants

The use of the topics (4–6) under the Right, and (7) under the Praiseworthy is explained in some detail.

(7) We now learn how to develop the deliberative cause as a whole, beginning with the Introduction and Statement of facts, and proceeding (8) to the Division, (8–9) the Proof and Refutation, and Conclusion.

ANALYSIS

(10) Epideictic, including praise and censure, deals with

1. External Circumstances	2. Physical Attributes	3. Qualities of Character
(a) Descent	(a) Agility	(a) Wisdom
(b) Ed·1cation	(b) Strength	(b) Justice
(c) Wealth	(c) Beauty	(c) Courage
(d) Kinds of power	(d) Health	(d) Temperance
(e) Titles to fame		
(f) Citizenship		
(g) Friendships		

(11) As for the Development of an epideictic discourse, the Introduction is drawn from (a) our own person, (b) the person we are discussing, (c) the person of our hearers, or (d) the subject-matter itself. (11–13) The topics for the Introduction are indicated, as also for (13) the Statement of facts, the Division, (13–15) the Proof and Refutation, and (15) the Conclusion. Epideictic, though seldom employed by itself independently in actual life, is yet worth our careful attention.

(16) Having finished with Invention, we turn to Arrangement, which is of two kinds: (a) that arising from the principles of rhetoric: (α) for the whole speech, (β) for individual arguments; and (b) that accommodated to particular circumstances (17).

(18) An appropriate Arrangement in Proof and Refutation would be to place: (a) the strongest arguments at the beginning and the end of the pleading, (b) arguments of medium force, and weak arguments, in the middle.

(19–20) Delivery, a faculty especially useful to the speaker, presents the following scheme:

ANALYSIS

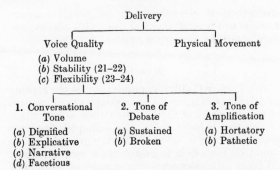

Delivery

Voice Quality   Physical Movement

(*a*) Volume
(*b*) Stability (21–22)
(*c*) Flexibility (23–24)

1. Conversational   2. Tone of   3. Tone of
    Tone   Debate   Amplification

(*a*) Dignified   (*a*) Sustained   (*a*) Hortatory
(*b*) Explicative   (*b*) Broken   (*b*) Pathetic
(*c*) Narrative
(*d*) Facetious

(24–25) Rules for the use of the voice in situations
representing each of these eight subdivisions are
offered, and (26–27) rules for bodily movement
appropriate to each.

(28–29) The two kinds of Memory, natural and
artificial, should supplement each other. The artificial memory includes backgrounds and images.
(30–32) To memorize a large number of items, we
must have a large number of backgrounds, in a
regular series, in a deserted region, clearly distinguishable, of moderate size and brightness, and at
intervals of about thirty feet. (33) Images should be
of both subject-matter and words; (33–34) the author
illustrates both kinds. (35–37) To acquire images
strong enough to awaken recollection we must
establish striking likenesses; and then in order to
revive the images, often and rapidly rehearse the
original backgrounds. (38–39) The author objects
for a number of reasons to listing images that
correspond to a great many words, yet (39–40)
regards the memorization of words as helpful in

strengthening the ability to memorize subject-matter, which is of practical use. (40) Essential in developing the memory is constant exercise.

BOOK IV

In a Preface (1–10) the author justifies the method he will follow of using his own examples in illustration of the Principles of Style. The Greek writers whom he opposes believe in drawing examples from the orators and poets, on the following grounds: (a) It would be immodest to create one's own examples. (b) Since examples serve the purpose of testimony, they should, like testimony, be drawn from writers of highest esteem. The prestige of the ancients excites the ambition to imitate their excellence. (c) It is proof of technical skill to select appropriate examples and to list these under the proper rubrics.

The author will refute these arguments as follows: (a) The argument on modesty is childish—why does not modesty keep these writers from writing anything at all? They are open rather to the charge of impudence, for extracting from the labour of authors praise for themselves. (b) Examples do not confirm or bear witness, but merely clarify the nature of a statement. Further, testimony must accord with the proposition, but the performance of these rhetoricians does not accord with their proposal. In writing a treatise they propose to teach to others what they have invented, but really show us what others have invented. (c) The choice from among many examples is not difficult, even for those who lack the highest art; the facile chooser will not necessarily write with skill himself.

liv

Furthermore, these writers are not only at fault in borrowing examples, but make an even greater mistake in borrowing from a great number of sources. If they must borrow examples at all, the selection should be made from one author alone, for (a) they might choose whom they would to supply examples for all cases, one on whose authority they could rely; (b) if a student believes that all qualities can exist in one man, he will be encouraged to strive for a mastery of them all.

Finally, the author will show that examples should not be borrowed at all: (a) an example cited by a writer on an art should be proof of his own skill in that art; (b) an example of one's own creation, draughted expressly to conform to the principle it is intended to clarify, makes for better understanding on the student's part.

The study of Style will consider (a) the kinds to which faultless oratorical style will confine itself, and (b) the qualities style should always have.

(11–14) The kinds of Style are three: (a) Grand, (b) Middle, and (c) Simple. Each is described and then illustrated by a passage. (15–16) Adjoining each of these styles is a defective style: (α) adjoining the Grand is the Swollen; (β) adjoining the Middle is the Slack or Drifting; (γ) adjoining the Simple is the Meagre. Again each is described and then illustrated by a passage.

Qualities of appropriate and finished Style:

(a) Taste (17)

(α) Correct Latinity, avoiding Solecisms Barbarisms	(β) Clarity, achieved by Current terms Proper terms

ANALYSIS

ANALYSIS

ANALYSIS

An epilogue (69) enjoins Herennius to exercise diligently, and summarizes the contents of the treatise.

LIST OF CICERO'S WORKS

SHOWING THEIR DIVISION INTO VOLUMES IN THIS SERIES

A. RHETORICAL TREATISES
Five volumes

B. ORATIONS
Ten volumes

LIST OF CICERO'S WORKS

LIST OF CICERO'S WORKS

LIST OF CICERO'S WORKS

BOOK I

[M. TULLI CICERONIS]

AD C. HERENNIUM

(DE RATIONE DICENDI)

LIBER PRIMUS

1 I. Etsi negotiis familiaribus inpediti vix satis
otium studio suppeditare possumus, et id ipsum quod
datur otii libentius in philosophia consumere consuevimus, tamen tua nos, Gai Herenni, voluntas
commovit ut de ratione dicendi conscriberemus, ne
aut tua causa noluisse aut fugisse nos laborem
putares. Et eo studiosius hoc negotium suscepimus,
quod te non sine causa velle cognoscere rhetoricam
intellegebamus; non enim in se parum fructus habet
copia dicendi et commoditas orationis, si recta in-
tellegentia et definita animi moderatione gubernetur.

Quas ob res illa quae Graeci scriptores inanis
adrogantiae causa sibi adsumpserunt reliquimus.
Nam illi, ne parum multa scisse viderentur, ea con-
quisierunt quae nihil adtinebant, ut ars difficilior
cognitu putaretur; nos autem ea quae videbantur ad

---

^a The beginning of Book 4 further sets forth the author's
attitude to the Greek writers on rhetoric (who these are
specifically is uncertain); *cf.* also 3. xxiii. 38. For his
attitude to philosophical studies see the end of Book 4.

[MARCUS TULLIUS CICERO]

TO GAIUS HERENNIUS

(ON THE THEORY OF PUBLIC SPEAKING)

BOOK I

1 I. My private affairs keep me so busy that I can hardly find enough leisure to devote to study, and the little that is vouchsafed to me I have usually preferred to spend on philosophy. Yet your desire, Gaius Herennius, has spurred me to compose a work on the Theory of Public Speaking, lest you should suppose that in a matter which concerns you I either lacked the will or shirked the labour. And I have undertaken this project the more gladly because I knew that you had good grounds in wishing to learn rhetoric, for it is true that copiousness and facility in expression bear abundant fruit, if controlled by proper knowledge and a strict discipline of the mind.

That is why I have omitted to treat those topics which, for the sake of futile self-assertion, Greek writers [a] have adopted. For they, from fear of appearing to know too little, have gone in quest of notions irrelevant to the art, in order that the art might seem more difficult to understand. I, on the other hand, have treated those topics which seemed

3

rationem dicendi pertinere sumpsimus. Non enim
spe quaestus aut gloria commoti venimus ad scribendum quemadmodum ceteri, sed ut industria nostra
tuae morem geramus voluntati.[a] Nunc, ne nimium
longa sumatur oratio, de re dicere incipiemus, si te
unum illud monuerimus, artem sine adsiduitate
dicendi non multum iuvare, ut intellegas hanc
rationem praeceptionis ad exercitationem adcommodari oportere.

2   II. Oratoris officium est de iis rebus posse dicere
quae res ad usum civilem moribus et legibus con-
stitutae sunt, cum adsensione auditorum quoad eius
fieri poterit.[b] Tria genera sunt causarum quae
recipere debet orator: demonstrativum, deliberativum, iudiciale.[c][d] Demonstrativum est quod tribuitur in alicuius certae personae laudem vel vituperationem. Deliberativum est in consultatione,
quod habet in se suasionem et dissuasionem.
Iudiciale est quod positum est in controversia, et
quod habet accusationem aut petitionem cum
defensione.

Nunc quas res oratorem habere oporteat docebimus, deinde quo modo has causas tractari conveniat
ostendemus.

---

   [a] Apparently text-books on public speaking sold well; see
Theodor Birt, *Rhein. Mus.* 72 (1917/18). 311–16.
   [b] The definition is that of Hermagoras, to whom the
function (ἔργον) of the perfect orator is τὸ τεθὲν πολιτικὸν
ζήτημα διατίθεσθαι κατὰ τὸ ἐνδεχόμενον πειστικῶς. See Sextus
Empiricus, *Adv. Rhet.* 62, ed. Fabricius, 2. 150.   *Cf.* Cicero,
De Inv. 1. v. 6.
   [c] γένη.
   [d] ἐπιδεικτικόν, συμβουλευτικόν, δικανικόν. The scheme is
Aristotelian (*Rhet.* 1. 3 , 1358b) but in essence older.   The

4

pertinent to the theory of public speaking. I have not been moved by hope of gain [a] or desire for glory, as the rest have been, in undertaking to write, but have done so in order that, by my painstaking work, I may gratify your wish. To avoid prolixity, I shall now begin my discussion of the subject, as soon as I have given you this one injunction: Theory without continuous practice in speaking is of little avail; from this you may understand that the precepts of theory here offered ought to be applied in practice.

2 II. The task of the public speaker is to discuss capably those matters which law and custom have fixed for the uses of citizenship, and to secure as far as possible the agreement of his hearers. [b] There are three kinds [c] of causes which the speaker must treat: Epideictic, Deliberative, and Judicial. [d] The epideictic kind is devoted to the praise or censure of some particular person. The deliberative consists in the discussion of policy and embraces persuasion and dissuasion. [e] The judicial is based on legal controversy, and comprises criminal prosecution or civil suit, and defence. [f]

Now I shall explain what faculties the speaker should possess, and then show the proper means of treating these causes. [g]

author's emphasis in the first two books, on the judicial kind, is characteristically Hellenistic (e.g., Hermagorean). The better tradition indicates that originally rhetoric was concerned with the judicial kind, and was later extended to the other two fields. For a study of the three *genera* see D. A. G. Hinks, *Class. Quarterly* 30 (1936). 170–6. *Cf.* Cicero, *De Inv.* 1. v. 7.

[e] προτροπή and ἀποτροπή.
[f] κατηγορία, δίκη, ἀπολογία.
[g] 2. ii. 2 below.

5

[CICERO]

3   Oportet igitur esse in oratore inventionem, dispositionem, elocutionem, memoriam, pronuntiationem. Inventio est excogitatio rerum verarum aut veri similium quae causam probabilem reddant. Dispositio est ordo et distributio rerum, quae demonstrat quid quibus locis sit conlocandum. Elocutio est idoneorum verborum et sententiarum ad inventionem adcommodatio. Memoria est firma animi rerum et verborum et dispositionis perceptio. Pronuntiatio est vocis, vultus, gestus moderatio cum venustate.

Haec omnia tribus rebus adsequi poterimus: arte, imitatione, exercitatione. Ars est praeceptio, quae

---

^a εὕρεσις, τάξις or οἰκονομία, λέξις or ἑρμηνεία or φράσις, μνήμη, ὑπόκρισις. The pre-Aristotelian rhetoric, represented by the *Rhet. ad Alexandrum*, treated the first three (without classifying them); Aristotle would add Delivery (*Rhet.* 3. 1, 1403 b), and his pupil Theophrastus did so (see note on 3. xi. 19 below). When precisely in the Hellenistic period Memory was added as a fifth division by the Rhodian or the Pergamene school, we do not know. These faculties (*res*; see also 1. ii. 3) are referred to in 2. i. 1 below (*cf.* 1. iii. 4) as the speaker's *functions* (*officia* = ἔργα τοῦ ῥήτορος). Quintilian, 3. 3. 11 ff., considers them as departments or constituent elements of the art (*partes rhetorices*) rather than as *opera* (= *officia*); so also here at 3. i. 1, 3. viii. 15, 3. xvi. 28, and Cicero, *De Inv.* 1. vii. 9. ἔργον is an Aristotelian concept (*cf.* the definition of rhetoric in *Rhet.* 1. 1–2, 1355b), and Aristotle was the first to classify the (major) functions. Our author here gives the usual order of the divisions; so also Cicero, *De Oratore* 1. 31. 142. Diogenes Laertius, 7. 43, presents the Stoic scheme: Invention, Style (φράσις), Arrangement, and Delivery. A goodly number of rhetorical systems were actually based on these ἔργα (*e.g.*, in most part Cicero's and Quintilian's); others were based on the divisions of the discourse (μόρια λόγου). See K. Barwick, *Hermes* 57 (1922). 1 ff.; Friedrich Solmsen, *Amer. Journ. Philol.* 62 (1941). 35–50, 169–90. Our author conflates the two schemes he has in-

6

3   The speaker, then, should possess the faculties of
Invention, Arrangement, Style, Memory, and Delivery.[a] Invention is the devising of matter, true
or plausible, that would make the case convincing.[b]
Arrangement is the ordering and distribution of the
matter, making clear the place to which each thing
is to be assigned.   Style is the adaptation of suitable
words and sentences to the matter devised.   Memory
is the firm retention in the mind of the matter, words,
and arrangement.   Delivery is the graceful regula-
tion of voice, countenance, and gesture.

All these faculties we can acquire by three means:
Theory, Imitation, and Practice.[c] By theory is meant

herited; see especially 1. ii. 3–iii. 4, 2. i. 1–ii. 2, and the
Introduction to the present volume, p. xviii.

[b] The concept goes back at least as far as Plato (e.g.,
Phaedrus 236 A); see Aristotle, Rhet. 1. 2 (1355b), on finding
artistic proofs.

[c] τέχνη (also παιδεία, ἐπιστήμη, μάθησις, scientia, doctrina),
μίμησις, γυμνασία (also ἄσκησις, μελέτη, ἐμπειρία, συνήθεια, declamatio).   The usual triad, Nature (φύσις, natura, ingenium,
facultas), Theory, and Practice, can be traced back to
Protagoras, Plato (Phaedrus 269 D), and Isocrates (e.g., Antid.
187; Adv. Soph. 14–18, where Imitation is also included).   Cf.
also Aristotle in Diogenes Laertius 5. 18; Cicero, De Inv. 1.
i. 2. De Oratore 1. 4. 14; Dionysius Halic. in Syrianus,
Scholia Hermog., ed. Rabe, 1. 4–5; Tacitus, Dialog. de
Orator., ch. 33; Plutarch, De liberis educ. 4 (2 A); and see
Paul Shorey, Trans. Am. Philol. Assn. 40 (1909). 185–201.
Imitation is presumed to have been emphasized in the Perga-
mene school of rhetors under Stoic influence.   Quintilian,
3. 5. 1, tells us that it was classed by some writers as a fourth
element, which he yet subordinates to Theory.   On Imitation
cf. Antonius in Cicero, De Oratore 2. 21. 89 ff.; Dionysius
Halic., De Imitat. (Opuscula 2. 197–217, ed. Usener-Radermacher); Quintilian, 10. 1. 20 ff.; Eduard Stemplinger, Das
Plagiat in der Griech. Lit., Leipzig and Berlin, 1912, pp. 81 ff.;
Kroll, "Rhetorik", coll. 1113 ff.; Paulus Otto, Quaestiones
selectae ad libellum qui est περὶ ὕψους spectantes, diss. Kiel, 1906,

[CICERO]

dat certam viam rationemque dicendi. Imitatio est qua impellimur, cum diligenti ratione, ut aliquorum similes in dicendo valeamus esse. Exercitatio est adsiduus usus consuetudoque dicendi.

Quoniam ergo demonstratum est quas causas oratorem recipere quasque res habere conveniat, nunc quemadmodum possit oratio ad rationem oratoris officii adcommodari dicendum videtur.

4 III. Inventio in sex partes orationis consumitur: in exordium, narrationem, divisionem, confirmationem, confutationem, conclusionem. Exordium est principium orationis, per quod animus auditoris constituitur ad audiendum. Narratio est rerum gestarum aut proinde ut gestarum expositio. Divisio est per quam aperimus quid conveniat, quid in controversia sit, et per quam exponimus quibus de rebus simus acturi. Confirmatio est nostrorum argumentorum expositio cum adseveratione. Confutatio

---

pp. 6–19; G. C. Fiske, *Lucilius and Horace*, Madison, 1920, ch. 1; J. F. D'Alton, *Roman Literary Theory and Criticism*, London, New York, and Toronto, 1931, pp. 426 ff.; Richard McKeon, " Literary Criticism and the Concept of Imitation in Antiquity," *Mod. Philol.* 34, 1 (1936). 1–35, and esp. pp. 26 ff.; D. L. Clark, " Imitation : Theory and Practice in Roman Rhetoric," *Quart. Journ. Speech* 37, 1 (1951). 11–22. " Exercise " refers to the *progymnasmata,* of which our treatise and Cicero's *De Inv.* show the first traces in Latin rhetoric, and to the " suasoriae " (*deliberationes*) and " controversiae " (*causae*) in which the treatise abounds. See also 4. xliv. 58 (Refining). The divorce between *praeexercitamenta* and *exercitationes* belongs to the Augustan period.

ᵃ The author's treatment of the parts of a discourse differs from that of Aristotle, who, in *Rhet.* 3. 13 (1414 a) ff., discusses them—Proem, Statement of Facts, Proof, and Conclusion—with all three kinds of oratory in view, not only the judicial, under Arrangement. Note that Invention is applied

a set of rules that provide a definite method and system of speaking. Imitation stimulates us to attain, in accordance with a studied method, the effectiveness of certain models in speaking. Practice is assiduous exercise and experience in speaking.

Since, then, I have shown what causes the speaker should treat and what kinds of competence he should possess, it seems that I now need to indicate how the speech can be adapted to the theory of the speaker's function.

4 III. Invention is used for the six parts of a discourse: the Introduction, Statement of Facts, Division, Proof, Refutation, and Conclusion.[a] The Introduction is the beginning of the discourse, and by it the hearer's mind is prepared[b] for attention. The Narration or Statement of Facts sets forth the events that have occurred or might have occurred.[c] By means of the Division we make clear what matters are agreed upon and what are contested, and announce what points we intend to take up. Proof is the presentation of our arguments, together with their corroboration.[d] Refutation is the destruction

---

[a] concretely to the parts of the discourse; in 1. xi. 18 ff. below the Issues are subjoined to Proof and Refutation. *Cf.* Cicero, *De Inv.* 1. xiv. 19. The Stoic scheme included Proem, Statement of Facts, Replies to Opponents, and Conclusion (Diogenes Laertius 7. 43).

[b] παρασκευάζεται. The concept is Isocratean. *Cf. Rhet. ad Alex.*, ch. 29 (1436a); Dionysius Halic., *De Lys.* 17; Anon. Seg. 5 and 9 (Spengel-Hammer 1 [2]. 353–4): Rufus 4 (Spengel-Hammer 1 [2]. 399); Anon., in Rabe, *Proleg. Sylloge*, p. 62.

[c] This definition is translated directly from a Greek original; see Hermogenes, *Progymn.* 2 (ed. Rabe, p. 4), Syrianus, *Scholia Hermog.* (ed. Rabe 2. 170), Theon 4 (Spengel 2. 78). *Cf.* Cicero, *De Inv.* 1. xix. 27.

[d] *Cf.* Cicero, *De Inv.* 1. xxiv. 34.

est contrariorum locorum dissolutio. Conclusio est
artificiosus orationis terminus.

Nunc quoniam una cum oratoris officiis, quo res
cognitu facilior esset, producti sumus ut de orationis
partibus loqueremur et eas ad inventionis rationem
adcommodaremus, de exordio primum dicendum
videtur.

5 Causa posita, quo commodius exordiri possimus
genus causae est considerandum. Genera causarum
sunt quattuor: honestum, turpe, dubium, humile.
Honestum causae genus putatur cum aut id defendimus quod ab omnibus defendendum videtur, aut
oppugnabimus quod ab omnibus videtur oppugnari
debere, ut pro viro forti, contra parricidam. Turpe
genus intellegitur cum aut honesta res oppugnatur
aut defenditur turpis. Dubium genus est cum habet
in se causa et honestatis et turpitudinis partem.
Humile genus est cum contempta res adfertur.

6 IV. Cum haec ita sint, conveniet exordiorum
rationem ad causae genus adcommodari. Exordiorum duo sunt genera: principium, quod Graece

---

ᵃ Cf. Cicero, De Inv. 1. xlii. 78 (reprehensio).
ᵇ πρόλογος, probably.
ᶜ ἔνδοξον, παράδοξον, ἀμφίδοξον, ἄδοξον, the σχήματα ὑποθέ-
σεων, later sometimes called figurae materiarum or controver-
siarum. The classification is on a moral basis. These genera
causarum are not to be confused with the three genera causarum treated in 1. ii. 2 above. Most rhetoricians (e.g., Cicero,
De Inv. 1. xv. 20) treated also a fifth kind, obscurum (δυσ-
παρακολούθητον), and some included six kinds (see Quintilian,
4. 1. 40). The division into four σχήματα is Hermagorean
(cf. Augustine, De Rhet. 1. 17 ff., in Halm, pp. 147 ff.), and

of our adversaries' arguments.[a] The Conclusion is
the end of the discourse, formed in accordance with
the principles of the art.

Along with the speaker's functions, in order to
make the subject easier to understand, I have been
led also to discuss the parts of a discourse, and to
adapt these to the theory of Invention. It seems,
then, that I must at this juncture first discuss the
Introduction.[b]

5 Given the cause, in order to be able to make a
more appropriate Introduction, we must consider
what kind of cause it is. The kinds of causes are
four: honourable, discreditable, doubtful, and petty.[c]
A cause is regarded as of the honourable kind when
we either defend what seems to deserve defence by
all men, or attack what all men seem in duty bound
to attack; for example, when we defend a hero, or
prosecute a parricide. A cause is understood to be
of the discreditable kind when something honourable
is under attack or when something discreditable is
being defended. A cause is of the doubtful kind
when it is partly honourable and partly discreditable.
A cause is of the petty kind when the matter brought
up is considered unimportant.

6 IV. In view of these considerations, it will be in
point to apply the theory of Introductions to the
kind of cause. There are two kinds of Introduction:
the Direct Opening, in Greek called the *Prooimion,*[d]

here our author conflates Hermagorean doctrine with the
pre-Aristotelian doctrine of the Proem; see Georg Thiele,
Hermagoras, Strassburg, 1893, pp. 113–121.

[d] προοίμιον, " Prelude"; see Aristotle, *Rhet.* 3. 14 (1414b),
Quintilian, 4. 1. 2 ff., Anon. Seg. 4, in Spengel-Hammer
1 (2). 352–3. *Cf.* Cicero, *De Inv.* 1. xv. 20.

prooemium[1] appellatur, et insinuatio, quae ephodos[2] nominatur. Principium est cum statim auditoris animum nobis idoneum reddimus ad audiendum. Id ita sumitur ut adtentos, ut dociles, ut benivolos auditores habere possimus. Si genus causae dubium habebimus, a benivolentia principium constituemus, ne quid illa turpitudinis pars nobis obesse possit. Sin humile genus erit causae, faciemus adtentos. Sin turpe causae genus erit, insinuatione utendum est, de qua posterius dicemus, nisi quid nacti erimus qua re adversarios criminando benivolentiam captare possimus. Sin honestum genus causae erit, licebit recte vel uti vel non uti principio. Si uti volemus, aut id oportebit ostendere qua re causa sit honesta, aut breviter quibus de rebus simus dicturi exponere. Sin principio uti nolemus, ab lege, ab scriptura, aut ab aliquo nostrae causae adiumento principium capere oportebit.

7 Quoniam igitur docilem, benivolum, adtentum auditorem habere volumus, quo modo quidque effici possit aperiemus. Dociles auditores habere poterimus, si summam causae breviter exponemus et si

---

[1] prohemium *MSS. Mx.*   [2] epodos *MSS. Mx.*

---

[a] ἔφοδος. The term is used in *Oxyr. Pap.* 3. 27, in a rhetorical treatise of perhaps the beginning of the fourth century B.C. In *Isaeus* 3, Dionysius Halic. comments on Isaeus' use of ἔφοδοι. *Cf.* also Anon., in Rabe, *Proleg. Syll.*, p. 206, and Anon., *Proleg. Invent.*, in Walz 7 (1). 54.

[b] The hearer is to be rendered προσεκτικός, εὐμαθής, εὔνους. *Cf.* Cicero, *De Inv.* 1. xvi. 22–3. The doctrine is pre-Aristotelian; see, *e.g.*, *Rhet. ad Alex.*, ch. 29 (1436a), and *Epist. Socrat.* 30. 4 on Isocrates. Aristotle, *Rhet.* 3. 14 (1415a), includes Receptiveness under Attention. Cicero, *Part. Orat.* 8. 28, gives three aims for the Direct Opening : *ut amice, ut*

and the Subtle Approach, called the *Ephodos*.[a] The Direct Opening straightway prepares the hearer to attend to our speech. Its purpose is to enable us to have hearers who are attentive, receptive, and well-disposed.[b] If our cause is of the doubtful kind, we shall build the Direct Opening upon goodwill, so that the discreditable part of the cause cannot be prejudicial to us. If our cause is of the petty kind, we shall make our hearers attentive. If our cause is of the discreditable kind, unless we have hit upon a means of capturing goodwill by attacking our adversaries, we must use the Subtle Approach, which I shall discuss later.[c] And finally, if our cause is of the honourable kind, it will be correct either to use the Direct Opening or not to use it.[d] If we wish to use it, we must show why the cause is honourable, or else briefly announce what matters we are going to discuss. But if we do not wish to use the Direct Opening, we must begin our speech with a law, a written document, or some argument supporting our cause.

7   Since, then, we wish to have our hearer receptive, well-disposed, and attentive, I shall disclose how each state can be brought about. We can have receptive hearers if we briefly summarise the cause and make

intellegenter, ut attente audiamur. For the importance of Attention in present-day rhetoric, *cf.* J. A. Winans, *Public Speaking*, New York, 1917, p. 194 : " Persuasion is the process of inducing others to give fair, favourable, or undivided attention to propositions."

[c] 1. vi. 9 ff.

[d] Cf. *Rhet. ad A¹ex.*, ch. 29 (1437b): " If there is no prejudice against ourselves or our speech or our subject, we shall set forth our Proposition immediately at the beginning, appealing for attention and a benevolent hearing afterwards."

[CICERO]

adtentos eos faciemus; nam docilis est qui adtente
vult audire. Adtentos habebimus, si pollicebimur
nos de rebus magnis, novis, inusitatis verba facturos,
aut de iis quae ad rem publicam pertineant, aut ad
eos ipsos qui audient, aut ad deorum immortalium
religionem; et si rogabimus ut adtente audiant; et
si numero exponemus res quibus de rebus dicturi
8 sumus. Benivolos auditores facere quattuor modis
possumus: ab nostra, ab adversariorum nostrorum,
ab auditorum persona, et ab rebus ipsis.

V. Ab nostra persona benivolentiam contrahemus
si nostrum officium sine adrogantia laudabimus,
atque in rem publicam quales fuerimus, aut in
parentes, aut in amicos, aut in eos qui audiunt
aperiemus et si . . .[1] aliquid referemus, dum haec
omnia ad eam ipsam rem qua de agitur sint adcommodata; item si nostra incommoda proferemus,
inopiam, solitudinem, calamitatem, et si orabimus
ut nobis sint auxilio, et simul ostendemus nos in aliis
noluisse spem habere.

Ab adversariorum persona benivolentia capta-
bitur si eos in odium, in invidiam, in contemptionem
adducemus. In odium rapiemus si quid eorum
spurce, superbe, perfidiose, crudeliter, confidenter,

[1] *Mx suggests* aperiemus et si *and fifteen additional words
to fill the lacuna.*

---

[a] So Aristotle, *Rhet.* 3. 14 (1415a), and Anon. Seg. 7
(Spengel-Hammer 1 [2]. 353-4): ἐκ τοῦ αὐτοῦ or τοῦ λέγοντος,
ἐκ τοῦ ἐναντίου or ἀντιδίκου, ἐκ τῶν ἀκροατῶν or δικαζόντων, ἐκ
τῶν πραγμάτων. Cf. also Cicero, *De Inv.* 1. xvi. 22. Here
as throughout the first two books the author is dealing with
judicial oratory.

[b] πάθος, here assigned to the Introduction, also has a place
in the Conclusion; see 2. xxx. 48-xxxi. 50 below. Thus the

14

them attentive; for the receptive hearer is one who is willing to listen attentively. We shall have attentive hearers by promising to discuss important, new, and unusual matters, or such as appertain to the commonwealth, or to the hearers themselves, or to the worship of the immortal gods; by bidding them listen attentively; and by enumerating the points 8 we are going to discuss. We can by four methods make our hearers well-disposed: by discussing our own person, the person of our adversaries, that of our hearers, and the facts themselves.[a]

V. From the discussion of our own person we shall secure goodwill by praising our services without arrogance and revealing also our past conduct toward the republic, or toward our parents, friends, or the audience, and by making some reference to . . . provided that all such references are pertinent to the matter in question; likewise by setting forth our disabilities, need, loneliness, and misfortune,[b] and pleading for our hearers' aid, and at the same time showing that we have been unwilling to place our hope in anyone else.

From the discussion of the person of our adversaries we shall secure goodwill by bringing them into hatred, unpopularity, or contempt.[c] We shall force hatred upon them by adducing some base, high-handed, treacherous, cruel, impudent, malicious, or

---

author accords with the early Greek rhetoric based on the divisions of the discourse. Nowhere does he make a profound analytical study of the emotions such as we find in Aristotle, *Rhet.*, Bk. II. In Anon. Seg. 6 (Spengel-Hammer 1 [2]. 353) are listed five emotions of the hearer which play a part in the function of the Proem: pity, anger, fear, hate, and desire.

[c] ἔχθρα or μῖσος, φθόνος, ὀργή.

malitiose, flagitiose factum proferemus. In invidiam
trahemus si vim, si potentiam, si factionem, divitias,
incontinentiam, nobilitatem, clientelas, hospitium,
sodalitatem, adfinitates adversariorum proferemus,
et his adiumentis magis quam veritati eos confidere
aperiemus. In contemptionem adducemus si inertiam, ignaviam, desidiam, luxuriam adversariorum
proferemus.

Ab auditorum persona benivolentia colligitur si
res eorum fortiter, sapienter, mansuete, magnifice
iudicatas proferemus; et si quae de iis existimatio,
quae iudicii expectatio sit aperiemus.

Ab rebus ipsis benivolum efficiemus auditorem si
nostram causam laudando extollemus, adversariorum
per contemptionem deprimemus.

9 VI. Deinceps de insinuatione aperiendum est.
Tria sunt tempora quibus principio uti non possumus,
quae diligenter sunt consideranda: aut cum turpem
causam habemus, hoc est, cum ipsa res animum
auditoris a nobis alienat; aut cum animus auditoris
persuasus esse videtur ab iis qui ante contra dixerunt;
aut cum defessus est eos audiendo qui ante dixerunt.

Si causa turpitudinem habebit, exordiri poterimus
his rationibus: hominem, non rem,[1] spectari oportere;
non placere nobis ipsis quae facta dicantur ab adver-

---

[1] hominem non rem *Thiele*: rem non hominem hominem
non rem *E*: rem hominem *PCMx*: rem non hominem *HP*[2] II.

---

[a] In Cicero, *De Inv.* 1. xvii. 23, the Subtle Approach is
specifically used in the *admirabile genus causae*. The three
causae of Cicero correspond to the " occasions " classified by
our author. Anon. Seg. 21 ff. (Spengel-Hammer 1 [2]. 357 ff.)
gives four occasions on which the Prooemion should be dispensed with, and discusses the view that it must always be
used.

shameful act of theirs. We shall make our adversaries unpopular by setting forth their violent behaviour, their dominance, factiousness, wealth, lack of self-restraint, high birth, clients, hospitality, club allegiance, or marriage alliances, and by making clear that they rely more upon these supports than upon the truth. We shall bring our adversaries into contempt by presenting their idleness, cowardice, sloth, and luxurious habits.

From the discussion of the person of our hearers goodwill is secured if we set forth the courage, wisdom, humanity, and nobility of past judgements they have rendered, and if we reveal what esteem they enjoy and with what interest their decision is awaited.

From the discussion of the facts themselves we shall render the hearer well-disposed by extolling our own cause with praise and by contemptuously disparaging that of our adversaries.

9 VI. Now I must explain the Subtle Approach.[a] There are three occasions on which we cannot use the Direct Opening, and these we must consider carefully: (1) when our cause is discreditable, that is, when the subject itself alienates the hearer from us; (2) when the hearer has apparently been won over by the previous speakers of the opposition; (3) or when the hearer has become wearied by listening to the previous speakers.

If the cause has a discreditable character,[b] we can make our Introduction with the following points: that the agent, not the action, ought to be considered; that we ourselves are displeased with the acts which our opponents say have been committed, and that

[b] *Cf.* Cicero, *De Inv.* 1. xvii. 24.

sariis, et esse indigna aut nefaria. Deinde cum diu
rem auxerimus, nihil simile a nobis factum ostendemus; aut aliquorum iudicium de simili causa aut
de eadem aut de minore aut de maiore proferemus,
deinde ad nostram causam pedetemptim accedemus
et similitudinem conferemus. Item si negabimus
nos de adversariis aut de aliqua re dicturos, et tamen
occulte dicemus interiectione verborum.

10   Si persuasus auditor, si¹ oratio adversariorum
fecerit fidem auditoribus—neque enim non facile
scire poterimus, quoniam non sumus nescii quibus
rebus fides fieri soleat—ergo si fidem factam puta-
bimus, his nos rebus insinuabimus ad causam: de eo
quod adversarii firmissimum sibi adiumentum
putarint primum nos dicturos pollicebimur; ab
adversarii dicto exordiemur, et ab eo maxime quod
ille nuperrime dixerit; dubitatione utemur quid
potissimum dicamus aut cui loco primum respon-
deamus, cum admiratione.

Si defessi erunt audiendo, ab aliqua re quae risum
movere possit, ab apologo, fabula veri simili, imitatione depravata, inversione, ambiguo, suspicione,
inrisione, stultitia, exsuperatione, collectione, lit-

¹ si *M*: fuerit id est si *EMx*.

ᵃ παραφθέγγεσθαι.
ᵇ *Cf.* Cicero, *De Inv.* 1. xvii. 25.
ᶜ See 4. xxix. 40 below.
ᵈ Note that humour enters the rhetorical system under the
Introduction.   Aristotle, *Rhet.* 3. 14 (1415a), also discusses
the place of laughter in the Proem.   This classification of
eighteen means of provoking laughter must have been a recent
accession to rhetorical theory; cf. the summary in Cicero, *De
Oratore* 2. 61. 248 ff.   On wit and humour in ancient rhetoric,
see E. Arndt, *De ridiculi doctrina rhetorica*, Bonn, 1904;

18

these are unworthy, yes, heinous. Next, when we
have for a time enlarged upon this idea, we shall
show that nothing of the kind has been committed by
us. Or we shall set forth the judgement rendered
by others in an analogous cause, whether that cause
be of equal, or less, or greater importance; then we
shall gradually approach our own cause and establish
the analogy. The same result is achieved if we deny
an intention to discuss our opponents or some extraneous matter and yet, by subtly inserting the words,[a]
do so.

10   If the hearers have been convinced,[b] if our
opponent's speech has gained their credence—and
this will not be hard for us to know, since we are
well aware of the means by which belief is ordinarily
effected—if, then, we think belief has been effected,
we shall make our Subtle Approach to the cause by
the following means: the point which our adversaries
have regarded as their strongest support we shall
promise to discuss first; we shall begin with a statement made by the opponent, and particularly with
that which he has made last; and we shall use
Indecision,[c] along with an exclamation of astonishment: " What had I best say ? " or " To what point
shall I first reply ? "

If the hearers have been fatigued by listening,
we shall open with something that may provoke
laughter [d]—a fable, a plausible fiction, a caricature,
an ironical inversion of the meaning of a word, an
ambiguity, innuendo, banter, a naïvety, an exaggera-

Mary A. Grant, *The Ancient Rhetorical Theories of the Laugh
able*, Madison, 1924; and Wilhelm Kroll in P.-W., art.
" Rhetorik," coll. 1076–7. *Cf.* also Wilhelm Süss, *Neue Jahrb.*
23 (1920). 28–45.

[CICERO]

terarum mutatione, praeter expectationem, similitudine, novitate, historia, versu, ab alicuius inter-
pellatione aut adrisione; si promiserimus aliter ac
parati fuerimus nos esse dicturos; nos non eodem
modo ut ceteri soleant verba facturos; quid alii
soleant, quid nos facturi simus [1] breviter exponemus.

11   VII. Inter insinuationem et principium hoc interest. Principium eiusmodi debet esse ut statim
apertis rationibus quibus praescripsimus aut benivolum aut adtentum aut docilem faciamus auditorem;
at insinuatio eiusmodi debet esse ut occulte, per dissimulationem, eadem illa omnia conficiamus, ut ad
eandem commoditatem in dicendi opere venire
possimus. Verum hae tres [2] utilitates tametsi in
tota oratione sunt conparandae, hoc est, ut auditores
sese perpetuo nobis adtentos, dociles, benivolos
praebeant, tamen id per exordium causae maxime
conparandum est.

Nunc, ne quando vitioso exordio utamur, quae vitia
vitanda sint docebo. Exordienda causa servandum
est ut lenis sit sermo et usitata verborum consuetudo,
ut non apparata videatur oratio esse. Vitiosum
exordium est quod in plures causas potest adcommodari, quod vulgare dicitur. Item vitiosum est quo
nihilo minus adversarius potest uti, quod commune

---

[1] simus *E*: sumus *MdMx*.
[2] hae tres *P²B²C* ΠE *Mx ed. mai.*: haec res *M*: haec tres
Mx.

---

[a] Of the adversary's arguments, perhaps.
[b] παρὰ προσδοκίαν.
[c] λαθραίως δι' ἑτέρων λόγων. Anon., *Proleg. Invent.*, in
Walz 7 (1). 54. 14–16, gives the same precept.

tion, a recapitulation,[a] a pun, an unexpected turn,[b] a comparison, a novel tale, a historical anecdote, a verse, or a challenge or a smile of approbation directed at some one. Or we shall promise to speak otherwise than as we have prepared, and not to talk as others usually do; we shall briefly explain what the other speakers do and what we intend to do.

11 VII. Between the Subtle Approach and the Direct Opening there is the following difference. The Direct Opening should be such that by the straightforward methods I have prescribed we immediately make the hearer well-disposed or attentive or receptive; whereas the Subtle Approach should be such that we effect all these results covertly, through dissimulation,[c] and so can arrive at the same vantage-point in the task of speaking. But though this three-fold advantage—that the hearers constantly show themselves attentive, receptive, and well-disposed to us—is to be secured throughout the discourse, it must in the main be won by the Introduction to the cause.

Now, for fear that we may at some time use a faulty Introduction, I shall show what faults must be avoided. In the Introduction of a cause we must make sure that our style is temperate and that the words are in current use,[d] so that the discourse seems unprepared. An Introduction is faulty if it can be applied as well to a number of causes;[e] that is called a banal Introduction. Again, an Introduction which the adversary can use no less well is faulty, and that

[d] Anon. Seg. 19 (Spengel-Hammer 1[2]. 356) makes the same point.
[e] *Cf.* Cicero, *De Inv.* 1. xviii. 26.

[CICERO]

appellatur; item illud quo adversarius ex contrario
poterit uti. Item vitiosum est quod nimium appara-
tis verbis [1] conpositum est, aut nimium longum est;
et quod non ex ipsa causa natum videatur ut proprie
cohaereat cum narratione; et quod neque benivolum
neque docilem neque adtentum facit auditorem.

VIII. De exordio satis erit dictum; deinceps ad
12 narrationem transeamus. Narrationum tria sunt
genera. Unum est cum exponimus rem gestam et
unum quidque trahimus ad utilitatem nostram
vincendi causa, quod pertinet ad eas causas de quibus
iudicium futurum est. Alterum genus est narrationis, quod intercurrit nonnumquam aut fidei aut
criminationis aut transitionis aut alicuius appara-
tionis causa. Tertium genus est id quod a causa
civili remotum est, in quo tamen exerceri convenit,
quo commodius illas superiores narrationes in causis
13 tractare possimus. Eius narrationis duo sunt genera:
unum quod in negotiis, alterum quod in personis
positum est.

Id quod in negotiorum expositione positum est tres
habet partes: fabulam, historiam, argumentum.
Fabula est quae neque veras neque veri similes
continet res, ut eae sunt quae tragoediis traditae

[1] verbis E Mx ed. mai.: M Mx omit.

---

[a] διήγησις. Cf. Cicero, De Inv. 1. xix. 27.
[b] διηγήσεις ἐπὶ κριτῶν λεγόμεναι.
[c] διαβολή.
[d] Incidental Narrative (παραδιήγησις); cf. Quintilian,
9. 2. 107, and Anon. Seg. 61 (Spengel-Hammer 1 [2]. 364–5),
who distinguishes it from Digression (παρέκβασις).

is called a common Introduction. That Introduction,
again, is faulty which the opponent can turn to his
own use against you. And again that is faulty which
has been composed in too laboured a style, or is too
long; and that which does not appear to have grown
out of the cause itself in such a way as to have an
intimate connection with the Statement of Facts; and,
finally, that which fails to make the hearer well-
disposed or receptive or attentive.

VIII. Concerning the Introduction I have said
enough; next let me turn to the Narration or State-
12 ment of Facts. There are three types of Statement
of Facts.[a] It is one type when we set forth the facts
and turn every detail to our advantage so as to win the
victory, and this kind appertains to the causes on
which a decision is to be rendered.[b] There is a
second type which often enters into a speech as a
means of winning belief or incriminating our adversary[c] or effecting a transition or setting the stage for
something.[d] The third type[e] is not used in a cause
actually pleaded in court, yet affords us convenient
practice[f] for handling the first two types more
13 advantageously in actual causes. Of such narratives
there are two kinds: one based on the facts, the other
on the persons.[g]

The kind of narrative based on the exposition of
the facts presents three forms: legendary, historical,
and realistic. The legendary tale comprises events
neither true nor probable, like those transmitted by

---

[e] διηγήσεις καθ᾽ ἑαυτάς.

[f] The reference is to the *progymnasmata* (*praeexercitamenta*). *Narratio* provided the first exercises imposed by
the rhetor; see Quintilian, 2. 4. 1, and Jean Cousin, *Études
sur Quintilien*, Paris, 1936, 1. 113.

[g] According to τὰ πράγματα or τὰ πρόσωπα.

23

sunt. Historia est gesta res, sed ab aetatis nostrae memoria remota. Argumentum est ficta res quae tamen fieri potuit, velut argumenta comoediarum.

Illud genus narrationis quod in personis positum est debet habere sermonis festivitatem, animorum dissimilitudinem, gravitatem lenitatem, spem metum, suspicionem desiderium, dissimulationem misericordiam, rerum varietates, fortunae commutationem, insperatum incommodum, subitam laetitiam, iucundum exitum rerum. Verum haec in exercendo transigentur; illud quod ad veritatem pertinet quomodo tractari conveniat aperiemus.

14 IX. Tres res convenit habere narrationem: ut brevis, ut dilucida, ut veri similis sit; quae quoniam fieri oportere scimus, quemadmodum faciamus cognoscendum est.

Rem breviter narrare poterimus si inde incipiemus narrare unde necesse erit; et si non ab ultimo initio repetere volemus; et si summatim, non parti-

---

[a] μῦθος, but see Cousin, *op. cit.*, 1. 113, note 4. *Cf.* Aristotle, *Poetics* 9 (1451a): "The poet's function is to describe, not the things that actually have happened, but the kind of things that might well happen—that are possible in the sense of being either probable or inevitable." But it is doubtless the miraculous element in tragedies that is here in mind; see the example of *fabula* in Cicero, *De Inv.* 1. xix. 27.

[b] ἱστορία.

[c] πλάσμα. *Cf. argumentum* (Presumptive Proof) in 2. ii. 3, and *argumentatio* (argument) in 2. ii. 2 below.

[d] *Cf.* the figure *notatio* (Character Delineation), 4. l. 63 below.

[e] *Cf.* Cicero, *Epist. ad Fam.* 5. 12. 4, on writing history: "For nothing is so suited to the delight of the reader as are shifting circumstances and the vicissitudes of fortune. Concerning our author's doctrine of *narratio* as reflecting Hellenistic ideas on historiography and story writing, see

tragedies.[a] The historical narrative is an account of exploits actually performed, but removed in time from the recollection of our age.[b] Realistic narrative recounts imaginary events, which yet could have occurred, like the plots of comedies.[c]

A narrative based on the persons should present a lively style and diverse traits of character,[d] such as austerity and gentleness, hope and fear, distrust and desire, hypocrisy and compassion, and the vicissitudes of life, such as reversal of fortune,[e] unexpected disaster, sudden joy, and a happy outcome. But it is in practice exercises that these types will be worked out.[f] How we should handle that type of Statement of Facts which belongs in actual causes I am about to explain.

14 IX. A Statement of Facts should have three qualities: brevity, clarity, and plausibility.[g] Since we know that these qualities are essential, we must learn how to achieve them.

We shall be able to make the Statement of Facts brief if we begin it at the place at which we need to begin; if we do not try to recount from the remotest beginning; if our Statement of Facts is summary and

R. Reitzenstein, *Hellenistische Wundererzählungen*, Leipzig, 1906, pp. 84 ff., and for further interpretations of these sections dealing with *narratio* (and of Cicero, *De Inv.* 1. xix. 27), Karl Barwick, *Hermes* 63, 3 (1928). 261–87, and Friedrich Pfister, *Hermes* 68, 4 (1933). 457–60.

[f] The *narratio* is developed (*tractatio* = ἐξεργασία) in the *progymnasmata*.

[g] συντομία, σαφήνεια, πιθανότης. The precept is Isocratean (see Quintilian, 4. 2. 31–2) or even older (see Octave Navarre, *Essai sur la rhétorique grecque avant Aristote*, Paris, 1900, p. 246). Aristotle, *Rhet.* 3. 16 (1416 b), scorns the injunction of brevity in favour of the " proper mean." *Cf.* Cicero, *De Inv.* 1. xx. 28.

culatim narrabimus; et si non ad extremum, sed usque eo quo opus erit persequemur; et si transitionibus nullis utemur, et si non deerrabimus ab eo quod coeperimus exponere; et si exitus rerum ita ponemus ut ante quoque quae facta sint sciri [1] possint, tametsi nos reticuerimus: quod genus, si dicam me ex provincia redisse, profectum quoque in provinciam intellegatur. Et omnino non modo id quod obest, sed etiam id quod neque obest neque adiuvat satius est praeterire. Et ne bis aut saepius idem dicamus cavendum est; etiam ne quid novissime quod diximus deinceps dicamus, hoc modo:

> Athenis Megaram vesperi advenit Simo;
> Ubi advenit Megaram, insidias fecit virgini;
> Insidias postquam fecit, vim in loco adtulit.

15 Rem dilucide narrabimus si ut quicquid primum gestum erit ita primum exponemus, et rerum ac temporum ordinem conservabimus ut gestae res erunt, aut ut potuisse geri videbuntur; hic erit considerandum ne quid perturbate, ne quid contorte, ne quid nove dicamus, ne quam in aliam rem transeamus, ne ab ultimo repetamus, ne longe persequamur, ne quid quod ad rem pertineat praetereamus; et si sequemur ea quae de brevitate praecepta sunt, nam quo brevior, dilucidior et cognitu facilior narratio fiet.

[1] sciri P^2BCE : scire HP^1Mx.

---

[a] Presented κεφαλαιωδῶς, not μερικῶς.

[b] Doxapatres (eleventh century), in Walz 2. 230, gives the same example; it is doubtless Greek in origin.

[c] The author of these iambic trimeters and the name of the comedy from which they come are both unknown. *Cf.* Plautus, *Miles Gloriosus* 439: *quae heri Athenis Ephesum adveni vesperi.*

not detailed;[a] if we carry it forward, not to the furthermost point, but to the point to which we need to go; if we use no digressions and do not wander from the account we have undertaken to set forth; and if we present the outcome in such a way that the facts that have preceded can also be known, although we have not spoken of them. For example, if I should say that I have returned from the province, it would also be understood that I had gone to the province.[b] And in general it is better to pass by not only that which weakens the cause but also that which neither weakens nor helps it. Furthermore, we must guard against saying a thing more than once, and certainly against repeating immediately what we have said already, as in the following: "Simo came from Athens to Megara in the evening; when he came to Megara, he laid a trap for the maiden: after laying the trap he ravished her then and there."[c]

15 Our Statement of Facts will be clear[d] if we set forth the facts in the precise order in which they occurred, observing their actual or probable sequence and chronology. Here we must see that our language is not confused,[e] involved, or unfamiliar, that we do not shift to another subject, that we do not trace the affair back to its remotest beginning, nor carry it too far forward, and that we do not omit anything pertinent. And our Statement of Facts will be clear if we follow the precepts on brevity that I have laid down,[f] for the shorter the Statement of Facts, the clearer will it be and the easier to follow.

[a] Cf. Cicero, De Inv. 1. xx. 29.
[e] ὑπερβατῶς, in inverted order.
[f] In 1. ix. 14 above.

16   Veri similis narratio erit si ut mos, ut opinio, ut
natura postulat dicemus; si spatia temporum, personarum dignitates, consiliorum rationes, locorum
opportunitates constabunt, ne refelli possit aut temporis parum fuisse, aut causam nullam, aut locum
idoneum non fuisse, aut homines ipsos facere aut pati
non potuisse. Si vera res erit, nihilominus haec
omnia narrando conservanda sunt, nam saepe veritas,
nisi haec servata sint, fidem non potest facere; sin
erunt ficta, eo magis erunt conservanda. De iis
rebus caute confingendum est quibus in rebus tabulae
aut alicuius firma auctoritas videbitur interfuisse.

Adhuc quae dicta sunt arbitror mihi constare cum
ceteris artis scriptoribus, nisi quia de insinuationibus
nova excogitavimus, quod eam soli nos praeter
ceteros in tria tempora divisimus, ut plane certam
viam et perspicuam rationem exordiorum haberemus.
X. Nunc, quod reliquum est—quoniam de rerum
inventione disputandum est, in quo singulare consumitur oratoris artificium—dabimus operam ut
nihilominus industrie quam rei utilitas postulabit
quaesisse videamur—si[1] prius pauca de divisione
causarum dixerimus.

---

[1] videamur si *MSS. Mx ed. mai.*: *lacuna before* si *Mx.*

---

[a] *Cf.* Cicero, *De Inv.* 1. xxi. 29–30.
[b] See note on 1. vi. 9 above. Our author's doctrine of the
Subtle Approach is Greek in origin, although we know no
specific Greek source for the three occasions. That Cicero
in *De Inv.* presents a like classification makes our author's

16   Our Statement of Facts will have plausibility [a] if it answers the requirements of the usual, the expected, and the natural; if account is strictly kept of the length of time, the standing of the persons involved, the motives in the planning, and the advantages offered by the scene of action, so as to obviate the argument in refutation that the time was too short, or that there was no motive, or that the place was unsuitable, or that the persons themselves could not have acted or been treated so. If the matter is true, all these precautions must none the less be observed in the Statement of Facts, for often the truth cannot gain credence otherwise. And if the matter is fictitious, these measures will have to be observed all the more scrupulously. Fabrication must be circumspect in those matters in which official documents or some person's unimpeachable guaranty will prove to have played a rôle.

In what I have thus far said I believe that I agree with the other writers on the art of rhetoric except for the innovations I have devised on Introductions by the Subtle Approach. I alone,[b] in contrast with the rest, have distinguished three occasions for the Subtle Approach, so as to provide us with a thoroughly sure method and a lucid theory of Introductions. X. Now as to the rest, since I must discuss the finding of arguments, a matter that makes unique demands upon the art of the speaker, I shall endeavour to exhibit an industry in research such as the importance of the subject demands—as soon as I have prefixed a few remarks on the Division of the cause.

claim difficult to explain; see the Introduction to the present volume, pp. xxix–xxx.

17   Causarum divisio in duas partes distributa est.
Primum perorata narratione [1] debemus aperire quid
nobis conveniat cum adversariis, si ea quae utilia
sunt nobis convenient, quid in controversia [2] relictum
sit, hoc modo : " Interfectam esse ab Oreste matrem
convenit mihi cum adversariis. Iure fecerit et licue-
ritne facere, id est in controversia." Item e contrario : " Agamemnonem esse a Clytemestra occisum
confitentur ; cum id ita sit, me ulcisci parentem
negant oportuisse."
      Deinde, cum hoc fecerimus, distributione uti
debemus. Ea dividitur in duas partes : enumerationem et expositionem. Enumeratione utemur cum
dicemus numero quot de rebus dicturi sumus. Eam
plus quam trium partium numero esse non oportet ;
nam et periculosum est ne quando plus minusve
dicamus, et suspicionem adfert auditori meditationis
et artificii, quae res fidem abrogat orationi. Expositio
est cum res quibus de rebus dicturi sumus exponimus
breviter et absolute.

        [1] perorata narratione *E* : per narrationem *M Mx*.
        [2] controversia *d* : controversiis *the other MSS. Mx*.

---

      [a] " Outlining of the case," the Analysis. προκατασκευή, a
combination of προέκθεσις and μερισμός. In Cicero, *De Inv.*
1. xxii. 31–xxiii. 33, *partitio. Cf.* the figure *divisio*, 4. xl. 52
below.
      [b] Martianus Capella, 5. 556, makes the same point for the
partitio.
      [c] A favourite theme of the rhetoricians ; *cf.* also 1. xv. 25
and 1. xvi. 26 below, Cicero, *De Inv.* 1. xiii. 18–xiv. 19,
1. xxii. 31, Quintilian, 3. 11. 4 ff., 3. 5. 11, 7. 4. 8.

17   The Division [a] of the cause falls into two parts. When
the Statement of Facts has been brought to an end,
we ought first to make clear what we and our opponents agree upon, if there is agreement on the points
useful to us,[b] and what remains contested, as follows :
" Orestes killed his mother; [c] on that I agree with
my opponents. But did he have the right to commit
the deed, and was he justified in committing it ? That
is in dispute." Likewise in reply : " They admit that
Agamemnon was killed by Clytemnestra ; yet despite
this they say that I ought not to have avenged my
father."

Then, when we have done this, we should use the
Distribution.[d] The Distribution has two parts : the
Enumeration [e] and the Exposition.[f] We shall be
using the Enumeration when we tell by number how
many points we are going to discuss. The number
ought not to exceed three ; for otherwise, besides the
danger that we may at some time include in the
speech more or fewer points than we enumerated,[g] it
instils in the hearer the suspicion of premeditation
and artifice,[h] and this robs the speech of conviction.
The Exposition consists in setting forth, briefly and
completely, the points we intend to discuss.

[d] Cf. the figure distributio, 4. xxxv. 47, and distributio, the
Broken Tone of Debate, 3. xiii. 23 below.

[e] Cf. the enumeratio (Summing Up) of 2. xxx. 47 below.
Quintilian, 4. 5. 24, praises Hortensius for the great pains he
took with his Partitions, " although Cicero often lightly
mocks him for counting his points on his fingers."

[f] ἔκθεσις. Cf. the expositio (Proposition of an argument)
in 2. xx. 32, and note on 2. xviii. 28 below.

[g] Cf. Cicero, Brutus 60. 217 on Curio : " His memory was so
altogether wanting that at times when he had announced three
points he would add a fourth or miss the third."

[h] See note on 4. vii. 10 below.

[CICERO]

18   Nunc ad confirmationem et confutationem transeamus. Tota spes vincendi ratioque persuadendi
posita est in confirmatione et in confutatione. Nam
cum adiumenta nostra exposuerimus contrariaque
dissolverimus, absolute nimirum munus oratorium
confecerimus. XI. Utrumque igitur facere poterimus, si constitutionem causae cognoverimus.
Causarum constitutiones alii quattuor fecerunt;
noster doctor tres putavit esse, non ut de illorum
quicquam detraheret inventione, sed ut ostenderet id
quod oportuisset simpliciter ac singulari modo docere
illos distribuisse dupliciter et bipertito. Constitutio
est prima deprecatio defensoris cum accusatoris in-
simulatione coniuncta. Constitutiones itaque, ut

---

a πίστις, κατασκευὴ κεφαλαίων.

b ἀνασκευή. In the *Rhet. ad Alex.*, ch. 7 (1428 a), Refutation is considered as one of seven subheads under Proof; see
also ch. 13 (1431 a).

c I follow the practice, perhaps begun by Thomas Wilson,
Arte of Rhetorique (first ed. 1553), ed. G. H. Mair, Oxford,
1910, p. 89, of translating *constitutio* (or *status* [= στάσις], the
term used by Cicero, except in *De Inv.*, and by most other
rhetoricians) as "Issue." The *constitutio* (= σύστασις, most
probably; see S. F. Bonner, *Class. Rev.* 61 [1947]. 84–6) is
the conjoining of two conflicting statements, thus forming the
centre of the argument and determining the character of the
case; for a study of the meaning of *status* and of *constitutio*
see A. O. L. Dieter, *Speech Monographs* 17, 4 (1950). 345–69.
Our author makes use of the *status* system only for judicial
oratory, the examples being drawn from both criminal and
civil causes. Adumbrated in pre-Aristotelian rhetoric
(where it was close to Attic procedure), as well as in Aristotle's
Rhetoric, it was developed principally by Hermagoras. Stoic
and Aristotelian dialectic exerted an influence in its evolution.
The terminology and Roman examples show that our author
assimilated the Greek theory. His system differs consider-
ably from that of Hermagoras; see Kroehnert, pp. 21 ff.;

18   Now let me pass to Proof [a] and Refutation.[b] The entire hope of victory and the entire method of persuasion rest on proof and refutation, for when we have submitted our arguments and destroyed those of the opposition, we have, of course, completely fulfilled the speaker's function. XI. We shall, then, be enabled to do both if we know the Type of Issue [c] which the cause presents. Others make these Types of Issue four.[d] My teacher [e] thought that there were three, not intending thereby to subtract any of the types they had discovered, but to demonstrate that one type which they should have taught as single and uncompounded they had divided into two distinct and separate types. The Issue is determined by the joining of the primary plea of the defence with the charge of the plaintiff. The Types of Issue

Hermann Netzker, *Hermagoras, Cicero, Cornificius quae docuerint de " statibus,"* Kiel diss., 1879, and " Die *constitutio legitima* des Cornificius," *Neue Jahrbücher* 133 (1886). 411–16; Heinrich Weber, *Ueber die Quellen der Rhet. ad Her. des Cornificius,* Zurich diss., 1886; Thiele, *Hermagoras*; Walter Jaeneke, *De statuum doctrina ab Hermogene tradita,* Leipzig, 1904; Claus Peters, *De rationibus inter artem rhetoricam quarti et primi saeculi intercedentibus,* Kiel diss., 1907, pp. 10 ff.; Kroll in P.-W., art. " Rhetorik," coll. 1090–5. Cicero's system in *De Inv.* 1. viii. 10 ff. differs from that of our author. *Cf.* Quintilian, 3. 6. 1 ff. Most critics see our author as a follower of Marcus Antonius in his system of *status*; *cf.* Quintilian, 3. 6. 45 ff. (note that *legalis,* not *legitimus* is the term used for the " Legal " Issue by the followers of Antonius), and Kroehnert, *loc. cit.* Modern students of Roman Law for the most part think that from the juristic point of view, as against the rhetorical, the *status* system was over-intricate and impractical; see note on 2. xiii. 19 below.

[d] Hermagoras taught four Types of Issue; see note on Transference, 1. xi. 19, below.

[e] See Introduction, pp. xxi ff., esp. p. xxiii.

ante diximus, tres sunt: coniecturalis, legitima,
iuridicalis.[a]

Coniecturalis est cum de facto controversia est, hoc
modo: Aiax in silva, postquam resciit quae fecisset
per insaniam, gladio incubuit. Ulixes intervenit,
occisum conspicatur, corpore telum cruentum educit.
Teucer intervenit, fratrem occisum, inimicum fratris
cum gladio cruento videt. Capitis arcessit. Hic
coniectura verum quaeritur. De facto erit controversia; ex eo constitutio causae coniecturalis
nominatur.[b][c]

19   Legitima est constitutio cum in scripto aut e
scripto aliquid controversiae nascitur. Ea dividitur
in partes sex: scriptum et sententiam, contrarias
leges, ambiguum, definitionem, translationem, ratiocinationem.[d]

Ex scripto et sententia controversia nascitur cum
videtur scriptoris voluntas cum scripto ipso dissentire,
hoc modo: si lex sit quae iubeat eos qui propter
tempestatem navem reliquerint omnia perdere, eorum
navem ceteraque esse, si, navis conservata sit, qui
remanserunt in navi. Magnitudine tempestatis
omnes perterriti navem reliquerunt, in scapham[e]

---

^a For the spelling *iuridicalis* see Stroebel, *Tulliana*, p. 20.

^b στοχασμός.   *Cf.* Cicero, *De Inv.* 1. viii. 11.

^c See the *progymnasma* in 2. xviii. 28–xix. 30 below.
Resenting the award of the arms of Achilles to Ulysses, Ajax
goes mad and slaughters a flock of sheep, thinking them his
enemies. *Cf.* Hermogenes, *De Stat.* 3 (ed. Rabe, pp. 49 and
54): A man is discovered burying in a lonely place the body
of a person recently slain, and is charged with murder;
Fortunatianus 1. 6 (Halm, p. 85) and 1. 8 (Halm, p. 87).

^d στάσις νομική.   *Cf.* Cicero, *De Inv.* 1. xiii. 17.

^e στάσις κατὰ ῥητὸν καὶ διάνοιαν.   *Cf.* the *sententia* (Maxim)
of 4. xvii. 24 below.

are then, as I have said above, three: Conjectural, Legal, and Juridical.[a]

The Issue is Conjectural[b] when the controversy concerns a question of fact, as follows: In the forest Ajax, after realizing what in his madness he had done, fell on his sword. Ulysses appears, perceives that Ajax is dead, draws the bloody weapon from the corpse. Teucer appears, sees his brother dead, and his brother's enemy with bloody sword in hand. He accuses Ulysses of a capital crime. Here the truth is sought by conjecture. The controversy will concern the fact.[c] And that is why the Issue in the cause is called Conjectural.

9   The Issue is Legal[d] when some controversy turns upon the letter of a text or arises from an implication therein. A Legal Issue is divided into six subtypes: Letter and Spirit,[e] Conflicting Laws,[f] Ambiguity,[g] Definition,[h] Transference,[i] and Reasoning from Analogy.[j]

A controversy from Letter and Spirit arises when the framer's intention appears to be at variance with the letter of the text, as follows: Suppose a law which decrees that whoever have abandoned their ship in a storm shall lose all rights of title, and that their ship, if saved, and cargo as well, belong to those who have remained on board. Terrified by the storm's violence, all deserted the ship and took to the

---

[f] ἀντινομία.

[g] ἀμφιβολία.

[h] ὅρος.

[i] μετάληψις. Procedural in nature. Cf. *translatio criminis*, 1. xiv. 24, and the figure *translatio*, 4. xxxiv. 45 below. Hermagoras was the first to enter this among the Types of Issue; see Cicero, *De Inv.* 1. xi. 16, and Quintilian, 3. 6. 60.

[j] συλλογισμός.

35

conscenderunt—praeter unum aegrotum; is propter
morbum exire et fugere non potuit. Casu et fortuitu
navis in portum incolumis delata est; illam aegrotus
possedit. Navem petit ille cuius fuerat. Haec constitutio legitima est ex scripto et sententia.

20 Ex contrariis legibus controversia constat cum alia
lex iubet aut permittit, alia vetat quippiam fieri, hoc
modo: Lex vetat eum qui de pecuniis repetundis
damnatus sit in contione orationem habere; altera
lex iubet augurem in demortui locum qui petat in
contione nominare. Augur quidam damnatus de
pecuniis repetundis in demortui locum nominavit;
petitur ab eo multa. Constitutio legitima ex contrariis legibus.

XII. Ex ambiguo controversia nascitur cum scriptum [1] duas aut plures sententias significat, hoc modo:
Paterfamilias cum filium heredem faceret, testamento
vasa argentea uxori legavit: "Heres meus uxori meae
xxx pondo vasorum argenteorum dato, quae [2]
volet." Post mortem eius vasa pretiosa et caelata
magnifice petit mulier. Filius se quae [3] ipse vellet in
xxx pondo ei debere dicit. Constitutio est legitima
ex ambiguo.

[1] scriptum *BCE* : res unam sententiam scripta scriptum
HP¹ Mx: res una sententia scripta scriptum Π.
[2] quae *BCE Mx ed. mai.* : qua *HP* Π *Mx.*
[3] quae *BCE Mx ed. mai.* : qua *HP* Π *Mx.*

---

[a] This *controversia* is of Greek origin; *cf.* Hermogenes,
De Stat. 2 (ed. Rabe, p. 41), Fortunatianus 1. 26 (Halm, pp.
100 f.), and Cicero, *De Inv.* 2. li. 153.
[b] On the importance of this type of rhetorical discussion
for juristic theory see note on 2. xiii. 19 below.

boat—all except one sick man who, on account of his
illness, could not leave the ship and escape. By
sheer chance the ship was driven safely to harbour.
The invalid has come into possession of the ship, and
the former owner claims it.[a] Here is a Legal Issue
based on Letter and Spirit.[b]

20   Controversy results from Conflicting Laws when one
law orders or permits a deed while another forbids it,
as follows : A law forbids one who has been convicted
of extortion to speak before the Assembly.[c] Another
law commands the augur to designate in the Assembly
the candidate for the place of a deceased augur.[d]
A certain augur convicted of extortion has designated
the candidate for the place of a deceased augur. A
penalty is demanded of him.[e] Here is a Legal Issue
established from Conflicting Laws.

XII. A controversy is created by Ambiguity when
a text presents two or more meanings, as follows :
The father of a family, when making his son his heir,
in his will bequeathed silver vessels to his wife :
" Let my heir give my wife thirty pounds' weight of
silver vessels, ' such as shall be selected '." After
his death the widow asks for some precious vessels of
magnificent relief-work. The son contends that he
owes her thirty pounds' weight of vessels " such as
shall be selected " by him.[f] Here is a Legal Issue
established from Ambiguity.

[c] Doubtless the law of C. Servilius Glaucia *de pecuniis
repetundis* (111 B.C.).
[d] The law of Cn. Domitius Ahenobarbus *de sacerdotiis*,
passed in 104 B.C. and repealed by Sulla in (?) 81 B.C., is here
indicated.
[e] When specifically the case came up we do not know;
Marx, *Proleg.*, p. 108, conjectures *c.* 100 B.C.
[f] *Cf.* Cicero, *De Inv.* 2. xl. 116; Lucilius 16. 552–3.

21   Definitione causa constat cum in controversia est
quo nomine factum appelletur.[1] Ea est huiusmodi:
Cum Lucius Saturninus legem frumentariam de
semissibus et trientibus laturus esset, Q. Caepio, qui
per id temporis quaestor urbanus erat, docuit
senatum aerarium pati non posse largitionem tantam.
Senatus decrevit, si eam legem ad populum ferat,
adversus rem publicam videri ea facere. Saturninus
ferre coepit. Collegae intercedere, ille nihilominus
sitellam detulit. Caepio, ut illum, contra intercedentibus collegis, adversus rem publicam vidit ferre,
cum viris bonis impetum facit, pontes disturbat, cistas
deicit, inpedimento est quo setius feratur. Arcessitur
Caepio maiestatis. Constitutio legitima ex definitione. Vocabulum enim definitur ipsum cum quaeritur quid sit minuere maiestatem.

22   Ex translatione controversia nascitur cum aut
tempus differendum aut accusatorem mutandum aut
iudices mutandos reus dicit. Hac parte constitu-

---

[1] appelletur *BCE Mx ed. mai.*: inpelletur *H*: inpelleretur
PB (in marg.) Π: conpelletur *Mx*.

---

[a] At the Comitia; over these the voters passed in single
file to the *saepta* in the Campus Martius to deposit their votes.
[b] Probably in his second tribunate in 100 B.C., L. Appuleius Saturninus proposed his law fixing the fee for grain at
five-sixths of an *as* (for a *modius*); the *lex Sempronia frumentaria* of 123 had set the price at almost eight times that
amount. It is uncertain whether the bill passed. Caepio
was in 99 B.C. charged with treason, but was acquitted. *Cf.*
2. xii. 17 (the supposed defence by Caepio), and for Saturninus
4. xxii. 31 and 4. liv. 67. This Q. Servilius Caepio was the
son of the Q. Servilius Caepio referred to in 1. xiv. 24 below.
[c] Literally, what constitutes " impairing the sovereign
majesty " of the state. *Cf.* 2. xii. 17 and 4. xxv. 35 below.
The *crimen maiestatis minutae* was invented probably in
103 B.C.; the *Lex Appuleia de maiestate* attempted to define

21   A cause rests on Definition when the name by
which an act should be called is in controversy. The
following is an example: When Lucius Saturninus
was about to introduce the grain law concerning the
five-sixths *as*, Quintus Caepio, who was city quaestor
during that time, explained to the Senate that the
treasury could not endure so great a largess. The
Senate decreed that if Saturninus should propose that
law before the people he would appear to be doing so
against the common weal. Saturninus proceeded
with his motion. His colleagues interposed a veto;
nevertheless he brought the lot-urn down for the
vote. Caepio, when he sees Saturninus presenting his
motion against the public welfare despite his colleagues' veto, attacks him with the assistance of some
Conservatives, destroys the bridges,[a] throws down
the ballot boxes, and blocks further action on the
motion. Caepio is brought to trial for treason.[b]
The Issue is Legal, and is established from Definition,
for we are defining the actual term when we investigate what constitutes treason.[c]

22   A controversy is based on Transference when the
defendant maintains that there must be a postpone-
ment of time or a change of plaintiff or judges.[d] This

the offence. See Hugh Last, *Cambr. Anc. History* 9. 160–1.
Cf. Antonius on the trial of Norbanus (95 B.C.) in Cicero,
De Oratore 2. 25. 107 ff., 2. 39. 164.
    [d] Anglo-American procedure has no specific analogue to
the term *translatio* as here defined, nor indeed was this *status*
suited to Roman juristic procedure. See Theodor Schwal-
bach, *Zeitschr. der Savigny-Stiftung für Rechtsgeschichte,
Romanist. Abt.*, 2 (1881). 209–32; Moriz Wlassak, *Der
Ursprung der römischen Einrede* (Festschr. Leopold Pfaff),
Vienna, 1910, pp. 12 ff.; and Artur Steinwenter, *Sav. Zeitschr.*
65 (1947). 69–120, esp. p. 81, and pp. 104–5. Note also *raro
venit in iudicium* below.

[CICERO]

tionis Graeci in iudiciis, nos in iure plerumque utimur. In iudiciis tamen nonnihil utimur, ut hoc modo: Si quis peculatus accusatur quod vasa argentea publica de loco privato dicatur sustulisse, possit dicere, cum definitione sit usus quid sit furtum, quid peculatus, secum furti agi, non peculatus oportere. Haec partitio legitimae constitutionis his de causis raro venit in iudicium, quod in privata actione praetoriae exceptiones sunt et causa cadit qui egit nisi habuit actionem, et in publicis quaestionibus cavetur legibus ut ante, si reo commodum sit, iudicium de accusatore fiat utrum illi liceat accusare necne.

23　XIII. Ex ratiocinatione controversia constat cum res sine propria lege venit in iudicium, quae tamen ab aliis legibus similitudine quadam aucupatur. Ea est huiusmodi: Lex: " Si furiosus existet, adgnatum gentiliumque in eo pecuniaque eius potestas esto." Et lex: " Qui parentem necasse iudicatus erit, ut is

---

a The Romans in the preliminary proceedings before the magistrate, where the issue is defined; the Greeks in the actual trial before the judge.

b Despite the alteration, the source of this *controversia* may originally have been Aristotle, *Rhet.* 1. 13 (1374 a) : " It often happens that a man may admit . . . theft, but not that the act was sacrilege (on the ground that the thing stolen was not the property of a god)." *Cf.* Cicero, *De Inv.* 1. viii. 11; Quintilian, 3. 6. 41 and 5. 10. 39; Hermogenes, *De Stat.* 2 (ed. Rabe, p. 37) and 4 (ed. Rabe, p. 62); Sopater, in Walz 8. 102–5; also Rabe, *Proleg. Syll.*, pp. 218, 253, and 336. On *peculatus publicus* see Mommsen, pp. 764 ff.

c *Cf.* Victorinus, in Halm, p. 276.

d These counterpleas accepted by the praetor allege new states of fact or of law; although the defendant accepts the *intentio* in the plaintiff's *formula*, he urges the praetor to permit the insertion of an *exceptio* in the *formula*. See

subtype of Issue the Greeks use in the proceedings before judges, we generally before the magistrate's tribunal.[a] We do, however, make some use of it in judicial proceedings. For example, if some one is accused of embezzlement, alleged to have removed silver vessels belonging to the state from a private place, he can say, when he has defined theft and embezzlement, that in his case the action ought to be one for theft and not embezzlement.[b] This subtype of Legal Issue rarely [c] presents itself in judicial proceedings for the following reasons: in a private action there are counterpleas accepted by the praetor,[d] and the plaintiff's case fails unless he has had a cause of action; in public investigations the laws provide that, if it suits the defendant, a decision is first passed on whether the plaintiff is, or is not, permitted to make the charge.

XIII. The controversy is based on Analogy when a matter that arises for adjudication lacks a specifically applicable law, but an analogy is sought from other existing laws on the basis of a certain similarity to the matter in question. For example, a law reads: " If a man is raving mad, authority over his person and property shall belong to his agnates, or to the members of his *gens*."[e] Another law reads: " He who has been convicted of murdering his parent shall

---

A. H. J. Greenidge, *The Legal Procedure of Cicero's Time*, Oxford, 1901, pp. 178–181, 229–235; E. Rabel, *Sav. Zeitschr.* 32 (1911). 413–23; Leopold Wenger, *Institutes of the Roman Law of Civil Procedure*, tr. O. H. Fisk, New York, 1940, pp. 155 ff. *Cf.* Cicero, *De Inv.* 1. viii. 10 and 2. xix. 57–xx. 61. Cicero in *De Inv.* (2. xix. 57) and our author supply the first references to the *exceptio* in extant literature. See Friedrich von Velsen, *Sav. Zeitschr.* 21 (1900). 104–5.

[e] *Twelve Tables* 5. 7 a.

obvolutus et obligatus corio devehatur in profluen-
tem." Et lex: "Paterfamilias uti super familia
pecuniave sua legaverit, ita ius esto." Et lex: " Si
paterfamilias intestato moritur, familia pecuniaque
eius adgnatum gentiliumque[1] esto."   Malleolus
iudicatus est matrem necasse. Ei damnato statim
folliculo lupino os obvolutum est et soleae ligneae
in pedibus inductae sunt; in carcerem ductus est.
Qui defendebant eum tabulas in carcerem adferunt,
testamentum ipso praesente conscribunt, testes recte
adfuerunt; de illo supplicium sumitur. Ii qui
heredes erant testamento hereditatem adeunt.
Frater minor Malleoli, qui eum oppugnaverat in eius
periculo, suam vocat hereditatem lege adgnationis.
Hic certa lex in rem nulla adfertur, et tamen multae
adferuntur, ex quibus ratiocinatio nascitur quare
potuerit aut non potuerit iure testamentum facere.
Constitutio legitima ex ratiocinatione.

Cuiusmodi partes essent legitimae constitutionis
ostendimus; nunc de iuridicali constitutione dicamus.
24   XIV. Iuridicalis constitutio est cum factum convenit, sed iure an iniuria factum sit quaeritur. Eius
constitutionis partes duae sunt, quarum una absoluta,
altera adsumptiva nominatur.

----

[1] gentiliumque d : et gentilium E : gentilium M Mx.

----

[a] Marx (Proleg., p. 107; see also R. Reitzenstein, Gnomon
5 [1929]. 605–6) affirms, and Mommsen (p. 643, note 6)
denies, the genuineness of this law; it is omitted in Cicero,
De Inv. 2. l. 148.
[b] Twelve Tables 5. 3.
[c] Cf. Twelve Tables 5. 4–5.
[d] Cf. Cicero, De Inv. 2. l. 149, and on this (ritualistic) form
of punishment Mommsen, pp. 921–3; Alfred Pernice, Sav.
Zeitschr. 17 (1896). 210 ff.; Max Radin, Journ. Rom. Studies
10 (1920). 119–30; Rudolf Düll, Atti del Congr. Internaz. di

be completely wrapped and bound in a leather sack and thrown into a running stream." *a* Another law : " As the head of a family has directed regarding his household or his property, so shall the law hold good." *b* Another law : " If the head of a family dies intestate, his household and property shall belong to his agnates, or to the members of his *gens*." *c* Malleolus was convicted of matricide. Immediately after he had received sentence, his head was wrapped in a bag of wolf's hide, the " wooden shoes " *d* were put upon his feet, and he was led away to prison. His defenders bring tablets into the jail, write his will in his presence, witnesses duly attending. The penalty is exacted of him. His testamentary heirs enter upon their inheritance. Malleolus' younger brother, who had been one of the accusers in his trial, claims his inheritance by the law of agnation. Here no one specific law is adduced, and yet many laws are adduced, which form the basis for a reasoning by analogy to prove that Malleolus had or had not the right to make a will. It is a Legal Issue established from Analogy.

I have explained the types of Legal Issue. Now let me discuss the Juridical Issue.

24 XIV. An Issue is Juridical *e* when there is agreement on the act, but the right or wrong of the act is in question. Of this Issue there are two subtypes, one called Absolute, *f* the other Assumptive. *g*

Diritto Rom. (Roma), Pavia, 1935, 2. 363–408. According to Livy, *Periochae* 68, Malleolus was the first (101 B.C.) to suffer this punishment.

e στάσις δικαιολογική. *Cf.* Cicero, *De Inv.* 1. xi. 15, 2. xxiii. 69 ff.

f κατ' ἀντίληψιν.

g κατ' ἀντίθεσιν.

[CICERO]

Absoluta est cum id ipsum quod factum est, ut aliud nihil foris adsumatur, recte factum esse dicemus, eiusmodi:[1] Mimus quidam nominatim Accium poetam conpellavit in scaena. Cum eo Accius iniuriarum agit. Hic nihil aliud defendit nisi licere nominari eum cuius nomine scripta dentur agenda.

Adsumptiva pars est cum per se defensio infirma est, adsumpta extraria re conprobatur. Adsumptivae partes sunt quattuor: concessio, remotio criminis, translatio criminis, conparatio.

Concessio est cum reus postulat ignosci. Ea dividitur in purgationem et deprecationem. Purgatio est cum consulto negat se reus fecisse. Ea dividitur in inprudentiam, fortunam, necessitatem: fortunam, ut Caepio ad tribunos plebis de exercitus amissione; inprudentiam, ut ille qui de eo servo qui dominum occiderat supplicium sumpsit, cui frater esset, ante-

---

[1] dicemus eiusmodi *l Mx ed. mai.*: eam dicemus eius modi *M*: dicemus ea eiusmodi (huiusmodi *C*) est *BCd*: dicemus ea est huiusmodi *b*: eam rem dicemus eiusmodi *Mx*.

---

[a] The mime was condemned; see 2. xiii. 19 below. This type of *controversia* is Greek in origin; *cf.* Hermogenes, *De Stat.* 11, ed Rabe, pp. 88–9 (but belonging to the subtype of Legal Issue based on Analogy; see 1. xiii. 23 above), and Sopater, in Walz 8. 383–4. See also Sulpitius Victor 39, in Halm, p. 337.

[b] συγγνώμη.　　　　　[c] μετάστασις.
[d] ἀντέγκλημα.　　　　[e] ἀντίστασις.
[f] *Cf.* 2. xvi. 23 and 2. xxvii. 43 below, and Cicero, *De Inv.* 1. xi. 15.
[g] κάθαρσις.
[h] παραίτησις.
[i] ἐκ προνοίας. Voluntary acts = τὰ ἑκούσια, involuntary = τὰ ἀκούσια.
[j] ἄγνοια.

44

It is an Absolute Issue when we contend that the act in and of itself, without our drawing on any extraneous considerations, was right. For example, a certain mime abused the poet Accius by name on the stage. Accius sues him on the ground of injuries. The player makes no defence except to maintain that it was permissible to name a person under whose name dramatic works were given to be performed on the stage.[a]

The Issue is Assumptive when the defence, in itself insufficient, is established by drawing on extraneous matter. The Assumptive subtypes are four: Acknowledgement of the Charge,[b] Rejection of the Responsibility,[c] Shifting of the Question of Guilt,[d] Comparison with the Alternative Course.[e]

The Acknowledgement[f] is the defendant's plea for pardon. The Acknowledgement includes the Exculpation[g] and the Plea for Mercy.[h] The Exculpation is the defendant's denial that he acted with intent.[i] Under Plea of Exculpation are three subheads: Ignorance,[j] Accident,[k] and Necessity;[l] accident, as in the case of Caepio[m] before the tribunes of the plebs on the loss of his army; ignorance, as in the case of the man who, before opening the tablets of the will by the terms of which his brother's slave had been

---

[k] τύχη, ἀτυχία, ἀτύχημα.

[l] ἀνάγκη, βία.

[m] In 105 B.C., Q. Servilius Caepio, through his failure to coöperate with his colleague Mallius, brought upon the army a disastrous defeat at Arausio at the hands of the Cimbri, Teutones, and their allies. Caepio's proconsular *imperium* was abrogated, and by the motion of the *tribunus plebis*, L. Cassius Longinus, he lost senatorial rank (104 B.C.). Cicero, *Brutus* 35. 135, says of Caepio that the fortunes of war were imputed to him as a crime.

quam tabulas testamenti aperuit, cum is servus testamento manu missus esset; necessitudinem, ut ille
qui ad diem commeatus non venit quod flumina vias
interclusissent. Deprecatio est cum et peccasse se et
consulto fecisse confitetur, et tamen postulat ut sui
misereantur. Hoc in iudicio fere non potest usu
venire, nisi quando pro eo dicimus cuius multa recte
facta extant, hoc modo—in loco communi per
amplificationem iniciemus: "Quodsi hoc fecisset,
tamen ei pro pristinis beneficiis ignosci conveniret;
verum nihil postulat ignosci." Ergo in iudicium non
venit, at in senatum, ad imperatorem et in consilium
talis causa potest venire.

25   XV. Ex translatione criminis causa constat cum
fecisse nos non negamus, sed aliorum peccatis coactos
fecisse dicimus; ut Orestes cum se defendit in
matrem conferens crimen.

Ex remotione criminis causa constat cum a nobis
non crimen, sed culpam ipsam amovemus, et vel in
hominem transferimus vel in rem quampiam conferi-
mus. In hominem transfertur, ut si accusetur is qui
Publium Sulpicium se fateatur occidisse, et id iussu
consulum defendat et eos dicat non modo imperasse,

---

[a] Manumitted, the slave was answerable for his crime to
the courts, and not subject to domestic punishment. The
controversia is doubtless Greek in origin. *Cf.* Quintilian,
7. 4. 14.

[b] The *controversia* is Greek in origin; the like situation
is presented in *De Inv.* 2. xxxi. 96. *Cf.* Quintilian, 7.
4. 14.

[c] *Cf.* Cicero, *De Inv.* 2. xxxiv. 104.

[d] The court was obliged to render a verdict strictly on the
law, and could not lessen the punishment. See also Quintilian, 5. 13. 5 and 7. 4. 17 ff.

manumitted, exacted punishment of the slave for
having slain his master;[a] necessity, as in the case of
the soldier who overstayed his leave because the
floods had blocked the roads.[b]   It is a Plea for Mercy
when the defendant confesses the crime and premeditation, yet begs for compassion.[c]   In the courts
this is rarely practicable,[d] except when we speak in
defence of one whose good deeds are numerous and
notable; for example, interposing as a commonplace
in amplification: "Even if he had done this, it
would still be appropriate to pardon him in view of
his past services; but he does not at all beg for
pardon."   Such a cause, then, is not admissible in
the courts, but is admissible before the Senate, or
a general, or a council.[e]

25   XV. A cause rests on the Shifting of the Question
of Guilt when we do not deny our act but plead that
we were driven to it by the crimes of others, as in
the case of Orestes when he defended himself by
diverting the issue of guilt from himself to his
mother.[f]

A cause rests on the Rejection of the Responsibility
when we repudiate, not the act charged, but the
responsibility, and either transfer it to another
person or attribute it to some circumstance.   An
example of the transference of responsibility to
another person: if an accusation should be brought
against the confessed slayer of Publius Sulpicius, and
he should defend his act by invoking an order of the
consuls, declaring that they not only commanded the

---

[e] Especially that of a magistrate; cf. Mommsen, pp. 149 f.
and note 5, and Wenger, *Institutes of the Roman Law of Civil
Procedure*, p. 32.
[f] Cf. 1. x. 17 above, and 1. xvi. 26 below.

[CICERO]

sed rationem quoque ostendisse quare id facere lice-
ret. In rem confertur, ut si quis ex testamento quod
facere iussus sit ex plebis scito vetetur.

Ex conparatione causa constat cum dicimus
necesse fuisse alterutrum facere, et id quod fecerimus
satius fuisse facere. Ea causa huiusmodi est : C.
Popilius, cum a Gallis obsideretur neque fugere ullo
modo posset, venit cum hostium ducibus in con-
locutionem ; ita discessit ut inpedimenta relinqueret,
exercitum educeret. Satius esse duxit amittere inpedimenta quam exercitum. Exercitum eduxit,
inpedimenta reliquit. Arcessitur maiestatis.

XVI. Quae constitutiones et quae constitutionum
partes sint videor ostendisse. Nunc quo modo eas et
qua via tractari conveniat demonstrandum est, si
prius aperuerimus quid oporteat ab ambobus in causa
destinari quo ratio omnis totius orationis conferatur.

---

^a P. Sulpicius Rufus was among those proscribed by Sulla
in 88 B.C. Pursued by Sulla's horsemen, he took refuge in a
villa at Laurentum, where he was betrayed by a slave and
murdered. His head was exhibited on the rostra. The
slave was set free by Sulla's orders and then hurled down the
Tarpeian Rock. *Cf.* Appian, *Bell. Civil.* 1. 7. 60 : "[Sul-
picius and others] had been voted enemies of Rome, and
anyone who came upon them had been authorized to kill
them with impunity or to bring them before the consuls
[Cornelius Sulla and Quintus Pompeius]." Velleius Paterculus, 2. 19, says that Sulpicius and his followers were declared
exiles by formal decree (*lege lata*). It was forbidden to bury
Sulpicius' body ; see 4. xxii. 31 below. If this *controversia* was
not merely a school exercise, and the murderer was actually
called to account, that may have been in the year 87, when
Sulpicius' party again came into power. See the notes on
4. xiv. 20, xxiv. 33, xxviii. 38, xxxiv. 45, lii. 65, and also
2. xxviii. 45.

^b *Cf.* Cicero, *De Inv.* 2. xxiv. 72. According to the
historians, after L. Cassius Longinus in the war against the

48

act but also gave reason why it was lawful.[a] An example of attribution to a circumstance: if a person should be forbidden by a plebiscite to do what a will has directed him to do.

A cause rests on Comparison with the Alternative Course when we declare that it was necessary for us to do one or the other of the two things, and that the one we did was the better. This cause is of the following sort: Gaius Popilius, hemmed in by the Gauls, and quite unable to escape, entered into a parley with the enemy's chiefs. He came away with consent to lead his army out on condition that he abandon his baggage. He considered it better to lose his baggage than his army. He led out his army and left the baggage behind. He is charged with treason.[b]

XVI. I believe that I have made clear what the Types of Issue are and what are their subdivisions. Now I must illustrate the proper ways and means of treating these, first indicating what both sides in a cause ought to fix upon as the point to which the complete economy of the entire speech should be directed.

Cimbri and their allies fell (in 107 B.C.) at the hands of the Tigurini in Gaul, C. Popilius Laenas, legate, made a pact: the Roman survivors would, in return for hostages and half of their possessions, leave in safety. The Roman band went under the yoke of the Tigurini. No mention is here made of the hostages nor of passing under the yoke, nor does the amount of the baggage agree precisely with that in the historical accounts. The charge of treason was made in 106 by the tribune C. Caelius Caldus; a fragment of the defence appears in 4. xxiv. 34 below. Popilius went into exile, but perhaps after a later trial under Saturninus' law of treason of 103 B.C.

26 Constitutione igitur reperta statim quaerenda ratio
est. Ratio est quae causam facit et continet defensionem, hoc modo—ut docendi causa in hac potissimum causa consistamus: Orestes confitetur se
occidisse matrem; nisi adtulerit facti rationem, per-
verterit defensionem. Ergo adfert eam, quae nisi
intercederet, ne causa quidem esset. " Illa enim,"
inquit, " patrem meum occiderat." Ergo, ut ostendi,
ratio ea est quae continet defensionem, sine qua ne
parva quidem dubitatio potest remorari damna-
tionem.

Inventa ratione firmamentum quaerendum est, id
est, quod continet accusationem, quod adfertur contra
rationem defensionis de qua ante dictum est. Id
constituetur hoc modo: Cum usus fuerit Orestes
ratione hoc pacto: " Iure occidi, illa enim patrem
meum occiderat," utetur accusator firmamento, hoc
modo: " At non abs te occidi neque indamnatam
poenas pendere oportuit."

Ex ratione defensionis et ex firmamento accusa-
tionis iudicii quaestio nascatur oportet, quam [1] nos

---

[1] quam *B C b l Mx ed. mai.*: tam *HP*: eam *Mx*: quod *d.*

---

[a] *Ratio* = τὸ συνέχον, *firmamentum* = τὸ αἴτιον. Cicero
misconstrued *firmamentum* in *De Inv.* 1. xiv. 19; cf. *Part.
Orat.* 29. 103, Quintilian, 3. 11. 19, Volkmann, pp. 100–108,
Thiele, *Hermagoras*, pp. 67–78, Jaeneke, *De statuum doctrina
ab Hermogene tradita*, p. 111.
[b] *Cf.* 1. x. 17 and 1. xv. 25 above.
[c] *Cf.* in Aristotle, *Rhet.* 2. 23 (1397ab), the third of the 28
topoi from which to draw enthymemes, the *topos* from corre-
lative terms : " And if ' well ' or ' justly ' is true of the person
to whom a thing is done, you may argue that it is true of the
doer. But here the argument may be fallacious; for,
granting that the man deserved what he got, it does not

26 Immediately upon finding the Type of Issue, then, we must seek the Justifying Motive.[a] It is this which determines the action and comprises the defence. Thus Orestes (for the sake of clarity, to adhere to this particular action) confesses that he slew his mother. Unless he has advanced a Justifying Motive for the act, he will have ruined his defence. He therefore advances one; were it not interposed, there would not even be an action. " For she," says he, " had slain my father." [b] Thus, as I have shown, the Justifying Motive is what comprises the defence; without it not even the slightest doubt could exist which would delay his condemnation.

Upon finding the Motive advanced in Justification we must seek the Central Point [a] of the Accusation, that is, that which comprises the accusation and is presented in opposition to the Justifying Motive of the defence which I have discussed above. This will be established as follows : When Orestes has used the Justifying Motive : " I had the right to kill my mother, for she had slain my father," the prosecutor will use his Central Point : " Yes, but not by your hand ought she to have been killed or punished without a trial." [c]

From the Justifying Motive of the defence and the Central Point of the Accusation must arise the Question for Decision, which we call the Point to

follow that he deserved it from you " (tr. Lane Cooper), and in 2. 24 (1401b), the fallacy of omission illustrated by the argument in Theodectes' *Orestes.* For the argument as used in other Greek tragedies, *cf.* Tyndareüs in Euripides, *Orestes* 538–9 : " My daughter, dying, paid her debt to justice, but that she died at his hand was not meet," and Castor, addressing Orestes in *Electra* 1244 : " Your mother now has but justice, but your deed is not just."

iudicationem, Graeci crinomenon appellant. Ea
constituetur ex coniunctione firmamenti et rationis,[1]
hoc modo: Cum dicat Orestes se patris ulciscendi
matrem occidisse, rectumne fuerit sine iudicio a
filio Clytemestram occidi? Ergo hac ratione iudicationem reperire convenit; reperta iudicatione
omnem rationem totius orationis eo conferri
oportebit.

27   XVII. In omnibus constitutionibus et partibus
constitutionum hac via iudicationes reperientur,
praeterquam in coniecturali constitutione; in ea nec
ratio qua re fecerit quaeritur, fecisse enim negatur,
nec firmamentum exquiritur, quoniam non subest
ratio. Quare ex intentione et infitiatione iudicatio
constituitur, hoc modo: Intentio: " Occidisti
Aiacem;" Infitiatio: " Non occidi;" Iudicatio:
" Occideritne?" Ratio omnis utriusque orationis,
ut ante dictum est, ad hanc iudicationem conferenda
est. Si plures erunt constitutiones aut partes constitutionum, iudicationes quoque plures erunt in una
causa, sed et omnes simili ratione reperientur.

Sedulo dedimus operam ut breviter et dilucide
quibus de rebus adhuc dicendum fuit diceremus.
Nunc quoniam satis huius voluminis magnitudo
crevit, commodius est in altero libro de ceteris rebus
deinceps exponere, ne qua propter multitudinem
litterarum possit animum tuum defatigatio retardare.
Si qua tardius haec quam studes absolventur, cum

---

[1] rationis defensione *MSS. Mx.*

[a] κρινόμενον, Hermagorean doctrine.
[b] *Cf.* Cicero, *De Inv.* 1. xiv. 19.
[c] κατάφασις.
[d] ἀπόφασις.

Adjudicate and the Greeks the *krinomenon.*[a] That will be established from the meeting of the prosecutor's Central Point and the defendant's Justifying Motive, as follows: When Orestes says that he killed his mother to avenge his father, was it right for Clytemnestra to be slain by her son without a trial? This, then, is the proper method of finding the Point to Adjudicate. Once the Point to Adjudicate is found, the complete economy of the entire speech ought to be directed to it.

27 XVII. The Points to Adjudicate will be found in this way in all Types of Issue and their subdivisions, except the conjectural.[b] Here the Justifying Motive for the act is not in question, for the act is denied, nor is the Central Point of the Accusation sought, for no Justifying Motive has been advanced. Therefore the Point to Adjudicate is established from the Accusation[c] and the Denial,[d] as follows: Accusation: "You killed Ajax." Denial: "I did not." The Point to Adjudicate: Did he kill him? The complete economy of both speeches must, as I have said above, be directed to this Point to Adjudicate. If there are several Types of Issue or their subdivisions in one cause, there will also be several Points to Adjudicate, but all these, too, will be determined by a like method.

I have taken great pains to discuss briefly and clearly the matters that have had to be treated up to this point. Now, since this Book has grown to sufficient length, it will be more convenient in turn to expound other matters in a second Book, so that the great amount of material may not tire you and slacken your attention. If I dispatch these matters too slowly for your eagerness, you will have to

rerum magnitudini tum nostris quoque occupationibus adsignare debebis. Verumtamen maturabimus, et quod negotio deminutum fuerit exaequabimus industria, ut pro tuo in nos officio et [1] nostro in te studio munus hoc adcumulatissime tuae largiamur voluntati.

[1] et *bd* : in *M* : *Cl Mx omit.*

attribute that to the magnitude of the subject and also to the demands of my other occupations. Yet I shall make speed, and compensate by diligence for the time taken up by my affairs, to the end that, by this gift, in token of your courtesy towards me and my own interest in you, I may grant your desire in most bountiful measure.

BOOK II

LIBER SECUNDUS

1 I. In primo libro, Herenni, breviter exposuimus
quas causas recipere oratorem oporteret et in
quibus officiis artis elaborare conveniret et ea officia
qua ratione facillime consequi posset. Verum quod
neque de omnibus rebus simul dici poterat et de
maximis rebus primum scribendum fuit quo cetera
tibi faciliora cognitu viderentur, ita nobis placitum
est ut ea quae difficillima essent potissimum conscriberemus.

Causarum tria genera sunt: demonstrativum,
deliberativum, iudiciale. Multo difficillimum iudiciale est; ergo id primum absolvimus hoc et priore
libro. De oratoris officiis quinque inventio et prima
et difficillima est. Ea quoque nobis erit hoc libro
propemodum absoluta; parvae partes eius in tertium
volumen transferentur.

2 De sex partibus orationis primum scribere in-
cepimus: in primo libro locuti sumus de exordio,
narratione, divisione, nec pluribus verbis quam
necesse fuit nec minus dilucide quam te velle existima-
bamus; deinde coniuncte de confirmatione et confutatione dicendum fuit. Quare genera constitutionum
et earum partes aperuimus; ex quo simul ostende-

---

a 1. ii. 2.
b 1. ii. 3.
c Cicero, *De Inv.* 1. vii. 9 : *princeps omnium partium.*
d 3. i. 1–viii. 15.
e 1. iii. 4–x. 18.

BOOK II

1   I. In the preceding Book, Herennius, I briefly set forth the causes with which the speaker must deal,[a] and also the functions of his art to which he may well devote his pains, and the means by which he can most easily fulfil these functions.[b] But since it was impossible to treat all the topics at once, and I had primarily to discuss the most important of them in order that the rest might prove easier for you to understand, I therefore decided to write first upon those that are the most difficult.

There are three kinds of causes: Epideictic, Deliberative, and Judicial. By far the most difficult is the judicial; that is why, in the present Book, and in the preceding Book, I have disposed of this kind first of all. Of the five tasks of the speaker Invention is the most important [c] and the most difficult. That topic too I shall virtually have disposed of in the present Book; small details will be postponed to Book III.[d]

2   I first undertook to discuss the six parts of a discourse. In the preceding Book I spoke about the Introduction, the Statement of Facts, and the Division,[e] at no greater length than was necessary nor with less clarity than I judged you desired. I had next to discuss Proof and Refutation, conjointly. Hence I expounded the different Types of Issue and their subdivisions,[f] and this at the same time showed

[f] I. x. 18– xv. 25.

[CICERO]

batur quomodo constitutionem et partem constitutionis causa posita reperiri oporteret. Deinde
docuimus iudicationem quemadmodum quaeri conveniret; qua inventa curandum ut omnis ratio
totius orationis ad eam conferatur. Postea admonui-
mus esse causas conplures in quas plures constitutiones aut partes constitutionum adcommodarentur.

II. Reliquum videbatur esse ut ostenderemus quae
ratio posset inventiones ad unam quamque constitutionem aut partem constitutionis adcommodare, et
item quales argumentationes, quas Graeci epichire-
mata [1] appellant, sequi, quales vitari oporteret;
quorum utrumque pertinet ad confirmationem et ad
confutationem. Deinde ad extremum docuimus
cuiusmodi conclusionibus orationum uti oporteat,
qui locus erat extremus de sex partibus orationis.

Primum ergo quaeremus quemadmodum quamque
causam tractare conveniat, et nimirum eam quae
prima quaeque difficillima est potissimum considerabimus.[2]

3　In causa coniecturali narratio accusatoris suspiciones interiectas et dispersas habere debet, ut nihil
actum, nihil dictum, nusquam ventum aut abitum,
nihil denique factum sine causa putetur. Defensoris
narratio simplicem et dilucidam expositionem debet
habere, cum adtenuatione suspicionis.

[1] epicheremata *MSS. Mx.*
[2] considerabimus *l* : consideremus *HPB* II *Mx.*

---

[a] 1. xvi. 25–xvii. 27.
[b] Implied in 1. xvii. 27.
[c] The scheme of organization under Proof and Refutation
is as follows : (a) the Types of Issue (1. x. 18 to end of Bk. 1);
(b) Invention applied to the Types of Issue (2. ii. 3–xvii. 26);

how the Type of Issue and its subdivision are to be found in a given cause. Then I explained how the Point to Adjudicate is properly sought; this found, we must see that the complete economy of the entire speech is directed to it.[a] After that I remarked that there are not a few causes [b] to which several Types of Issue or their subdivisions are applicable.

II. It remained for me, as it seemed, to show by what method we can adapt the means of invention to each type of issue or its subdivision,[c] and likewise what sort of technical arguments (which the Greeks call *epicheiremata*) [d] one ought to seek [e] or avoid; [f] both of these departments belong to Proof and Refutation. Then finally I have explained what kind of Conclusions to speeches one ought to employ; [g] the Conclusion was the last of the six parts of a discourse.

First, then, I shall investigate how we should handle causes representing each Type of Issue, and of course shall give primary consideration to that type which is the most important and most difficult.

3 In a Conjectural cause the prosecutor's Statement of Facts should contain, intermingled and interspersed in it, material inciting suspicion of the defendant, so that no act, no word, no coming or going, in short nothing that he has done may be thought to lack a motive. The Statement of Facts of the defendant's counsel should contain a simple and clear account, and should also weaken suspicion.

(c) the *tractatio* of the arguments devised by Invention (2. xviii. 27–xxix. 46).

[d] ἐπιχειρήματα.

[e] 2. xviii. 27–xix. 30.

[f] 2. xx. 31–xxix. 46.

[g] 2. xxx. 47–xxxi. 50.

[CICERO]

Huius constitutionis ratio in sex partes est distributa: probabile, conlationem, signum, argumentum, consecutionem, approbationem. Horum unum quodque quid [1] valeat aperiemus.

Probabile est per quod probatur expedisse peccare, et ab simili turpitudine hominem numquam afuisse. Id dividitur in causam et in vitam.

Causa est ea quae induxit ad maleficium commodorum spe aut incommodorum vitatione, cum quaeritur num quod commodum maleficio appetierit, num honorem, num pecuniam, num dominationem; num aliquam cupiditatem aut amoris aut eiusmodi libidinis voluerit explere, aut num quod incommodum vitarit: inimicitias, infamiam, dolorem, supplicium.

4 III. Hic accusator in spe commodi cupiditatem ostendet adversarii, in vitatione incommodi formidinem augebit. Defensor autem negabit fuisse causam si poterit, aut eam vehementer extenuabit; deinde iniquum esse dicet omnes ad quos aliquid emolumenti ex aliqua re pervenerit in suspicionem maleficii devocari.

---

[1] quodq(ue) quid B^2CE: quodque quod P^2: quodq(ue) quidq(ue) B^1: quid quid H: quid quod II: quidqu P^1: quidquid quid Mx.

The scheme of the Conjectural Issue includes six divisions: Probability, Comparison, Sign, Presumptive Proof, Subsequent Behaviour, and Confirmatory Proof. I shall explain the meaning of each of these terms.

Through Probability [a] one proves that the crime was profitable to the defendant, and that he has never abstained from this kind of foul practice. The subheads under Probability are Motive and Manner of Life.[b]

The Motive [c] is what led the defendant to commit the crime, through the hope it gave him of winning advantages or avoiding disadvantages.[d] The question is: Did he seek some benefit from the crime—honour, money, or power? Did he wish to satisfy some passion—love or a like overpowering desire? Or did he seek to avoid some disadvantage—enmities, ill repute, pain, or punishment? III. Here the prosecutor, if the hope of gaining an advantage is in question, will disclose his opponent's passion; if the avoidance of a disadvantage is in question, he will enlarge upon his opponent's fear. The defendant's counsel, on the other hand, will, if possible, deny that there was a motive, or will at least vigorously belittle its importance; then he will say that it is unfair to bring under suspicion of wrongdoing every one to whom some profit has come from an act.

act, distinguishing in motive passion (*impulsio*) and premeditation (*ratiocinatio*). Quintilian, 7. 2. 7 ff., treats conjecture from the point of view of the act and the author (his identity, his intention [*animus*]).

[c] *Cf.* Cicero, *De Inv.* 2. v. 17–viii. 28.

[d] *Cf.* in Aristotle, *Rhet.* 2. 23 (1399b 30 ff.), the *topos* of Inducements and Deterrents; and see note on 2. xxi. 34 below.

5 Deinde vita hominis ex ante factis spectabitur.
Primum considerabit accusator num quando simile
quid fecerit. Si id non reperiet, quaeret num quando
venerit in similem suspicionem; et in eo debebit esse
occupatus ut ad eam causam peccati quam paulo
ante exposuerit vita hominis possit adcommodari, hoc
modo: si dicet pecuniae causa fecisse, ostendat eum
semper avarum fuisse, si honoris, ambitiosum; ita
poterit animi vitium cum causa peccati conglutinare.
Si non poterit par vitium cum causa reperire, reperiat
dispar. Si non poterit avarum demonstrare, demonstret corruptorem perfidiosum, si quo modo poterit
denique aliquo aut quam plurimis vitiis contaminare;
deinde qui illud fecerit tam nequiter eundem hunc
tam perperam fecisse non esse mirandum. Si vehementer castus et [1] integer [2] existimabitur adversarius, dicet facta, non famam spectari oportere;
illum ante occultasse sua flagitia; se planum fac-
turum ab eo maleficium non abesse. Defensor
primum demonstrabit vitam integram, si poterit; id
si non poterit, confugiet ad inprudentiam, stultitiam,
adulescentiam, vim, persuasionem; quibus de rebus
. . . vituperatio eorum quae extra id crimen erunt
non debeat adsignari. Sin vehementer hominis

---

[1] et *P²b d* : *other MSS. Mx omit.*
[2] integer *MSS.* : *Mx brackets.*

---

[a] *Cf.* Cicero, *De Inv.* 2. x. 32.
[b] *Cf.* Cicero, *De Inv.* 2. x. 33.
[c] Quintilian, 7. 2. 34, discusses charges based on the past
life of the defendant.
[d] *Cf.* Cicero, *De Inv.* 2. x. 33 and 2. xvi. 50.
[e] *Cf.* Cicero, *De Inv.* 2. x. 34.
[f] *Cf.* Cicero, *De Inv.* 2. xi. 35.

64

5   Next the defendant's Manner of Life will be examined in the light of his previous conduct. First the
prosecutor will consider whether the accused has ever
committed a similar offence.[a] If he does not find any,
he will seek to learn whether the accused has ever incurred the suspicion of any similar guilt; and it will
devolve upon him to make every effort to relate the
defendant's manner of life to the motive which he has
just exposed. For example, if the prosecutor contends that the motive for the crime was money, let him
show that the defendant has always been covetous;
if the motive was public honour, ambitious; he will
thus be able to link the flaw in the defendant's
character with the motive for the crime. If he cannot find a flaw consistent with the motive, let him
find one that is not. If he cannot show that the
defendant is covetous,[b] let him show that he is a
treacherous seducer; in short, if he possibly can, let
him brand the defendant with the stigma of some one
fault, or indeed, of as many faults as possible.[c] Then,
he will say, it is no wonder that the man who in
that other instance acted so basely should have acted
so criminally in this instance too.[d] If the adversary
enjoys a high reputation for purity and integrity, the
prosecutor will say that deeds, not reputation, ought
to be considered; that the defendant has previously
concealed his misdeeds,[e] and he will make it plain
that the defendant is not guiltless of misbehaviour.
The defendant's counsel will first show his client's
upright life,[f] if he can; if he cannot, he will have
recourse to thoughtlessness, folly, youth, force, or
undue influence. On these matters . . . censure
ought not to be imposed for conduct extraneous to
the present charge. If the speaker is seriously

65

turpitudine inpedietur et infamia, prius dabit operam
ut falsos rumores dissipatos esse dicat de innocente,
et utetur loco communi rumoribus credi non oportere.
Sin nihil eorum fieri potest, utatur extrema defensione : dicat non se de moribus eius apud censores, sed
de criminibus adversariorum apud iudices dicere.

6 IV. Conlatio est cum accusator id quod adversarium fecisse criminatur alii nemini nisi reo bono
fuisse demonstrat, aut alium neminem potuisse perficere nisi adversarium, aut eum ipsum aliis rationibus
aut non potuisse aut non aeque commode potuisse,
aut eum fugisse alias rationes commodiores propter
cupiditatem.   Hoc loco defensor demonstret oportet
aut aliis quoque bono fuisse, aut alios quoque id quod
ipse insimuletur facere potuisse.

Signum est per quod ostenditur idonea perficiendi
facultas esse quaesita. Id dividitur in partes sex :
locum, tempus, spatium, occasionem, spem perficiendi, spem celandi.

7 Locus quaeritur, celebris an desertus, semper
desertus an tum cum id factum sit, fuerit in eo loco
solitudo, sacer an profanus, publicus an privatus
fuerit; cuiusmodi loci adtingant; num qui est
passus perspectus, exauditus esse possit. Horum

---

^a *Cf.* Cicero, *De Inv.* 2. xi. 37.   In Gellius, 14. 2. 8, a man
against whom the claim of a sum of money was made pleads
that the case concerns a claim before a private judge, and
not a question of morals before the censors.

^b *Cf.* Cicero, *De Inv.* 2. vii. 24.

^c σημεῖον. Different from the usual *signum* of the rhetori-
cians ; see *Rhet. ad Alex.*, chaps. 7 (1428a), 12 (1430b–1431a),
and 14 (1431ab), Aristotle, *Rhet.* 1. 2 (1357ab) ; Cicero, *De Inv.*
1. xxx. 48, and Quintilian, 5. 9. 1 ff. ; also Kroll, *Philologus*
89 (1934). 334–341. *Cf.* Cicero, *Pro Caelio* 22. 53 : " I might

handicapped by the man's baseness and notoriety, he
will first take care to say that false rumours have
been spread about an innocent man, and will use the
commonplace that rumours ought not to be believed.
If none of these pleas is practicable, let him use the
last resource of defence; let him say that he is not
discussing the man's morals before censors, but the
charges of his opponents before jurors.[a]

6 IV. Comparison [b] is used when the prosecutor
shows that the act charged by him against his
adversary has benefited no one but the defendant;
or that no one but his adversary could have committed
it; or that his adversary could not have committed it,
or at least not so easily, by other means; or that,
blinded by passion, his adversary failed to see any
easier means. To meet this point the defendant's
counsel ought to show that the crime benefited others
as well, or that others as well could have done what is
imputed to his client.

By Signs one shows that the accused sought an
opportunity favourable to success. Sign [c] has six
divisions: the Place, the Point of Time, the Duration
of Time, the Occasion, the Hope of Success, the
Hope of Escaping Detection.

7 The Place is examined as follows: Was it fre-
quented or deserted, always a lonely place, or
deserted then at the moment of the crime? A sacred
place or profane, public or private? What sort of
places are adjacent? Could the victim have been
seen or heard? I should willingly describe in detail

in my speech search every lurking-place of suspicion. No
motive, no place, no opportunity, no accomplice, no hope of
succeeding in the crime, no hope of escaping detection, no
means at all, no trace of heinous guilt will be found."

quid reo, quid accusatori conveniat perscribere non
gravaremur, nisi facile quivis causa posita posset
iudicare. Initia enim inventionis ab arte debent
proficisci; cetera facile conparabit exercitatio.

Tempus ita quaeritur: quid anni, qua hora—noctu
an interdiu—et qua die, qua noctis hora factum esse
dicatur, et cur eiusmodi temporibus.

Spatium ita considerabitur: satisne longum fuerit
ad eam rem transigendam, scieritne satis ad id perficiendum spatii futurum; nam parvi refert satis
spatii fuisse ad id perficiendum si id ante sciri et
ratione provideri non potuit.

Occasio quaeritur, idoneane fuerit ad rem adori-
endam, an alia melior quae aut praeterita sit aut non
expectata.

Spes perficiendi ecqua fuerit spectabitur hoc modo:
si quae supra dicta sunt signa concurrent, si praeterea
ex altera parte vires, pecunia, consilium, scientia,
apparatio videbitur esse, ex altera parte inbecillitas,
inopia, stultitia, inprudentia, inapparatio demonstrabitur fuisse; qua re scire poterit [1] utrum diffidendum
an confidendum fuerit.

Spes celandi quae fuerit quaeritur ex consciis,
arbitris, adiutoribus, liberis aut servis aut utrisque.

[1] poterit *M* : potuerit *E Mx.*

---

[a] For the genitive form *die*, see W. M. Lindsay, *The Latin
Language*, Oxford, 1894, pp. 382–3; Neue-Wagener, *Formen-
lehre der latein. Sprache* (3rd ed., Leipzig, 1902), 1. 573–4;
Kühner-Holzweissig, *Ausführliche Grammatik der latein.
Sprache* (2nd ed., Hannover, 1912), 1. 405–6.

[b] *Cf.* Aristotle, *Rhet.* 2. 5 (1383a): "We feel confidence
if . . . there are means of aid—either numerous means or
great, or both numerous and great."

AD HERENNIUM, II. iv. 7

which of these points is serviceable to the defence, and
which to the prosecution, were it not that any one
would in a given cause find this easy to determine.
For of Invention it is only the first principles which
ought to originate in theory; all the rest will readily
be supplied by practice.

The Point of Time is examined as follows: In what
season of the year, in what part of the day—whether
at night or in the daytime—at what hour of the day *a*
or night, is the act alleged to have been committed,
and why at such a time?

The Duration of Time will be considered in the
following fashion: Was it long enough to carry this
act through, and did the defendant know that there
would be enough time to accomplish it? For it is
only of slight importance that he had enough time to
carry out the crime if he could not in advance have
known or have forecast that that would be so.

The Occasion is examined as follows: Was it
favourable for the undertaking, or was there a
better occasion which was either let pass or not
awaited?

Whether there was any Hope of Success will be in-
vestigated as follows: Do the above-mentioned signs
coincide? Especially, do power, money, good judgement, foreknowledge, and preparedness appear on
one side, and is it proved that on the other there were
weakness, need, stupidity, lack of foresight, and
unpreparedness? Hereby one will know whether
the defendant should have had confidence in his
success or not.

What Hope there was of Escaping Detection we
seek to learn from confidants, eye-witnesses, or
accomplices, freemen or slaves or both.*b*

69

[CICERO]

8 V. Argumentum est per quod res coarguitur certioribus argumentis et magis firma suspicione. Id dividitur in tempora tria: praeteritum, instans, consequens.

In praeterito tempore oportet considerare ubi fuerit, ubi visus sit, quicum visus sit, num quid appararit, num quem convenerit, num quid dixerit, num quid habuerit de consciis, de adiutoribus, de adiumentis; num quo in loco praeter consuetudinem fuerit aut alieno tempore. In instanti tempore quaeretur num visus sit cum faciebat, num qui strepitus, clamor, crepitus exauditus, aut denique num quid aliquo sensu perceptum sit, aspectu, auditu, tactu, odoratu, gustatu; nam quivis horum sensus potest conflare suspicionem. In consequenti tempore spectabitur num quid re transacta relictum sit quod indicet aut factum esse maleficium aut ab quo factum sit. Factum esse, hoc modo: si tumore et livore decoloratum corpus est mortui, significat eum veneno necatum. A quo factum sit, hoc modo: si telum, si vestimentum, si quid eiusmodi relictum aut si

---

ᵃ *Cf.* Cicero, *De Inv.* 2. xiii. 43. *Argumentum* is virtually equivalent to the σημεῖον (fallible sign) of the *Rhet. ad Alex.* (ch. 12, 1430b). The tradition thus antedates Aristotle and persisted against his theory of σημεῖον, which joined with εἰκός (the probable proposition) in forming the material of the enthymeme (E. M. Cope, *An Introd. to Aristotle's Rhetoric*, London and Cambridge, 1867, pp. 160 ff.). The *communes loci* dealing with the περιστάσεις are akin to the Aristotelian kind of *topoi*, but are not specifically Aristotelian. They belong in the Hermagorean system of Issues, but the specific division of σημεῖα into three periods goes back to pre-Aristotelian rhetorical theory (*Rhet. ad Alex., l.c.*). Neocles (first or second Christian century) in Anon. Seg. 153 (Spengel-Hammer 1 [2]. 379) divides probabilities, signs, and examples

8 V. Through Presumptive Proof guilt is demonstrated by means of indications that increase certainty and strengthen suspicion. It falls into three periods: preceding the crime, contemporaneous with the crime, following the crime.[a]

In respect to the period preceding the crime, one ought to consider where the defendant was, where he was seen, with whom seen, whether he made some preparation, met any one, said anything, or showed any sign of having confidants, accomplices, or means of assistance; whether he was in a place, or there at a time, at variance with his custom. In respect to the period contemporaneous with the crime, we shall seek to learn whether he was seen in the act; whether some noise, outcry, or crash was heard; or, in short, whether anything was perceived by one of the senses—sight, hearing, touch, smell, or taste. For any type of sense-experience can arouse suspicion. In respect to the period following the crime, one will seek to discover whether after the act was completed there was left behind anything indicating that a crime was committed, or by whom it was committed. Indicating that it was committed: for example, if the body of the deceased is swollen and black and blue it signifies that the man was killed by poison. Indicating by whom it was committed: for example, if a weapon, or clothing, or something of the kind was left behind, or a footprint of the accused was dis-

into three types according to the same chronological scheme, " as cloud indicating storm, smoke fire, and blood murder." Σημεῖα and εἰκότα were used by the Attic orators as early as Antiphon, and by Thucydides; see Friedrich Solmsen, *Die Entwicklung der aristotelischen Logik und Rhetorik* (Neue Philol. Untersuch. 4), Berlin, 1929, pp. 26-7, and *Antiphonstudien* (Neue Philol. Untersuch. 8), Berlin, 1931, pp. 50 ff.

vestigium rei repertum fuerit; si cruor in vestimentis;
si in eo loco conprehensus aut visus, transacto negotio,
quo in loco res gesta dicitur.

Consecutio est cum quaeritur quae signa nocentis
et innocentis consequi soleant. Accusator dicet,
si poterit, adversarium, cum ad eum ventum sit,
erubuisse, expalluisse, titubasse, inconstanter locutum
esse, concidisse, pollicitum esse aliquid; quae signa
conscientiae sint. Si reus horum nihil fecerit,
accusator dicet eum usque adeo praemeditatum
fuisse quid sibi esset usu venturum ut confidentissime
resisteret, responderet;[1] quae signa confidentiae,
non innocentiae sint. Defensor, si pertimuerit,
magnitudine periculi, non conscientia peccati se
commotum esse dicet; si non pertimuerit, fretum
innocentia negabit esse commotum.

9   VI. Approbatio est qua utimur ad extremum
confirmata suspicione. Ea habet locos proprios
atque communes. Proprii sunt ii quibus nisi accusator nemo potest uti, et ii quibus nisi defensor. Communes sunt qui alia in causa ab reo, alia ab accusatore
tractantur. In causa coniecturali proprius locus

[1] responderet *Mx brackets*.

---

[a] *Cf.* Galen, *De symptom. different.* (ed. Kühn, 7. 43), " the
symptom (σύμπτωμα) which some physicians call ἐπιγέννημα "
(after-symptom); Chrysippus, fragm. 125, ed. Alfred Gercke,
Jahrbücher für Class. Philol., Suppl. 14 (1885), 738: κατ'
ἐπακολούθημά τι καὶ σύμπτωμα.

[b] *Defensor* is here used as if it meant *reus*. *Cf.* also the
last sentence under Comparison in 2. iv. 6, and in 2. xiv. 22;
2. xv. 22, end; Cicero, *De Inv.* 2. xxviii. 83 and 86, and 2.
xxix. 88; and Wenger, *Institutes of the Roman Law of Civil
Procedure*, p. 91, note 44.

covered; if there was blood on his clothes; or if, after the deed was done, he was caught or seen in the spot where the crime is alleged to have been perpetrated.

For Subsequent Behaviour we investigate the signs which usually attend guilt or innocence.[a] The prosecutor will, if possible, say that his adversary, when come upon, blushed, paled, faltered, spoke uncertainly, collapsed, or made some offer—signs of a guilty conscience. If the accused has done none of these things, the prosecutor will say his adversary had even so far in advance calculated what would actually happen to him that he stood his ground and replied with the greatest self-assurance—signs of audacity, and not of innocence. The defendant's counsel, if his client has shown fear, will say that he was moved,[b] not by a guilty conscience, but by the magnitude of his peril; if his client has not shown fear, counsel will say that he was unmoved because he relied on his innocence.

9   VI. Confirmatory Proof[c] is what we employ finally, when suspicion has been established. It has special and common topics.[d] The special topics are those which only the prosecution, or those which only the defence, can use. The common topics are those which are used now by the defence, and now by the prosecution, depending on the case. In a conjectural

---

[c] βεβαίωσις in *Rhet. ad Alex.*, ch. 36 (1442b).

[d] The treatment of commonplaces goes back to Protagoras and Gorgias (Cicero, *Brutus* 12. 46–7, Quintilian, 3. 1. 12). On the *topoi* of Aristotle see Cope, *An Introd. to Aristotle's Rhetoric*, pp. 124–131. *Cf.* Cicero, *De Inv.* 2. xv. 48, who makes a twofold classification of the matters amplified: doubtful and certain; Quintilian, 5. 12. 15–16; and note on 2. xxx. 47 below.

accusatoris est cum dicit malorum misereri non
oportere, et cum auget peccati atrocitatem. Defensoris proprius locus est cum misericordiam captat et
cum accusatorem calumniari criminatur. Communes loci sunt cum accusatoris tum defensoris : abs
testibus, contra testes; abs quaestionibus, contra
quaestiones; ab argumentis, contra argumenta; ab
rumoribus, contra rumores.

A testibus dicemus secundum auctoritatem et
vitam testium et constantiam testimoniorum. Contra
testes : secundum [1] vitae turpitudinem, testimoniorum
inconstantiam; si aut fieri non potuisse dicemus aut
non factum esse quod dicant, aut scire illos non
potuisse, aut cupide dicere et argumentari. Haec et
ad inprobationem et ad interrogationem testium
pertinebunt.

10   VII. A quaestionibus dicemus cum demonstrabimus maiores veri inveniendi causa tormentis et
cruciatu voluisse quaeri, et summo dolore homines
cogi ut quicquid sciant dicant; et praeterea con-

---

[1] *lacuna*; secundum *inserted by Schuetz.*

---

[a] For *a, ab* meaning *on the side of* cf. 2. xxvii. 43 (*ab reo*),
and see Schmalz-Hofmann, p. 523.
[b] The non-technical means of persuasion (πίστεις ἄτεχνοι),
those that are not inherent in the art, that are not supplied by
our own efforts. See Aristotle, *Rhet.* 1. 2 (1355b) and 1. 15
(1375a), who lists five : laws, witnesses, contracts, evidence
given under torture, and the oath. The theory is pre-Aristotelian; cf. *Rhet. ad Alex.*, chaps. 7 (1428a) and 14 (1431b)
ff., on the supplementary proofs (ἐπίθετοι πίστεις) : the
speaker's own opinion, witnesses, admissions under torture,
and oaths. The employment of these proofs long antedated

cause the prosecutor uses a special topic when he says that wicked men ought not to be pitied, and expatiates upon the atrocity of the crime. The defendant's counsel uses a special topic when he tries to win pity, and charges the prosecutor with slander. These topics are common to both prosecution and defence: to speak for[a] or against witnesses, for or against the testimony given under torture, for or against presumptive proof, and for or against rumours.[b]

In favour of witnesses[c] we shall speak under the heads: (a) authority and manner of life of the witnesses, and (b) the consistency of their evidence. Against witnesses, under the heads: (a) their base manner of living; (b) the contradictory character of their testimony; (c) if we contend that what they allege to have happened either could not have happened or did not happen, or that they could not have known it. or that it is partiality which inspires their words and inferences. These topics will appertain both to the discrediting and to the examination of witnesses.

10 VII. We shall speak in favour of the testimony given under torture[d] when we show that it was in order to discover the truth that our ancestors wished investigations to make use of torture and the rack, and that men are compelled by violent pain to tell all they know. Moreover, such reasoning will have

argumentation in the law-courts; when argumentation came into being its first function was to interpret these " already existing " proofs.

[c] μάρτυρες.
[d] βάσανοι. To be distinguished from *iudicii quaestio* (1. xvi. 26). Torture was administered under the direction of the court, but not in the presence of the jury. The torture of free men was not legal.

firmatior haec erit disputatio si quae dicta erunt argumentando isdem viis quibus omnis coniectura tractatur trahemus ad veri similem suspicionem; idemque hoc in testimoniis facere oportebit. Contra quaestiones hoc modo dicemus: primum maiores voluisse certis in rebus interponi quaestiones cum quae vere dicerentur sciri, quae falso in quaestione pronuntiarentur refelli possent, hoc modo: quo in loco quid positum sit, et si quid esset simile quod videri aut vestigiis probari [1] aut aliquo simili signo percipi posset; deinde dolori credi non oportere, quod alius alio recentior sit in dolore, quod ingeniosior ad eminiscendum, quod denique saepe scire aut suspicari possit quid quaesitor velit audire; quod cum dixerit, intellegat sibi finem doloris futurum. Haec disputatio conprobabitur si refellemus quae in quaestionibus erunt dicta probabili argumentatione; idque partibus coniecturae quas ante exposuimus facere oportebit.

11 Ab argumentis et signis et ceteris locis quibus augetur suspicio dicere hoc modo convenit: Cum multa concurrant argumenta et signa quae inter se consentiant, rem perspicuam, non suspiciosam videri oportere. Item plus oportere signis et argumentis credi quam testibus, haec enim eo modo exponi quo

---

[1] *lac.*; aut vestigiis probari *suggested by Mx.*

a 2. ii. 3–v. 8.

the greater force if we give the confessions elicited under torture an appearance of plausibility by the same argumentative procedure as is used in treating any question of fact. And this, too, we shall have to do with the evidence of witnesses. Against the testimony given under torture we shall speak as follows: In the first place, our ancestors wished inquisitions to be introduced only in connection with unambiguous matters, when the true statement in the inquisition could be recognized and the false reply refuted; for example, if they sought to learn in what place some object was put, or if there was in question something like that which could be seen, or be verified by means of footprints, or be perceived by some like sign. We then shall say that pain ought not to be relied upon, because one person is less exhausted by pain, or more resourceful in fabrication, than another, and also because it is often possible to know or divine what the presiding justice wishes to hear, and the witness knows that when he has said this his pain will be at an end. Such reasoning will find favour, if, by a plausible argument, we refute the statements made in the testimony given under torture; and to accomplish this we should use the divisions under the Conjectural Issue which I have set forth above.[a]

11   In favour of presumptive proof, signs, and the other means of increasing suspicion it is advantageous to speak as follows: When there is a concurrence of many circumstantial indications and signs that agree with one another, the result ought to appear as clear fact, not surmise. Again, signs and presumptive proof deserve more credence than witnesses, for these first are presented precisely as they occurred in

modo re vera sint gesta, testes corrumpi posse vel pretio vel gratia vel metu vel simultate. Contra argumenta et signa et ceteras suspiciones dicemus hoc modo: si demonstrabimus nullam rem esse quam non suspicionibus quivis possit criminari; deinde unam quamque suspicionem extenuabimus et dabimus operam ut ostendamus nihilo magis in nos eam quam in alium quempiam convenire; indignum facinus esse sine testibus coniecturam et suspicionem firmamenti satis habere.

12   VIII. A rumoribus dicemus si negabimus temere famam nasci solere quin subsit aliquid; et si dicemus causam non fuisse quare quispiam confingeret et eminisceretur; et praeterea, si ceteri falsi soleant esse, argumentabimur hunc esse verum. Contra rumores dicemus primum si docebimus multos esse falsos rumores, et exemplis utemur de quibus falsa fama fuerit; et aut iniquos nostros aut homines natura malivolos et maledicos confinxisse dicemus; et aliquam aut fictam fabulam in adversarios adferemus quam dicamus omnibus in ore esse, aut verum rumorem proferemus qui illis aliquid turpitudinis adferat, neque tamen ei rumori nos fidem habere dicemus, ideo quod quivis unus homo possit quamvis turpem de quolibet rumorem proferre et confictam fabulam dissipare. Verumtamen si rumor vehementer probabilis esse videbitur, argumentando famae fidem poterimus abrogare.

ᵃ For the same sentiment *cf.* Anon. Seg. 189, in Spengel-Hammer 1 (2). 386; Hermogenes, *De Stat.* 3 (ed. Rabe, pp. 45–6); also Aristotle, *Rhet.* 1. 15 (1376 a): The speaker who

reality, whereas witnesses can be corrupted by bribery, or partiality, or intimidation, or animosity.[a] Against presumptive proof, signs, and the other provocatives of suspicion we shall speak in the following fashion: we shall show that nothing is safe from attack by suspicion, and then we shall weaken each and every reason for suspicion and try to show that it applies to us no more than to any one else; it is a shameful outrage to consider suspicion and conjecture, in the absence of witnesses, as sufficiently corroborative.

12 VIII. We shall speak in favour of rumours by saying that a report is not wont to be created recklessly and without some foundation, and that there was no reason for anybody wholly to invent and fabricate one; and, moreover, if other rumours usually are lies, we shall prove by argument that this one is true. We shall speak against rumours if we first show that many rumours are false, and cite examples of false report; if we say that the rumours were the invention of our enemies or of other men malicious and slanderous by nature; and if we either present some story invented against our adversaries which we declare to be in every mouth, or produce a true report carrying some disgrace to them, and say we yet have no faith in it for the reason that any person at all can produce and spread any disgraceful rumour or fiction about any other person. If, nevertheless, a rumour seems highly plausible, we can destroy its authority by logical argument.

lacks witnesses on his side will argue " that probabilities cannot be bribed to mislead the court, and are never convicted of false witness."

Quod et difficillima tractatu est constitutio coniecturalis et in veris causis saepissime tractanda est, eo
diligentius omnes eius partes perscrutati sumus, ut ne
parvula quidem titubatione aut offensatione inpedire-
mur, si ad hanc rationem praeceptionis adsiduitatem
exercitationis adcommodassemus.   Nunc ad legitimae
constitutionis partes transeamus.

13   IX. Cum voluntas scriptoris cum scripto dissidere
videbitur, si a scripto dicemus, his locis utemur:
secundum narrationem primum scriptoris conlaudatione, deinde scripti recitatione, deinde percontatione
scirentne idonee adversarii id scriptum fuisse in lege
aut testamento aut stipulatione aut quolibet scripto
quod ad eam rem pertinebit; deinde conlatione quid
scriptum sit, quid adversarii se fecisse dicant: quid
iudicem sequi conveniat, utrum id quod diligenter
perscriptum sit, an id quod acute sit excogitatum;
deinde ea sententia quae ab adversariis sit excogitata
et scripto adtributa contemnetur et infirmabitur.
Deinde quaeretur quid periculi fuerit si id voluisset
adscribere, aut num non potuerit perscribi.   Deinde
a nobis sententia reperietur et causa proferetur quare
id scriptor senserit quod scripserit; et demonstrabitur
scriptum illud esse dilucide, breviter, commode, perfecte, cum ratione cauta.   Deinde exempla profe-
rentur quae res, cum ab adversariis sententia et
voluntas adferretur, ab scripto potius iudicatae sint.
Deinde ostendetur quam periculosum sit ab scripto
recedere.   Locus communis est contra eum qui, cum

---

[a] ἀληθινὰ πράγματα (Longinus, in Spengel-Hammer 1 [2].
195. 18), as distinguished from school exercises; cf. 4. xliv. 58.
[b] Cf. Cicero, De Inv. 2. xliii. 125.

80

Because the Conjectural Issue is the hardest to treat and in actual causes [a] needs to be treated most often, I have the more carefully examined all its divisions, in order that we may not be hindered by even the slightest hesitation or blunder, if only we have applied these precepts of theory in assiduous practice. Now let me turn to the subtypes of Legal Issue.

13 IX. When the intention of the framer appears at variance with the letter of a text, speaking in support of the letter [b] we shall employ the following topics: first, after the Statement of Facts, a eulogy of the framer and then the reading aloud of the text; next the questioning of our adversaries: Are they duly aware that this text was in a law, will, contract, or any other document involved in the cause?; then a comparison of the text with the admitted act of our adversaries: Which should the judge follow—a document carefully draughted, or an interpretation cunningly invented? After that the interpretation devised and given to the text by our adversaries will be disparaged and weakened. Then the question will be raised: What risk would the writer have run by adding an entry of that kind had he really intended it, or was it impossible to write it out in full? Then we shall ascertain the writer's intention and present the reason why he had in mind what he wrote, and show that that text is clear, concise, apt, complete, and planned with precision. Thereupon we shall cite examples of judgements rendered in favour of the text, although adversaries raised the issue of spirit and intention. Finally, we shall show the danger of departing from the letter of the text. The commonplace here is that against one who, though confessing

fateatur se contra quod legibus sanctum aut testamento perscriptum sit fecisse, tamen facti quaerat defensionem.

14   X. Ab sententia sic dicemus: primum laudabimus scriptoris commoditatem atque brevitatem, quod tantum scripserit quod necesse fuerit; illud quod sine scripto intellegi potuerit non necessario scribendum putarit.   Deinde dicemus calumniatoris esse officium verba et litteras sequi, neglegere voluntatem. Deinde id quod scriptum sit aut non posse fieri aut non lege, non more, non natura, non aequo et bono posse fieri, quae omnia noluisse scriptorem quam rectissime fieri nemo dicet; at ea quae a nobis facta sint iustissime facta.   Deinde contrariam sententiam aut nullam esse aut stultam aut iniustam aut non posse fieri aut non constare cum superioribus et inferioribus sententiis aut cum iure communi aut cum aliis legibus communibus aut cum rebus iudicatis dissentire.   Deinde exemplorum a voluntate et contra scriptum iudicatorum enumeratione, deinde legum aut stipulationum breviter exscriptarum in quibus

---

^{a} ἀκριβοδίκαιος.   Cf. Cicero, Pro Caecina 23. 65 : [People who feel that they have equity on their side say that] " a pettifogger follows the letter; a good juror defends the will and intention of the framer."

^{b} The departments of Law, considered in 2. xiii. 19–20 below.

^{c} κοινὸν δίκαιον, the " unwritten statutes of heaven that stand fast for ever " (ἄγραπτα κάσφαλῆ θεῶν νόμιμα) of Sophocles, Antig. 454–5. (Sophocles apparently echoes an argument used by Pericles in an actual case; see Lysias, Adv. Andoc. 10). Cf. Aristotle, Rhet. 1. 10 (1368b) : " By universal law I mean all the unwritten principles that are supposed to be acknowledged by all mankind "; 1. 13 (1373b) : " For indeed there is, as all men to some extent divine, a natural and universal

that he has violated the mandates of a statute or
the directions of a will, yet seeks to defend his act.

14 X. In favour of the intention we shall speak as
follows: first we shall praise the framer for deft
conciseness in having written only what was necessary;
he did not think it necessary to write what could be
understood without a text. Next we shall say that
to follow the words literally and to neglect the
intention is the method of a pettifogger.[a] Then,
we shall contend, the letter either cannot be
carried out, or at least not without violation of
Statute Law, Legal Custom, the Law of Nature, or
Equity [b]—all these, as no one will deny, the writer
wished to be most strictly observed; but on the
contrary, what we have done is absolutely just.
Further, the interpretation of our adversaries is
either no interpretation, or is unreasonable, unjust,
impracticable, or inconsistent with past or subsequent interpretations, or is in disagreement with
the common law [c] or with other generally binding
rules of law or with previous decisions. Next we
shall cite instances of decisions rendered in favour of
the intention and contrary to the letter, and then

notion of right and wrong, binding on them even if they
have no mutual intercourse or covenant "; 1. 15 (1375a):
" It is clear that if the written law is adverse to our case, he
[the speaker] must appeal to the universal law, and to the
principles of equity as representing a higher order of justice.
[He must say] that [the judge's obligation to decide] ' according to my best judgement ' means that the judge will not be
guided simply and solely by the letter of the statute " (tr.
Lane Cooper); Cope, *An Introd. to Aristotle's Rhetoric*, pp.
239–44. *Cf.* also the Stoic Chrysippus in Diogenes Laertius
7. 88 : " The common law, the right reason pervading all
things; " and Cicero, *De Offic.* 3. 17. 69.

intellegatur scriptorum voluntas et recitatione utemur et [1] expositione. Locus communis contra eum
qui scriptum recitet et scriptoris voluntatem non
interpretetur.

15   Cum duae leges inter se discrepant,[2] videndum est
primum num quae obrogatio aut derogatio sit, deinde
utrum leges ita dissentiant ut altera iubeat, altera
vetet, an ita ut altera cogat, altera permittat. Infirma
enim erit eius defensio qui negabit se fecisse quod
cogeretur, cum altera lex permitteret; plus enim
valet sanctio permissione. Item illa defensio tenuis
est, cum ostenditur id factum esse quod ea lex
sanciat cui legi obrogatum aut derogatum sit, id quod
posteriore lege sanctum sit esse neglectum. Cum
haec erunt considerata, statim nostrae legis expositione, recitatione, conlaudatione utemur. Deinde
contrariae legis enodabimus voluntatem et eam
trahemus ad nostrae causae commodum. Dein de
iuridicali absoluta sumemus rationem iuris et
quaeremus partes iuris utrocum faciant; de qua parte
iuridicalis posterius disseremus.

16   XI. Si ambiguum esse scriptum putabitur, quod in
duas aut plures sententias trahi possit, hoc modo
tractandum est: primum sitne ambiguum quaeren-
dumst; deinde quomodo scriptum esset si id quod
adversarii interpretantur scriptor fieri voluisset
ostendendum est; deinde id quod nos interpretemur
et fieri posse et honeste, recte, lege, more, natura,

---

[1] *lac.*; recitatione utemur et *sugg. Mx.*
[2] discrepant *E* : discrepent *other MSS. Mx.*

---

[a] See 2. xiii. 19–20.

read and explain laws or contracts which had been
written down in concise form and yet in which the
intention of the framer is understood. The commonplace here is that against one who reads a text and
does not interpret the writer's intention.

15 When two laws conflict, we must first see whether
they have been superseded or restricted, and then
whether their disagreement is such that one commands
and the other prohibits, or one compels and the other
allows. It will be a weak defence indeed for a
person to say that he failed to do what one law
ordained, because another law made it optional; for
obligation is more binding than mere permission. So
also it is a meagre defence for a person to show
that he has observed the obligation of a law which
has been superseded or restricted, without heeding
the obligation of the later law. After these considerations we shall at once pass to the exposition, reading,
and warm recommendation of the law favourable to
us. Then we shall elucidate the intention of the
opposing law and appropriate it for the advantage of
our cause. Finally, we shall take over the theory of
Law from the Absolute Juridical Issue, and examine
with which side the departments of Law hold; this
subtype of a Juridical Issue I shall discuss later.[a]

16 XI. If a text is regarded as ambiguous, because it
can be interpreted in two or more meanings, the
treatment is as follows: first we must examine
whether it is indeed ambiguous; then we must show
how it would have been written if the writer had
wished it to have the meaning which our adversaries
give to it; next, that our interpretation is practicable,
and practicable in conformity with the Honourable
and the Right, with Statute Law, Legal Custom,

bono et aequo fieri posse; quod adversarii inter-
pretentur ex contrario; nec esse ambigue scriptum
cum intellegatur utra sententia vera sit. Sunt qui
arbitrentur ad hanc causam tractandam vehementer
pertinere cognitionem amphiboliarum eam quae ab
dialecticis proferatur. Nos vero arbitramur non
modo nullo adiumento esse, sed potius maximo inpedimento. Omnes enim illi amphibolias aucupantur,
eas etiam quae ex altera parte sententiam nullam
possunt interpretari. Itaque et alieni sermonis
molesti interpellatores, et scripti cum odiosi tum
obscuri interpretes sunt; et dum caute et expedite
loqui volunt, infantissimi reperiuntur. Ita dum
metuunt in dicendo ne quid ambiguum dicant,
nomen suum pronuntiare non possunt. Verum horum
pueriles opiniones rectissimis rationibus, cum voles,
refellemus. In praesentiarum hoc intercedere non
alienum fuit, ut huius infantiae garrulam disciplinam
contemneremus.

17 XII. Cum definitione utemur, primum adferemus
brevem vocabuli definitionem, hoc modo: " Maiestatem is minuit qui ea tollit ex quibus rebus civitatis
amplitudo constat. Quae sunt ea, Q. Caepio?

---

a *Honesta res* and *rectum* are defined in 3. ii. 3 below, the
departments of Law in 2. xiii. 19–20 below.

b Isocrates, *Panath.* 26–28, on the so-called eristic discussions " which our young men take greater pleasure in than
they ought," holds them unsuitable for grown men. In
Cicero, *De Oratore* 2. 26. 111, Antonius blames the rhetoricians
for not knowing ambiguities as well as the dialecticians
understood them (see also *Orator* 32. 115), whereas Dionysius
Halic., *De Composit. Verb.*, ch. 4, says that treatises such as
those of Chrysippus dealing, among others, with ambiguous
propositions offer no benefit to civil oratory, at least with
respect to charm and beauty of style. The contempt for

the Law of Nature, or Equity;[a] of our adversaries' interpretation the opposite is true; and the text is not ambiguous since one well understands which is the true sense. There are some who think that for the development of this kind of cause a knowledge of amphibolies as taught by the dialecticians is highly useful. I, however, believe that this knowledge is of no help at all, and is, I may even say, a most serious hindrance. In fact these writers are on the lookout for all amphibolies, even for such as yield no sense at all in one of the two interpretations. Accordingly, when some one else speaks, they are his annoying hecklers, and when he writes, they are his boring and also misty interpreters. And when they themselves speak, wishing to do so cautiously and deftly, they prove to be utterly inarticulate. Thus, in their fear to utter some ambiguity while speaking, they cannot even pronounce their own names. Indeed I shall refute the childish opinions of these writers by the most straightforward proofs whenever you wish. For the present it has not been out of place to make this protest, in order to express my contempt for the wordy learning of this school of inarticulateness.[b]

17 XII. When we deal with the Issue of Definition, we shall first briefly define the term in question, as follows: "He impairs the sovereign majesty of the state who destroys the elements constituting its dignity. What are these, Quintus Caepio? The

dialectic is Epicurean; cf. Diogenes Laertius 10. 31: "Dialectic the Epicureans reject as superfluous"; Cicero, De Fin. 1. 7. 22, on Epicurus: "He does not show how to detect ambiguities"; ibid., 2. 6. 18. Chrysippus maintained that every word is by nature ambiguous, while Diodorus Cronus asserted that no word is ambiguous (Gellius 11. 12).

[CICERO]

Suffragia populi et magistratus consilium.[1] Nempe igitur tu et populum suffragio et magistratum consilio privasti cum pontes disturbasti." Item ex contrario: " Maiestatem is minuit qui amplitudinem civitatis detrimento adficit. Ego non adfeci, sed prohibui detrimento; aerarium enim conservavi, libidini malorum restiti, maiestatem omnem interire non passus sum." Primum igitur vocabuli sententia breviter et ad utilitatem adcommodate causae describitur; deinde factum nostrum cum verbi descriptione coniungetur; deinde contrariae descriptionis ratio refelletur, si aut falsa erit aut inutilis aut turpis aut iniuriosa—id quod ex iuris partibus sumetur de iuridicali absoluta, de qua iam loquemur.

18 Quaeritur in translationibus primum num aliquis eius rei actionem, petitionem, aut persecutionem habeat, num alio tempore, num alia lege, num alio quaerente. Haec legibus et moribus, aequo et bono reperientur; de quibus dicetur in iuridicali absoluta.

In causa ratiocinali primum quaeretur ecquid in rebus maioribus aut minoribus aut similibus [2] similiter

---

[1] suffragia populi et magistratus consilium *E* : suffragia magistratus *M Mx.*

[2] similibus *E* : dissimilibus *M Mx.*

---

a Our author here resumes the controversy between Saturninus and Caepio treated in 1. xii. 21 above.

b 2. xiii. 19–20 below.

c For the meaning of these terms see Moriz Wlassak, *Sav. Zeitschr.* 42 (1921). 408 ff., and *Sitzungsb. Akad. der Wissensch. in Wien (Philos.-hist. Kl.)* 202, 3 (1924). 168, note 37; Wenger, *Institutes of the Roman Law of Civil Procedure*, p. 259, note 10, and p. 416. All enforceable rights are exhausted by the triad : *actio* refers to the *legis actio, petitio* comprehends obligations without regard to the form of the legal procedure, and *persecutio* refers probably to rights in general embraced under prosecution, including such praetorian remedies outside

suffrage of the people and the counsel of the magistracy. No doubt, then, in demolishing the bridges of
the Comitium, you have deprived the people of their
suffrage and the magistracy of their counselling." [a]
Likewise, in reply: "He impairs the sovereign
majesty of the state who inflicts damage upon its
dignity. I have not inflicted, but rather prevented,
damage, for I have saved the Treasury, resisted the
license of wicked men, and kept the majesty of the
state from perishing utterly." Thus the meaning of
the term is first explained briefly, and adapted to the
advantage of our cause; then we shall connect our
conduct with the explanation of the term; finally,
the principle underlying the contrary definition will
be refuted, as being false, inexpedient, disgraceful,
or harmful—and here we shall borrow our means
from the departments of Law treated under the
Absolute Juridical Issue, which I shall soon discuss. [b]

18 In causes based on Transference we first examine
whether one has the right to institute an action, claim,
or prosecution [c] in this matter, or whether it should
not rather be instituted at another time, or under
another law, or before another examiner. The
pertinent means will be provided by Statute Law,
Legal Custom, and Equity, which I shall discuss in
connection with the Absolute Juridical Issue. [d]

In a cause based on Analogy [e] we shall first seek
to know whether there exists any like text or decision
on matters of greater, less, or like importance; next

an ordinary lawsuit as *interdicta* (see Greenidge, *The Legal
Procedure of Cicero's Time*, pp. 75-8, Wenger, pp. 245 ff.)
and *in integrum restitutiones* (see Wenger, pp. 244-5).

[d] 2. xiii. 19-20 below.

[e] Arising from a gap in the law, which is filled by a process
of deduction.

scriptum aut iudicatum sit; deinde utrum ea res
similis sit ei rei qua de agitur an dissimilis; deinde
utrum consulto de ea re scriptum non sit, quod
noluerit cavere, an quod satis cautum putarit propter
ceterorum scriptorum similitudinem.

De partibus legitimae constitutionis satis dictum
est; nunc ad iuridicalem revertemur.

19 XIII. Absoluta iuridicali constitutione utemur cum
ipsam rem quam nos fecisse confitemur iure factam [1]
dicemus, sine ulla adsumptione extrariae defensionis.
In ea convenit quaeri iurene sit factum. De eo
causa posita dicere poterimus si ex quibus partibus
ius constet cognoverimus. Constat igitur ex his
partibus : natura, lege, consuetudine, iudicato,
aequo et bono, pacto.

[1] factam *E* : factum *M Mx.*

---

[a] See l. xiv. 24 above.
[b] *Cf.* Cicero, *De Inv.* 2. liii. 160 ff. Johannes Stroux
("Summum ius summa iniuria," in *Festschr. Speiser-Sarasin,*
Leipzig, 1926, and "Griechische Einflüsse auf die Entwickl.
der röm. Rechtswissensch. gegen Ende der republikan. Zeit,"
in *Atti del Congr. Internaz. di diritto Rom.* (Roma), Pavia,
1934, 1. 111–132; now both printed as *Röm. Rechtswissensch.
und Rhetorik,* Potsdam, 1949) argues that rhetorical theory
had a substantial influence on Roman jurisprudence (the
sequence being from Greek philosophy to Greek rhetoric,
thence to Roman rhetoric, and finally to Roman juristic
theory and practice), but many students of Roman Law
believe that, though useful for pleading, it was not of real
significance for directing judicial decisions. Thus the *status*
system as a whole seems to have had no influence upon the
jurists, with the possible exception of the doctrines of Letter
and Spirit and of Definition (1. xi. 19, 2. ix. 13–x. 14; 1. xii. 21,

whether that matter is in fact like or unlike the matter in question; then whether the absence of a text concerning the matter here involved was intentional, because the framer was unwilling to make any provision, or because he thought that there was provision enough thanks to the similar provisions in the other legal texts.

On the subdivisions of the Legal Issue I have said enough; now I shall turn back to the Juridical.[a]

19   XIII. We shall be dealing with an Absolute Juridical Issue when, without any recourse to a defence extraneous to the cause, we contend that the act itself which we confess having committed was lawful. Herein it is proper to examine whether the act was in accord with the Law. We can discuss this question, once a cause is given, when we know the departments of which the Law is constituted. The constituent departments, then, are the following: Nature, Statute, Custom, Previous Judgements, Equity, and Agreement.[b]

2. xii. 17); *cf.*, for example, Quintilian, 7. 6. 1. The rhetorician's method of interpretation is rationalistic and schematic, the jurist's is casuistic. See A. A. Schiller, *Virginia Law Rev.* 27 (1941). 733–768, esp. 750 ff.; Fritz Schulz, *Principles of Roman Law*, Oxford, 1936, pp. 129 ff., and *History of Roman Legal Science*, Oxford, 1946, pp. 53 ff., 71 ff.; J. Himmelschein, "Studien zu der antiken Hermeneutica iuris," in *Symbolae Friburgens. in honorem Ottonis Lenel*, Leipzig, 1935, pp. 373–424; Artur Steinwenter, "Rhetorik und römischer Zivilprozess," *Sav. Zeitschr.* 67 (1947). 69–120; H. F. Jolowicz, *Historical Introduction to the Study of Roman Law*, 2nd ed., Cambridge, 1952, pp. 576 f. Note, too, that such sources of Law as the Edict and the *responsa prudentium* are missing from our author's list; see Jolowicz, ch. 5. On the philosophical (Stoic) background of our author's theory of Law see also Kroll, *Philologus* 90 (1935). 211–215.

[CICERO]

Natura ius est quod cognationis aut pietatis causa observatur, quo iure parentes a liberis et a parentibus liberi coluntur.

Lege ius est id quod populi iussu sanctum est; quod genus, ut in ius eas cum voceris.

Consuetudine ius est id quod sine lege aeque ac si legitimum sit usitatum est; quod genus, id quod argentario tuleris expensum ab socio eius recte petere possis.

Iudicatum est id de quo sententia lata est aut decretum interpositum. Ea saepe diversa sunt, ut aliud alio iudici aut praetori aut consuli aut tribuno plebis placitum sit; et fit ut de eadem re saepe alius aliud decreverit aut iudicarit, quod genus: M. Drusus, praetor urbanus, quod cum herede mandati ageretur iudicium reddidit, Sex. Iulius non reddidit.

---

a φύσις. In the Roman conception *ius civile* is the Law which each people forms for itself and is peculiar to its state; the *ius gentium* (not the modern law of nations), on the other hand, is the Law common to all peoples. The latter became identified with Natural Law, which was originally a Greek concept. See Gaius, *Inst.* 1. 1, and Elemér Balogh, in *Studi in onore di Pietro Bonfante* (Milan, 1930), 4. 677-9. Alfred Pernice, *Sav. Zeitschr.* 22 (1901). 62-3, denying the juristic value of these "sources of Law," points out that Nature cannot be a source of *positive* Law. *Cf.* Cicero, *De Inv.* 2. xxii. 67.

b νόμος. The definition, as against the others in this section, is Roman; *cf.* Gaius, *Inst.* 1. 3: "A statute is a command and ordinance of the people." But our author's definition seems too inclusive; for example, not every action of a Popular Assembly made Law. On *sanctio* (consecration) see Mommsen, p. 882, and p. 901, note 5.

c *Twelve Tables* 1. 1.

d συνήθεια. Students of Roman jurisprudence deny that the concept of customary law held by the rhetoricians (to

To the Law of Nature [a] belong the duties observed because of kinship or family loyalty. In accordance with this kind of Law parents are cherished by their children, and children by their parents.

Statute Law [b] is that kind of Law which is sanctioned by the will of the people; for example, you are to appear before the court when summoned to do so.[c]

Legal Custom [d] is that which, in the absence of any statute, is by usage endowed with the force of statute law; for example, the money you have deposited with a banker you may rightly seek from his partner.[e]

It is a Previous Judgement [f] when on the same question a sentence has been passed or a decree interposed. These are often contradictory, according as one judge, praetor, consul, or tribune of the plebs has determined differently from another; and it often happens that on the very same matter one has decreed or decided differently from another. For example, Marcus Drusus, city praetor, granted an action on breach of contract against an heir, whereas Sextus Julius refused to do so.[g] Again, Gaius

whom it was useful, for tradition is a valid source for argumentation) was as such employed by the jurists of this period. See Pernice, *Sav. Zeitschr.* 22 (1901). 59 ff.; Artur Steinwenter, in *Studi in onore di Pietro Bonfante*, 2.421–40; A. A. Schiller, *Virginia Law Rev.* 24 (1938). 268–82; Fritz Schulz, *History of Roman Legal Science*, p. 74; C. W. Westrup, *Introd. to Early Roman Law* III, 1 (Copenhagen and London, 1939). 127 ff.

[e] One of only a few situations in Roman private law described as of customary origin; see Schiller, *Virg. Law Rev.* 24. 275.

[f] κεκριμένον.

[g] M. Livius Drusus was *praetor urbanus* c. 115 B.C., Sextus Julius Caesar in 123 B.C.

Item: C. Caelius iudex absolvit iniuriarum eum qui Lucilium poetam in scaena nominatim laeserat, P. Mucius eum qui L. Accium poetam nominaverat 20 condemnavit. Ergo, quia possunt res simili de causa dissimiliter iudicatae proferri, cum id usu venerit, iudicem cum iudice, tempus cum tempore, numerum cum numero iudiciorum conferemus.

Ex aequo et bono ius constat quod ad veritatem et utilitatem communem videtur pertinere; quod genus, ut maior annis LX et cui morbus causa est cognitorem det. Ex eo vel novum ius constitui convenit ex tempore et ex hominis dignitate.

Ex pacto ius est si quid inter se pepigerunt, si quid inter quos convenit. Pacta sunt quae legibus observanda sunt, hoc modo: "Rem ubi pagunt, orato; ni pagunt, in comitio aut in foro ante meridiem causam coicito." Sunt item pacta quae sine legibus

---

a C. Caelius (Caldus? See P. F. Girard, *Mélanges de droit romain* [Paris, 1923] 2. 398, note 2), before 103 B.C. The *mimi* specialised in broad and coarse humour (*iocus illiberalis*). Lucilius used licence in attacking other men (*e.g.*, the poets Accius and Pacuvius), but resented attacks upon himself.

b See R. E. Smith, "The Law of Libel at Rome," *Class. Quart.* 44 (1951). 171–2.

c Publius Mucius Scaevola, probably in 136 B.C. See l. xiv. 24 above.

d Corresponds to καλὸν καὶ δίκαιον, ἐπιεικές, ἴσον, yet the Roman term emphasizes the social point of view, implying more than "fairness." The *bonum* is connected with *bona fides*. See Fritz Pringsheim, "Bonum et Aequum," *Sav. Zeitschr.* 52 (1932). 78–155; Westrup, *op. cit.*, III, 1. 21 ff. The definition is philosophical, and Greek in origin, but the illustration is from Roman law. According to Stroux, "Summum ius summa iniuria," the Aristotelian doctrine of equity came to the Roman Forum through the Peripatetic and Academic writers, and thence to the *interpretatio iuris*, but most students deny such an influence upon the Roman

Caelius, sitting in judgement, acquitted *a* of the charge of injury *b* the man who had by name attacked the poet Lucilius on the stage, while Publius Mucius condemned *c* the man who had specifically named the
20 poet Lucius Accius. Therefore, because different past judgements can be offered for a like case, we shall, when this comes to pass, compare the judges, the circumstances, and the number of decisions.

The Law rests on Equity *d* when it seems to agree with truth and the general welfare; for example, a man who is more than sixty years old, and pleads illness, shall substitute an attorney for himself.*e* Thus according to circumstances and a person's status virtually a new kind of Law may well be established.

It is Law founded on Agreement *f* if the parties have made some contract between themselves—if there is some covenant between parties. There are agreements which must be observed according to statutes, as for example: " When parties have contract on the matter, party shall plead; if they do not have contract, party shall state outline of cause in the Comitium or the Forum before midday." *g* There are also agreements which, independently of statutes,

jurists, or minimize it. See Ernst Levy, *Sav. Zeitschr.* 48 (1928). 668–78; Schiller, *Virg. Law Rev.* 27. 753 ff.; Schulz, *History of Roman Legal Science*, pp. 74 f.

e This is the earliest text expressly mentioning substitution in Roman procedure. On procedural representation see Wenger, *Institutes of the Roman Law of Civil Procedure*, pp. 88 ff.

f συνάλλαγμα.

g *Twelve Tables* 1. 6–9. The Comitium adjoined the Forum on the northwest; although the two areas were not separated by a natural line, each kept its separate identity until the middle of the second century B.C.

[CICERO]

observantur ex convento, quae iure praestare dicuntur.

His igitur partibus iniuriam demonstrari, ius confirmari convenit, id quod in absoluta iuridicali faciendum videtur.

21 XIV. Cum ex conparatione quaereretur utrum satius fuerit facere id quod reus dicat se fecisse, an id quod accusator dicat oportuisse fieri, primum quaeri conveniet utrum fuerit utilius ex contentione, hoc est, utrum honestius, facilius, conducibilius. Deinde oportebit quaeri ipsumne oportuerit iudicare utrum fuerit utilius, an aliorum fuerit utilius statuendi potestas. Deinde interponetur ab accusatore suspicio ex constitutione coniecturali qua re putetur non ea ratione factum esse quo melius deteriori anteponeretur, sed[1] dolo malo negotium gestum de aliqua probabili causa. Ab defensore contra refellatur argumentatio coniecturalis de qua ante dictum est. Deinde quaereretur potueritne vitari ne in eum
22 locum veniretur. His sic tractatis accusator utetur loco communi in eum qui inutile utili praeposuerit cum statuendi non habuerit potestatem. Defensor contra eos qui aequum censeant rem perniciosam utili praeponi utetur loco communi per conquestionem; et simul quaerat ab accusatoribus, ab iudicibus ipsis,

---

[1] sed *b l d* : sed in eo II *Mx* : si in eo *P*[1] : sine eo *H* : si sine *C*[2] : sine *B* : ine *C*[1].

---

[a] Our author now turns to the Assumptive Juridical Issue. *Cf.* 1. xiv. 24 and 1. xv. 25 above, and Cicero's fuller, and generally clearer, treatment in *De Inv.* 2. xxiv. 72 ff.; also the figure Comparison (*similitudo*), 4. xlv. 59 below.
[b] *Cf.* the definition of Advantage, 3. ii. 3 below.

are binding by virtue of the covenant itself; these are said to obtain at Law.

These, then, are the divisions of Law by means of which one should demonstrate the injustice or establish the justice of an act—which we see to be the end sought in an Absolute Juridical cause.

XIV. When Comparison [a] is used to examine whether it was better to do that which the defendant says he did, or that which the prosecutor says should have been done, it will be proper first to ascertain from the conflict which was the more advantageous, that is, more honourable, practicable, and profitable.[b] Next we ought to discover whether the defendant himself should have decided which was the more advantageous, or whether the right to determine this belonged to others. Then the prosecutor, in accordance with the procedure in a conjectural issue, will interpose a suspicion leading to the belief that the defendant had not by his act intended to prefer the better to the worse, but had carried out the business with wilful fraud on some plausible ground. Let the defendant's counsel, on his side, refute the conjectural argument referred to above. Then the question will be whether this development could have been prevented from reaching such a pass. These points thus treated, the prosecutor will use the commonplace against one who has preferred the disadvantageous to the advantageous when he lacked the right of decision. The defendant's counsel, on his part, will use a commonplace in the form of a complaint against those who deem it equitable to prefer the ruinous to the advantageous; and at the same time let him ask the accusers, and the jurors themselves, what they would have done had they been in the defendant's place,

97

quid facturi essent si in eo loco fuissent, et tempus, locum, rem, deliberationem suam ponet ante oculos.

XV. Translatio criminis est cum ab reo facti causa in aliorum peccatum transfertur. Primum quaerendum est iurene in alium crimen transferatur; deinde spectandum est aeque magnum sit illud peccatum quod in alium transferatur atque illud quod reus suscepisse dicatur; deinde, oportueritne in ea re peccare in qua alius ante peccarit; deinde, oportueritne iudicium ante fieri; deinde, cum factum iudicium non sit de illo crimine quod in alium transferatur, oporteatne de ea re iudicium fieri quae res in iudicium non devenerit. Locus communis accusatoris contra eum qui plus censeat vim quam iudicia valere oportere. Et ab adversariis percontabitur accusator quid futurum sit si idem ceteri faciant ut de indemnatis supplicia sumant, quod eos idem fecisse dicant. Quid si ipse accusator idem facere voluisset? Defensor eorum peccati atrocitatem proferet in quos crimen transferet; rem, locum, tempus ante oculos ponet, ut ii qui audient existiment aut non potuisse aut inutile [1] fuisse rem in iudicium venire.

23 XVI. Concessio est per quam nobis ignosci postulamus. Ea dividitur in purgationem et deprecationem.

---

[1] inutile *CE* : non inutile *M Mx.*

---

a Cf. 1. xv. 25 above, and Cicero, *De Inv.* 2. xxvi. 78 ff. (*relatio criminis*).
b Cf. Cicero, *De Inv.* 2. xxvii. 80 f.
c The problem is that exploited in tragedy, concerning the right to take justice into one's own hands.
d Cf. Cicero, *De Inv.* 2. xxviii. 84 f.
e Cf. Cicero, *De Inv.* 2. xxxi. 94.

and he will set before their eyes the time, the place, the circumstances, and the defendant's deliberations.

XV. Shifting of the Question of Guilt takes place when the defendant refers the reason for his act to the crime committed by others.[a] First we must examine whether the Law permits the shifting of the issue of guilt to another; next we must see whether the offence which is being imputed to another is as serious as that with which the defendant is charged; then whether the defendant ought to have transgressed in the same way as another had previously; next, whether a judicial decision ought not to have been rendered before he committed his act; then, in the absence of a judicial decision on the offence which is being imputed to another, whether a decision ought now to be rendered on a matter which has never come to trial.[b] Here the prosecutor's commonplace is against one who believes that violence ought to prevail over judicial decisions.[c] Furthermore, he will ask his adversaries what would happen if everyone else should do the same as they, and should inflict punishment upon persons who have not been convicted, contending that the adversaries have set the example. What if the accuser himself had wished to do likewise? The defendant's counsel will set forth the atrocity of the crime committed by those to whom he is shifting the issue of guilt; he will present before the eyes of the hearers the circumstances, the place, and the time so that they may think that it was either impossible or inexpedient for the matter to come to trial.[d]

23   XVI. Through the Acknowledgement [e] we plead for pardon. The Acknowledgement includes the Exculpation and the Plea for Mercy.

99

Purgatio est cum consulto a nobis factum negamus.
Ea dividitur in necessitudinem, fortunam, inprudentiam. De his partibus primum ostendendum est;
deinde ad deprecationem revertendum videtur.
Primum considerandum est num culpa ventum sit in
necessitudinem. Deinde quaerendum est quo modo
vis illa vitari potuerit ac levari. Deinde is qui in
necessitudinem causam conferet expertusne sit quid
contra facere aut excogitare posset. Deinde num
quae suspiciones ex coniecturali constitutione trahi
possint, quae significent id consulto factum esse
quod necessario cecidisse dicitur. Deinde, si maxime
necessitudo quaepiam fuerit, conveniatne eam satis
idoneam causam putari.

24   Si inprudentia reus se peccasse dicet, primum
quaeretur utrum potuerit nescire an non potuerit;
deinde utrum data sit opera ut sciretur an non;
deinde utrum casu nescierit an culpa. Nam qui se
propter vinum aut amorem aut iracundiam fugisse
rationem dicet, is animi vitio videbitur nescisse, non
inprudentia; quare non inprudentia se defendet, sed
culpa contaminabit. Deinde coniecturali constitutione quaeretur utrum scierit an ignoraverit, et
considerabitur satisne inprudentia praesidii debeat
esse cum factum esse constet.

---

    a *Cf.* Cicero, *De Inv.* 2. xxxii. 98 ff.
    b *Cf.* Cicero, *De Inv.* 2. xxxi. 95, and *Rhet. ad Alex.*, ch. 4
(1427 a).
    c *Cf.* Aristotle, *Eth. Nic.* 3. 3 (1111 a 24) : " For it is
perhaps a mistake to say that acts committed through anger
or desire are involuntary."

The Exculpation is our denial that we acted with
intent. Subheads under Plea of Exculpation are
Necessity, Accident, and Ignorance. These are to be
explained first, and then, as it seems, it will be best
to return to the Plea for Mercy. One must first
consider whether it was the defendant's fault that
he was brought to this necessity.[a] After that we
must inquire what means he had to avoid or lighten
this superior force. Next, did he who offers necessity
as an excuse try to do, or to contrive, what he could
against it? Then, cannot some grounds for suspicion
be drawn from the procedure in a conjectural issue,
which would signify that the deed attributed to
necessity was premeditated? Finally, if there was
some extreme necessity, is it proper to deem this a
sufficient excuse?

24   If the defendant says that he erred through
ignorance,[b] the first question will be: Could he or
could he not have been uninformed? Next, did he
or did he not make an effort to inform himself?
Then, is his ignorance attributable to accident or to
his own fault? For a person who declares that his
reason fled because of wine or love or anger, will
appear to have lacked comprehension through fault
of character rather than ignorance [c]; he will therefore not justify himself on the ground of ignorance,
but will taint himself with guilt.[d] Finally, by means
of the procedure in a conjectural issue, we shall seek
to discover whether he was or was not informed, and
consider whether ignorance should be sufficient
justification when it is established that the deed was
committed.

[d] The *Rhet. ad Alex.*, ch. 7 (1429 a), admits such a defence
as a last resort.

[CICERO]

Cum in fortunam causa confertur et ea re defensor ignosci reo dicet oportere, eadem omnia videntur consideranda quae de necessitudine praescripta sunt. Etenim omnes hae [1] tres partes purgationis inter se finitimae sunt, ut in omnes eadem fere possint adcommodari.

Loci communes in his causis: accusatoris contra eum qui, cum peccasse confiteatur, tamen oratione iudices demoretur; defensoris de humanitate, misericordia: voluntatem in omnibus rebus spectari convenire; quae consulto facta non sint, ea fraudi [2] esse non oportere.

25 XVII. Deprecatione utemur cum fatebimur nos peccasse, neque id inprudentes aut fortuito aut necessario fecisse dicemus, et tamen ignosci nobis postulabimus. Hic ignoscendi ratio quaeritur ex his locis: si plura aut maiora officia quam maleficia videbuntur constare; si qua virtus aut nobilitas erit in eo qui supplicabit; si qua spes erit usui futurum si sine supplicio discesserit; si ipse ille supplex mansuetus et misericors in potestatibus ostendetur fuisse; si ea quae peccavit non odio neque crudelitate, sed officio et recto studio commotus fecit; si tali de causa aliis quoque ignotum est; si nihil ab eo periculi nobis

---

[1] hae *E Mx ed. mai.* : haec *p Mx.*
[2] ea fraudi *E* : an ea fraude *M* : an ea fraudei *Mx.*

---

[a] *Cf.* Cicero, *De Inv.* 2. xxxi. 96.
[b] *Cf.* Cicero, *De Inv.* 2. xxxiii. 101 f.
[c] For the commonplaces on pity see also 2. xvii. 26 and especially 2. xxxi. 50 below.
[d] *Cf.* Cicero, *De Inv.* 2. xxxv. 106, and *Pro Ligario.*

When the cause of the crime is attributed to accident,[a] and counsel for the defence maintains that his client should be pardoned on that ground, it appears that all the points to be considered are precisely those prescribed above for necessity; for all these three divisions of Exculpation are so closely interrelated that virtually the same rules can be applied to them all.

Commonplaces [b] in these causes are the following: that of the prosecutor against one who confesses a crime, yet holds the jurors up by prolix speech-making; for the defence, on humanity and pity,[c] that it is the intention which should always be considered, and that unintentional acts ought not to be regarded as crimes.

25   XVII. We shall use the Plea for Mercy [d] when we confess the crime without attributing it to ignorance, chance, or necessity, and yet beg for pardon. Here the ground for pardoning is sought in the following topics: if it seems evident that the good deeds of the suppliant have been more numerous or more weighty than the bad; if he is endowed with some virtue, or with good birth; if there is any hope that he will be of service in the event that he departs unpunished; if the suppliant himself is shown to have been gentle and compassionate [e] in power; if in committing his mistakes he was moved not by hatred or cruelty, but by a sense of duty and right endeavour; if on a similar ground others also have been pardoned; if, in the event that we acquit him, no peril from him appears likely to be our lot in

    [e] For *mansuetus et misericors* cf. Sallust, *Cat.* 54. 2 (on Caesar), 52. 11 and 52. 27 (Cato), and 34. 1 (Q. Marcius); Cicero, *Pro Murena* 41. 90, *Pro Sulla* 33. 93.

futurum videbitur si eum missum fecerimus; si nulla
aut a nostris civibus aut ab aliqua civitate vituperatio
26 ex ea re suscipietur. Loci communes: de humanitate, fortuna, misericordia, rerum commutatione. His
locis omnibus ex contrario utetur is qui contra dicet,
cum amplificatione et enumeratione peccatorum.
Haec causa iudicialis fieri non potest, ut in libro primo
ostendimus, sed, quod potest vel ad senatum vel ad
consilium venire, non visa est supersedenda.

Cum ab nobis crimen removere volemus, aut in rem
aut in hominem nostri peccati causam conferemus.
Si causa in hominem conferetur, quaerendum erit
primum potueritne tantum quantum reus demonstrabit is in quem causa conferetur; et quone modo aut
honeste aut sine periculo potuerit obsisti; si maxime
ita sit, num ea re concedi reo conveniat quod alieno
inductu fecerit. Deinde in coniecturalem trahetur
controversiam et edisseretur num consulto factum sit.
Si causa in rem quandam conferetur, et haec eadem
fere et omnia quae de necessitudine praecepimus
consideranda erunt.

27   XVIII. Quoniam satis ostendisse videamur quibus
argumentationibus in uno quoque genere causae
iudicialis uti conveniret, consequi videtur ut doceamus

---

[a] 1. xiv. 24. *Cf*. Cicero, *De Inv*. 2. xxxiv. 105.

[b] Cicero, *De Inv*. 2. xxix. 86–xxx. 94, considers also the
situation (*remotio rei*) in which the defendant denies that the
act he is charged with concerned him or his duty. *Cf*. also
Exculpation, 2. xvi. 23 above.

the future; if as a result of that acquittal no censure
will accrue either from our fellow-citizens or from
26 some other state.   Commonplaces: on humanity,
fortune, pity, and the mutability of things.   All these
commonplaces, reversed, will be used by the adversary, who will also amplify and recount the defendant's transgressions.   Such a cause is not admissible
in the courts, as I showed in Book I,[a] but because
it is admissible either before the Senate or a
council, I have decided that I should not pass it
over.

When we wish to Reject the Responsibility, we
shall throw the blame for our crime either upon some
circumstance or upon another person.[b]   If upon a
person, we must first examine whether the person
to whom the responsibility is transferred had as
much influence as the defendant will represent; next,
whether the defendant could somehow have resisted
this influence honourably or safely;[c] and, even if the
conditions are in fullest measure such as the defendant represents them to be, whether it is nevertheless
proper to make allowances to him just because he
acted on another's persuasion.   Then we shall turn
the controversy into one of fact and examine in
detail whether there was premeditation.   If the
responsibility is transferred to some circumstance,
virtually these same precepts and all those that I
have set forth on Necessity[d] are to be observed.

27   XVIII. Since I believe that I have fully shown
what arguments are advantageously used in each
type of judicial cause, it seems to follow that I should

[c] See the definition of Advantage, 3. ii. 3 below.
[d] 2. xvi. 23 above.

quemadmodum ipsas argumentationes ornate et
absolute tractare possimus. Nam fere non difficile
invenire quid sit causae adiumento, difficillimum vero
est [1] inventum expolire et expedite pronuntiare.
Haec enim res facit ut neque diutius quam satis sit in
isdem locis commoremur, nec eodem identidem
revolvamur, neque inchoatam argumentationem relin-
quamus, neque incommode ad aliam deinceps
transeamus. Itaque hac ratione et ipsi meminisse
poterimus quid quoque loco dixerimus, et auditor cum
totius causae tum unius cuiusque argumentationis
distributionem percipere et meminisse poterit.

28   Ergo absolutissima et perfectissima est argumentatio ea quae in quinque partes est distributa:
propositionem, rationem, rationis confirmationem,
exornationem, conplexionem. Propositio est per

---

[1] vero est *PB C* Π *d* : est vero *b l* : est *H Mx.*

---

[a] *Tractatio* and *inventio* supplement each other; Cicero,
De Oratore 2. 41. 176 : " We now see that it is by no means
enough to *find* what to say, unless you are able to *handle* it
(*id inventum tractare*) skilfully once found ; " *cf.* also
ibid., 2. 27. 120. The tradition is Isocratean ; *Paneg.* 9 :
" For the deeds of the past are a heritage common to us all,
but the ability to make full use (= χρῆσις) of them at the
proper time, in each instance to form the right conceptions
about them, and to set these forth in a finished style, is the
special gift of them that know." *Cf.* 1. ii. 2, 2. ii. 2, 3. iv. 7,
3. vi. 11.

[b] Cicero, *De Inv.* 1. xxxvii. 67, divides the deductive argument (*argumentatio per ratiocinationem*) into *propositio*,
propositionis approbatio, *assumptio*, *assumptionis approbatio*,
and *complexio*.

While Aristotle in forming arguments constructs the
enthymeme in close analogy with the logical syllogism (e.g.,
Rhet. 1. 2, 1356 b), our author, with the practical speaker in
mind in this meagre treatment, shows little interest in the
syllogistic form. The epicheireme is more complicated than

explain how to develop[a] these arguments elegantly
and completely. To be sure, it is in general not hard
to devise matter which should serve to support a
cause, but to polish what has been devised and to
give it a ready delivery is very hard. Indeed it is
this faculty which keeps us from dwelling longer
than necessary on the same topics, from returning
again and again to the same place, abandoning a
chain of argument before it has been completed, and
making an inappropriate transition to the next argument. By the following method, therefore, we can
ourselves remember what we have said in each place,
and the hearer can perceive and remember the
distribution of the parts in the whole cause and also
in each particular argument.

8   The most complete and perfect argument, then,
is that which is comprised of five parts: the Proposition, the Reason, the Proof of the Reason, the
Embellishment, and the Résumé.[b] Through the

the enthymeme (of which it is a later name). Aristotle's
enthymeme (and, later, also Quintilian's [epicheireme]; see
5. 14. 6) comprised two premises and conclusion; the epicheireme normally comprised four premises. Aristotle took
the premises for granted; the later rhetoricians thought it
necessary to prove each. The epicheireme may have
developed under Stoic influence. Cicero, *De Inv.* 1. xxxv. 61,
makes it clear that the quinquepartite epicheireme grew out
of Aristotle's syllogism; Theophrastus, following observations of Isocrates, may have been the first to introduce it into
rhetoric. Cicero's syllogistic form (*ratiocinatio*) is logical;
he treats it on a par with Socratic induction. See Cicero,
De Inv. 1. xxxiv. 57 ff.; Quintilian, 5. 10. 1 ff. and 5. 14. 5 ff.;
Wilhelm Kroll, *Das Epicheirema*, in *Sitzungsb. Akad. der
Wissensch. in Wien (Philos.-histor.Kl.)*, 216. 2 (1936);
Friedrich Solmsen, *Amer. Journ. Philol.* 62 (1941). 39 ff.,
169 ff. It is doubtful whether the epicheireme as here
described was very widely used in actual oratory.

quam ostendimus summatim quid sit quod probari volumus. Ratio est quae causam demonstrat verum esse id quod intendimus, brevi subiectione. Rationis confirmatio est ea quae pluribus argumentis corroborat breviter expositam rationem. Exornatio est qua utimur rei honestandae et conlocupletandae causa, confirmata argumentatione. Conplexio est quae concludit breviter, colligens partes argumentationis.

Hisce igitur quinque partibus ut absolutissime utamur, hoc modo tractabimus argumentationem:

XIX. " Causam ostendemus Ulixi fuisse quare interfecerit Aiacem.

" Inimicum enim acerrimum de medio tollere volebat, a quo sibi non iniuria summum periculum metuebat.

" Videbat illo incolumi se incolumem non futurum; sperabat illius morte se salutem sibi conparare; consueverat, si iure non potuerat, iniuria quavis inimico exitium machinari, cui rei mors indigna Palamedis testimonium dat. Ergo et metus periculi

---

^a πρότασις, λῆμμα, hereafter in Book 2 called *expositio* by our author.

^b *Cf.* Cicero, *De Inv.* 1. xxxviii. 68.

^c The Proposition. Here begins a *progymnasma* (σύγκρισις of persons). The theme was first taken up in 1. xi. 18 above. Thiele, *Hermagoras*, pp. 159–163, conjectures that the source of both theme (originally a ὅπλων κρίσις or an Αἴας of tragedy) and treatment by five-fold epicheireme is Hermagoras. *Cf.* Quintilian, 4. 2. 13; Ulysses replies that he did not do the deed, and had no quarrel with Ajax, and that their conflict was concerned only with renown.

^d The Reason.

^e Ulysses hated Palamedes because he had exposed Ulysses' deceit in feigning madness so as to avoid joining the

Proposition[a] we set forth summarily what we intend to prove. The Reason, by means of a brief explanation subjoined, sets forth the causal basis for the Proposition, establishing the truth of what we are urging. The Proof of the Reason corroborates, by means of additional arguments, the briefly presented Reason. Embellishment we use in order to adorn and enrich the argument, after the Proof has been established. The Résumé is a brief conclusion, drawing together the parts of the argument.

Hence, to make the most complete use of these five parts, we shall develop an argument as follows:[b]

XIX. " We shall show that Ulysses had a motive in killing Ajax.[c]

" Indeed he wished to rid himself of his bitterest enemy, from whom, with good cause, he feared extreme danger to himself.[d]

" He saw that, with Ajax alive, his own life would be unsafe; he hoped by the death of Ajax to secure his own safety; it was his habit to plan an enemy's destruction by whatsoever wrongful means, when he could not by rightful, as the undeserved death of Palamedes bears witness.[e] Thus the fear of danger

Greek expedition to Troy, and because Ulysses envied his fame for wisdom. According to another tradition this hatred arose from the severe reproof Palamedes dealt out to Ulysses for returning empty-handed from a foraging expedition. The stories of the vengeance also differ. Ulysses and Diomedes induced him to descend into a well in order to find alleged treasure, and then stoned him; or they drowned him while he was fishing; or with Agamemnon they bribed a servant of Palamedes to conceal under Palamedes' bed a forged letter from Priam offering a bribe of gold, accused Palamedes of treachery, and when the letter (or gold) was discovered, caused him to be stoned by the Greeks.

hortabatur eum interimere a quo supplicium vere-
batur, et consuetudo peccandi maleficii suscipiendi
removebat dubitationem.

29   " Omnes enim cum minima peccata cum causa
suscipiunt, tum vero illa quae multo maxima sunt
maleficia aliquo certo emolumento inducti suscipere
conantur. Si multos induxit in peccatum pecuniae
spes, si conplures scelere se contaminarunt imperii
cupiditate, si multi leve conpendium fraude maxima
commutarunt, cui mirum videbitur istum a maleficio
propter acerrunam formidinem non temperasse?
Virum fortissimum, integerrimum, inimicitiarum
persequentissimum, iniuria lacessitum, ira exsuscita-
tum homo timidus, nocens, conscius sui peccati,
insidiosus voluit interimere; acerrimum homo perfidiosus [1] inimicum incolumem esse noluit.   Cui [2]
tandem hoc mirum videbitur? Nam cum feras
bestias videamus alacres et erectas vadere ut alteri
bestiae noceant, non est incredibile putandum istius
quoque animum ferum, crudelem atque inhumanum
cupide ad inimici perniciem profectum, praesertim
cum in bestiis nullam neque bonam neque malam
rationem videamus, in isto plurimas et pessumas
rationes semper fuisse intellegamus.

30   " Si ergo pollicitus sum me daturum causam qua
inductus Ulixes accesserit ad maleficium, et si
inimicitiarum acerrimam rationem et periculi metum

----

[1] *lac.*; voluit interimere acerrimum homo perfidiosus *sugg.*
Mx.
[2] Cui *E* : qui *M Mx.*

110

encouraged him to slay the man from whom he dreaded vengeance, and, in addition, the habit of wrong-doing robbed him of his scruples at undertaking the evil deed.[a]

29 " Now not only do all men have a motive even in their least peccadillos, but certainly they are attracted by some sure reward when they enter upon crimes which are by far the most heinous. If the hope of gaining money has led many a man to wrong-doing, if from greed for power not a few have tainted themselves with crime, if numerous men have trafficked for a paltry profit with arrant deceit, who will find it strange that Ulysses, when under stress of acute terror, did not refrain from crime? A hero most brave, most upright, most implacable against his foes, harassed by a wrong, roused to anger—him the frightened, malevolent, guilt-conscious, guileful man wished to destroy; the treacherous man did not wish his bitter enemy to stay alive. To whom, pray, will this seem strange? For when we see wild beasts rush eagerly and resolutely to attack one another, we must not think it incredible that this creature, too—a wild, cruel, inhuman spirit—set out passionately to destroy his enemy; especially since in beasts we see no reasoning, good or bad, while he, we know, always had designs, ever so many, and ever so base.[b]

30 " If, then, I have promised to give the motive which impelled Ulysses to enter upon the crime, and if I have shown that the reckoning of a bitter enmity and the fear of danger were the factors, it must

[a] The Proof of the Reason.
[b] The Embellishment. Quintilian, 5. 14. 6, knows of the *exornatio* as a part of the epicheireme.

intercessisse demonstravi, non est dubium quin confiteatur causam maleficii fuisse."

Ergo absolutissima est argumentatio ea quae ex quinque partibus constat, sed ea non semper necesse est uti. Est cum conplexione supersedendum est, si res brevis est, ut facile memoria conprehendatur; est cum exornatio praetermittenda est, si parum locuples ad amplificandum et exornandum res videtur esse. Sin et brevis erit argumentatio et res tenuis aut humilis, tum et exornatione et conplexione supersedendum est. In omni argumentatione de duabus partibus postremis haec quam exposui ratio est habenda. Ergo amplissima est argumentatio quinquepertita; brevissima est tripertita; mediocris, sublata aut exornatione aut conplexione, quadripertita.

31   XX. Duo genera sunt vitiosarum argumentationum: unum quod ab adversario reprehendi potest, id quod pertinet ad causam; alterum quod tametsi nugatorium est, tamen non indiget reprehensionis. Quae sint quae reprehensione confutari conveniat, quae tacite contemni atque vitari sine reprehensione, nisi exempla subiecero, intellegere dilucide non poteris. Haec cognitio vitiosarum argumentationum duplicem utilitatem adferet. Nam et vitare in argumentatione vitium admonebit et ab aliis non vitatum commode reprehendere docebit.

Quoniam igitur ostendimus perfectam et plenam argumentationem ex quinque partibus constare, in

---

a The Résumé.

b Arrangement accommodated to circumstance, as in 3. ix. 17 below. *Cf.* Cicero, *De Inv.* 1. xxxix. 70 ff.

c Our author omitted to use a transition here. Cicero, *De Inv.* 1. xlii. 78 ff., rightly considers the defective arguments under Refutation (*reprehensio*).

unquestionably be acknowledged that he had a motive for his crime." [a]

An argument comprised of the five parts is, then, the most complete, but its use is not always necessary. There is a time when the Résumé should be dispensed with—if the matter is brief enough to be readily embraced by the memory. There is a situation, too, in which the Embellishment should be omitted—if the matter proves to be too meagre for amplification and adornment. And if the argument is brief and the matter also slight or insignificant, then both the Embellishment and the Résumé should be left out. This rule which I have just set forth is to be observed for the last two parts in every argument. [b] The fullest argument, therefore, is fivefold, the briefest threefold, and the mean fourfold, lacking either the Embellishment or the Résumé.

31 XX. Defective arguments [c] are of two kinds: one can be refuted [d] by the adversary, and so belongs to the cause proper; the other, although likewise invalid, does not need to be refuted. If I do not add examples, you will be unable clearly to distinguish those arguments which it is proper to refute in rebuttal, and those which it is proper to ignore in disdainful silence and to abstain from refuting. This knowledge of defective arguments will confer a double advantage. It will warn us to avoid a fault in arguing, and teach us skilfully to reprehend a fault not avoided by others.

Since, then, I have shown that a perfect and full argument consists of five parts, [e] let us consider the

[d] *Reprehensio* = λύσις.
[e] *Cf.* Cicero, *De Inv.* 1. xlii. 79.

una quaque parte argumentationis quae vitia vitanda
sunt consideremus, ut et ipsi ab his vitiis recedere, et
adversariorum argumentationes hac praeceptione in
omnibus partibus temptare et ab aliqua parte labefactare possimus.

32   Expositio vitiosa est cum ab aliqua aut a maiore
parte ad omnes confertur id quod non necessario est
omnibus adtributum; ut si quis hoc modo exponat:
" Omnes qui in paupertate sunt malunt maleficio
parare divitias quam officio paupertatem tueri." Si
qui hoc modo exposuerit argumentationem, ut non
curet quaerere qualis ratio aut rationis confirmatio sit,
ipsam facile reprehendemus expositionem cum
ostendemus id quod in aliquo paupere inprobo sit in
omnes pauperes falso et iniuria conferri.

33   Item vitiosa expositio est cum id quod raro fit
fieri omnino negatur, hoc modo: " Nemo potest uno
aspectu neque praeteriens in amorem incidere."
Nam cum nonnemo devenerit in amorem uno aspectu,
et cum ille neminem dixerit, omnino nihil differt raro
id fieri, dummodo aliquando fieri aut posse modo fieri
intellegatur.

XXI. Item vitiosa expositio est cum omnes res
ostendemus nos collegisse et aliquam rem idoneam
praeterimus, hoc modo: " Quoniam igitur hominem
occisum constat esse, necesse est aut a praedonibus
aut ab inimicis occisum esse aut abs te, quem ille

ᵃ The fallacy of False Generalization. *Cf.* Cicero, *De Inv.*
1. xliii. 80.

ᵇ In Cicero, *De Inv.* 1. xliii. 80, this observation is assigned
to the speech delivered by C. Scribonius Curio (first of the
three orators of that name, praetor in 121 B.C.) in defence of
Servius Fulvius in a prosecution for incest. According to Cicero,
Brutus 32. 122, the speech was once esteemed a masterpiece.

faults to be avoided in each single part of the argument, so that we may ourselves be able to shun these faults, and by the following rules test the argument of our adversaries in all its parts and undermine it in some one of these.

32 The Proposition is defective when an assertion based on some one part or on a majority of individuals, but not necessarily applicable to all, is referred to all, as if one should argue as follows : " All the poor would rather do wrong and acquire riches than do right and remain poor." If a speaker has presented this sort of Proposition in an argument, without caring to ask of what nature the Reason or the Proof of the Reason is to be, we shall easily refute his Proposition by showing that what is true of one dishonest poor man is being falsely and unjustly applied to all the poor.[a]

33 Again, the Proposition is defective when a rare occurrence is declared to be absolutely impossible, as follows : " No one can fall in love at a single glance, or as he is passing by." [b] For inasmuch as some have fallen in love at first sight, and yet the speaker has said " no one," it is of no significance whatsoever that the experience occurs but rarely, provided we understand that it sometimes does occur, or even only that it can occur.

XXI. Again, the Proposition is defective when we submit that we have made a complete enumeration of the possibilities and pass by some pertinent one,[c] as follows : " Since, then, it is established that the man was killed, he must have been killed by robbers, or by enemies, or by you, whom in his will he made

[c] The fallacy of Incomplete Disjunction. *Cf.* Cicero, *De Inv.* l. xlv. 84.

heredem testamento ex parte faciebat. Praedones in illo loco visi numquam sunt; inimicum nullum habebat; relinquitur, si neque a praedonibus neque ab inimicis occisus est, quod alteri non erant, alteros non habebat, ut abs te sit interemptus." Nam in huiuscemodi expositione reprehensione utemur si quos praeterquam quos ille conlegerit potuisse suscipere maleficium ostenderimus; velut in hoc exemplo, cum dixerit necesse esse aut a praedonibus aut ab inimicis aut a nobis occisum esse, dicemus potuisse vel a familia vel a coheredibus nostris. Cum hoc modo illorum conlectionem disturbaverimus, nobis latiorem locum defendendi reliquerimus. Ergo hoc quoque vitandum est in expositione, ne quando, cum omnia collegisse videamur, aliquam idoneam partem reliquerimus.

34   Item vitiosa expositio est quae constat ex falsa enumeratione, si aut cum plura sunt pauciora dicamus, hoc modo: "Duae res sunt, iudices, quae omnes ad maleficium impellant: luxuries et avaritia." "Quid amor?" inquiet quispiam, "quid ambitio? quid religio? quid metus mortis? quid imperii

---

[a] Cf. Cicero, De Inv. 1. xlv. 85.
[b] Cf. Cato in Livy, 34. 4. 1 ff.: "Often have you heard me complain . . . that the state is suffering from the two opposing vices, luxury and greed, which have been the curse and destruction of every great empire;" Cicero, Pro S. Rosc. Am. 27. 75: "The city creates luxury; from luxury greed inevitably springs, and from greed bursts forth audacity, the source of every crime and wrong;" Longinus, De Sublim. 46. 6: "For the love of money . . . and the love of pleasure enslave us;" Isocrates, Antid. 217: "Well then, I say that every man does everything he does for the sake of pleasure or gain or glory;" Aristotle, Rhet. 1. 10 (1369 a):

part-heir. In that place robbers have never been seen. He had no enemy. If he was not killed by robbers, of whom there were none, nor by enemies, of whom he had none, it remains that he was slain by you." We shall refute a Proposition of this type by showing that others besides those whom the speaker has enumerated could have undertaken the crime.[a] Here, for example, when he has said that the murder must have been committed by robbers, or by enemies, or by us, we shall say that it could have been committed by the man's slaves or by our co-heirs. When we have in this way upset the enumeration made by our accusers, we have left ourselves wider room for defence. This then is another mistake always to be avoided in the Proposition—the omission of some pertinent item when we think that we have included all.

34 Again, the Proposition is defective if it is based on a false enumeration and we present fewer possibilities than there are in reality, as follows : " There are two things, men of the jury, which ever impel men to crime : luxury and greed." [b] " But what about love ?," some one will say, " ambition,[c] superstition, the fear of death,[d] the passion for power, and, in short,

---

" Thus every act of men is necessarily done from one or other of seven causes : chance, nature, compulsion, habit, calculation, passion, or desire."

[c] Aristotle, *Polit.* 2. 9 (1271 a), declares greed and ambition to be the commonest motives of crime; *cf.* also Timon the Misanthrope in Stobaeus, 3. 10. 53 : " The components of evil are greed and the love of glory "; and Horace, *Serm.* 1. 4. 25–6 : " Take anyone at all from amid a crowd—he is suffering from either greed or some wretched ambition."

[d] The sentiment is Epicurean; *cf.*, for example, Lucretius 1. 80 ff., 3. 59 ff.

cupiditas? quid denique alia permulta?" Item
falsa enumeratio est cum pauciora sunt et plura
dicimus, hoc modo: "Tres res sunt quae omnes
homines sollicitent: metus, cupiditas, aegritudo."
Satis enim fuerat dixisse metum, cupiditatem,
quoniam aegritudinem cum utraque re coniunctam
esse necesse est.

XXII. Item vitiosa expositio est quae nimium
longe repetitur, hoc modo: "Omnium malorum
stultitia est mater atque materies. Ea parit immen-
sas cupiditates. Immensae porro cupiditates infinitae,
immoderatae sunt. Hae[1] pariunt avaritiam. Avaritia porro hominem ad quodvis maleficium impellit.
Ergo avaritia inducti adversarii nostri hoc in se
facinus admiserunt." Hic id quod extremum dictum
est satis fuit exponere, ne Ennium et ceteros poetas
imitemur, quibus hoc modo loqui concessum est:

> Utinam ne in nemore Pelio securibus
> Caesae accidissent abiegnae ad terram trabes,
> Neve inde navis inchoandi exordium
> Coepisset quae nunc nominatur nomine
> Argo, quia Argivi in ea delecti viri
> Vecti petebant pellem inauratam arietis
> Colchis, imperio regis Peliae, per dolum;
> Nam numquam era errans mea domo efferret
> pedem.

[1] hae *E* : haec *M Mx.*

---

[a] In Theon 5 (Spengel 2. 99 and 105) and in Stobaeus, 3. 10. 37,
Bion of Borysthenes (first half 3rd century B.C.) is quoted as
saying that avarice is mother city (μητρόπολις) of all evil; in
Diogenes Laertius, 6. 50, the saying is attributed to Diogenes
the Cynic (fourth century B.C.). This sentiment was popular
in the rhetorical schools and philosophical diatribes. *Cf.* Sallust,

the great multitude of other motives? " Again the enumeration is false when the possibilities are fewer than we present, as follows : " There are three emotions that agitate all men : fear, desire, and worry." Indeed it had been enough to say fear and desire, since worry is necessarily conjoined with both.

XXII. Again, the Proposition is defective if it traces things too far back, as follows : " Stupidity is the mother and matter of all evils. She gives birth to boundless desires. Furthermore, boundless desires have neither end nor limit. They breed avarice. Avarice, further, drives men to any crime you will. Thus it is avarice which has led our adversaries to take this crime upon themselves." [a] Here what was said last was enough for a Proposition, lest we copy Ennius and the other poets, who are licensed to speak as follows : " O that in Pelion's woods the firwood timbers had not fallen to the ground, cut down by axes, and that therefrom had not commenced the undertaking to begin the ship which now is named with the name of Argo, because in it sailed the picked Argive heroes who were seeking the golden fleece of the ram from the Colchians, with guile, at King Pelias' command. For then never would my mistress, misled, have set foot away from home." [b] Indeed here

---

Cat. 10 : " These [the lust for money and the lust for power] were, I might say, the source (*materies*) of all evils "; Calpurnius Flaccus 8 : " A man long happy is substance (*materia*) for all disasters," and see also Otto, *s.v.* " avaritia " 5, p. 51.

[b] Medea's nurse in the Prologue of Ennius' *Medea Exul*, which was a reproduction of Euripides' *Medea*. Ennius here observed the sequence of causes more carefully than Euripides had done; see *Schol. in Eurip., Med.* 1. 1 ff., ed. Ed. Schwartz, 2. 140 ff. *Cf.* Cicero, *De Inv.* 1. xlix. 91; Quintilian, 5. 10. 83; Ribbeck, 1. 49–50.

[CICERO]

Nam hic satis erat dicere, si id modo quod satis esset
curarent poetae:

Utinam ne era errans mea domo efferret pedem.
Ergo hac quoque ab ultimo repetitione in expositioni-
bus magnopere supersedendum est. Non enim
reprehensionis [1] sicut [2] aliae conplures indiget, sed [3]
sua sponte vitiosa est.

35   XXIII. Vitiosa ratio est quae ad expositionem non
est adcommodata vel propter infirmitatem vel
propter vanitatem. Infirma ratio est quae non
necessario ostendit ita esse quemadmodum expositum
est, velut apud Plautum:

Amicum castigare ob meritam noxiam
Inmune est facinus, verum in aetate utile
Et conducibile.

Haec expositio est.   Videamus quae ratio adferatur:

Nam ego amicum hodie meum
Concastigabo pro commerita noxia.

Ex eo quod ipse facturus est, non ex eo quod fieri
convenit, utile quid sit ratiocinatur. Vana ratio est
quae ex falsa causa constat, hoc modo: " Amor
fugiendus non est, nam ex eo verissima nascitur
amicitia."   Aut hoc modo: " Philosophia vitanda

----

[1] reprehensionis *sugg. Mx* : reprehensione *MSS.*
[2] sicut *BCl* : sed sicut *HP* Π *b d Mx.*
[3] *lac.*; indiget sed *sugg. Mx.*

----

[a] Its faultiness is self-evident. *Cf.* Plato, *Sophist* 252 C:
" They do not need others to refute them, but, as the saying
goes, they have an enemy and adversary who dwells in the
same house with them."

AD HERENNIUM, II. xxii. 34–xxiii. 35

it were adequate, if poets had a care for mere
adequacy, to say: "Would that my misled mistress
had not set foot away from home." In the Proposition, then, we must also carefully guard against
this tracing of things back to their remotest origin;
for the Proposition does not, like many others,
need to be refuted, but is on its own account
defective.[a]

35   XXIII. The Reason is defective if it is inappropriate
to the Proposition because either weak or groundless.
It is weak when it does not conclusively demonstrate
the correctness of the Proposition, as in Plautus:
"To reprove a friend for a fault that deserves reproof
is a thankless task, but in season useful and profitable." That is the Proposition. Let us see what
Reason is presented: "For [b] today I shall severely
reprove my friend for a fault that much deserves
reproof." His reckoning of what is useful is based on
what he himself is about to do, and not on what it is
proper to do. A Reason is groundless when it rests
on a false supposition, as follows: "One must not
flee from love, for it engenders the truest friendship." [c]
Or as follows: "One must spurn philosophy, for it

[b] *Trinummus* 23–6. A proper translation would be:
"For instance, today." *Nam*, here appearing in colloquial
speech, introduces a particular instance of a general statement; it is transitional rather than confirmatory, and so the
charge that Megaronides uses a false syllogism is unjust.
Cicero, *De Inv.* 1. 1. 95, is guilty of the same misunderstanding.
See W. M. Lindsay, *Syntax of Plautus*, Oxford, 1907, p. 100.
[c] *Cf.* Aristotle, *Rhet.* 2. 24 (1401 b), illustrating, among the
sham enthymemes, the *topos* from a sign (a single instance
used to prove the rule): "For example, one might say that
lovers are of service to their countries, for it was the love of
Harmodius and Aristogeiton which brought about the down-
fall of the tyrant Hipparchus."

[CICERO]

est, adfert enim socordiam atque desidiam." Nam
hae rationes nisi falsae essent, expositiones quoque
earum veras esse confiteremur.

36   Itemque infirma ratio est quae non necessariam
causam adfert expositionis, velut Pacuvius:

> Fortunam insanam esse et caecam et brutam per-
> hibent philosophi
> Saxoque instare in globoso praedicant volubili;
> Id quo saxum inpulerit Fors, eo cadere Fortunam
> autumant.
> Caecam ob eam rem esse iterant, quia nihil cernat
> quo sese adplicet;
> Insanam autem esse aiunt, quia atrox, incerta
> instabilisque sit;
> Brutam, quia dignum atque indignum nequeat
> internoscere.
> Sunt autem alii philosophi qui contra Fortunam
> negant
> Ullam misera in aetate esse; Temeritatem esse
> autumant.
> Id magis veri simile esse usus reapse experiundo
> edocet;
> Velut Orestes modo fuit rex, factust mendicus
> modo.
> Naufragio nempe re ergo id factum, hau Forte aut
> Fortuna obtigit.

Nam hic Pacuvius infirma ratione utitur cum ait
verius esse Temeritate quam Fortuna res geri.   Nam

---

a Cf. R. W. Emerson in "The American Scholar":
"Inaction is cowardice, but there can be no scholar without
the heroic mind." For other echoes of the opposition to
philosophy and art see 2. xxvii. 43 and 4. xxxii. 43.

produces inactivity and sloth." [a]   If all these Reasons were not false, we should also be obliged to admit the truth of their Propositions.

36   Again, a Reason is weak if the causal basis which it submits for the Proposition is not a compelling one. For example, Pacuvius: " The goddess Fortune is mad, blind, and stupid, some philosophers maintain. They declare that she stands upon a revolving globe of stone; [b] whither Chance impels this stone, thither, they say, does Fortune fall. She is blind, they repeat, for that she fails wholly to perceive whereto she attaches herself. Moreover they declare that she is mad because she is cruel, uncertain, and inconstant; stupid because she knows not how to tell worthy from unworthy. But there are other philosophers who, on the contrary, deny that in our wretched life there is any such thing as Fortune; there is, they say, Blind Accident. That this is more like the truth, is proved by the actual experience of life; even as Orestes now was king, and now became a beggar. Surely by the shipwreck of his property was this brought to pass, and did not befall by Chance or Fortune." [c] Pacuvius here uses a weak Reason when he says that it is truer to ascribe the guidance of events to Accident rather than to Fortune, for whichever of these philosophical theories

[b] Cf. the like portrayal of Fortune in *Cebetis Tabula* (probably first Christian century), ch. 7 (ed. Praechter, p. 6), and Shakespeare, *Henry V*, 3. 6. 26 ff.; also Otto, *s.v.* " fortuna " 1, p. 142.

[c] We do not know to which play this fragment (from a prologue, perhaps) is to be assigned. Ribbeck, 1. 145, conjectures *Chryses*; Marx, and Warmington, 2. 319, *Dulorestes*; L. A. Post, *Hermiona*. For the genitive form *re* (last verse) see p. 68, note *a*.

utraque opinione philosophorum fieri potuit ut is qui
rex fuisset mendicus factus esset.

37   XXIV. Item infirma ratio est cum videtur pro
ratione adferri, sed idem dicit quod in expositione
dictum est, hoc modo : " Magno malo est hominibus
avaritia, idcirco quod homines magnis et multis
incommodis conflictantur propter immensam pecuniae
cupiditatem." Nam hic aliis verbis idem per rationem dicitur quod dictum est per expositionem.

Item infirma ratio est quae minus idoneam quam
res postulat causam subicit expositionis, hoc modo :
" Utilis est sapientia, propterea quod qui sapientes
sunt pietatem colere consuerunt." Item: " Utile
est amicos veros habere, habeas enim quibuscum
iocari possis." Nam in huiusmodi rationibus non
universa neque absoluta, sed extenuata ratione
expositio confirmatur.

Item infirma ratio est quae vel alii expositioni
potest adcommodari, ut facit Pacuvius, qui eandem
adfert rationem quare caeca, eandem quare bruta
Fortuna dicatur.[1]

38   In confirmatione rationis multa et vitanda in
nostra et observanda in adversariorum oratione sunt
vitia, proptereaque diligentius consideranda quod
adcurata confirmatio rationis totam vehementissime
conprobat argumentationem.

---

[1] dicatur ΠE : dicitur *other MSS. Mx.*

you hold, it could have happened that one who had been a king became a beggar.

37 XXIV. Again, a Reason is weak when it appears to be presented as the Reason, but says precisely the same as was said in the Proposition,[a] as follows : " A great evil to mankind is greed, for the reason that men wrestle with great and many ills on account of the boundless passion for money." Here the Reason merely repeats in other words what has been said in the Proposition.

Again, a Reason is weak if the causal basis which it submits for the Proposition is inadequate to the demands of the subject,[b] as follows : " Wisdom is useful because the wise have been in the habit of cultivating a sense of duty." Or, " It is useful to have true friends, for thus you may have persons with whom you can jest." In Reasons of this kind the Proposition is supported not by a universal or absolute reason, but by a feeble one.

Again, the Reason is weak if it can at choice be applied to another Proposition,[c] as in the case of Pacuvius, who presents the same reason for calling Fortune blind as for calling her stupid.[d]

38 In the Proof of the Reason, there are many faults to be avoided in our discourse and also to be watched for in that of our adversaries. These must be considered the more carefully because an accurate Proof of the Reason supplies the most cogent support of the whole argument.

[a] Cf. Cicero, De Inv. 1. l. 95.
[b] Very like the type of fallacy in 2. xxiii. 36 above.
[c] An Introduction similarly defective is called banal in 1. vii. 11 above.
[d] 2. xxiii. 36 above.

Utuntur igitur studiosi in confirmanda ratione duplici conclusione, hoc modo :

Iniuria abs te adficior indigna, pater ;
Nam si inprobum esse Cresphontem [1] existimas,
Cur me huic locabas nuptiis ? Sin est probus,
Cur talem invitam invitum cogis linquere ?

Quae hoc modo concludentur aut ex contrario convertentur aut ex simplici parte reprehendentur. Ex contrario, hoc modo :

Nulla te indigna, nata, adficio iniuria.
Si probus est, te locavi ; sin est inprobus,
Divortio te liberabo incommodis.

Ex simplici parte reprehendetur si ex duplici conclusione alterutra pars diluitur, hoc modo :

" Nam si inprobum esse Cresphontem [2] existimas,
Cur me huic locabas nuptiis ? " " Duxi probum ;
Erravi ; post cognovi, et fugio cognitum."

39 XXV. Ergo reprehensio huiusmodi conclusionis duplex est ; auctior illa superior, facilior haec posterior ad excogitandum.

[1] chresponthem *P* Π : chrespontem *B C Mx ed. mai.* : chresponthe *H* : threspontem *E* : Chresponten *Mx.*
[2] chrespontem *M Mx ed. mai.* : threspontem *ld* : trespontem *b* : Chresponten *Mx.*

---

[a] δίλημμα, διλήμματον. *Complexio* in Cicero, *De Inv.* 1. xxix. 45, and in Servius on Virgil, *Aen.* 2. 675. *Cf.* in Aristotle, *Rhet.* 2. 23 (1399 a), No. 14 of the 28 lines of argument from which to draw enthymemes, the *topos* of criss-cross consequences ; Hermogenes, *De Inv.* 4. 6 (ed. Rabe, pp. 192–4) ; and also the figure Division, 4. xl. 52 below.

Students in the rhetorical schools, therefore, in Proving the Reason, use a Dilemma,*a* as follows: "You treat me, father, with undeserved wrong. For if you think Cresphontes wicked, why did you give me to him for wife? But if he is honourable, why do you force me to leave such a one against his will and mine?" Such a Dilemma will either be reversed against the user, or be rebutted in a single term.*b* Reversed, as follows: "My daughter, I do not treat you with any undeserved wrong. If he is honourable, I have given him you in marriage; but if he is wicked, I shall by divorce free you from your ills." It will be a rebuttal in a single term if one or the other alternative is confuted, as follows: "You say: 'For if you think Cresphontes wicked, why did you give me to him for wife?' I thought him honourable. I erred. Too late I came to know him, and knowing him, I fly from him." *c* XXV. Thus the rebuttal of a dilemma of this type is twofold: the first fuller, the second easier to invent.

b Cf. Cicero, De Inv. 1. xlv. 83; he uses an example which our author gives in 2. xxvi. 42 to illustrate the vice of inconsistency.

c The verses in this section have been referred either to a Greek school of rhetoric where exercises were set on the *Cresphontes* of Euripides or to Ennius' *Cresphontes*; see Marx, *Proleg.*, p. 132, and Ribbeck, 1. 33, but also Johannes Tolkiehn, *Berl. philol. Wochenschr.* 37 (1917). 828–9, who believes that the first four verses belong to the Ennian play. Our author seems here to have forgotten what precisely constitutes Proof of the Reason; cf. his definition in 2. xviii. 28 above, and the illustration in 2. xix. 29.

In the event that the conditions here mirrored are Roman, the daughter must have remained in the *potestas* of her father if he divorced her from her husband without her consent. This, then, would be an early reference to marriage without *manus*.

[CICERO]

Item vitiosa confirmatio est rationis cum ea re quae plures res significat abutimur pro certo unius rei signo, hoc modo: " Necesse est, quoniam pallet, aegrotasse ; " aut " Necesse est peperisse, quoniam sustinet puerum infantem." Nam haec sua sponte certa signa non habent; sin cetera quoque similia concurrunt, nonnihil illiusmodi signa adaugent suspicionem.

Item vitiosum est quando [1] vel in alium vel in eum ipsum qui dicit id [2] quod in adversarium dicitur [3] potest convenire, hoc modo:

" Miseri sunt qui [4] uxores ducunt." " At tu duxisti alteram."

Item vitiosum est id quod vulgarem habet defensionem, hoc modo: " Iracundia deductus peccavit aut adulescentia aut amore." Huiuscemodi enim deprecationes si probabuntur, inpune maxima peccata dilabentur.

Item vitiosum est cum id pro certo sumitur, quod inter omnes constat, quod etiam nunc in controversia est, [5] hoc modo:

Eho tu, dii quibus est potestas motus superum atque inferum
Pacem inter [6] sese conciliant, conferunt concordiam.

---

[1] quando d : quod *other MSS. Mx.*
[2] id E : M Mx omit.
[3] dicitur d : dicit *other MSS. Mx.*
[4] qui P²CE : si MMx.
[5] est Cbl : sit d : *other MSS. Mx omit.*
[6] inter E : enim inter *other MSS. Mx.*

---

[a] *Cf.* Cicero, *De Inv.* 1. xliii. 81.

Again, the Proof of the Reason is faulty when we misapply a sign designating a variety of things in such a way as to indicate specifically a single thing,[a] as follows: " Since he is pale, he must have been sick," or: " She must have become a mother, since she is holding a baby boy in her arms." [b] These indications do not of themselves offer definite proof, but if there is concurrence of other like indications, such signs increase probability not a little.

Again, there is a fault when that which is directed against the adversary can as well fit some one else or the speaker himself,[c] as follows: " Wretched are they who marry wives." " Yet you have married a second." [d]

Again, that is faulty which presents a banal defence, as follows: " He was led into crime by anger—or youth—or love." [e] For if excuses of this sort are admitted, the greatest crimes will escape unpunished.

Again it is a fault to assume as certain, on the ground that " it is universally agreed upon," a thing which is still in dispute, as follows: " Ho! Look you, the gods who guide the movements of the beings that dwell above and below keep peace among themselves

---

[b] Cf. Aristotle's examples of the infallible kind of sign in *Rhet.* 1. 2 (1357 b): " He is sick, for he has a fever," and " She has had a child, for she has milk "; also *Anal. Pr.* 2. 27 (70 a).

[c] This is the " common " argument; cf. Cicero, *De Inv.* 1. xlviii. 90, and Quintilian, 5. 13. 29. Faults such as those treated from here on are described briefly by Quintilian in 5. 13. 34 f.

[d] From a comedy (?) by an unknown author; yet Ribbeck, 1. 300–1, suspects that the verse may belong to a dispute between Jason and Medea in Ennius' *Medea.*

[e] Cf. 2. xvi. 24 above.

[CICERO]

Nam ita pro suo iure hoc exemplo utentem Thesprotum [1] Ennius induxit, quasi iam satis certis rationibus ita esse demonstrasset.

40   Item vitiosum est quod iam quasi sero atque acto negotio dici videtur, hoc modo: " In mentem mihi si venisset, Quirites, non commisissem ut in hunc locum res veniret, nam hoc aut hoc fecissem; sed me tum haec ratio fugit."

Item vitiosum est cum id quod in aperto delicto positum est tamen aliqua tegitur defensione, hoc modo:

Cum te expetebant omnes florentissimo
Regno, reliqui; nunc desertum ab omnibus
Summo periclo sola ut restituam paro.

XXVI. Item vitiosum est quod in aliam partem ac dictum sit potest accipi.   Id est huiusmodi, ut si quis potens ac factiosus in contione dixerit: " Satius est uti regibus quam uti malis legibus."   Nam et hoc, tametsi rei augendae causa potest sine malitia dici, tamen propter potentiam eius qui dicit non dicitur sine atroci suspicione.

41   Item vitiosum est falsis aut vulgaribus definitionibus uti.   Falsae sunt huiusmodi, ut si quis dicat iniuriam

[1] thesprotum *M* : threspontem *E* (thespontem *d*) : Chrespontem *Mx*.

a Probably from the *Thyestes* of Ennius; see Vahlen, pp. ccx and 183.   Thesprotus is perhaps interceding to reconcile the estranged brothers Atreus and Thyestes.   But if the reading *Chrespontem* (E *threspontem*) is correct, the verses are from the *Cresphontes* of Ennius; see Ribbeck, l. 34.   *Cf.* Cicero, De Inv. 1. xlix. 91.
b *Cf.* Cicero, De Inv. 1. xlviii. 90.
c *Cf.* Cicero, De Inv. 1. xlviii. 90.

130

and join in concord."[a] Thus Thesprotus, as Ennius has presented him, uses this example on his own authority, as though he had already demonstrated the fact by reasons sufficiently conclusive.

40   Again, that is faulty which appears to be pronounced too late, as it were, and after the matter has been concluded,[b] as follows: " If it had entered my mind, fellow-citizens, I should not have been guilty of allowing the matter to come to such a pass, for I should have done this or that; but at the time this thought escaped me."

Again, there is a fault when that which stands as a manifest transgression is yet cloaked by some defence,[c] as follows: " When all men were seeking you out and you had a most prosperous kingdom, I forsook you; now that all have deserted you, I, alone, in greatest peril, prepare to restore you." [d]

XXVI. Again, that is faulty which can be taken in another sense than the speaker intended;[e] for example, if some influential demagogue should in a speech before the Assembly say: " It is better to submit to kings than to bad laws." In fact, these words, though they may be uttered by way of amplification without sinister intent, are nevertheless because of the speaker's influence sure to breed a terrible suspicion.

41   Again, it is a fault to use false or general definitions;[f] false, as if one should say that there is no

---

[d] Assigned to the *Medus* of Pacuvius; Medea is speaking to Aeetes.

[e] Cicero, *De Inv.* 1. xlvii. 88, gives a different treatment of ambiguity.

[f] *Cf.* Cicero, *De Inv.* 1. lxix. 91. The " general definition " represents the same kind of fault as the last type of weak Reason in 2. xxiv. 37 above.

esse nullam nisi quae ex pulsatione aut convicio constet. Vulgares sunt quae nihilominus in aliam rem transferri possunt, ut si quis dicat: "Quadruplator, ut breviter scribam, capitalis est,[1] est enim inprobus et pestifer civis." Nam nihilo magis quadruplatoris quam furis, quam sicarii aut proditoris adtulit definitionem.

Item vitiosum est pro argumento sumere quod in disquisitione positum est, ut si quis quem furti arguat et ita dicat eum esse hominem inprobum, avarum, fraudulentem; ei rei testimonium esse quod sibi furtum fecerit.

Item vitiosum est controversiam controversia dissolvere, hoc modo; "Non convenit, censores, istum vobis satis facere quod ait se non potuisse adesse ita ut iuratus fuerit.[2] Quid? si ad exercitum non venisset, idemne tribuno militum diceret?" Hoc ideo vitiosum est quia non expedita aut iudicata res, sed inpedita et in simili controversia posita exempli loco profertur.

42 Item vitiosum est cum id de quo summa controversia est parum expeditur et quasi transactum sit relinquitur, hoc modo:

Aperte fatur dictio, si intellegas:
Tali dari arma qualis qui gessit fuit
Iubet, potiri si studeamus Pergamum.
Quem ego me profiteor esse; me est aecum frui

---

[1] est *CE* : *other MSS. Mx omit.*
[2] fuerit *M* : fuerat *E Mx.*

---

a See the definition of *iniuria* in 4. xxv. 35 below.
b The fallacy of Begging the Question.
c Cf. Aristotle, *Rhet.* 2. 24 (1401 b), illustrating, among the sham enthymemes, the *topos* from a "sign": "Suppose that

injury except in the form of battery or of insulting language;[a] general, like that which can be equally well applied to something else, as if one should say: "An informer, in short, is worthy of death; for he is a wicked and dangerous citizen." The speaker has offered a definition no more appropriate to an informer than to a thief, assassin, or traitor.

Again, it is a fault to advance as proof what has been put in question,[b] as if one should charge another with theft, and accordingly declare that he is a wicked, greedy, and deceitful man—and the evidence for this is that he has stolen from the speaker.[c]

Again, it is a fault to refute one disputed point by another disputed point,[d] as follows: "You should not be satisfied, Censors, when this defendant says that he was unable to be present as he had sworn he would be. I ask, would he have given this same excuse to the tribune of the soldiers if he had failed to appear for military duty?" This is faulty because a matter not clearly settled or adjudged, but entangled with difficulties and based on a like point of dispute is cited as an example.

Again, a fault is present when a matter about which there is the sharpest controversy is not clearly settled and is allowed to pass as though it were agreed upon, as follows: "Plainly speaks the oracle's response if you would understand. He commands that the arms be given to a warrior such as was he who bore them, should we be zealous to take Pergamum. This warrior I profess to be. It is but fair

some one calls Dionysius a thief 'because he is a rogue.' There is, of course, no logical argument here; not every rogue is a thief, though every thief is a rogue."

[d] Cf. the last fault considered in 2. xxv. 39 above.

Fraternis armis mihique adiudicarier,
Vel quod propinquus vel quod virtute aemulus.

Item vitiosum est ipsum sibi in sua oratione dissentire et contra atque ante dixerit dicere, hoc
modo : " Qua causa accusem hunc ? ", tum id
exputando evolvere :

Nam si veretur, quid eum accuses qui est probus ?
Sin inverecundum animi ingenium possidet,
Quid autem eum accuses qui id parvi auditum
aestimet ?

XXVII. Non incommoda ratione videtur sibi ostendisse quare non accusaret. Quid postea ? quid ait ?

Nunc ego te ab summo iam detexam exordio.

43 Item vitiosum est quod dicitur contra iudicis
voluntatem aut eorum qui audiunt, si aut partes
quibus illi student, aut homines quos illi caros habent
laedantur, aut aliquo eiusmodi vitio laeditur auditoris
voluntas.

Item vitiosum est non omnes res confirmare quas
pollicitus sis in expositione.

Item verendum est ne de alia re dicatur, cum alia
de re controversia sit ; inque eiusmodi vitio considerandum est ne aut ad rem addatur quid, aut
quippiam de re detrahatur, aut tota causa mutata in

---

[a] Perhaps from the *Armorum Iudicium* of Accius (Warmington, 2. 362) rather than from the play of the same name
by Pacuvius (Marx, *Proleg.*, p. 132) ; see Tolkiehn, *Berl.
Philol. Wochenschr.* 37 (1917). 827–8. Ajax speaks for the
arms of Achilles which Agamemnon, on Athena's advice,
later awarded to Ulysses.

[b] The fragment is from a tragedy by an unknown author,
The example was a favourite of the rhetoricians. *Cf.* Cicero,

that I have the use of my cousin's arms and that they be awarded me, either because I am his kin or, if you will, because I rival him in valour." [a]

Again, it is a fault to be inconsistent with oneself in one's own discourse and to contradict what one has said before, as follows: " On what ground shall I impeach him? ", and then to develop this thought by the following reflection: " For if he has a conscience, why should you impeach an honourable man? But if he has a shameless character, to what avail then would you impeach one who, when he has heard the charge, deems it of little account? " XXVII. He seems to have provided himself with a sound enough reason for not making the accusation. What does he say next? " Now at last I will finish you off from the very first thread." [b]

43 Again, that is faulty which is said against the convictions of the judge or the audience [c]—if the party to which they are devoted, or men whom they hold dear, should be attacked, or the sentiments of the hearer outraged by some fault of this kind.

Again, it is a fault not to prove everything which in the Proposition you have promised to prove.[d]

Again, one must beware of talking on a different subject from the one in dispute [e]—and in regard to this kind of fault one must take care not to add anything to, or omit anything from, the subject, and not to change the question at issue and turn to quite

De Inv. 1. xlv. 83, 1. l. 93; Victorinus, in Halm, p. 253; C. Julius Victor, ch. 12, in Halm, p. 414.

[c] Cf. Cicero, De Inv. 1. xlix. 92, and De Oratore 2. 75. 304–5.

[d] Cf. Cicero, De Inv. 1. l. 94.

[e] The fallacy of Shifting Ground. Cf. Cicero, De Inv. 1. l. 94.

aliam causam derivetur; uti apud Pacuvium Zethus [1] cum Amphione, quorum controversia de musica inducta disputatione in sapientiae rationem et virtutis utilitatem consumitur.

Item considerandum est ne aliud accusatoris criminatio contineat, aliud defensoris purgatio purget, quod saepe consulto multi ab reo faciunt angustiis causae coacti; ut si quis, cum accusetur ambitu magistratum petisse, ab imperatoribus saepe numero apud exercitum donis militaribus se dicat [2] donatum esse. Hoc si diligenter in oratione adversariorum observaverimus, saepe deprehendemus eos de ea re quod dicant non habere.

44 Item vitiosum est artem aut scientiam aut studium quodpiam vituperare propter eorum vitia qui in eo studio sunt; veluti qui rhetoricam vituperant propter alicuius oratoris vituperandam vitam.

Item vitiosum est ex eo, quia perperam factum constet esse, putare ostendi a certo homine factum esse, hoc modo: " Mortuum deformatum, tumore praeditum, corpore decoloratum constat fuisse; ergo veneno necatus est." Deinde si sit usque in eo

---

[1] Zethus *MSS.*: faciunt Zethus *Mx.*
[2] *lac.;* donis militaribus se dicat *sugg. Mx.*

---

[a] The twins in the *Antiopa* (as in the *Antiope* of Euripides) engage in a famous debate: the practical Zethus, hostile to culture, finds fault with Amphion's love of music, and urges the virile active life of farming, cattle breeding, and war; the cultivated Amphion praises music and the life of contemplation. Amphion yields " to his brother's mood " so far as to still his lyre; see Horace, *Epist.* 1. 18. 43–4. *Cf.* Cicero, *De Inv.* 1. 1. 94, *De Oratore* 2. 37. 155, *De Re Publ.* 1. 18, and Callicles in Plato, *Gorgias* 485 E ff. The separation of musical from philosophical studies represents a Roman point of view.

another; like the case of Zethus and Amphion in
Pacuvius—their controversy, begun on the subject
of music, ends in a disputation on the theory of
wisdom and the utility of virtue.[a]

Again, care must be taken that the prosecutor's
charge shall not bear on one point, and the Exculpation of the defence on another. Many speakers on
the side of the defence are often intentionally guilty
of this irrelevance when pressed by the difficulties of
their cause; for example, if a man accused of having
sought a magistracy by bribery should say that in
the army he had often received military gifts from
generals. If we carefully watch for this fault in the
speech of our adversaries we shall often detect that
they have nothing to say to the point.

Again, it is a fault to disparage an art or science or
any occupation because of the faults of those engaged
in it,[b] as in the case of those who blame rhetoric
because of the blameworthy life of some orator.[c]

Again, it is a fault, when you establish that a
crime was committed, to believe you are thereby
proving that it was committed by a specific person, as
follows: " It is established that the corpse was dis-
figured, swollen, and discoloured; therefore the man
was killed by poison." Then, if the speaker con-

[b] The argument is not *ad rem* but *ad hominem*; the fallacy
of Ignoring the Question. *Cf.* Cicero, *De Inv.* 1. l. 94.
[c] *Cf.* Quintilian, 12. 1. 32: " Let us banish from our hearts
the notion that eloquence, the fairest of all things, can combine with vicious character "; Philodemus, *Rhet.* 2. 270, ed.
Sudhaus: " But it is clear to all that many orators are very
able, yet in character thoroughly depraved; " Plato, *Gorgias*
457 A, and Ludwig Radermacher, *Artium Scriptores*, Sitzungsber. Österreich. Akad. (philos.-hist. Klasse) 227, 3 (Vienna,
1951). 45.

occupatus, ut multi faciunt, venenum datum, vitio
non mediocri conflictetur. Non enim factumne sit
quaeritur, sed a quo factum sit.

45 XXVIII. Item vitiosum est in conparandis rebus
alteram rem efferre, de re altera mentionem non
facere aut neglegentius disputare; ut si cum conparetur utrum satius sit populum frumentum accipere
an non accipere, quae commoda sint in altera re vera
curet enumeret, quae in altera incommoda sint et
quae velit depressa praetereat, aut ea quae minima
sint dicat.

Item vitiosum est in rebus conparandis necesse
putare[1] alteram rem vituperare[2] cum alteram laudes;
quod genus, si quaeratur utris maior honor habendus
sit, Albensibus an Vestinis Pennensibus, quod[3] rei
publicae populi Romani profuerint, et is qui dicat
alteros laedat. Non enim necesse est, si alteros
praeponas, alteros vituperare; fieri enim potest ut,
cum alteros magis laudaris, aliquam alteris partem
laudis adtribuas, ne cupide depugnasse contra veritatem puteris.

[1] putare *Lambinus* : putari *MSS. Mx.*
[2] vituperare *E* : vituperari *other MSS. Mx.*
[3] quod *P²BC²l Mx ed. mai.* : quo *M Mx* : qui *b d.*

---

[a] *Cf.* Cicero, *De Inv.* 1. 1. 94. Yet this procedure is not
faulty when followed in the Statement of Facts; see *De Inv.*
1. xxi. 30.
[b] A deliberative problem; our author has in the first two
books been emphasizing the judicial kind.

centrates, as many do, on proving that poison was administered, he will be harassed by a not insignificant fault. The question is not whether the crime was committed, but who committed it.

XXVIII. Again, it is a fault in making a comparison to bring out one term and either suppress mention of the other, or treat it rather cursorily; [a] for example, if in deciding by a comparison whether it is better for the populace to receive, or not to receive, wheat, the speaker should on the one hand really take care to enumerate the benefits, but on the other should pass over the disadvantages and whatever he wishes to suppress, or should mention only those disadvantages which are least serious. [b]

Again, it is a fault in making a comparison to think it necessary to disparage one thing when you praise the other; [c] for example, if the question should arise, who are to be held in greater honour for services to the Roman republic, the Albensians or the Pinnensian Vestini, [d] and the speaker should attack one or the other. Indeed it is not necessary, if you prefer one, to disparage the other; for you can manage, when you have given greater praise to one, to allot some portion of praise to the other, so that you may not be thought to have combated the truth under influence of partiality.

[c] Cf. Cicero, De Inv. 1. l. 94.
[d] Most probably for her faithfulness to Rome in the Marsic war, in which she gallantly withstood a siege, Alba Fucens, a city of the Aequi on the borders of the Marsi in Central Italy, was rewarded with the status of municipium; Pinna (or Penna), at the foot of the Apennines, a chief city of the Vestini, was also faithful to Rome (although the other Vestini were in revolt) and endured a hard siege.

Item vitiosum est de nomine et vocabulo controversiam struere quam rem consuetudo optime potest
iudicare; velut Sulpicius, qui intercesserat ne exules
quibus causam dicere non licuisset reducerentur,
idem posterius, immutata voluntate, cum eandem
legem ferret, aliam se ferre [1] dicebat propter nominum
commutationem; nam non exules, sed vi eiectos se
reducere aiebat. Proinde quasi id fuisset in controversia, quo illi nomine appellarentur, aut proinde
quasi non omnes quibus aqua et igni interdictum est
exules appellentur. Verum illi fortasse ignoscimus si
cum causa fecit; nos tamen intellegamus vitiosum
esse intendere controversiam propter nominum
mutationem.

46   **XXIX.** Quoniam exornatio constat ex similibus et
exemplis et amplificationibus et rebus iudicatis et
ceteris rebus quae pertinent ad exaugendam et con-
locupletandam argumentationem, quae sint his rebus
vitia consideremus.

---

[1] aliam se ferre ΠCP² Mx ed. mai.: aliam sese ferre E:
alios efferre H: aliose ferre P: alio se ferre Mx: aliis e
ferre B.

---

[a] Cf. Horace, Ars Poet. 72: " Usage (usus = consuetudo =
συνήθεια), in whose hands lie the decision (arbitrium), rights
(ius), and standard (norma) of speaking "; Demetrius, De
Elocut. 2. 86: " Usage, which is our teacher always," and
2. 87, in which he makes usage his " standard " (κανών =
norma).

[b] In 90 B.C., after the outbreak of the Marsic War, the
tribune Q. Varius Hybrida introduced a law on treason
directed against the senatorial leaders; it inquired into the
actions of those who helped or advised the allies to take up
arms against Rome. Sulpicius' law in 88 restored the exiles
who had been condemned without a hearing either by the
Varian Commission or by the court established under the Lex

Again, it is a fault to build upon a name or appellation a dispute which usage can best decide.[a] For example, Sulpicius [b] had opposed his veto to the recall of the exiles who had not been permitted to plead their cause; later he changed his mind, and proposing the same law, said he was offering a different proposal, because he had changed the name. For, he said, he was recalling not " exiles," but " those ejected by violence "—as though the dispute concerned the name by which to call those people, or as though all to whom water and fire have been formally forbidden are not called exiles. True, we perhaps excuse Sulpicius if he had a reason for doing this.[c] Yet let us understand that it is a fault to raise a controversy on account of a change in names.

XXIX. Since Embellishment consists of similes, examples, amplifications, previous judgements, and the other means which serve to expand and enrich the argument, let us consider the faults which attach to these.

Plautia Iudiciaria of 90/89, but was itself later in the year repealed by Sulla. Why Sulpicius had earlier vetoed a proposal to recall the exiles is not clear, for many of these belonged to his own party. The grounds for the veto were probably constitutional, and the new form of the proposal may have been intended to avoid constitutional objections that the decisions of the courts were being nullified; or perhaps popular opinion pressed him to change his mind. It was through the interdiction of fire and water, the symbol of the community, that the capital sentence was carried into effect. See Ernst Levy, *Die röm. Kapitalstrafe*, Sitzungsber. Heidelberg. Akad. (philos.-hist. Klasse) 21, 5 (1930–31). 14 ff.

 [c] The author here seems to betray bias in favour of the Popular party; but see the Introduction to the present volume, pp. xxiii f.

[CICERO]

Simile vitiosum est quod ex [1] aliqua parte dissimile est nec habet parem rationem conparationis aut sibi ipsi obest qui adfert.

Exemplum vitiosum est si aut falsum est, ut reprehendatur, aut inprobum, ut non sit imitandum, aut maius aut minus quam res postulat.

Res iudicata vitiose proferetur si aut dissimili de re proferetur, aut de ea re qua de controversia non est, aut inproba, aut eiusmodi ut aut plures aut magis idoneae res iudicatae ab adversariis proferri possint.

Item vitiosum est id quod adversarii factum esse confiteantur, de eo argumentari et planum facere factum esse; nam id augeri oportet.

Item vitiosum est id augere quod convenit docere, hoc modo: ut si quis quem arguat hominem occidisse et, antequam satis idoneas argumentationes adtulerit, augeat peccatum et dicat nihil indignius esse quam hominem occidere. Non enim utrum indignum sit an non, sed factumne sit quaeritur.

Conplexio vitiosa est quae non quidque quod [2] primum dictum est primum conplectitur, et quae non breviter concluditur, et quae non ex enumeratione certum et constans aliquid relinquit, ut intellegatur quid propositum in argumentatione sit, quid deinde

---

[1] quod ex $B\,C\,\Pi$: id quod ex E: quode P: quod de $H\,Mx$.

[2] non quidque quod C^2d: non quique quod C^1: non quod quique P^1Mx: non quod quidque $P^2\,\Pi\,B\,l$: quod non quodque b: quod quique H.

---

[a] Cf. Cicero, *De Inv.* 1. lxiv. 82.

[b] Aristotle, *Rhet.* 2. 25 (1403 a), Quintilian, 5. 13. 24, Anon. Seg. 187 (Spengel-Hammer 1 [2]. 385), and Apsines, *Ars Rhet.* 9 (Spengel-Hammer 1 [2]. 283–5) treat the invalidation of examples (λύσεις παραδειγμάτων).

A Simile is defective if it is inexact in any aspect, and lacks a proper ground for the comparison, or is prejudicial to him who presents it.[a]

An Example is defective if it is either false, and hence refutable, or base, and hence not to be imitated, or if it implies more or less than the matter demands.[b]

The citing of a Previous Judgement will be faulty [c] if the judgement applies to an unlike matter, or one not in dispute, or if it is discreditable, or is of such a kind that previous decisions either in greater number or of greater appropriateness can be offered by our adversaries.

Again, it is a fault, when our adversaries admit a fact, to devote an argument to establishing it as a fact; [d] for it should rather be amplified.

Again, it is a fault to amplify what one should prove; [e] for example, if a man should charge another with homicide, and before he has presented conclusive arguments, should amplify the crime, avowing that there is nothing more shameful than homicide. The question is, in fact, not whether the deed is or is not shameful, but whether it was committed.

The Résumé is defective if it does not include every point in the exact order in which it has been presented; if it does not come to a conclusion briefly; [f] and if the summary does not leave something precise and stable, so as to make clear what the Proposition

---

[c] Cf. Cicero, De Inv. 1. xliv. 82.

[d] Cf. Cicero, De Inv. 1. xlix. 92.

[e] Two functions are differentiated, the logical and emotional; see 2. xxx. 47 ff. below. Cf. Cicero, De Inv. 1. xlix. 92; in Aristotle, Rhet. 2. 24 (1401 b), the topos (among the sham enthymemes) of indignation (δείνωσις)—the speaker amplifies the deed without having proved his case.

[f] Cf. Cicero, De Inv. 1. xxxvii. 67.

[CICERO]

ratione, quid rationis confirmatione, quid tota argumentatione demonstratum.

47 XXX. Conclusiones, quae apud Graecos epilogi
nominantur, tripertitae sunt. Nam constant ex
enumeratione, amplificatione, et commiseratione.
Quattuor locis uti possumus conclusionibus: in
principio, secundum narrationem, secundum firmis-
simam argumentationem, in conclusione.

Enumeratio est per quam colligimus et com-
monemus quibus de rebus verba fecerimus, breviter,
ut renovetur, non redintegretur oratio; et ordine ut
quicquid erit dictum referemus, ut auditor, si
memoriae mandaverit, ad idem quod ipse meminerit
reducatur. Item curandum est ne aut ab exordio
aut narratione repetatur orationis enumeratio. Ficta

---

a ἐπίλογοι. The Isocratic theory of the Conclusion was
also tripartite; to Theodectes (whose rhetorical system was
based on the parts of the discourse) its functions are to stir
the emotions, especially anger and pity, to praise or blame,
and to recall what has been said. See Hugo Rabe, *Proleg.
Syll.*, Leipzig, 1931, pp. 32 and 216; Anon. Seg. 208-9, in
Spengel-Hammer 1 (2). 389; Friedrich Solmsen in *Hermes*
67 (1932). 144-151. The *Rhet. ad Alex.*, ch. 36 (1444 b–
1445 a), discusses the part played in Conclusions by the
Summary and the Conciliation of the Audience (including the
Appeal to Pity), together with Discrediting the Opponent.
To Aristotle, *Rhet.* 3. 19 (1419 b), the Conclusion has four
functions: to conciliate the audience and discredit the
opponent, to magnify and depreciate, to excite the emotions
required by the case, and to review what has been said.
Cicero, *De Inv.* 1. lii. 98, divides *conclusio* into Summing Up,
Invective (*indignatio*, δείνωσις), and Appeal to Pity (*conquestio*); in *Part. Orat.* 15. 52 ff. the *peroratio* is restricted
(doubtless because the work is in the form of an isagogic
dialogue) to two divisions, Amplification and Summing Up,
Invective and Appeal to Pity being subordinate to Amplification. Anon. Seg. 203 (Spengel-Hammer 1 [2]. 454) considers the Conclusion as dealing with either facts (τὸ πρακτικόν)

was, then what has been established by the Reason, by the Proof of the Reason, and by the argument as a whole.

47   XXX. Conclusions, among the Greeks called *epilogoi*,[a] are tripartite, consisting of the Summing Up, Amplification, and Appeal to Pity. We can in four places use a Conclusion: in the Direct Opening, after the Statement of Facts, after the strongest argument, and in the Conclusion of the speech.

The Summing Up[b] gathers together and recalls the points we have made—briefly, that the speech may not be repeated in entirety, but that the memory of it may be refreshed; and we shall reproduce all the points in the order in which they have been presented, so that the hearer, if he has committed them to memory, is brought back to what he remembers. Again, we must take care that the Summary should not be carried back to the Introduction or the Statement of Facts. Otherwise the speech will appear to

or emotions (τὸ παθητικόν), placing the Summary in the former class; so also Quintilian, 6. 1. 1.

[b] ἀνάμνησις, ἀνακεφαλαίωσις. In *Rhet. ad Alex.*, ch. 20 (1433 b), παλιλλογία. Cf. *Rhet. ad Alex.*, *l.c.*: " When Summing Up we shall recapitulate either in the form of a division or a recommendation of policy or of a question or of an enumeration;" Cicero, *Part. Orat.* 17. 59 : " There are two occasions for the Summing Up—if you mistrust the memory of those before whom you are pleading whether on account of the length of time elapsed [since the events you have been discussing took place] or on account of the length of your speech, or if, by repeatedly presenting arguments that strengthen your speech and setting these forth briefly, your case will have more force; " Quintilian, 6. 1. 1 : " The Summing Up . . . both refreshes the memory of the *iudex* and at the same time places the whole case before his eyes." Cf. the *enumeratio* of 1. x. 17 above, and *complexio*, the Résumé of an argument, 2. xviii. 28 above.

enim et dedita opera conparata oratio videbitur esse
artificii significandi, ingenii venditandi, memoriae
ostendendae causa. Quapropter initium enumera-
tionis sumendum est a divisione. Dein¹ ordine
breviter exponendae res sunt quae tractatae erunt in
confirmatione et confutatione.

Amplificatio est res quae per locum communem
instigationis auditorum causa sumitur. Loci communes ex decem praeceptis commodissime sumentur
adaugendi criminis causa.

48 Primus locus sumitur ab auctoritate, cum com-
memoramus quantae curae ea res fuerit dis im-
mortalibus aut maioribus nostris, regibus, civitatibus,
nationibus, hominibus sapientissimis, senatui; item
maxime quo modo de his rebus legibus sanctum sit.

Secundus locus est cum consideramus illae res de
quibus criminamur ad quos pertineant; utrum ad
omnes, quod atrocissimum est; an ad superiores,

---

¹ dein P² C Π b l : de M : deinde Omnibonus Mx : deinde
ex d.

ᵃ See note on 4. vii. 10 below.
ᵇ The purpose of Amplification is δείνωσις (indignatio in
4. xv. 22 and 4. xxxix. 51, iracundia in 3. xiii. 24). Note that
the loci communes (see note on 2. vi. 9 above) are here attached
to Amplification (αὔξησις), which, in turn, is a subhead under
the Conclusion. The theory of Amplification was first formed
for epideictic; Gorgias, Tisias (Plato, Phaedrus 267 A), and
Isocrates gave it prominence. Cf. Cicero, Part. Orat. 15. 52 :
" The right place for Amplification is in the Peroration; but
also in the course of the speech there are opportunities to
digress for the sake of amplification, when some point has
been proved or refuted. Amplification is, then, a more
impressive affirmation, so to speak, which by moving the
mind wins belief in speaking;" 8. 27 : " Although Amplification has its own proper place, often in the opening of a

146

have been fabricated [a] and devised with elaborate pains so as to demonstrate the speaker's skill, advertise his wit, and display his memory. Therefore the Summary must take its beginning from the Division. Then we must in order and briefly set forth the points treated in the Proof and Refutation.

Amplification is the principle of using Commonplaces to stir [b] the hearers. To amplify an accusation it will be most advantageous to draw commonplaces from ten formulae.

48 (1) The first commonplace [c] is taken from authority, when we call to mind of what great concern the matter under discussion has been to the immortal gods, or to our ancestors, or kings, states, barbarous nations, sages, the Senate; and again, especially how sanction has been provided in these matters by laws.

(2) The second commonplace [c] is used when we consider who are affected by these acts on which our charge rests; whether all men, which is a most shocking thing; or our superiors, such as are those

speech, and almost always at the end, yet it is to be used also in other parts of the discourse, especially when a point has been proved or refuted." Cicero, De Inv. 1. liii. 100–liv. 105, gives five additional loci for invective; his No. 12 is like our author's No. 8. There are correspondences between our author's commonplaces and those listed in Aristotle, Rhet. 1. 14 (1374 b–1375 a); cf., e.g., μόνος ἢ πρῶτος (our author's No. 8), τὸ θηριωδέστερον ἀδίκημα (No. 7), ἐκ προνοίας (No. 6), ἴασις (No. 5); on correspondences with those in the Rhet. ad Alex. see Claus Peters, pp. 100–101. Peters, and Octave Navarre, Essai sur la Rhétorique Grecque avant Aristote, Paris, 1900, pp. 304 ff., illustrate the use made of several of these commonplaces by Greek orators. See Walter Plöbst, Die Auxesis, diss. Munich, 1911.

[c] Cf. Cicero, De Inv. 1. liii. 101.

quod genus ii sunt a quibus auctoritatis locus communis sumitur; an ad pares, hoc est, in isdem partibus animi, corporis, fortunarum positos; an ad
inferiores, qui his omnibus rebus antecelluntur.

Tertius locus est quo percontamur quid sit even-
turum si omnibus idem concedatur, et, ea re neglecta,
ostendemus quid periculorum atque incommodorum
consequatur.

Quartus locus est quo demonstratur, si huic sit
permissum, multos alacriores ad maleficium futuros,
quod adhuc expectatio iudicii remoratur.

Quintus locus est cum ostendimus, si semel aliter
iudicatum sit, nullam rem fore quae incommodo
mederi aut erratum iudicum corrigere possit. Quo in
loco non incommodum erit uti ceterarum rerum conparatione, ut ostendamus alias res posse aut vetustate
sedari aut consilio corrigi, huius rei aut leniendae aut
corrigendae nullam rem adiumento futuram.

49   Sextus est locus cum ostendimus et consulto
factum et dicimus voluntario facinori nullam esse
excusationem, inprudentiae iustam deprecationem
paratam.

Septimus locus est quo ostendimus taetrum facinus,
crudele, nefarium, tyrannicum esse; quod genus
iniuria mulierum, aut earum rerum aliquid quarum
rerum causa bella suscipiuntur et cum hostibus de
vita dimicatur.

---

a *Cf.* 3. vi. 10 below.

b *Cf.* Cicero, *De Inv.* 1. liii. 101 and 2. xxxii. 100; the *locus
qui efficitur ex causis* in *Top.* 18. 67.

c *Cf.* Cicero, *De Inv.* 1. liii. 102; *Rhet. ad Alex.*, ch. 4
(1427 a).

d *Cf.* Cicero, *De Inv.* 1. liii. 102.

from whom the commonplace of authority is taken; or our peers, those in the same situation as we with respect to qualities of character, physical attributes, and external circumstances; [a] or our inferiors, whom in all these respects we excel.

(3) By means of the third commonplace [b] we ask what would happen if the same indulgence should be granted to all culprits, and show what perils and disadvantages would ensue from indifference to this crime.

(4) By means of the fourth commonplace [c] we show that if we indulge this man, many others will be the more emboldened to commit crimes—something which the anticipation of a judicial sentence has hitherto checked.

(5) By the fifth commonplace [d] we show that if once judgement is pronounced otherwise than as we urge, there will be nothing which can remedy the harm or correct the jurors' error. Here it will be in point for us to make a comparison with other mistakes, so as to show that other mistakes can either be moderated by time or corrected designedly, but that so far as the present mistake is concerned, nothing will serve either to alleviate or to amend it.

(6) By means of the sixth commonplace [d] we show that the act was done with premeditation, and declare that for an intentional crime there is no excuse, although a rightful plea of mercy is provided for an unpremeditated act.

(7) By means of the seventh commonplace [d] we show that it is a foul crime, cruel, sacrilegious, and tyrannical; such a crime as the outraging of women, or one of those crimes that incite wars and life-and-death struggles with enemies of the state.

149

[CICERO]

Octavus locus est quo ostendimus non vulgare, sed singulare esse maleficium, spurcum, nefarium, inusitatum; quo maturius et atrocius vindicandum est.

Nonus locus est qui constat ex peccatorum conparatione, quasi cum dicemus maius esse maleficium stuprare ingenuum quam sacrum legere, quod alterum propter egestatem, alterum propter intemperantem superbiam fiat.

Decimus locus est per quem omnia quae in negotio gerundo acta sunt quaeque rem consequi solent exputamus acriter et criminose et diligenter, ut agi res et geri negotium videatur rerum consequentium enumeratione.

50   XXXI. Misericordia commovebitur auditoribus si variam fortunarum commutationem dicemus; si ostendemus in quibus commodis fuerimus quibusque incommodis simus, conparatione; si quae nobis futura sint nisi causam obtinuerimus enumerabimus et ostendemus; si supplicabimus et nos sub eorum quorum misericordiam captabimus potestatem subiciemus: si quid nostris parentibus, liberis, ceteris necessariis casurum sit propter nostras calamitates

---

a Cf. Cicero, *De Inv.* 1. liv. 103.

b ἀντιπαραβολή. See the example of the grand style, 4. viii. 12 below, for a use of this commonplace. *Cf.* Quintilian, 6. 2. 21 : " For some things are heinous in themselves, such as parricide, murder, poisoning, but other things have to be made to seem heinous; " and Cicero, *De Inv.* 1. liv. 104.

c ἐκτύπωσις. *Cf.* the figures *descriptio*, 4. xxxix. 51, and *demonstratio*, 4. lv. 68 below; Cicero, *De Inv.* 1. liv. 104.

d ἔλεος, οἶκτος. Cicero's treatment in *De Inv.* 1. lv. 106–lvi. 109 is fuller, listing sixteen *loci* of *conques'io*. Karl Aulitzky, *Wiener Studien* 39 (1917). 26–49, believes that Cicero and our author here use a common Roman source which may derive from Apollonius ὁ μαλακός. That the

(8) By means of the eighth commonplace [a] we show that it is not a common but a unique crime, base, nefarious, and unheard-of, and therefore must be the more promptly and drastically avenged.

(9) The ninth commonplace consists of a comparison [b] of wrongs, as when we shall say it is a more heinous crime to debauch a free-born person than to steal a sacred object, because the one is done from unbridled licentiousness and the other from need.

(10) By the tenth commonplace we shall examine sharply, incriminatingly, and precisely, everything that took place in the actual execution of the deed and all the circumstances that usually attend such an act, so that by the enumeration of the attendant circumstances the crime may seem to be taking place and the action to unfold before our eyes. [c]

XXXI. We shall stir Pity [d] in our hearers by recalling the vicissitudes of fortune; by comparing the prosperity we once enjoyed with our present adversity; [e] by enumerating and explaining the results that will follow for us if we lose the case; [f] by entreating those whose pity we seek to win, and by submitting ourselves to their mercy; by revealing what will befall our parents, children, and other kinsmen through our disgrace, [g] and at the same time

---

Appeal to Pity belongs in the Conclusion of a forensic speech is a concept of pre-Aristotelian rhetoric; cf. *Rhet. ad Alex.*, ch. 36 (1445 a).

[e] Cf. Cicero, *Part. Orat.* 17. 57 : " For nothing is so pitiable as a man who has become pitiable after having been happy ; " Aristotle, *Poetics*, ch. 13 (1452 b–1453 a).

[f] So also *Rhet. ad Alex.*, ch. 36 (1445 a), and Quintilian, 6. 1. 19.

[g] Quintilian, 6. 1. 18, offers similar advice to the accuser who is exciting pity for the man he is seeking to avenge.

aperiemus, et simul ostendemus illorum nos sollici-
tudine et miseria, non nostris incommodis dolere;
si de clementia, humanitate, misericordia nostra
qua in alios usi sumus aperiemus; si nos semper aut
diu in malis fuisse ostendemus; si nostrum fatum aut
fortunam conqueremur; si animum nostrum fortem,
patientem incommodorum ostendemus futurum.
Commiserationem brevem esse oportet, nihil enim
lacrima citius arescit.

Fere locos obscurissimos totius artificii tractavimus
in hoc libro; quapropter huic volumini modus hic sit.
Reliquas praeceptiones, quoad videbitur, in tertium
librum transferemus. Haec si, ut conquisite conscripsimus, ita tu diligenter et nobiscum et sine nobis
considerabis, et nos industriae fructus ex tua conscientia capiemus, et tute nostram diligentiam lauda-
bis tuaque [1] perceptione laetabere; tu scientior eris
praeceptorum artificii, nos alacriores ad reliquum
persolvendum. Verum haec futura satis scio, te
enim non ignoro. Nos deinceps ad cetera praecepta
transeamus, ut, quod libentissime faciamus, tuae
rectissimae [2] voluntati morem geramus.

---

[1] tuaque *P²CE* : tua *M Mx*.
[2] rectissimae *Md* : rectissime *b l Mx*.

showing that we grieve not because of our own straits but because of their anxiety and misery; by disclosing the kindness, humanity, and sympathy we have dispensed to others; by showing that we have ever, or for a long time, been in adverse circumstances; by deploring our fate or bad fortune; by showing that our heart will be brave and patient of adversities. The Appeal to Pity must be brief, for nothing dries more quickly than a tear.[a]

In the present Book I have treated virtually the most obscure topics in the whole art of rhetoric; therefore this Book must end here. The remaining rules, so far as seems best, I shall carry over to Book III. If you study the material that I have presented, both with and without me, with care equal to the pains I have taken in assembling it, I, on my part, shall reap the fruit of my labour in your sharing the knowledge with me, and you, on yours, will praise my diligence and rejoice in the learning you have acquired. You will have greater understanding of the precepts of rhetoric, and I shall be more eager to discharge the rest of my task. But that this will be so I know quite well, for I know you well. Let me turn at once to the other rules, so that I may gratify your very proper wish—and this it gives me the greatest pleasure to do.

[a] The proverb is attributed by Cicero, in *De Inv.* 1. lvi. 109, to Apollonius the rhetorician, who is perhaps to be identified with Apollonius ὁ μαλακός (born *c.* 160 B.C.) rather than with Apollonius Molon, Cicero's teacher. Both ὁ μαλακός and Molon (later) taught at Rhodes. For a study of the proverb see G. D. Kellogg, *Amer. Journ. Philol.* 28 (1907). 301–10.

BOOK III

LIBER TERTIUS

1   I. Ad omnem iudicialem causam quemadmodum
conveniret inventionem rerum adcommodari satis
abundanter arbitror superioribus libris demonstratum.
Nunc earum rationem rerum inveniendarum quae
pertinebant ad causas deliberativas et demonstrativas
in hunc librum transtulimus, ut omnis inveniendi
praeceptio tibi quam primum persolveretur.

Reliquae quattuor partes erant artificii. De
tribus partibus in hoc libro dictum est: dispositione,[a]
pronuntiatione, memoria. De elocutione, quia plura
dicenda videbantur, in quarto libro conscribere
maluimus, quem, ut arbitror, tibi librum celeriter
absolutum mittemus, ne quid tibi rhetoricae artis
deesse possit. Interea prima quaeque et nobiscum
cum voles, et interdum sine nobis legendo consequere,
ne quid inpediare quin ad hanc utilitatem pariter
nobiscum progredi possis. Nunc tu fac adtentum te
praebeas; nos proficisci ad instituta pergemus.

2   II. Deliberationes partim sunt eiusmodi ut quaeratur utrum potius faciendum sit, partim eiusmodi ut
quid potissimum faciendum sit consideretur. Utrum

---

    [a] 3. ii. 2–v. 9, vi. 10–viii. 15.
    [b] 3. ix. 16–x. 18 below.
    [c] 3. xi. 19–xv. 27 below.
    [d] 3. xvi. 28–xxiv. 40 below.
    [e] Style would ordinarily have preceded Delivery and
Memory; *cf.* 1. ii. 3 above.

BOOK III

1 I. In the preceding Books I have, as I believe, shown amply enough how to apply the Invention of topics to any judicial cause. The method of finding the topics appropriate to deliberative and epideictic causes I now carry over to the present Book,[a] in order that I may as speedily as possible discharge my task of explaining to you all the rules of Invention.

Four departments of rhetoric are left us to consider. Three are treated in the present Book: Arrangement,[b] Delivery,[c] and Memory.[d] Style, because it seems to require a fuller treatment, I prefer to discuss in Book IV,[e] which I hope to complete quickly and send to you, so that you may not lack anything on the art of rhetoric. Meanwhile you will learn all the principles I first set forth,[f] with me, when you wish, and at times without me, by reading, so that you may in no way be kept from equal progress with me towards the mastery of this useful art. It is now for you to give attention, while I resume progress towards our goal.

2 II. Deliberative [g] speeches are either of the kind in which the question concerns a choice between two courses of action, or of the kind in which a choice among several is considered. An example of a

---

[f] Of judicial oratory, the most difficult and important kind; cf. 2. i. 1 above.

[g] See note on the epideictic kind, 3. vi. 10 below.

[CICERO]

potius, hoc modo: Kartago tollenda an relinquenda
videatur. Quid potissimum, hoc pacto: ut si Hannibal consultet, cum ex Italia Kartaginem arcessatur,
an in Italia remaneat, an domum redeat, an in
Aegyptum profectus occupet Alexandriam.

Item deliberationes partim ipsae propter se
consultandae sunt, ut si deliberet senatus captivos
ab hostibus redimat an non; partim propter aliquam
extraneam causam veniunt in deliberationem et consultationem, ut si deliberet senatus solvatne legibus
Scipionem ut eum liceat ante tempus consulem fieri;
partim et propter se sunt deliberandae et magis
propter extraneam causam veniunt in consultationem,
ut si deliberet senatus bello Italico sociis civitatem

---

^a Cato the Elder and Publius Scipio Nasica always ended
their speeches, on no matter what question, the one with
" In my opinion, Carthage must be destroyed," and the other
with " In my opinion, Carthage must be spared "; see
Plutarch, *Marcus Cato* 27 (352), and Appian, *Pun.* 8 (1). 10. 69.
This *suasoria* was common among the rhetoricians; *cf.* Cicero,
De Inv. 1. viii. 11 and 1. xii. 17.

^b When, in 203 B.C., the Carthaginians were in danger from
Scipio, they summoned Hannibal to Africa. Appian, *Hann.*
7. 9. 58, reports Hannibal's fear of the perfidy and ingratitude
of his countrymen. Alexandria, once captured, might have
appeared to him as a safe refuge from the Romans and his
enemies at home. Egypt had been weakened by the war
with Antiochus the Great. The deliberations are not referred to in any historical account that has come down to
us; the source may have been L. Coelius Antipater.

^c A *suasoria* referring to the aftermath of Cannae in 216
B.C., as described in Livy 22. 60 ff. Some wished to ransom

158

choice between two courses of action: Does it seem better to destroy Carthage, or to leave her standing? [a] An example of a choice among several: If Hannibal, when recalled to Carthage from Italy, should deliberate whether to remain in Italy, or return home, or invade Egypt and seize Alexandria.[b]

Again, a question under deliberation is sometimes to be examined on its own account; for example, if the Senate should deliberate whether or not to redeem the captives from the enemy.[c] Or sometimes a question becomes one for deliberation and inquiry on account of some motive extraneous to the question itself; for example, if the Senate should deliberate whether to exempt Scipio from the law so as to permit him to become consul while under age.[d] And sometimes a question comes under deliberation on its own account and then provokes debate even more because of an extraneous motive; for example, if in the Italic War the Senate should deliberate

the prisoners at public cost; others opposed the disbursement of money by the state, but not ransoming at the expense of individuals, and would have granted, on surety, loans from the treasury to those who needed money. T. Manlius Torquatus spoke against the proposal, which failed. This *suasoria* was popular with the rhetoricians; *cf.* Cicero, *De Oratore* 3. 28. 109, *De Offic.* 1. 13. 40 and 3. 32. 113.

[d] Although Scipio Aemilianus was in fact seeking the aedileship, and not the consulship, for 147 B.C., he was exempted from the law requiring a candidate for the consulship to have been praetor (and at least two years previously); at 36 (or 37) he was also well under the age required (in Cicero's day 43 years) for holding the consulship. He was elected consul in order to deal with Carthage.

Our author's consistent rule is to refer to the younger Scipio simply as *Scipio* (see also 4. v. 7, 4. xiii. 19, and 4. xxxii. 43 below) and to the elder as *Africanus* (see 4. xv. 22, 4. xxv. 34, and 4. xxxi. 42).

det an non. In quibus causis rei natura faciet deliberationem omnis oratio ad ipsam rem adcommodabitur; in quibus extranea causa conficiet deliberationem, in his ea ipsa causa erit adaugenda aut deprimenda.

3 Omnem orationem eorum qui sententiam dicent finem sibi conveniet utilitatis proponere, ut omnis eorum ad eam totius orationis ratio conferatur.

Utilitas in duas partes in civili consultatione dividitur: tutam, honestam.

Tuta est quae conficit instantis aut consequentis periculi vitationem qualibet ratione. Haec tribuitur in vim et dolum, quorum aut alterum separatim aut utrumque sumemus coniuncte. Vis decernitur per exercitus, classes, arma, tormenta, evocationes hominum, et alias huiusmodi res. Dolus consumitur in pecunia, pollicitatione, dissimulatione, maturatione, mentitione, et ceteris rebus de quibus magis

---

^a When examined on its own account, this question might, for example, be considered as involving a radical change in Roman institutions; a motive " extraneous " to the question itself might be the effect of the measure upon other allies now threatening defection. In 90 B.C., L. Julius Caesar put through his law offering full Roman citizenship to all corporate communities in Italy that had not revolted; in the next year the *lex Plautia-Papiria* was passed, granting citizenship to any individual who (a) belonged to a city of Italy allied with Rome, and (b) resided permanently in Italy, and (c) applied for citizenship within sixty days.

^b τὸ συμφέρον (and Injury, τὸ βλαβερόν) in Aristotle, *Rhet.* 1. 3 (1358 b). *Cf.* Cicero, *De Oratore* 2. 82. 334 : " Thus in an advisory speech there is nothing more desirable than Worth (*dignitas*) . . . but Advantage generally gains the upper hand."

whether or not to grant citizenship to the Allies.[a] In causes in which the subject of itself engenders the deliberation, the entire discourse will be devoted to the subject itself. In those in which an extraneous motive gives rise to the deliberation, it is this motive which will have to be emphasized or depreciated.

3 The orator who gives counsel will throughout his speech properly set up Advantage [b] as his aim,[c] so that the complete economy of his entire speech may be directed to it.

Advantage in political deliberation has two aspects: Security [d] and Honour.[e]

To consider Security is to provide some plan or other for ensuring the avoidance of a present or imminent danger. Subheads under Security are Might and Craft, which we shall consider either separately or conjointly. Might is determined by armies, fleets, arms, engines of war, recruiting of man power, and the like. Craft is exercised by means of money, promises, dissimulation, accelerated speed, deception, and the other means, topics which

---

[e] τέλος. In Aristotle, *Rhet.* 1. 6 (1362 a), σκοπός. The topics drawn from the " ends " of the three different branches of oratory were later called τελικὰ κεφάλαια. Volkmann, pp. 299 ff., discusses the treatment of these by different rhetoricians. *Cf.* Cicero, *De Inv.* 2. li. 156 ff.

[d] τὸ χρήσιμον, ἀναγκαῖον, ἀκίνδυνον.

[e] τὸ καλόν. Aristotle, *Rhet.* 1. 3 (1358 b), makes Honour (and Justice) subsidiary to Advantage, but Cicero in *De Inv.* 2. li. 156 sets forth Honour and Advantage as coördinate aims, and Antonius in *De Oratore* 2. 82. 335 considers the situation in which Advantage and Honour oppose each other. The Stoics believed a conflict between Honour and Advantage to be impossible; see Cicero, *De Offic.* 3. 2. 9 ff. Perhaps because of Stoic influence, Cicero makes Advantage the sole aim in *Part. Orat.* 24. 83.

idoneo tempore loquemur si quando de re militari aut
de administratione rei publicae scribere velimus.

Honesta res dividitur in rectum et laudabile.
Rectum est quod cum virtute et officio fit.   Id dividitur in prudentiam, iustitiam, fortitudinem, modestiam.   Prudentia est calliditas quae ratione quadam
potest dilectum habere bonorum et malorum.   Dicitur item prudentia scientia cuiusdam artificii; item
appellatur prudentia rerum multarum memoria et
usus conplurium negotiorum.   Iustitia est aequitas
ius uni cuique rei tribuens pro dignitate cuiusque.
Fortitudo est rerum magnarum appetitio et rerum
humilium contemptio et laboris cum utilitatis ratione
perpessio.   Modestia est in animo continens moderatio cupiditatem.

4   III. Prudentiae partibus utemur in dicendo si
commoda cum incommodis conferemus, cum alterum
sequi, vitare alterum cohortemur; aut si qua in re

---

^a Whether our author ever wrote on these subjects we do
not know.   See notes on 3. xvi. 28 and 4. xii. 17 below.

^b ὀρθόν and ἐπαινετόν (Aristotle, *Eth. Nic.* 2. 7. 11, 1108 a).

^c To be distinguished from *ius* (2. xiii. 19).

^d σοφία (and φρόνησις—the definition shows that *prudentia*
partakes of the nature of both), δικαιοσύνη, ἀνδρεία, σωφροσύνη.
Here rhetoric draws upon philosophy for a catalogue of the
virtues; see Plato, *Republic* 4. 428 ff.   After Plato's example,
the Stoics treated these as the primary virtues; see *e.g.*, the
Epitome of Didymus in Stobaeus, 2. 7. 5 b 2 (ed. Wachsmuth,
2. 60), and Diogenes Laertius 7. 92.   *Cf.* also Hippolytus,
Ref. Omn. Haer. 1. 20.   Aristotle, *Rhet.* 1. 9 (1366 b), lists
Prudence as well as Wisdom among the elements of Virtue,
and   adds   Magnificence,   Magnanimity,   Liberality,   and
Gentleness.   See note on 3. vi. 10 below, and Kroll, *Philologus* 90 (1935). 206 ff.

^e *Cf.* 3. iii. 4 below; Cicero, *De Inv.* 2. liii. 160, *De Nat.
Deor.* 3. 15. 38, *De Offic.* 1. 5. 15, *De Leg.* 1. 6. 19; Ulpian in

I shall discuss at a more appropriate time, if ever I attempt to write on the art of war or on state administration.[a]

The Honourable is divided into the Right and the Praiseworthy.[b] The Right [c] is that which is done in accord with Virtue and Duty. Subheads under the Right are Wisdom, Justice, Courage, and Temperance.[d] Wisdom is intelligence capable, by a certain judicious method, of distinguishing good and bad; likewise the knowledge of an art is called Wisdom; and again, a well-furnished memory, or experience in diverse matters, is termed Wisdom. Justice is equity, giving to each thing what it is entitled to in proportion to its worth.[e] Courage is the reaching for great things and contempt for what is mean; also the endurance of hardship in expectation of profit.[f] Temperance is self-control that moderates our desires.[g]

4   III. We shall be using the topics of Wisdom in our discourse if we compare advantages and disadvantages, counselling the pursuit of the one and the avoidance of the other; if we urge a course in a field in which we

Justinian, *Dig.* 1. 1. 10. On this concept (which was Greek in origin; cf., *e.g.*, Aristotle, *Top.* 6. 5 [143 a 16], 6. 7 [145 b 36], *Eth. Nic.* 5. 9 [1133 b], *Rhet.* 1. 9 [1366 b 9], and the Stoic definition in Stobaeus, *loc. cit.*) see Leopold Wenger, " Suum Cuique in antiken Urkunden," in *Aus der Geisteswelt des Mittelalters* (Grabmann Festschrift), Münster, 1935, 1. 1415–25, and Felix Senn, *De la justice et du droit*, Paris, 1927, pp. 1–54.

[f] *Cf.* 3. iii. 6 and 4. xxv. 35 below, and the definition in Cicero, *De Inv.* 2. liv. 163.

[g] *Cf.* Plutarch, *De virt. mor.* 2 (441 A) : " Virtue, when it moderates our desires (ἐπιθυμίαν κοσμοῦσα) and defines the mean and the seasonable in our pleasures, is called Temperance."

cohortemur aliquid cuius rei aliquam disciplinam poterimus habere quo modo aut qua quidque ratione fieri
oporteat; aut si suadebimus quippiam cuius rei gestae
aut praesentem aut auditam memoriam poterimus
habere—qua in re facile id quod velimus exemplo
allato persuadere possumus.

Iustitiae partibus utemur si aut innocentium aut
supplicium misereri dicemus oportere; si ostendemus
bene merentibus gratiam referre convenire; si
demonstrabimus ulcisci male meritos oportere; si
fidem magnopere censebimus conservandam; si leges
et mores civitatis egregie dicemus oportere servari; si
societates atque amicitias studiose dicemus coli
convenire; si quod ius in parentes, deos, patriam
natura conparavit, id religiose colendum demonstrabimus; si hospitia, clientelas, cognationes, adfinitates
caste colenda esse dicemus; si nec pretio nec gratia
nec periculo nec simultate a via recta ostendemus
deduci oportere; si dicemus in omnibus aequabile
ius statui convenire. His atque huiusmodi partibus
iustitiae si quam rem in contione aut in consilio
faciendam censebimus iustam esse ostendemus,
contrariis iniustam. Ita fiet ut isdem locis et ad
suadendum et ad dissuadendum simus conparati.

5   Sin fortitudinis retinendae causa faciendum quid [1]
esse dicemus, ostendemus res magnas et celsas sequi

---

[1] quid *d* : *other MSS. Mx omit.*

[a] ἤθη καὶ νόμοι, ἔθη καὶ νόμιμα.   *Cf.* 1. ii. 2 and 2. xii. 19
above.

have a technical knowledge of the ways and means whereby each detail should be carried out; or if we recommend some policy in a matter whose history we can recall either from direct experience or hearsay—in this instance we can easily persuade our hearers to the course we wish by adducing the precedent.

We shall be using the topics of Justice if we say that we ought to pity innocent persons and suppliants; if we show that it is proper to repay the well-deserving with gratitude; if we explain that we ought to punish the guilty; if we urge that faith ought zealously to be kept; if we say that the laws and customs*a* of the state ought especially to be preserved; if we contend that alliances and friendships should scrupulously be honoured; if we make it clear that the duty imposed by nature toward parents, gods, and fatherland must be religiously observed; if we maintain that ties of hospitality, clientage, kinship, and relationship by marriage must inviolably be cherished; if we show that neither reward nor favour nor peril nor animosity ought to lead us astray from the right path; if we say that in all cases a principle of dealing alike with all should be established. With these and like topics of Justice we shall demonstrate that an action of which we are sponsors in Assembly or council is just, and by their contraries we shall demonstrate that an action is unjust. As a result we shall be provided with the same commonplaces for both persuasion and dissuasion.

5 When we invoke as motive for a course of action steadfastness in Courage, we shall make it clear that men ought to follow and strive after noble and lofty

et appeti oportere; et item res humiles et indignas viris fortibus viros[1] fortes propterea contemnere oportere nec idoneas dignitate sua iudicare. Item ab nulla re honesta periculi aut laboris magnitudine deduci oportere; antiquiorem mortem turpitudine haberi; nullo dolore cogi ut ab officio recedatur; nullius pro rei veritate metuere inimicitias; quodlibet pro patria, parentibus, hospitibus, amicis, iis rebus quas iustitia colere cogit, adire periculum et quemlibet suscipere laborem.

Modestiae partibus utemur si nimias libidines honoris, pecuniae, similium rerum vituperabimus; si unam quamque rem certo naturae termino definiemus; si quoad cuique satis sit ostendemus, nimium progredi dissuadebimus, modum uni cuique rei statuemus.

6 Huiusmodi partes sunt virtutis amplificandae is suadebimus, adtenuandae[2] si ab his dehortabimur, ut haec adtenuentur quae supra demonstravi. Nam nemo erit qui censeat a virtute recedendum; verum aut res non eiusmodi dicatur esse ut virtutem possimus egregiam experiri, aut in contrariis potius rebus quam in his virtus constare quae ostendantur. Item, si quo pacto poterimus, quam is qui contra dicet iustitiam vocabit, nos demonstrabimus ignaviam esse et inertiam ac pravam liberalitatem; quam prudentiam appellarit, ineptam et garrulam et odiosam scientiam esse dicemus; quam ille modestiam dicet esse, eam nos inertiam et dissolutam neglegentiam esse dicemus; quam ille fortitudinem

---

[1] viros *E* : vel viros *M* : *lac. followed by* vel viros *Mx.*

[2] adtenuandae *E* : omnibus verbis adtenuandae *M Mx.*

actions, and that, by the same token, actions base
and unworthy of the brave ought therefore to be
despised by brave men and considered as beneath
their dignity. Again, from an honourable act no
peril or toil, however great, should divert us;
death ought to be preferred to disgrace; no pain
should force an abandonment of duty; no man's
enmity should be feared in defence of truth; for
country, for parents, guest-friends, intimates, and
for the things justice commands us to respect, it
behoves us to brave any peril and endure any
toil.

We shall be using the topics of Temperance if we
censure the inordinate desire for office, money, or the
like; if we restrict each thing to its definite natural
bounds; if we show how much is enough in each case,
advise against going too far, and set the due limit to
every matter.

6   Virtues of this kind are to be enlarged upon if we
are recommending them, but depreciated if we are
urging that they be disregarded, so that the points
which I have made above [a] will be belittled. To be
sure, no one will propose the abandonment of virtue,
but let the speaker say that the affair is not of such
a sort that we can put any extraordinary virtue to the
test; or that the virtue consists rather of qualities
contrary to those here evinced. Again, if it is at all
possible, we shall show that what our opponent calls
justice is cowardice, and sloth, and perverse generosity; what he has called wisdom we shall term
impertinent, babbling, and offensive cleverness; what
he declares to be temperance we shall declare to be
inaction and lax indifference; what he has named

[a] 3. iii. 4–5.

nominarit, eam nos gladiatoriam et inconsideratam appellabimus temeritatem.

7 IV. Laudabile est quod conficit honestam et praesentem et consequentem commemorationem. Hoc nos eo separavimus a recto non quod hae quattuor partes quae subiciuntur sub vocabulum recti hanc honestatis commemorationem dare non soleant, sed quamquam ex recto laudabile nascitur, tamen in dicendo seorsum tractandum est hoc ab illo. Neque enim solum laudis causa rectum sequi convenit, sed si laus consequitur, duplicatur recti appetendi voluntas. Cum igitur erit demonstratum rectum esse, laudabile esse demonstrabimus aut ab idoneis hominibus—ut si qua res honestiori ordini placeat quae a deteriore ordine inprobetur—aut quibus sociis aut omnibus civibus, exteris nationibus, posterisque nostris.

Cum huiusmodi divisio sit locorum in consultatione, breviter aperienda erit totius tractatio causae.

Exordiri licebit vel a principio vel ab insinuatione vel isdem rationibus quibus in iudiciali causa. Si cuius rei narratio incidet, eadem ratione narrari oportebit.

8 Quoniam in huiusmodi causis finis est utilitas et ea dividitur in rationem tutam atque honestam, si utrumque poterimus ostendere, utrumque pollice-

---

ᵃ Thucydides, 3. 82, describing the moral effects of the revolutions in the Hellenic world during the fifth year of the Peloponnesian war (427–6 B.C.), tells how men changed as they thought fit the accepted value of words in their relation to things : " For reckless audacity came to be regarded as the courage of self-sacrifice for party, cautious delay as fair-seeming cowardice, moderation as a screen for unmanliness,

courage we shall term the reckless temerity of a gladiator.[a]

7   IV. The Praiseworthy is what produces an honourable remembrance, at the time of the event and afterwards. I have separated the Praiseworthy from the Right, not because the four categories which I list under the appellative Right usually fail to engender this honourable remembrance, but because, although the praiseworthy has its source in the right, we must nevertheless in speaking treat one apart from the other. Indeed we should pursue the right not alone for the sake of praise; but if praise accrues, the desire to strive after the right is doubled. When, therefore, a thing is shown to be right, we shall show that it is also praiseworthy, whether in the opinion of qualified persons (if, for example, something should please a more honourable class of men, and be disapproved by a lower class), or of certain allies, or all our fellow citizens, or foreign nations, or our descendants.

Such being the division of topics in deliberative speaking, I must briefly explain how to develop the cause as a whole.

The Introduction may be made by means of the Direct Opening or of the Subtle Approach, or by the same means as in a judicial cause. If there happens to be a Statement of Facts, the same method will properly be followed in the narrative.

8   Since in causes of this kind the end is Advantage, and Advantage is divided into the consideration of Security and the consideration of Honour, if we can prove that both ends will be served, we shall promise

and sagacity in all things as general fecklessness;" see also Cato in Sallust, *Cat.* 52. 11. Our author here uses the figure *distinctio* (παραδιαστολή); see note on 4. xxv. 35 below.

bimur nos in dicendo demonstraturos esse ; si alterum
erimus demonstraturi, simpliciter quid dicturi sumus
ostendemus. At si nostram rationem tutam esse
dicemus, divisione utemur in vim et consilium. Nam
quod in docendo rei dilucide [1] magnificandae causa
dolum appellavimus, id in dicendo honestius consilium appellabimus. Si rationem nostrae sententiae
rectam esse dicemus, et omnes partes recti incident,
quadripertita divisione utemur ; si non incident, quot
erunt, tot exponemus in dicendo.

Confirmatione et confutatione utemur nostris locis
quos ante ostendimus confirmandis, contrariis con-
futandis. Argumentationis artificiose tractandae
ratio de secundo libro petetur. V. Sed si acciderit
ut in consultatione alteri ab tuta ratione, alteri ab
honesta sententia sit, ut in deliberatione eorum qui a
Poeno circumsessi deliberant quid agant, qui tutam
rationem sequi suadebit his locis utetur : Nullam rem
utiliorem esse incolumitate ; virtutibus uti neminem
posse qui suas rationes in tuto non conlocarit ; ne
deos quidem esse auxilio iis qui se inconsulto in
periculum mittant ; honestum nihil oportere existi-
9 mari quod non salutem pariat. Qui tutae rei prae-
ponet rationem honestam his locis utetur : Virtutem
nullo tempore relinquendam ; vel dolorem, si is
timeatur, vel mortem, si ea formidetur, dedecore et

---

[1] dilucide *b* : dilucidae *most other MSS. Mx* : dilucidandae *d*.

[a] 2. xviii. 28 ff.

to make this twofold proof in our discourse; if we are
going to prove that one of the two will be served, we
shall indicate simply the one thing we intend to
affirm. If, now, we say that our aim is Security, we
shall use its subdivisions, Might and Strategy. For
that which, in instructing, I have, in order to give
clarity and emphasis called Craft, we shall in speaking call by the more honourable name of Strategy.
If we say that our counsel aims at the Right, and all
four categories of Right apply, we shall use them all.
If these categories do not all apply, we shall in
speaking set forth as many as do.

We shall use Proof and Refutation when we
establish in our favour the topics explained above,
and refute the contrary topics. The rules for developing an argument artistically will be found in
Book II.[a] V. But if it happens that in a deliberation
the counsel of one side is based on the consideration
of security and that of the other on honour, as in the
case of those who, surrounded by Carthaginians,
deliberate on a course of action,[b] then the speaker
who advocates security will use the following topics:
Nothing is more useful than safety; no one can make
use of his virtues if he has not based his plans upon
safety; not even the gods help those who thought-
lessly commit themselves to danger; nothing ought
to be deemed honourable which does not produce
9 safety. One who prefers the considerations of
honour to security will use the following topics:
Virtue ought never to be renounced; either pain,
if that is feared, or death, if that is dreaded, is more

[b] A *suasoria* used also by Cicero, in *De Inv.* 2. lvii. 171,
concerning the inhabitants of Casilinum in Campania, after
the heroic defence of 216 B.C. against Hannibal.

infamia leviorem esse ; considerare quae sit turpitudo consecutura—at non immortalitatem neque aeternam incolumitatem consequi, nec esse exploratum illo vitato periculo nullum in aliud periculum venturum ; virtuti vel ultra mortem proficisci esse praeclarum ; fortitudini fortunam quoque esse adiumento solere ; eum tute vivere qui honeste vivat, non qui in praesentia incolumis, et eum qui turpiter vivat incolumem in perpetuum esse non posse.

Conclusionibus fere similibus in his et in iudicialibus causis uti solemus, nisi quod his maxime conducit quam plurima rerum ante gestarum exempla proferre.

10 VI. Nunc ad demonstrativum genus causae transeamus. Quoniam haec causa dividitur in laudem et vituperationem, quibus ex rebus laudem constituerimus, ex contrariis rebus erit vituperatio

---

a The proverb was extremely common in Greek and Latin literature; see Otto, *s.v.* " fortuna " 9, p. 144.

b *Cf.* Cicero, *De Inv.* 2. lix. 177–8. The epideictic kind, like the deliberative (3. ii. 2–v. 9 above), receives only a sketchy treatment from our author—evidence of the dominant position which the judicial kind, with its *status* system, held in Hellenistic rhetoric. Despite the Epicurean notion that only epideictic was amenable to rules, the judicial kind was in fact the easiest to systematize, even as it was by far the most often employed in Hellenistic times. The Greek term " epideictic " did not primarily emphasize the speaker's virtuosity, nor was the Latin equivalent *demonstrativum* intended to imply logical demonstration. Whereas in both

tolerable than disgrace and infamy; one must consider the shame which will ensue—indeed neither immortality nor a life everlasting is achieved, nor is it proved that, once this peril is avoided, another will not be encountered; virtue finds it noble to go even beyond death; fortune, too, habitually favours the brave;[a] not he who is safe in the present, but he who lives honourably, lives safely—whereas he who lives shamefully cannot be secure for ever.

As a general rule we employ virtually the same Conclusions in these as in judicial causes, except that here especially it is useful to present examples from the past in the greatest possible number.

VI. Let us now turn to the Epideictic kind of cause.[b] Since epideictic includes Praise and Censure, the topics on which praise is founded will, by their contraries, serve us as the bases for censure. The following, then, can be subject to praise: External

deliberative and judicial causes the speaker seeks to persuade his hearers to a course of action, in epideictic his primary purpose is by means of his art to impress his ideas upon them, without action as a goal. On the scope and purpose of epideictic, and on the discrepancies between our author's treatment and that of Aristotle (*Rhet.* 1. 3, 1358 b), see D. A. G. Hinks, *Class. Quart.* 30 (1936). 170–6; *cf.* also Quintilian, 3. 4. 1 ff., and Volkmann, pp. 19 ff. In the Stoic scheme " encomiastic " was used instead of " epideictic "; see Diogenes Laertius 7. 42. This term, for which *laudativum* (see Cicero, *Part. Orat.* 3. 10, and Quintilian, 3. 3. 14, 3. 4. 12) would be the Latin equivalent, actually corresponds more closely to our author's definition of the *genus* than does *demonstrativum*. Doxapatres (Rabe, *Proleg. Syll.*, pp. 149 ff.) argues for the primacy of the deliberative kind, setting the judicial in the second place, and the epideictic (panegyric) last; *cf.* Isocrates, *Paneg.* 4, *Antid.* 46 ff., *Panath.* 271. See also Stanley Wilcox, *Harvard Studies in Class. Philol.* 53 (1942). 121–155.

conparata. Laus igitur potest esse rerum externarum, corporis, animi.

Rerum externarum sunt ea quae casu aut fortuna secunda aut adversa accidere possunt: genus, educatio, divitiae, potestates, gloriae, civitas, amicitiae, et quae huiusmodi sunt et quae his contraria. Corporis sunt ea quae natura corpori adtribuit commoda aut incommoda: velocitas, vires, dignitas, valetudo, et quae contraria sunt. Animi sunt ea quae consilio et cogitatione nostra constant: prudentia, iustitia, fortitudo, modestia, et quae contraria sunt. 11 Erit igitur haec confirmatio et confutatio nobis in huiusmodi causa.

Principium sumitur aut ab nostra, aut ab eius de quo loquemur, aut ab eorum qui audient persona, aut ab re.

---

a The classification is Platonic and Aristotelian; see, *e.g.*, Plato, *Gorgias* 477 C, *Euthyd.* 279, *Philebus* 48 E, *Laws* 697 B, 727 A ff., *Epist.* 8. 355 B (*cf.* also *Phaedrus* 241 C); Aristotle, *Eth. Nic.* 1. 8, 1098 b ("an ancient classification and one accepted by philosophers"), *Magna Moral.* 1. 3 (1184 b), *Protrepticus* (see *Oxyrh. Pap.* 4. 82 ff.). It also appears early in rhetorical theory; see *Rhet. ad Alex.* 1 (1422 a). *Cf.* also Areius Didymus in Stobaeus, 2. 7. 14; Diogenes Laertius 5. 30 ff.; Clemens Alex., *Paedagogus* 2. 10. 102; Hippolytus, *Ref. Omn. Haer.* 1. 20; Sextus Empiricus, *Adv. Ethic.* 3. 45; Aelius Aristides 45. 17; Cicero, *De Fin.* 3. 14. 43, *De Inv.* 1. liii. 101 and 2. lix. 177, *De Oratore* 3. 29. 115, *Part. Orat.* 11. 38, *Top.* 23. 89; Apsines, *Ars Rhet.*, in Spengel-Hammer 1 (2). 312. 7 ff.; and see Claus Peters, pp. 71–83.

b τὰ ἐκτὸς ἀγαθά, τὰ ἐπίκτητα.

c εὐγένεια.

d παιδεία.

e πλοῦτος, χρήματα, κτήματα.

f δυνάμεις, δυναστεία.

Circumstances, Physical Attributes, and Qualities of Character.[a]

To External Circumstances [b] belong such as can happen by chance, or by fortune, favourable or adverse: descent,[c] education,[d] wealth,[e] kinds of power,[f] titles to fame,[g] citizenship,[h] friendships,[i] and the like, and their contraries. Physical Attributes [j] are merits or defects bestowed upon the body by nature: agility,[k] strength,[l] beauty,[m] health,[n] and their contraries. Qualities of Character [o] rest upon our judgement and thought: wisdom, justice,

11 courage, temperance, and their contraries. Such, then, in a cause of this kind, will be our Proof and Refutation.

The Introduction [p] is drawn from our own person, or the person we are discussing, or the person of our hearers, or from the subject-matter itself.

---

[g] εὐδοξία, τιμή.

[h] πατρίς, πόλις, ἔθνος, πολιτεία.

[i] φίλοι. Cf. Eutychus in Plautus, Mercator 845–6: " What I kept seeking was at home. There I found six companions : life, friendship, native land, gladness, fun, and sport."

[j] σῶμα.

[k] ποδώκεια.

[l] ἰσχύς, ῥώμη.

[m] κάλλος.

[n] ὑγίεια, εὐεξία.

[o] ἀρεταὶ ψυχῆς—properly, Virtues of the Soul. See note on 3. ii. 3 above. Our author and Cicero in De Inv. differ from the Rhet. ad Alex., Aristotle, and Theon in including only the " primary " virtues; see Georg Reichel, Quaestiones Progymnasm., diss. Leipzig, 1909, pp. 90 ff.

[p] The tractatio is based upon the parts of the discourse, and thus follows the pre-Aristotelian rhetorical theory.

Note that unlike judicial (see 1. iv. 6) and deliberative (3. iv. 7) oratory, epideictic lacks the Subtle Approach (insinuatio).

[CICERO]

Ab nostra, si laudabimus: aut officio facere, quod causa necessitudinis intercedat; aut studio, quod eiusmodi virtute sit ut omnes commemorare debeant velle; aut quod rectum sit [1] ex aliorum laude ostendere qualis ipsius animus sit. Si vituperabimus: aut merito facere, quod ita tractati simus; [2] aut studio, quod utile putemus esse ab omnibus unicam malitiam atque nequitiam cognosci; aut quod placeat ostendi quod nobis placeat ex aliorum vituperatione.

Ab eius persona de quo loquemur, si laudabimus: vereri nos ut illius facta verbis consequi possimus; omnes homines illius virtutes praedicare oportere; ipsa facta omnium laudatorum eloquentiam anteire. Si vituperabimus, ea quae videmus contrarie paucis verbis commutatis dici posse dicemus, ut paulo supra exempli causa demonstratum est.

12   Ab auditorum persona, si laudabimus: quoniam non apud ignotos laudemus, nos monendi causa pauca dicturos; aut si erunt ignoti, ut talem virum velint cognoscere petemus; quoniam in eodem virtutis studio sint apud quos laudemus atque ille qui laudatur fuerit aut sit, sperare nos facile iis quibus velimus huius facta probaturos. Contraria vituperatio:

---

[1] aut quod rectum sit *Aldus* : quod rectum sit aut *MSS. Mx.*

[2] simus *E* : sumus *other MSS. Mx.*

---

[a] Or perhaps : " from one's praise of others what one's own character is."

[b] *Cf.* Isocrates, *Paneg.* 13 : " For I notice that the other speakers in their Introductions mollify their audience and make excuses for what they are going to say . . . some saying that it is hard to find words to match the greatness of the deeds ", and *Panath.* 36; Demosthenes, *Phil.* 2. 11; and also 4. viii. 12 and 4. xxxix. 51 below.

From our own person: if we speak in praise, we shall say that we are doing so from a sense of duty, because ties of friendship exist; or from goodwill, because such is the virtue of the person under discussion that every one should wish to call it to mind; or because it is appropriate to show, from the praise accorded him by others, what his character is.[a] If we speak in censure, we shall say that we are justified in doing so, because of the treatment we have suffered; or that we are doing so from goodwill, because we think it useful that all men should be apprised of a wickedness and a worthlessness without parallel; or because it is pleasing to show by our censure of others what conduct is pleasing to ourselves.

When we draw our Introduction from the person being discussed: if we speak in praise, we shall say that we fear our inability to match his deeds with words;[b] all men ought to proclaim his virtues; his very deeds transcend the eloquence of all eulogists. If we speak in censure, we shall, as obviously we can by the change of a few words, and as I have demonstrated just above, express sentiments to the contrary effect.

12 When the Introduction is drawn from the person of the hearers: if we speak in praise, we shall say that since we are not delivering an encomium amongst people unacquainted with the man, we shall speak but briefly, to refresh their memories; or if they do not know him, we shall try to make them desire to know a man of such excellence; since the hearers of our eulogy have the same zeal for virtue as the subject of the eulogy had or now has, we hope easily to win the approval of his deeds from those whose approval we desire. The opposite, if it is censure: we shall say that since

177

quoniam norint, pauca de nequitia eius dicturos;
quod si ignorent, petemus uti gnoscant, uti malitiam
vitare possint; quoniam dissimiles sint qui audiant
atque ille qui vituperatur, sperare eos illius vitam
vehementer inprobaturos.

Ab rebus ipsis: incertos esse quid potissimum
laudemus; vereri ne, cum multa dixerimus, plura
praetereamus. et quae similes sententias habebunt;
quibus sententiis contraria sumuntur a vituperatione.

13   VII. Principio tractato aliqua harum quas ante
commemoravimus ratione, narratio non erit ulla quae
necessario consequatur; sed si qua inciderit, cum
aliquod factum eius de quo loquemur nobis narrandum
sit cum laude aut vituperatione, praeceptio narrandi
de primo libro repetetur.

Divisione hac utemur: exponemus quas res lauda-
turi sumus aut vituperaturi; deinde ut quaeque
quove tempore res erit gesta ordine dicemus, ut quid
quamque tute cauteque egerit intellegatur. Sed
exponere oportebit animi virtutes aut vitia; deinde
commoda aut incommoda corporis aut rerum externarum quomodo ab animo tractata sint [1] demonstrare.
Ordinem hunc adhibere in demonstranda vita
debemus:

---

[1] tractata sint $H^2P^2B\ C\ d$: tracta sint Π: tractata sunt b
Mx: sunt tractata l: tractata H.

our hearers know the man, we shall confine ourselves
to a few words on the subject of his worthlessness;
but if they do not, we shall try to make them know
him, in order that they may avoid his wickedness;
since our hearers are unlike the subject of our
censure, we express the hope that they will vigorously
disapprove his way of life.

When the Introduction is drawn from the subject-
matter itself: we shall say that we do not know what
to praise in particular; we fear that in discussing a
number of things we shall pass by even more; and
add whatever will carry like sentiments. The sentiments opposite to these are drawn upon, if we
censure.

13   VII. If the Introduction has been developed in
accordance with any of the methods just mentioned,
there will be no need for a Statement of Facts to
follow it; but if there is occasion for one, when we
must recount with either praise or censure some deed
of the person discussed, the instructions for Stating
the Facts will be found in Book I.[a]

The Division we shall make is the following: we
shall set forth the things we intend to praise or
censure; then recount the events, observing their
precise sequence and chronology, so that one may
understand what the person under discussion did and
with what prudence and caution. But it will first
be necessary to set forth his virtues or faults of
character, and then to explain how, such being his
character, he has used the advantages or disadvantages, physical or of external circumstances. The
following is the order we must keep when portraying
a life:

[a] 1. viii. 12–ix. 16.

[CICERO]

Ab externis rebus: genus—in laude: quibus maioribus natus sit; si bono genere, parem aut excelsiorem fuisse; si humili genere, ipsum in suis, non in maiorum virtutibus habuisse praesidium. In vituperatione: si bono genere, dedecori maioribus fuisse; si malo, tamen his ipsis detrimento fuisse. Educatio—in laude: bene et [1] honeste in bonis disciplinis per omnem pueritiam educatum.[2] In vituperatione: . . .

14   Deinde transire oportet ad corporis commoda: natura si sit dignitas atque forma, laudi fuisse eam, non quemadmodum ceteris detrimento atque dedecori; si vires atque velocitas egregia, honestis haec exercitationibus et industriis dicemus conparata; si valetudo perpetua, diligentia et temperantia cupiditatum. In vituperatione, si erunt haec corporis commoda, male [3] his usum dicemus quae casu et natura tamquam quilibet gladiator habuerit; si non erunt, praeter formam omnia ipsius culpa et intemperantia afuisse dicemus.

Deinde revertemur ad extraneas res, et in his animi virtutes aut vitia quae fuerint considerabimus; divitiae an paupertas fuerit, et quae potestates, quae gloriae, quae amicitiae, quae inimicitiae, et quid fortiter inimicitiis gerundis fecerit; cuius causa susceperit inimicitias; qua fide, benivolentia, officio

---

[1] bene et *E* : *M omits* : *lac. Mx.*
[2] per omnem puericiam educatum *E* : totius pueritiae fuerit *M Mx.*
[3] male *E* : de *M Mx.*

(1) External Circumstances: Descent—in praise: the ancestors of whom he is sprung; if he is of illustrious descent, he has been their peer or superior; if of humble descent, he has had his support, not in the virtues of his ancestors, but in his own. In censure: if he is of illustrious descent, he has been a disgrace to his forebears; if of low descent, he is none the less a dishonour even to these. Education—in praise: that he was well and honourably trained in worthy studies throughout his boyhood. In censure: . . .

14 (2) Next we must pass to the Physical Advantages: if by nature he has impressiveness and beauty, these have served him to his credit, and not, as in the case of others, to his detriment and shame; if he has exceptional strength and agility, we shall point out that these were acquired by worthy and diligent exercise; if he has continual good health, that was acquired by care and by control over his passions. In censure, if the subject has these physical advantages, we shall declare that he has abused what, like the meanest gladiator, he has had by chance and nature. If he lacks them, we shall say that to his own fault and want of self-control is his lack of every physical advantage, beauty apart, attributable.

(3) Then we shall return to External Circumstances and consider his virtues and defects of Character evinced with respect to these: Has he been rich or poor? What kinds of power has he wielded? What have been his titles to fame? What his friendships? Or what his private feuds, and what act of bravery has he performed in conducting these feuds? With what motive has he entered into feuds? With what loyalty, goodwill, and sense of duty has he

[CICERO]

gesserit amicitias; in divitiis qualis aut paupertate cuiusmodi fuerit; quemadmodum habuerit in potestatibus gerundis animum. Si interierit, cuiusmodi mors eius fuerit, cuiusmodi res mortem eius sit 15 consecuta. VIII. Ad omnes autem res in quibus animus hominis maxime consideratur illae quattuor animi virtutes erunt adcommodandae; ut, si laudemus, aliud iuste, aliud fortiter, aliud modeste, aliud [1] prudenter factum esse dicamus; si vituperabimus, aliud iniuste, aliud immodeste, aliud ignave, aliud stulte factum praedicemus.

Perspicuum est iam nimirum ex hac dispositione quemadmodum sit tractanda tripertita divisio laudis et vituperationis, si illud etiam adsumpserimus, non necesse esse nos omnes has partes in laudem aut in vituperationem transferre, propterea quod saepe ne incidunt quidem, saepe ita tenuiter incidunt ut non sint necessariae [2] dictu. Quapropter eas partes quae firmissimae videbuntur legere oportebit.

Conclusionibus brevibus utemur, enumeratione ad exitum causae; in ipsa causa crebras et breves amplificationes interponemus per locos communes.

Nec hoc genus causae eo quod raro accidit in vita neglegentius commendandum est; neque enim id quod potest accidere ut faciendum sit aliquando, non oportet velle quam adcommodatissime posse facere; et si separatim haec causa minus saepe tractatur, at in iudicialibus et in deliberativis causis saepe magnae partes versantur laudis aut vitu-

---

[1] aliud *E* : et aliud *M Mx.*
[2] necessariae *E* : necessaria *other MSS. Mx.*

---

[a] If a noble death, εὐθανασία.
[b] *I.e.*, the epideictic. As a *progymnasma* it is the type περὶ ἐγκωμίου καὶ ψόγου.

conducted his friendships? What character of man
has he been in wealth, or in poverty? What has been
his attitude in the exercise of his prerogatives? If
he is dead, what sort of death did he die,[a] and what
15 sort of consequences followed upon it? VIII. In
all circumstances, moreover, in which human character is chiefly studied, those four above-mentioned
virtues of character will have to be applied. Thus,
if we speak in praise, we shall say that one act was
just, another courageous, another temperate, and
another wise; if we speak in censure, we shall declare
that one was unjust, another intemperate, another
cowardly, and another stupid.

From this arrangement it is now no doubt clear
how we are to treat the three categories of praise and
censure—with the added proviso that we need not use
all three for praise or for censure, because often not
all of them even apply, and often, too, when they do,
the application is so slight that it is unnecessary to
refer to them. We shall therefore need to choose
those categories which seem to provide the greatest
force.

Our Conclusions will be brief, in the form of a
Summary at the end of the discourse; in the discourse itself we shall by means of commonplaces
frequently insert brief amplifications.

Nor should this kind of cause [b] be the less strongly
recommended just because it presents itself only
seldom in life. Indeed when a task may present
itself, be it only occasionally, the ability to perform it
as skilfully as possible must seem desirable. And if
epideictic is only seldom employed by itself independently, still in judicial and deliberative causes
extensive sections are often devoted to praise or

perationis. Quare in hoc quoque causae genere
nonnihil industriae consumendum putemus.

Nunc, absoluta a nobis difficillima parte rhetoricae,
hoc est inventione perpolita atque ad omne causae
genus [1] adcommodata, tempus est ad ceteras partes
proficisci. Deinceps igitur de dispositione dicemus.

16   IX. Quoniam dispositio est per quam illa quae
invenimus in ordinem redigimus ut certo quicquid
loco pronuntietur, videndum est cuiusmodi rationem
in disponendo habere conveniat. Genera disposi-
tionum sunt duo: unum ab institutione artis profectum, alterum ad casum temporis adcommodatum.

Ex institutione artis disponemus cum sequemur
eam praeceptionem quam in primo libro exposuimus,
hoc est ut utamur principio, narratione, divisione,
confirmatione, confutatione, conclusione, et ut hunc
ordinem quemadmodum praeceptum est ante in
dicendo sequamur. Item ex institutione artis non
modo totas causas per orationem, sed singulas quoque
argumentationes disponemus, quemadmodum in libro
secundo docuimus: in expositionem, rationem, confirmationem rationis, exornationem, conclusionem.

17 Haec igitur duplex dispositio est: una per orationes,

[1] atque ad omne causae genus $B^2C\,d$: atque omne causae
genus $P^1B\,\Pi\,Mx$: ad que omne causae genus H: adq(ue)
omne causae genus P^2: atque omne causae ad genus $b\,l$.

---

[a] In the Peripatetic order of the *officia oratoris* Style
followed Invention in second place, Arrangement being
third; *cf.* 1. ii. 3 above, and the note on 3. i. 1.

[b] τάξις, οἰκονομία. Corax and Tisias were the first to
set up a theory of Arrangement. Sulpitius Victor 14 (Halm,
p. 320) distinguishes between the Natural Arrangement
(*ordo naturalis*) and the Artistic (*ordo artificiosus*, οἰκονομία),
the former corresponding to our author's *ordo artificiosus*
(see 3. ix. 17 below), the *genus ab institutione artis profectum*, and

censure. Therefore let us believe that this kind of cause also must claim some measure of our industry.

Now that I have completed the most difficult part of rhetoric—thoroughly treating Invention and applying it to every kind of cause—it is time to proceed to the other parts. I shall therefore next [a] discuss the Arrangement.

16   IX. Since it is through the Arrangement [b] that we set in order the topics we have invented so that there may be a definite place for each in the delivery, we must see what kind of method one should follow in the process of arranging. The kinds of Arrangement are two: one arising from the principles of rhetoric, the other accommodated to particular circumstances.

Our Arrangement will be based on the principles of rhetoric when we observe the instructions that I have set forth in Book I [c]—to use the Introduction, Statement of Facts, Division, Proof, Refutation, and Conclusion, and in speaking to follow the order enjoined above. It is likewise on the principles of the art that we shall be basing our Arrangement, not only of the whole case throughout the discourse, but also of the individual arguments, according to Proposition, Reason, Proof of the Reason, Embellishment, and Résumé, as I have explained in Book II. [d]

17   This Arrangement, then, is twofold—one for the whole speech, and the other for the individual

the latter to our author's *genus ad casum temporis adcommodatum. Cf.* Quintilian's *oeconomica dispositio* in 7. 10. 11. Athanasius (probably fourth Christian century), in Rabe, *Proleg. Syll.*, p. 176, distinguishes τάξις from οἰκονομία on the same principle.

[c] 1. iii. 4.

[d] 2. xviii. 28. *Conclusio* is there called *complexio*.

altera per argumentationes, ab institutione artis profecta.

Est autem alia dispositio, quae, cum ab ordine artificioso recedendum est, oratoris iudicio ad tempus adcommodatur; ut si ab narratione dicere incipiamus aut ab aliqua firmissima argumentatione aut litterarum aliquarum recitatione; aut si secundum principium confirmatione utamur, deinde narratione; aut si quam eiusmodi permutationem ordinis faciemus; quorum nihil, nisi causa postulat, fieri oportebit. Nam si vehementer aures auditorum obtunsae videbuntur atque animi defatigati ab adversariis multitudine verborum, commode poterimus principio supersedere et [1] exordiri causam aut a narratione aut aliqua firma argumentatione. Deinde, si commodum erit, quod non semper necesse est, ad principii sententiam reverti licebit. X. Si causa nostra magnam difficultatem videbitur habere, ut nemo aequo animo principium possit audire, ab narratione cum inceperimus, ad principii sententiam revertemus. Si narratio parum probabilis, exordiemur ab aliqua firma argumentatione. His commutationibus et translationibus saepe uti necesse est cum ipsa res artificiosam dispositionem artificiose commutare cogit.

[1] et *BCE* : *H*PΠ *Mx omit.*

---

[a] On the principle of " anomaly " rather than " analogy."

arguments—and is based upon the principles of rhetoric.

But there is also another Arrangement, which, when we must depart from the order imposed by the rules of the art, is accommodated to circumstance in accordance with the speaker's judgement;[a] for example, if we should begin our speech with the Statement of Facts, or with some very strong argument, or the reading of some documents; or if straightway after the Introduction we should use the Proof and then the Statement of Facts; or if we should make some other change of this kind in the order. But none of these changes ought to be made except when our cause demands them. For if the ears of the audience seem to have been deafened and their attention wearied by the wordiness of our adversaries, we can advantageously omit the Introduction,[b] and begin the speech with either the Statement of Facts or some strong argument. Then, if it is advantageous—for it is not always necessary—one may recur to the idea intended for the Introduction. X. If our cause seems to present so great a difficulty that no one can listen to the Introduction with patience, we shall begin with the Statement of Facts and then recur to the idea intended for the Introduction. If the Statement of Facts is not quite plausible, we shall begin with some strong argument. It is often necessary to employ such changes and transpositions when the cause itself obliges us to modify with art the Arrangement prescribed by the rules of the art.

[b] But in 1. vi. 10 our author advises us in such circumstances to use the Subtle Approach, and to open with something that may provoke laughter.

[CICERO]

18   In confirmatione et confutatione argumentationum
dispositionem [1] huiusmodi convenit habere: firmissi-
mas argumentationes in primis et in postremis causae
partibus conlocare; mediocres, et neque inutiles
ad dicendum neque necessarias ad probandum, quae
si separatim ac singulae dicantur infirmae sint, cum
ceteris coniunctae firmae et probabiles fiunt, interponi oportet. Nam et statim re narrata expectat
animus auditoris si qua re causa confirmari possit—
quapropter continuo firmam aliquam oportet inferre
argumentationem; et reliqua, quoniam nuperrime
dictum facile memoriae mandatur, utile est, cum
dicere desinamus, recentem aliquam relinquere in
animis auditorum bene firmam argumentationem.
Haec dispositio locorum, tamquam instructio militum, facillime in dicendo, sicut illa in pugnando,
parere poterit victoriam.

19   XI. Pronuntiationem multi maxime utilem oratori
dixerunt esse et ad persuadendum plurimum valere.
Nos quidem unum de quinque rebus plurimum posse
non facile dixerimus; egregie [2] magnam esse utilitatem in pronuntiatione audacter confirmaverimus.

[1] dispositionem *BC*[2] : dispositiones *HE Mx* : disputationes
*PC*II.

[2] egregie *M* : nec egregie *other MSS. Mx*.

---

[a] Quintilian, 5. 12. 14, calls this the Homeric disposition,
from *Il.* 4. 297-9 : " And first he [Nestor] arrayed the horsemen with horses and chariots, and behind them the foot-
soldiers, many and valiant, to be a bulwark of battle. But
the weaklings he drove into the midst." *Cf.* also Longinus,
in Spengel-Hammer 1 (2). 185. 16 ff.

[b] *Cf.* 1. ii. 3 above.

[c] *Cf.* Quintilian, 11. 3. 2 : " But delivery itself has a
marvellously powerful effect in oratory; for the nature of the
material we have composed in our minds is not so important

18 In the Proof and Refutation of arguments it is appropriate to adopt an Arrangement of the following sort : (1) the strongest arguments should be placed at the beginning and at the end of the pleading ; (2) those of medium force, and also those that are neither useless to the discourse nor essential to the proof, which are weak if presented separately and individually, but become strong and plausible when conjoined with the others, should be placed in the middle.[a] For immediately after the facts have been stated the hearer waits to see whether the cause can by some means be proved, and that is why we ought straightway to present some strong argument. (3) And as for the rest, since what has been said last is easily committed to memory, it is useful, when ceasing to speak, to leave some very strong argument fresh in the hearer's mind. This arrangement of topics in speaking, like the arraying of soldiers in battle, can readily bring victory.

19 XI. Many have said that the faculty of greatest use to the speaker and the most valuable for persuasion is Delivery. For my part, I should not readily say that any one of the five faculties [b] is the most important ; that an exceptionally great usefulness resides in the delivery I should boldly affirm.[c] For

as how we deliver it ; " 11. 3. 7 : " Cicero also thinks action to be the dominant element in oratory ; " 11. 3. 5–6 : " For my part I would affirm that a mediocre speech supported by all the power of delivery will have more force than the best speech devoid of that power. That is why Demosthenes, asked what was primary in the whole task of oratory, gave the palm to delivery, and gave it second and third place as well. . . . So that we may assume that he thought it to be not merely the first, but the only virtue of oratory " (cf. also Philodemus, Rhet., ed. Sudhaus, 1. 196 ; Cicero, Brutus 37.

Nam commodae inventiones et concinnae verborum elocutiones et partium causae artificiosae dispositiones et horum omnium diligens memoria sine pronuntatione non plus quam sine his rebus pronuntiatio sola valere poterit. Quare, et quia nemo de ea re diligenter scripsit—nam omnes vix posse putarunt de voce et vultu et gestu dilucide scribi, cum eae res ad sensus nostros pertinerent—et quia magnopere ea pars a nobis ad dicendum conparanda est, non neglegenter videtur tota res consideranda.

Dividitur igitur pronuntiatio in vocis figuram et in corporis motum. Figura vocis est ea quae suum quendam possidet habitum ratione et industria 20 conparatum. Ea dividitur in tres partes: magnitudinem, firmitudinem, mollitudinem. Magnitudinem vocis maxime conparat natura; nonnihil auget, sed maxime conservat adcuratio.[1] Firmitudinem

---

[1] conservat accuratio *MS. used by Lambinus*: amplificat (amplificet *b*) accuratio (adcuratio *Mx*) *bl Mx*: curatur conservat *HP*: cura conservat *P²IIB²C²d*: conservat *BC*.

142, *Orator* 17. 56; Plutarch, *Vitae Dec. Orat.* 845 B; Longinus, in Spengel-Hammer 1 (2). 195; Theon 5, in Spengel 2. 104 f.). Our author is probably following Theophrastus; Athanasius (Rabe, *Proleg. Syll.*, p. 177) says that to Theophrastus " the most important thing for persuasion in rhetoric is delivery." *Cf.* Philodemus, *Rhet.*, ed. Sudhaus 1. 193 (I use Gomperz' restoration): " Of the six, or as some hold, seven parts of rhetoric, Athenaeus [second century B.C.] said that the most important is delivery; " Longinus, in Spengel-Hammer 1 (2). 194 : " Delivery is of greatest importance for proof." Thrasymachus maintained that delivery is given us by nature, not by art (Quintilian, 3. 3. 4).

ᵃ Diogenes Laertius, 5. 48, lists a work on delivery by Theophrastus. L. Plotius Gallus, friend of Marius, wrote about Gesture as practised in his day (Quintilian, 11. 3. 143); whether this work antedated our treatise we do not know. Theophrastus was probably the first to make Delivery a

skilful invention, elegant style, the artistic arrangement of the parts comprising the case, and the careful
memory of all these will be of no more value without
delivery, than delivery alone and independent of
these. Therefore, because no one has written carefully on this subject [a]—all have thought it scarcely
possible for voice, mien, and gesture to be lucidly
described, as appertaining to our sense-experience—
and because the mastery of delivery is a very
important requisite for speaking, the whole subject,
as I believe, deserves serious consideration.

Delivery, then, includes Voice Quality and Physical
Movement.[b] Voice Quality [c] has a certain character
20 of its own, acquired by method and application. It
has three aspects: Volume, Stability, and Flexibility.
Vocal volume is primarily the gift of nature; cultivation [d] augments it somewhat, but chiefly conserves it.

fourth *officium oratoris* (adding to it Invention, Style, and
Arrangement, Aristotle's scheme in the *Rhetoric*); Aristotle
(see *Rhet.* 3. 1, 1403 b) did not fully develop the theory of
delivery. The Stoics followed Theophrastus; for their
scheme see note on 1. ii. 3 above. See also Philodemus on
delivery, in H. M. Hubbell, *The Rhetorica of Philodemus*,
New Haven, 1920, pp. 300-1.

[b] The divisions are probably Theophrastan (ἡ κίνησις τοῦ
σώματος καὶ ὁ τόνος τῆς φωνῆς); 'see Athanasius, in Rabe,
Proleg. Syll., p. 177. *Cf.* Longinus, in Spengel-Hammer
1 (2). 194 : διάθεσις σώματός τε καὶ τόνου φωνῆς, and Dionysius
Halic., *De Demosth.* 53 : τὰ πάθη τὰ τῆς φωνῆς καὶ τὰ σχήματα
τοῦ σώματος.

[c] *Cf.* Cicero's study of Voice in *De Oratore* 3. 56. 213-
58. 219, 3. 60. 224-61. 227, and *Orator* 17. 55-18. 60; Quintilian's in 11. 3. 14-65.

[d] *Cura* comprised methods derived from rhetoric, music,
and acting, but was in part also dietetic and medical in
nature; see Armin Krumbacher, *Die Stimmbildung der Redner
im Altertum bis auf die Zeit Quintilians*, Paderborn, 1920,
esp. pp. 101-7.

vocis maxime conparat cura; nonnihil adauget, et
maxime conservat exercitatio declamationis.[1] Mollitudinem vocis, hoc est ut eam torquere in dicendo
nostro commodo possimus, maxime faciet exercitatio
declamationis. Quapropter de magnitudine vocis et
firmitudinis parte, quoniam altera natura paritur,
altera cura conparatur, nihil nos adtinet commonere
nisi ut ab iis qui non inscii sunt eius artificii ratio
curandae vocis petatur. XII. De ea parte firmitudinis quae conservatur ratione declamationis, et de
mollitudine vocis, quae maxime necessaria est oratori,
quoniam ea quoque moderatione declamationis conparatur, dicendum videtur.

21   Firmam ergo maxime poterimus in dicendo vocem
conservare si quam maxime sedata et depressa voce
principia dicemus. Nam laeditur arteria si antequam
voce leni permulsa est acri clamore completur. Et
intervallis longioribus uti convenit; recreatur enim
spiritu vox et arteriae reticendo adquiescunt. Et in
continuo clamore remittere et ad sermonem transire
oportet; commutationes enim faciunt ut nullo genere
vocis effuso in omni voce integri simus. Et acutas
vocis exclamationes vitare debemus; ictus enim fit
et vulnus arteriae acuta atque adtenuata nimis
adclamatione, et qui splendor est vocis consumitur
uno clamore universus. Et uno spiritu continenter
multa dicere in extrema convenit oratione; fauces

---

[1] declamationis P^2B^2E : imitationis M Mx.

---

[a] Note that these references to *declamatio*, the earliest in
extant Latin literature, appear in connection with delivery.
Declamatio = probably ἀναφώνησις. See S. F. Bonner,
Roman Declamation in the Late Republic and Early Empire,
Liverpool, 1949, p. 20, note 3.

[b] The *phonasci*, teachers of singing and declamation.

Stability is primarily gained by cultivation; declamatory exercise augments it somewhat, but chiefly conserves it. Vocal flexibility—the ability in speaking to vary the intonations of the voice at pleasure—is primarily achieved by declamatory exercise.[a] Thus with regard to vocal volume, and in a degree also to stability, since one is the gift of nature and the other is acquired by cultivation, it is pointless to give any other advice than that the method of cultivating the voice should be sought from those skilled in this art.[b] XII. It seems, however, that I must discuss stability in the degree that it is conserved by a system of declamation, and also vocal flexibility (this is especially necessary to the speaker), because it too is acquired by the discipline of declamation.

21   We can, then, in speaking conserve stability mainly by using for the Introduction a voice as calm and composed as possible. For the windpipe is injured if filled with a violent outburst of sound before it has been soothed by soft intonations. And it is appropriate to use rather long pauses—the voice is refreshed by respiration and the windpipe is rested by silence. We should also relax from continual use of the full voice and pass to the tone of conversation; for, as the result of changes, no one kind of tone is spent, and we are complete in the entire range. Again, we ought to avoid piercing exclamations, for a shock that wounds the windpipe is produced by shouting which is excessively sharp and shrill,[c] and the brilliance of the voice is altogether used up by one outburst. Again, at the end of the speech it is proper to deliver long periods in one unbroken

[c] The Rhodian school opposed the overloud delivery of the Asiatic orators.

enim calefiunt, et arteriae conplentur, et vox, quae tractata varie est, reducitur in quendam sonum aequabilem atque constantem. Quam saepe rerum naturae gratia quaedam iure debetur, velut accidit in hac re! Nam quae dicimus ad vocem servandam prodesse, eadem adtinent ad suavitudinem pronuntiationis, ut quod nostrae voci prosit idem voluntati 22 auditoris probetur. Utile est ad firmitudinem sedata vox in principio. Quid insuavius quam clamor in exordio causae? Intervalla vocem confirmant; eadem sententias concinniores divisione reddunt et auditori spatium cogitandi relinquunt. Conservat vocem continui clamoris remissio, et auditorem quidem varietas maxime delectat, cum sermone animum retinet aut exsuscitat clamore. Acuta exclamatio vocem vulnerat; eadem laedit auditorem, habet enim quiddam inliberale et ad muliebrem potius vociferationem quam ad virilem dignitatem in dicendo adcommodatum. In extrema oratione continens vox remedio est voci. Quid? haec eadem nonne animum vehementissime calefacit auditoris in totius conclusione causae? Quoniam igitur eadem vocis firmitudini et pronuntiationis suavitudini prosunt, de utraque re simul erit in praesentia dictum—de firmitudine quae visa sunt, de suavitudine quae coniuncta fuerunt; cetera suo loco paulo post dicemus.

---

[a] *Cf.* Dionysius Halic., *De Composit. Verb.*, ch. 23, on the smooth mode of composition : " It limits . . . the measure of the period so that a man's full breath will be able to encompass it; " Cicero, *Brutus* 8. 34.

[b] Our author repeats the thought of the first sentence of Sect. 21 immediately above.

[c] He proceeds at once to do so; see 3. xiii. 23–xiv. 25. The detailed rules that follow belong to a rhetoric later than that of Theophrastus, who apparently did not hand down many

breath,[a] for then the throat becomes warm, the windpipe is filled, and the voice, which has been used in a variety of tones, is restored to a kind of uniform and constant tone. How often must we be duly thankful to nature, as here! Indeed what we declare to be beneficial for conserving the voice applies also to agreeableness of delivery, and, as a result, what benefits our voice likewise finds favour in the hearer's taste. A useful thing for stability is a calm tone in the Introduction.[b] What is more disagreeable than the full voice in the Introduction to a discourse? Pauses strengthen the voice. They also render the thoughts more clear-cut by separating them, and leave the hearer time to think. Relaxation from a continuous full tone conserves the voice, and the variety gives extreme pleasure to the hearer too, since now the conversational tone holds the attention and now the full voice rouses it. Sharp exclamation injures the voice and likewise jars the hearer, for it has about it something ignoble, suited rather to feminine outcry than to manly dignity in speaking. At the end of the speech a sustained flow is beneficial to the voice. And does not this, too, most vigorously stir the hearer at the Conclusion of the entire discourse? Since, then, the same means serve the stability of the voice and agreeableness of delivery, my present discussion will have dealt with both at once, offering as it does the observations that have seemed appropriate on stability, and the related observations on agreeableness. The rest I shall set forth somewhat later, in its proper place.[c]

precepts of delivery. See Johannes Stroux, *De Theophrasti virtutibus dicendi*, Leipzig, 1912, p. 70; Maximilian Schmidt, *Commentatio de Theophrasto rhetore*, Halle, 1839, p. 61.

[CICERO]

23 XIII. Mollitudo igitur vocis, quoniam omnis ad
rhetoris praeceptionem pertinet, diligentius nobis
consideranda est. Eam dividimus in sermonem,
contentionem, amplificationem. Sermo est oratio
remissa et finitima cotidianae locutioni. Contentio est
oratio acris et ad confirmandum et ad confutandum
adcommodata. Amplificatio est oratio quae aut in
iracundiam inducit, aut ad misericordiam trahit
auditoris animum.

Sermo dividitur in partes quattuor: dignitatem,
demonstrationem, narrationem, iocationem. Dignitas
est oratio cum aliqua gravitate et vocis remissione.
Demonstratio est oratio quae docet remissa voce
quomodo quid fieri potuerit aut non potuerit. Narratio est rerum gestarum aut proinde ut gestarum
expositio. Iocatio est oratio quae ex aliqua re risum
pudentem et liberalem potest conparare.

Contentio dividitur in continuationem et in
distributionem. Continuatio est orationis enunti-
andae adceleratio clamosa. Distributio est in contentione oratio frequens cum raris et brevibus intervallis, acri vociferatione.

24 Amplificatio dividitur in cohortationem et conquestionem. Cohortatio est oratio quae aliquod

---

a ἀνειμένη.

b Contentio (ἐναγώνιος λόγος) represents the impassioned,
vehement address of formal debate, *sermo* the informal
language of ordinary conversation (Cicero, *De Offic.* 1. 37. 132 :
*sermo in circulis, disputationibus, congressionibus familiarium
versetur, sequatur etiam convivia*). Our author's treatment
seems to have a Peripatetic cast; see Aristotle, *Rhet.* 3. 12
(1413 b). *Cf.* Cicero, *l.c.* (in *De Offic.*, Bk. 1, he follows the
Stoic philosopher Panaetius) : " Rules for *contentio* we have
from the rhetoricians. There are none for *sermo*; yet I do
not know why there cannot be for *sermo*, too."

23   XIII. Now the flexibility of the voice, since it depends entirely on rhetorical rules, deserves our more careful consideration. The aspects of Flexibility are Conversational Tone, Tone of Debate, and Tone of Amplification. The Tone of Conversation is relaxed,[a] and is closest to daily speech. The Tone of Debate is energetic, and is suited to both proof and refutation.[b] The Tone of Amplification either rouses the hearer to wrath or moves him to pity.

Conversational tone comprises four kinds: the Dignified,[c] the Explicative, the Narrative, and the Facetious. The Dignified, or Serious, Tone of Conversation is marked by some degree of impressiveness and by vocal restraint. The Explicative in a calm voice explains how something could or could not have been brought to pass. The Narrative sets forth events that have occurred or might have occurred.[d] The Facetious can on the basis of some circumstance elicit a laugh which is modest and refined.[e]

In the Tone of Debate are distinguishable the Sustained and the Broken. The Sustained is full-voiced and accelerated delivery. The Broken Tone of Debate is punctuated repeatedly with short, intermittent pauses, and is vociferated sharply.

24   The Tone of Amplification includes the Hortatory and the Pathetic. The Hortatory, by amplifying

---

[c] Cf. the definition of *dignitas*, 4. xiii. 18 below.

[d] The same definition of *narratio* as in 1. iii. 4 above.

[e] The Facetious belongs naturally to *sermo*; see note on *contentio* above. The definition recalls the difference (*e.g.*, Aristotle, *Eth. Nic.* 4. 14, 1128) between the wit whose jests are in good taste (εὐτράπελος), and the buffoon (βωμολόχος).

peccatum amplificans auditorem ad iracundiam
adducit. Conquestio est oratio quae incommodorum
amplificatione animum auditoris ad misericordiam
perducit.

Quoniam igitur mollitudo vocis in tres partes
divisa est, et eae partes ipsae sunt in octo partes
alias distributae, harum octo partium quae cuiusque
idonea pronuntiatio sit demonstrandum videtur.

XIV. Sermo cum est in dignitate, plenis faucibus
quam sedatissima et depressissima voce uti conveniet,
ita tamen ut ne ab oratoria consuetudine ad tragicam
transeamus. Cum autem est in demonstratione,
voce paululum attenuata, crebris intervallis et
divisionibus oportet uti, ut in ipsa pronuntiatione
eas res quas demonstrabimus inserere atque insecare
videamur in animis auditorum. Cum autem est sermo
in narratione, vocum varietates opus sunt, ut quo
quidque pacto gestum sit ita narrare videamur.[1]
Strenue quod volumus ostendere factum, celeriuscule
dicemus; at aliud otiose, retardabimus. Deinde
modo acriter, tum clementer, maeste, hilare in
omnes partes commutabimus ut verba item pronuntiationem. Si qua inciderint in narrationem
dicta, rogata, responsa, si quae admirationes de
quibus nos narrabimus, diligenter animum adver-
temus ut omnium personarum sensus atque animos

---

[1] videamur *ld* : videatur *other MSS. Mx.*

---

[a] Amplification and Appeal to Pity are separated in 2. xxx.
47 and 2. xxxi. 50 above; *cf.* 4. viii. 11 (the Grand Style),
4. xxviii. 38 (Reduplication), 4. liii. 66 (Personification), and
also 4. xxxix. 51 (Vivid Description) below.

some fault, incites the hearer to indignation. The Pathetic, by amplifying misfortunes, wins the hearer over to pity.[a]

Since, then, vocal flexibility is divided into three tones, and these in turn subdivide into eight others, it appears that we must explain what delivery is appropriate to each of these eight subdivisions.

XIV. (1) For the Dignified Conversational Tone it will be proper to use the full throat but the calmest and most subdued voice possible, yet not in such a fashion that we pass from the practice of the orator to that of the tragedian.[b] (2) For the Explicative Conversational Tone one ought to use a rather thin-toned voice, and frequent pauses and intermissions, so that we seem by means of the delivery itself to implant and engrave in the hearer's mind the points we are making in our explanation. (3) For the Narrative Conversational Tone varied intonations are necessary, so that we seem to recount everything just as it took place. Our delivery will be somewhat rapid when we narrate what we wish to show was done vigorously, and it will be slower when we narrate something else done in leisurely fashion. Then, corresponding to the content of the words, we shall modify the delivery in all the kinds of tone, now to sharpness, now to kindness, or now to sadness, and now to gaiety. If in the Statement of Facts there occur any declarations, demands, replies, or exclamations of astonishment concerning the facts we are narrating, we shall give careful attention to expressing with the voice the

[b] On the speaker's delivery as against the actor's see 3. xv. 26 below; Cicero, *Orator* 25. 86; Quintilian, 11. 3. 57, 181 ff.

[CICERO]

25 voce exprimamus. Sin erit sermo in iocatione,
leviter tremebunda voce, cum parva significatione
risus, sine ulla suspicione nimiae cachinnationis
leniter oportebit ab sermone serio torquere verba
ad liberalem iocum.

Cum autem contendere oportebit, quoniam id aut
per continuationem aut per distributionem facien-
dumst, in continuatione, adaucto mediocriter sono
vocis,[1] verbis continuandis vocem quoque iungere [2]
oportebit et torquere sonum et celeriter cum clamore
verba conficere, ut vim volubilem orationis vociferatio
consequi possit. In distributione vocis ab imis
faucibus exclamationem quam clarissimam adhibere
oportet, et quantum spatii in singulas exclamationes
sumpserimus, tantum in singula intervalla spatii
consumere iubemur.

In amplificationibus cum cohortatione utemur voce
adtenuatissima, clamore leni, sono aequabili, commutationibus crebris, maxima celeritate. In con-
questione utemur voce depressa, inclinato sono,
crebris intervallis, longis spatiis, magnis commutationibus.

XV. De figura vocis satis dictum est; nunc de
corporis motu dicendum videtur.

26 Motus est corporis gestus et vultus moderatio
quaedam quae probabiliora reddit ea quae pro-
nuntiantur. Convenit igitur in vultu pudorem et
acrimoniam esse, in gestu nec venustatem conspi-

---

[1] vocis P^2 C Π E Mx ed. mai. : voci M Mx.
[2] iungere P^2B^2Π : adiungere d : augere CE Mx : rugere M.

---

[a] For the fullest extant treatment of gesture in ancient
rhetoric see Quintilian, Bk. 11, ch. 3.

25 feelings and thoughts of each personage. (4) For the Facetious Conversational Tone, with a gentle quiver in the voice, and a slight suggestion of a smile, but without any trace of immoderate laughter, one ought to shift one's utterance smoothly from the Serious Conversational tone to the tone of gentlemanly jest.

Since the Tone of Debate is to be expressed either through the Sustained or the Broken, when the (5) Sustained Tone of Debate is required, one ought moderately to increase the vocal volume, and, in maintaining an uninterrupted flow of words, also to bring the voice into harmony with them, to inflect the tone accordingly, and to deliver the words rapidly in a full voice, so that the voice production can follow the fluent energy of the speech. (6) For the Broken Tone of Debate we must with deepest chest tones produce the clearest possible exclamations, and I advise giving as much time to each pause as to each exclamation.

For (7) the Hortatory Tone of Amplification we shall use a very thin-toned voice, moderate loudness, an even flow of sound, frequent modulations, and the utmost speed. (8) For the Pathetic Tone of Amplification we shall use a restrained voice, deep tone, frequent intermissions, long pauses, and marked changes.

XV. On Voice Quality enough has been said. Now it seems best to discuss Physical Movement.

26 Physical movement [a] consists in a certain control of gesture and mien which renders what is delivered more plausible. Accordingly the facial expression should show modesty and animation, and the gestures should not be conspicuous for either elegance or

[CICERO]

ciendam nec turpitudinem esse, ne aut histriones aut
operarii videamur esse. Ad easdem igitur partes in
quas vox est distributa motus quoque corporis ratio
videtur esse adcommodanda. Nam si erit sermo
cum dignitate, stantis in vestigio, levi dexterae motu,
loqui oportebit, hilaritate, tristitia, mediocritate
vultus ad sermonis sententias adcommodata. Sin
erit in demonstratione sermo, paululum corpus a
cervicibus demittemus; nam est hoc datum ut quam
proxime tum vultum admoveamus ad auditores si
quam rem docere eos et vehementer instigare
velimus. Sin erit in narratione sermo, idem motus
poterit idoneus esse qui paulo ante demonstrabatur in
dignitate. Sin in iocatione, vultu quandam debe-
bimus hilaritatem significare sine commutatione
gestus.

27 Sin contendemus per continuationem, brachio celeri, mobili vultu, acri aspectu utemur. Sin contentio
fiet per distributionem, porrectione perceleri brachii,
inambulatione, pedis dexteri rara supplausione,[1] acri
et defixo aspectu uti oportet.

Sin utemur amplificatione per cohortationem,
paulo tardiore et consideratiore gestu conveniet uti,
similibus ceteris rebus atque in contentione per
continuationem. Sin utemur amplificatione per

---

[1] supplausione *bl*, subplausione *P²ΠB²* : supplausione *Hd*,
subplusione *PBMx* : subplosione *C*.

---

[a] Here doubtless is the Theophrastan tradition of τὸ
πρέπον (see note on 4. x. 15 below); yet Athenaeus, 1. 20, says
202

grossness,[a] lest we give the impression that we are either actors or day labourers. It seems, then, that the rules regulating bodily movement ought to correspond to the several divisions of tone comprising voice. To illustrate: (1) For the Dignified Conversational Tone, the speaker must stay in position when he speaks, lightly moving his right hand, his countenance expressing an emotion corresponding to the sentiments of the subject—gaiety or sadness or an emotion intermediate. (2) For the Explicative Conversational Tone, we shall incline the body forward a little from the shoulders, since it is natural to bring the face as close as possible to our hearers when we wish to prove a point and arouse them vigorously. (3) For the Narrative Conversational Tone, the same physical movement as I have just set forth for the Dignified will be appropriate. (4) For the Facetious Conversational Tone, we should by our countenance express a certain gaiety, without changing gestures.

27   (5) For the Sustained Tone of Debate, we shall use a quick gesture of the arm, a mobile countenance, and a keen glance. (6) For the Broken Tone of Debate, one must extend the arm very quickly, walk up and down, occasionally stamp the right foot, and adopt a keen and fixed look.

   (7) For the Hortatory Tone of Amplification, it will be appropriate to use a somewhat slower and more deliberate gesticulation, but otherwise to follow the procedure for the Sustained Tone of Debate. (8) For the Pathetic Tone of Amplification,

that Theophrastus gave free play to gestures in his own delivery. *Cf.* 3. xiv. 24 above; also Cicero, *De Oratore* 2. 59. 242, 3. 59. 220; Quintilian, 11. 3. 89; Gellius 1. 5.

conquestionem, feminis plangore et capitis ictu, nonnumquam sedato et constanti gestu, maesto et conturbato vultu uti oportebit.

Non sum nescius quantum susceperim negotii qui motus corporis exprimere verbis et imitari scriptura conatus sim voces. Verum nec hoc confisus sum posse fieri ut de his rebus satis commode scribi posset, nec, si id fieri non posset, hoc quod feci fore inutile putabam, propterea quod hic admonere voluimus quid oporteret; reliqua trademus exercitationi. Hoc tamen scire oportet, pronuntiationem bonam id proficere,[1] ut res ex animo agi videatur.

28 XVI. Nunc ad thesaurum inventorum atque ad omnium partium rhetoricae custodem, memoriam, transeamus.

Memoria utrum habeat quiddam artificiosi, an omnis ab natura proficiscatur, aliud dicendi tempus magis idoneum dabitur. Nunc proinde atque constet in hac re multum valere artem et praeceptionem, ita de ea re loquemur. Placet enim nobis esse artificium

---

[1] proficere M : perficere *other MSS. Mx.*

---

[a] *Cf.* Quintilian, 11. 3. 123 : " Slapping the thigh, which, it is believed, Cleon [see Plutarch, *Nicias* 8] was the first to introduce at Athens, is in common use; it is becoming as a sign of indignation and also excites the hearer. Cicero [*Brutus* 80. 278] misses this in Calidius." In Lucian, *Rhetor. Praeceptor* 19, the young learner is satirically encouraged to make use of this gesture.

[b] On ancient mnemonics see Helga Hajdu, *Das mnemotechnische Schrifttum des Mittelalters* (Vienna, Amsterdam, and Leipzig, 1936), pp. 11–33, and L. A. Post, *Class. Weekly*

one ought to slap one's thigh [a] and beat one's head, and sometimes to use a calm and uniform gesticulation and a sad and disturbed expression.

I am not unaware how great a task I have undertaken in trying to express physical movements in words and portray vocal intonations in writing. True, I was not confident that it was possible to treat these matters adequately in writing. Yet neither did I suppose that, if such a treatment were impossible, it would follow that what I have done here would be useless, for it has been my purpose merely to suggest what ought to be done. The rest I shall leave to practice. This, nevertheless, one must remember: good delivery ensures that what the orator is saying seems to come from his heart.

28 XVI. Now let me turn to the treasure-house of the ideas supplied by Invention, to the guardian of all the parts of rhetoric, the Memory.[b]

The question whether memory has some artificial quality, or comes entirely from nature, we shall have another, more favourable, opportunity to discuss. At present I shall accept as proved that in this matter art and method are of great importance, and shall treat the subject accordingly. For my part, I am

25 (1932). 105–110; on Memory in oral literature, J. A. Notopoulos, *Trans. Am. Philol. Assn.* 69 (1938). 465–493. The rhetorical interest in *memoria* appears early, among the sophists, who valued its uses in the learning of commonplaces and for improvisation. Our author's mnemonic system is the oldest extant. Whether such pictorial methods were widely used by the orators we do not know, but the theory persists to this day. See also Longinus, in Spengel-Hammer 1 (2). 197–206; Cicero, *De Oratore* 2. 85. 350–88. 360; and esp. Quintilian's historical and critical treatment, 11. 2. 1–51.

[CICERO]

memoriae—quare placeat alias ostendemus; in praesentia cuiusmodi sit ea aperiemus.

Sunt igitur duae memoriae: una naturalis, altera artificiosa. Naturalis est ea quae nostris animis insita est et simul cum cogitatione nata; artificiosa est ea quam confirmat inductio quaedam et ratio praeceptionis. Sed qua via in ceteris rebus ingenii bonitas imitatur saepe doctrinam, ars porro naturae commoda confirmat et auget, item fit in hac re ut nonnumquam naturalis memoria, si cui data est 29 egregia, similis sit huic artificiosae, porro haec artificiosa naturae commoda retineat et amplificet ratione doctrinae. Quapropter et naturalis memoria praeceptione confirmanda est ut sit egregia, et haec quae doctrina datur indiget ingenii. Nec hoc magis aut minus in hac re quam in ceteris artibus fit, ut ingenio doctrina, praeceptione natura nitescat. Quare et illis qui natura memores sunt utilis haec erit institutio, quod tute paulo post poteris intellegere; et si illi, freti ingenio, nostri non indigerent, tamen iusta causa daretur quare iis qui minus ingenii habent adiumento velimus esse. Nunc de artificiosa memoria loquemur.

---

^a Whether our author ever published such an explanation we do not know. See notes on 3. ii. 3 and 4. xii. 17.

^b For the commonplace *cf.* Isocrates, *Adv. Soph.* 14 ff., *Antid.* 189 ff.; Plato, *Phaedrus* 269 D; Cicero, *Pro Archia* 7. 15, *Tusc. Disp.* 2. 13, Crassus in *De Oratore* 1. 25. 113 ff.; Horace, *Ars Poet.* 408-11; the comic (?) poet Simylus, in Stobaeus, 4. 18 *a* 4; Longinus, *De Sublim.* 36. 4; Quintilian, 2. 19. 1 ff., and (on Delivery) 11. 3. 11 ff.; and for its applica-

satisfied that there is an art of memory—the grounds of my belief I shall explain elsewhere.[a] For the present I shall disclose what sort of thing memory is.

There are, then, two kinds of memory: one natural, and the other the product of art. The natural memory is that memory which is imbedded in our minds, born simultaneously with thought. The artificial memory is that memory which is strengthened by a kind of training and system of discipline. But just as in everything else the merit of natural excellence often rivals acquired learning, and art, in its turn, reinforces and develops the natural advantages,[b] so does it happen in this instance. The natural memory, if a person is

29 endowed with an exceptional one, is often like this artificial memory, and this artificial memory, in its turn, retains and develops the natural advantages by a method of discipline. Thus the natural memory must be strengthened by discipline so as to become exceptional, and, on the other hand, this memory provided by discipline requires natural ability. It is neither more nor less true in this instance than in the other arts that science thrives by the aid of innate ability, and nature by the aid of the rules of art. The training here offered will therefore also be useful to those who by nature have a good memory, as you will yourself soon come to understand.[c] But even if these, relying on their natural talent, did not need our help, we should still be justified in wishing to aid the less well-endowed. Now I shall discuss the artificial memory.

tion to *memoria* Antonius in Cicero, *De Oratore* 2. 88. 360, and Longinus, in Spengel-Hammer 1 (2). 204.

[c] *Cf.* 3. xxii. 36 below.

[CICERO]

Constat igitur artificiosa memoria ex locis et[1] imaginibus. Locos appellamus eos qui breviter, perfecte, insignite aut natura aut manu sunt absoluti, ut eos facile naturali memoria conprehendere et amplecti queamus: ut aedes, intercolumnium, angulum, fornicem, et alia quae his similia sunt. Imagines sunt formae quaedam et notae et simulacra eius rei quam meminisse volumus; quod genus equi, leonis, aquilae memoriam si volemus habere, imagines 30 eorum locis certis conlocare oportebit. Nunc cuiusmodi locos invenire et quo pacto reperire et in locis imagines constituere oporteat ostendemus.

XVII. Quemadmodum igitur qui litteras sciunt possunt id quod dictatur eis scribere, et recitare quod scripserunt, item qui mnemonica[2] didicerunt possunt quod audierunt in locis conlocare et ex his memoriter pronuntiare. Nam loci cerae aut chartae simillimi sunt, imagines litteris, dispositio et conlocatio imaginum scripturae, pronuntiatio lectioni. Oportet igitur, si volumus multa meminisse, multos nos nobis locos conparare, uti multis locis multas imagines conlocare possimus. Item putamus oportere ex ordine hos locos habere, ne quando perturbatione ordinis

---

[1] ex locis *M* : locis et *E Mx*.
[2] qui mnemonica *Aldus* : qui nemonica *Mx* : quinimmodica *P* : qui inmodica *Hb* : qui immodica II*B C l d*.

---

[a] *Cf.* "the table of my memory," Shakespeare, *Hamlet* 1. 5. 98. For the analogy with wax *cf.* Socrates in Plato, *Theaet.* 191 CD; Cicero, *Part. Orat.* 6. 26, and in *De Oratore* 2. 88. 360, Charmadas (*fl.* 107 B.C.) and Metrodorus (born *c.* 150 B.C.); and the seal-ring in Aristotle, *De Mem. et Recollect.*

The artificial memory includes backgrounds and images. By backgrounds I mean such scenes as are naturally or artificially set off on a small scale, complete and conspicuous, so that we can grasp and embrace them easily by the natural memory—for example, a house, an intercolumnar space, a recess, an arch, or the like. An image is, as it were, a figure, mark, or portrait of the object we wish to remember; for example, if we wish to recall a horse, a lion, or an eagle, we must place its image in a definite back-
30 ground. Now I shall show what kind of backgrounds we should invent and how we should discover the images and set them therein.

XVII. Those who know the letters of the alphabet can thereby write out what is dictated to them and read aloud what they have written. Likewise, those who have learned mnemonics can set in backgrounds what they have heard, and from these backgrounds deliver it by memory. For the backgrounds are very much like wax tablets [a] or papyrus, the images like the letters, the arrangement and disposition of the images like the script, and the delivery is like the reading. We should therefore, if we desire to memorize a large number of items, equip ourselves with a large number of backgrounds, so that in these we may set a large number of images. I likewise think it obligatory to have these backgrounds in a series, so that we may never by confusion in their order be prevented from following the images—

---

450 ab. *Cf.* also, in Theophrastus, *De Sens.* 51–2, Democritus' theory that in vision the air is moulded like wax, and see the interpretation of this passage by Paul Friedländer, *Die platonischen Schriften*, Berlin and Leipzig, 1930, p. 448, note 1.

[CICERO]

inpediamur quo setius quoto quoque loco [1] libebit,
vel ab superiore vel ab inferiore parte, imagines
sequi, et ea quae mandata locis erunt edere possimus;
XVIII. nam ut, si in ordine stantes notos complures
viderimus, nihil nostra intersit utrum ab summo an ab
imo an ab medio nomina eorum dicere incipiamus,
item in locis ex ordine conlocatis eveniet ut in
quamlibebit partem quoque loco libebit, imaginibus
commoniti, dicere possimus id quod locis manda-
31 verimus.   Quare placet et ex ordine locos conparare.

Locos quos sumpserimus egregie commeditari
oportebit, ut perpetuo nobis haerere possint; nam
imagines, sicuti litterae, delentur ubi nihil utimur;
loci, tamquam cera, remanere debent.   Et ne forte in
numero locorum falli possimus, quintum quemque
placet notari; quod genus si in quinto loco manum
auream conlocemus, si in decimo aliquem notum
cui praenomen sit Decimo, deinde facile erit deinceps [2] similis notas quinto quoque [3] loco conlocare.
XIX. Item commodius est in derelicta quam in celebri
regione locos conparare, propterea quod frequentia et
obambulatio hominum conturbat et infirmat imaginum notas, solitudo conservat integras simulacrorum figuras.   Praeterea dissimiles forma atque
natura loci conparandi sunt, ut distincti interlucere

[1] quoq(ue) loco *l* : loco quoque *H* : quoq(ue) *P* Π :
quidq(ue) loco *C* : quidq(ue) *B* : quoquo loco *E Mx.*
[2] deinceps *P*²Π*B*²*CE* : inceps *HPB Mx.*
[3] quoque *M* : quoquo *E Mx.*

210

proceeding from any background we wish, whatsoever its place in the series, and whether we go
forwards or backwards—nor from delivering orally
what has been committed to the backgrounds.
XVIII. For example, if we should see a great
number of our acquaintances standing in a certain
order, it would not make any difference to us whether
we should tell their names beginning with the person
standing at the head of the line or at the foot or in
the middle. So with respect to the backgrounds.
If these have been arranged in order, the result will
be that, reminded by the images, we can repeat orally
what we have committed to the backgrounds, pro-
31 ceeding in either direction from any background we
please. That is why it also seems best to arrange
the backgrounds in a series.

We shall need to study with special care the backgrounds we have adopted so that they may cling
lastingly in our memory, for the images, like letters,
are effaced when we make no use of them, but the
backgrounds, like wax tablets, should abide. And
that we may by no chance err in the number of
backgrounds, each fifth background should be
marked. For example, if in the fifth we should set a
golden hand, and in the tenth some acquaintance
whose first name is Decimus, it will then be easy to
station like marks in each successive fifth background.
XIX. Again, it will be more advantageous to
obtain backgrounds in a deserted than in a populous
region, because the crowding and passing to and fro
of people confuse and weaken the impress of the
images, while solitude keeps their outlines sharp.
Further, backgrounds differing in form and nature
must be secured, so that, thus distinguished, they

possint; nam si qui multa intercolumnia sumpserit, conturbabitur similitudine ut ignoret quid in quoque [1] loco conlocarit. Et magnitudine modica et mediocres locos habere oportet; nam et praeter modum ampli vagas imagines reddunt, et nimis angusti saepe non videntur posse capere imaginum con-
32 locationem. Tum nec nimis inlustres nec vehementer obscuros locos habere oportet, ne aut obcaecentur tenebris imagines aut splendore praefulgeant. Intervalla locorum mediocria placet esse, fere paulo plus aut minus pedum tricenum; nam ut aspectus item cogitatio minus valet sive nimis procul removeris sive vehementer prope admoveris id quod oportet videri.

Sed quamquam facile est ei qui paulo plura noverit quamvis multos et idoneos locos conparare, tamen si qui satis idoneos invenire se non putabit, ipse sibi constituat quam volet multos licebit. Cogitatio enim quamvis regionem potest amplecti, et in ea situm loci cuiusdam ad suum arbitrium fabricari et architectari. Quare licebit, si hac prompta copia contenti non erimus, nosmet ipsos nobis cogitatione nostra regionem constituere, et idoneorum locorum commodissimam distinctionem conparare.

De locis satis dictum est; nunc ad imaginum rationem transeamus.

33 XX. Quoniam ergo rerum similes imagines esse oportet, ex omnibus rebus nosmet nobis similitudines eligere debemus. Duplices igitur similitudines esse

[1] quoque *Ml*: uno quoque *d*: quoquo *bMx*.

may be clearly visible; for if a person has adopted
many intercolumnar spaces, their resemblance to one
another will so confuse him that he will no longer
know what he has set in each background. And
these backgrounds ought to be of moderate size and
medium extent, for when excessively large they
render the images vague, and when too small often
seem incapable of receiving an arrangement of
32 images. Then the backgrounds ought to be neither
too bright nor too dim, so that the shadows may not
obscure the images nor the lustre make them glitter.
I believe that the intervals between backgrounds
should be of moderate extent, approximately thirty
feet; for, like the external eye, so the inner eye of
thought is less powerful when you have moved the
object of sight too near or too far away.

Although it is easy for a person with a relatively
large experience to equip himself with as many and as
suitable backgrounds as he may desire, even a person
who believes that he finds no store of backgrounds
that are good enough, may succeed in fashioning as
many such as he wishes. For the imagination can
embrace any region whatsoever and in it at will
fashion and construct the setting of some background. Hence, if we are not content with our
ready-made supply of backgrounds, we may in our
imagination create a region for ourselves and obtain
a most serviceable distribution of appropriate
backgrounds.

On the subject of backgrounds enough has been
said; let me now turn to the theory of images.

33 XX. Since, then, images must resemble objects,
we ought ourselves to choose from all objects likenesses for our use. Hence likenesses are bound to

debent, unae rerum, alterae verborum. Rerum similitudines exprimuntur cum summatim ipsorum negotiorum imagines conparamus; verborum similitudines constituuntur cum unius cuiusque nominis et
vocabuli memoria imagine notatur.

Rei totius memoriam saepe una nota et imagine
simplici conprehendimus; hoc modo, ut si accusator
dixerit ab reo hominem veneno necatum et hereditatis
causa factum arguerit et eius rei multos dixerit testes
et conscios esse. Si hoc primum, ut ad defendendum
nobis expeditum sit, meminisse volemus, in primo
loco rei totius imaginem conformabimus; aegrotum
in lecto cubantem faciemus ipsum illum de quo
agetur, si formam eius detinebimus; si eum non
agnoverimus,[1] at aliquem aegrotum non de minimo
loco sumemus, ut cito in mentem venire possit.
Et reum ad lectum eius adstituemus, dextera pocu-
lum, sinistra tabulas, medico testiculos arietinos
tenentem. Hoc modo et testium et hereditatis et
34 veneno necati memoriam habere poterimus. Item
deinceps cetera crimina ex ordine in locis ponemus
et quotienscumque rem meminisse volemus, si for-
marum dispositione et imaginum diligenti notatione
utemur, facile ea quae volemus memoria consequemur.

[1] agnoverimus *E* : *other MSS. Mx omit.*

---

a Thus *memoria* embraces the speaker's command of his
material as well as of the words.
b According to Macrobius, *Sat.* 7. 13. 7–8, the anatomists
spoke of a nerve which extends from the heart to the fourth
finger of the left hand (the *digitus medicinalis*), where it
interlaces into the other nerves of that finger; the finger was
therefore ringed, as with a crown. *Testiculi* suggests *testes*

be of two kinds, one of subject-matter,[a] the other of words. Likenesses of matter are formed when we enlist images that present a general view of the matter with which we are dealing; likenesses of words are established when the record of each single noun or appellative is kept by an image.

Often we encompass the record of an entire matter by one notation, a single image. For example, the prosecutor has said that the defendant killed a man by poison, has charged that the motive for the crime was an inheritance, and declared that there are many witnesses and accessories to this act. If in order to facilitate our defence we wish to remember this first point, we shall in our first background form an image of the whole matter. We shall picture the man in question as lying ill in bed, if we know his person. If we do not know him, we shall yet take some one to be our invalid, but not a man of the lowest class, so that he may come to mind at once. And we shall place the defendant at the bedside, holding in his right hand a cup, and in his left tablets, and on the fourth finger [b] a ram's testicles. In this way we can record the man who was poisoned, the inheritance, and the witnesses. In like fashion we shall set the other counts of the charge in backgrounds successively, following their order, and whenever we wish to remember a point, by properly arranging the patterns of the backgrounds [c] and carefully imprinting the images, we shall easily succeed in calling back to mind what we wish.

(witnesses). Of the scrotum of the ram purses were made; thus the money used for bribing the witnesses may perhaps also be suggested.

[c] At 3. xvi. 29 above *formae* is used to describe the images.

[CICERO]

XXI. Cum verborum similitudines imaginibus exprimere volemus, plus negotii suscipiemus et magis ingenium nostrum exercebimus. Id nos hoc modo facere oportebit :

Iam domum itionem reges Atridae parant.[a]

Hunc versum meminisse si volemus, conveniet primo[1] in loco constituere manus ad caelum tollentem Domitium cum a Regibus Marciis loris caedatur— hoc erit " Iam domum itionem reges ; " in altero loco Aesopum et Cimbrum subornari ut ad Iphigeniam[2] in Agamemnonem et Menelaum—hoc erit " Atridae parant." Hoc modo omnia verba erunt expressa. Sed haec imaginum conformatio tum valet si naturalem memoriam exsuscitaverimus hac notatione, ut versu posito ipsi nobiscum primum transeamus bis aut ter eum versum, deinde tum imaginibus verba exprimamus. Hoc modo naturae suppeditabitur doctrina. Nam utraque altera separata minus erit firma, ita tamen ut multo plus in doctrina atque arte praesidii sit. Quod docere non gravaremur, ni

[1] *lac.*; hunc versum meminisse si volemus conveniet primo *sugg. Mx.*

[2] Ephigeniam *MSS. Mx.*

---

[a] An iambic senarius, whether our author's own creation or from a tragedy by an unknown author (the *Iphigenia* mentioned below?) is uncertain. Note that here the play is upon the form of the word, not its meaning, and that no special provision is made for the adverb *iam*. Quintilian, 11. 2. 25, doubts the efficacy of symbols to record a series of connected words : " I do not mention the fact that some things, certainly conjunctions, for example, cannot be represented by images."

XXI. When we wish to represent by images the likenesses of words, we shall be undertaking a greater task and exercising our ingenuity the more. This we ought to effect in the following way:

Iam domum itionem reges Atridae parant.[a]

" And now their home-coming the kings, the sons of Atreus, are making ready."

If we wish to remember this verse, in our first background we should put Domitius, raising hands to heaven while he is lashed by the Marcii Reges [b]— that will represent " Iam domum itionem reges " (" And now their home-coming the kings,"); in the second background, Aesopus and Cimber,[c] being dressed as for the rôles of Agamemnon and Menelaüs in *Iphigenia*—that will represent " Atridae parant " (" the sons of Atreus, are making ready "). By this method all the words will be represented. But such an arrangement of images succeeds only if we use our notation to stimulate the natural memory, so that we first go over a given verse twice or three times to ourselves and then represent the words by means of images. In this way art will supplement nature. For neither by itself will be strong enough, though we must note that theory and technique are much the more reliable. I should not hesitate to

[b] The scene is doubtless our author's own creation. Rex was the name of one of the most distinguished families of the Marcian *gens*; the Domitian (of plebeian origin) was likewise a celebrated *gens*.

[c] Clodius Aesopus (a friend of Cicero) was the greatest tragic actor of the first half of the first century B.C.; Cimber, mentioned only here, was no doubt also a favourite of the day. See Otto Ribbeck, *Die römische Tragödie im Zeitalter der Republik*, Leipzig, 1875, pp. 674–6.

metueremus ne, cum ab instituto nostro recessis-
semus, minus commode servaretur haec dilucida
brevitas praeceptionis.

35   Nunc, quoniam solet accidere ut imagines partim
firmae et acres et ad monendum idoneae sint, partim
inbecillae et infirmae quae vix memoriam possint
excitare, qua de causa utrumque fiat considerandum
est, ut, cognita causa, quas vitemus et quas sequamur
imagines scire possimus.

   XXII. Docet igitur nos ipsa natura quid oporteat
fieri. Nam si quas res in vita videmus parvas, usitatas, cotidianas, meminisse non solemus, propterea
quod nulla nova nec admirabili re commovetur
animus; at si quid videmus aut audimus egregie
turpe, inhonestum, inusitatum, magnum, incredibile,
ridiculum, id diu meminisse consuevimus. Itaque
quas res ante ora videmus aut audimus obliviscimur
plerumque; quae acciderunt in pueritia meminimus
optime saepe; nec hoc alia de causa potest accidere
nisi quod usitatae res facile e memoria elabuntur, in-
36 signes et novae diutius manent in animo. Solis
exortus, cursus, occasus nemo admiratur propterea
quia cotidie fiunt; at eclipses [1] solis mirantur quia
raro accidunt, et solis eclipses [2] magis mirantur quam
lunae propterea quod hae [3] crebriores sunt. Docet
ergo se natura vulgari et usitata re non exsuscitari,
novitate et insigni quodam negotio commoveri.
Imitetur ars igitur naturam, et quod ea desiderat id

---

[1] eclipsis Π *b d Mx* : eclypsis *HBCl* : aeglypsis *P*.
[2] eclipses *b* : eclipsis Π *d Mx* : eclypsis *HB l* : aeclipsis *C* :
aeglypsis *P*.
[3] hae *P²B C b d* : haec *l Mx*.

---

[a] *Cf.* Jerome, *Apol. adv. libr. Rufini* 1. 30.

demonstrate this in detail, did I not fear that, once having departed from my plan, I should not so well preserve the clear conciseness of my instruction.

35 Now, since in normal cases some images are strong and sharp and suitable for awakening recollection, and others so weak and feeble as hardly to succeed in stimulating memory, we must therefore consider the cause of these differences, so that, by knowing the cause, we may know which images to avoid and which to seek.

XXII. Now nature herself teaches us what we should do. When we see in everyday life things that are petty, ordinary, and banal, we generally fail to remember them, because the mind is not being stirred by anything novel or marvellous. But if we see or hear something exceptionally base, dishonourable, extraordinary, great, unbelievable, or laughable, that we are likely to remember a long time. Accordingly, things immediate to our eye or ear we commonly forget; incidents of our childhood we often remember best.[a] Nor could this be so for any other reason than that ordinary things easily slip from the memory while the striking and novel stay longer in 36 mind. A sunrise, the sun's course, a sunset, are marvellous to no one because they occur daily.[b] But solar eclipses are a source of wonder because they occur seldom, and indeed are more marvellous than lunar eclipses, because these are more frequent. Thus nature shows that she is not aroused by the common, ordinary event, but is moved by a new or

[b] *Cf.* Lucretius 2. 1037–8 : " So wondrous would this sight have been. Yet, wearied as all are with satiety of seeing, how truly no one now deigns to gaze up at the bright quarters of heaven ! "

inveniat, quod ostendit sequatur. Nihil est enim quod aut natura extremum invenerit aut doctrina primum; sed rerum principia ab ingenio profecta sunt, exitus disciplina conparantur.

37 Imagines igitur nos in eo genere constituere oportebit quod genus in memoria diutissime potest haerere. Id accidet si quam maxime notatas similitudines constituemus; si non multas nec vagas, sed aliquid agentes imagines ponemus; si egregiam pulcritudinem aut unicam turpitudinem eis adtribuemus; si aliquas exornabimus, ut si coronis aut veste purpurea, quo nobis notatior sit similitudo; aut si qua re deformabimus, ut si cruentam aut caeno oblitam aut rubrica delibutam inducamus, quo magis insignita sit forma, aut ridiculas res aliquas imaginibus adtribuamus, nam ea res quoque faciet ut facilius meminisse valeamus. Nam quas res veras facile meminimus,[1] easdem fictas et diligenter notatas meminisse non difficile est. Sed illud facere oportebit, ut identidem primos quosque locos imaginum renovandarum causa celeriter animo pervagemus.

38 XXIII. Scio plerosque Graecos qui de memoria scripserunt fecisse ut multorum verborum imagines conscriberent, uti qui ediscere vellent paratas haberent, ne quid in quaerendo consumerent operae. Quorum rationem aliquot de causis inprobamus:

---

[1] meminimus $P^2BC\Pi d$: minus HP : meminerimus $blMx$.

---

[a] The idea is a commonplace in a variety of schools of thought : e.g., Democritus, fragm. 154, in Diels-Kranz, *Die Fragmente der Vorsokratiker*, 6th ed., 2. 173, and Lucretius 5. 1102, 1354, 1361 ff., 1379; Aristotle, *Physica* 2. 2(194 a) and 2. 8 (199 a), *Meteor.* 4. 3 (381 b), *De mundo* 5 (396 b, in Diels-Kranz 1. 153); Theophrastus, *De Caus. Plant.* 2. 18. 2; Dionysius Halic., *Isaeus*, ch. 16; Seneca, *Epist.* 65. 3; Marcus

striking occurrence. Let art, then, imitate nature,[a]
find what she desires, and follow as she directs.
For in invention nature is never last, education never
first; rather the beginnings of things arise from
natural talent, and the ends are reached by discipline.

37 We ought, then, to set up images of a kind that can
adhere longest in the memory. And we shall do so if
we establish likenesses as striking as possible; if we
set up images that are not many or vague, but doing
something; if we assign to them exceptional beauty
or singular ugliness; if we dress some of them with
crowns or purple cloaks, for example, so that the
likeness may be more distinct to us; or if we somehow disfigure them, as by introducing one stained
with blood or soiled with mud or smeared with red
paint, so that its form is more striking, or by assigning
certain comic effects to our images, for that, too, will
ensure our remembering them more readily. The
things we easily remember when they are real we
likewise remember without difficulty when they are
figments, if they have been carefully delineated.
But this will be essential—again and again to run
over rapidly in the mind all the original backgrounds
in order to refresh the images.

38 XXIII. I know that most of the Greeks who have
written on the memory [b] have taken the course of
listing images that correspond to a great many words,
so that persons who wished to learn these images by
heart would have them ready without expending
effort on a search for them. I disapprove of their
method on several grounds. First, among the

Aurelius, *Medit.* 11. 10; Plotinus, *Enn.* 5. 8. 1; Cicero,
Orator 18. 58; Quintilian, 8. 3. 71; Dante, *Inferno* 11. 97 ff.
 [b] Precisely who these predecessors were we do not know.

primum, quod in verborum innumerabili multitudine
ridiculumst mille verborum imagines conparare.
Quantulum enim poterunt haec valere, cum ex
infinita verborum copia modo aliud modo aliud nos
verbum meminisse oportebit? Deinde, cur volumus
ab industria quemquam removere, ut, ne quid ipse
quaerat, nos illi omnia parata quaesita tradamus?
Praeterea, similitudine alia alius magis commovetur.
Nam ut saepe, formam si quam similem cuipiam
dixerimus esse, non omnes habemus adsensores, quod
alii videtur aliud, item fit in imaginibus ut quae nobis
diligenter notata sit, ea parum videatur insignis aliis.
39 Quare sibi quemque suo commodo convenit imagines
conparare. Postremo, praeceptoris est docere quemadmodum quaeri quidque conveniat, et unum aliquod
aut alterum, non omnia quae eius generis erunt
exempli causa subicere, quo res possit esse dilucidior; ut cum de prooemiis [1] quaerendis disputamus,
rationem damus quaerendi, non mille prooemiorum [2]
genera conscribimus, item arbitramur de imaginibus
fieri convenire.

XXIV. Nunc, ne forte verborum memoriam aut
nimis difficilem aut parum utilem arbitrere, rerum
ipsarum memoria contentus sis, quod et utilior sit et
plus habeat facultatis, admonendus es quare verborum
memoriam non inprobemus. Nam putamus oportere
eos qui velint res faciliores sine labore et molestia
facere in rebus difficilioribus esse ante exercitatos.
Nec nos hanc verborum memoriam inducimus ut versus

[1] prohemiis *PΠBC Mx* : proemiis *C²E* : praemiis *H*.
[2] prohemiorum *PΠBC Mx*: proemiorum *C²E*: premiorum *H*.

innumerable multitude of words it is ridiculous to collect images for a thousand. How meagre is the value these can have, when out of the infinite store of words we shall need to remember now one, and now another? Secondly, why do we wish to rob anybody of his initiative, so that, to save him from making any search himself, we deliver to him everything searched out and ready? Then again, one person is more struck by one likeness, and another more by another. Often in fact when we declare that some one form resembles another, we fail to receive universal assent, because things seem different to different persons. The same is true with respect to images: one that is well-defined to us appears relatively

39 inconspicuous to others. Everybody, therefore, should in equipping himself with images suit his own convenience. Finally, it is the instructor's duty to teach the proper method of search in each case, and, for the sake of greater clarity, to add in illustration some one or two examples of its kind, but not all. For instance, when I discuss the search for Introductions, I give a method of search and do not draught a thousand kinds of Introductions. The same procedure I believe should be followed with respect to images.

XXIV. Now, lest you should perchance regard the memorizing of words either as too difficult or as of too little use, and so rest content with the memorizing of matter, as being easier and more useful, I must advise you why I do not disapprove of memorizing words. I believe that they who wish to do easy things without trouble and toil must previously have been trained in more difficult things. Nor have I included memorization of words to enable us to get

meminisse possimus, sed ut hac exercitatione illa
rerum memoria quae pertinet ad utilitatem confirme-
tur, ut ab hac difficili consuetudine sine labore ad
40 illam facultatem transire possimus. Sed cum in
omni disciplina infirma est artis praeceptio sine
summa adsiduitate exercitationis, tum vero in
mnemonicis [1] minimum valet doctrina, nisi industria,
studio, labore, diligentia conprobatur. Quam pluri-
mos locos ut habeas et quam maxime ad praecepta
adcommodatos curare poteris; in imaginibus con-
locandis exerceri cotidie convenit. Non enim, sicut a
ceteris studiis abducimur nonnumquam occupatione,
item ab hac re nos potest causa deducere aliqua.
Numquam est enim quin aliquid memoriae tradere
velimus, et tum maxime cum aliquo maiore negotio
detinemur. Quare, cum sit utile facile meminisse,
non te fallit quod tantopere utile sit quanto labore sit
appetendum; quod poteris existimare utilitate cognita.
Pluribus verbis ad eam te hortari non est sententia,
ne aut tuo studio diffisi aut minus quam res postulat
dixisse videamur.

De quinta parte rhetoricae deinceps dicemus. Tu
primas quasque partes in animo frequenta et, quod
maxime necesse est, exercitatione confirma.

[1] mnemonicis *Aldus* : nemonicis *HP* Π *B Mx* : memoriis
P²CE.

verse by rote, but rather as an exercise whereby to strengthen that other kind of memory, the memory of matter, which is of practical use. Thus we may without effort pass from this difficult training to ease
40 in that other memory. In every discipline artistic theory is of little avail without unremitting exercise, but especially in mnemonics theory is almost valueless unless made good by industry, devotion, toil, and care. You can make sure that you have as many backgrounds as possible and that these conform as much as possible to the rules; in placing the images you should exercise every day. While an engrossing preoccupation may often distract us from our other pursuits, from this activity nothing whatever can divert us. Indeed there is never a moment when we do not wish to commit something to memory, and we wish it most of all when our attention is held by business of special importance. So, since a ready memory is a useful thing, you see clearly with what great pains we must strive to acquire so useful a faculty. Once you know its uses you will be able to appreciate this advice. To exhort you further in the matter of memory is not my intention, for I should appear either to have lacked confidence in your zeal or to have discussed the subject less fully than it demands.

I shall next discuss the fifth part of rhetoric. You might rehearse in your mind each of the first four divisions, and—what is especially necessary—fortify your knowledge of them with exercise.

BOOK IV

LIBER QUARTUS

1 I. Quoniam in hoc libro, Herenni, de elocutione
conscripsimus, et quibus in rebus opus fuit exemplis
uti, nostris exemplis usi sumus, et id fecimus praeter
consuetudinem Graecorum qui de hac re scripserunt,
necessario faciendum est ut paucis rationem nostri
consilii demus. Atque hoc necessitudine nos [1]
facere, non studio, satis erit signi quod in superioribus
libris nihil neque ante rem neque praeter rem locuti
sumus. Nunc, si pauca quae res postulat dixerimus,
tibi id quod reliquum est artis, ita uti instituimus,
persolvemus. Sed facilius nostram rationem intel-
leges si prius quid illi dicant cognoveris.

Compluribus de causis putant oportere, cum ipsi
praeceperint quo pacto oporteat ornare elocutionem,
unius cuiusque generis ab oratore aut poëta probato
sumptum ponere exemplum. Et primum se id

---

[1] necessitudine nos *E* : nos necessitudine *PBCΠd* : necessitudine *H Mx*.

---

[a] See note on 4. v. 7 below.
[b] *Cf.* the long prefaces to the books of Cicero, *De Inv.*
[c] The character of this Introduction to Book 4 (only the
final argument and some of the illustrations are Roman)
suggests a Greek origin. It reflects the debates between
Greeks and Greeks—on Atticism as against Asianism, or the
old rhetoric, based on the imitation of the ancients (μίμησις
τῶν ἀρχαίων), as against the modern (νεωτερισμός). Hermagoras, to whose reliance on the ancients Cicero, *De Inv.*
I. vi. 8, refers, and whom Cicero in his Introduction to that

BOOK IV

1   I. Inasmuch as in the present Book, Herennius, I have written about Style, and wherever there was need of examples, I have used those of my own making, and in so doing have departed from the practice of the Greek writers [a] on the subject, I must in a few words justify my method. And that I make this explanation from necessity, and not from choice, is sufficiently indicated by the fact that in the preceding Books I have said nothing by way either of preface [b] or of digression. Now, after a few indispensable observations, I shall, as I undertook to do, discharge my task of explaining to you the rest of the art. But you will more readily understand my method when you have learned what the Greeks say.[c]

On several grounds they think that, after they have given their own precepts on how to embellish style, they must for each kind of embellishment offer an example drawn from a reputable orator or poet.[d] And their first ground is that in doing so they are

---

work attacks, was doubtless also in the author's mind. See Paul Wendland, *Quaestiones Rhetoricae*, Göttingen, 1914. As our notes show, in spite of the argument in this Introduction, Book 4 contains numerous examples taken (though often with considerable changes) from a variety of sources, both Roman and Greek.

  [d] Rhetoric and poetry meet expressly also in 4. i. 2, ii. 3, iii. 5, iv. 7, v. 7, v. 8, xxxii. 43, xxxii. 44, and 2. xxii. 34. The Peripatetic school encouraged the close relationship between the two.

[CICERO]

modestia commotos facere dicunt, propterea quod videatur esse ostentatio quaedam non satis habere praecipere de artificio, sed etiam ipsos videri velle artificiose gignere exempla; hoc est, inquiunt, osten-

2 tare se, non ostendere artem. Quare pudor in primis est ad eam rem inpedimento, ne nos[1] solos probare, nos amare, alios contemnere et deridere videamur. Etenim cum possimus ab Ennio sumere aut a Gracco ponere exemplum, videtur esse adrogantia illa relinquere, ad sua devenire.

Praeterea, exempla testimoniorum locum obtinent. Id enim quod admonuerit et leviter fecerit praeceptio exemplo, sicut testimonio, conprobatur. Non igitur ridiculus sit si quis in lite aut in iudicio domesticis testimoniis pugnet? Ut enim testimonium, sic exemplum rei confirmandae causa sumitur. Non ergo oportet hoc nisi a probatissimo sumi, ne quod aliud confirmare debeat egeat id ipsum confirmationis. Etenim necesse est aut se omnibus anteponant et sua maxime probent, aut negent optima esse exempla quae a probatissimis oratoribus aut poëtis sumpta sint. Si se omnibus anteponant, intolerabili adrogantia sunt; si quos sibi praeponant et eorum

[1] ne nos *P²Πbd* : ne ut nos et *HMx* : ne ut nos *PBC* : ne sibi nos *l*.

---

[a] *Cf.* Horace, *Ars Poet.* 444.
[b] Ennius and Gracchus served as models for Crassus in his youth; *cf.* Cicero, *De Oratore* 1. 34. 154.
[c] See note on 4. iii. 5 below.
[d] Whether civil or criminal.

prompted by modesty, because it seems a kind of ostentation not to be content to teach the art, but to appear desirous themselves of creating examples artificially. That, they say, would be showing 2 themselves off, not showing what the art is. Hence it is in the first place a sense of shame which keeps us from following this practice, for we should appear to be approving of ourselves alone,[a] to be prizing ourselves, scorning and scoffing at others. For when we can take an example from Ennius, or offer one from Gracchus,[b] it seems presumptuous to neglect these and to have recourse to our own examples.

In the second place, examples, they say, serve the purpose of testimony; for, like the testimony of a witness, the example enforces what the precept has suggested and only to a slight degree effected.[c] Would not a man be ridiculous, then, if in a trial[d] or in a domestic procedure[e] he should contest the issue on the basis of his own personal testimony? For an example is used just like testimony to prove a point; it should properly therefore be taken only from a writer of highest reputation, lest what ought to serve as proof of something else should itself require proof. In fact, inventors of examples must either prefer themselves to all others and esteem their own products most of all, or else deny that the best examples are those taken from the orators or poets of highest reputation. If they should set themselves above all others, they are unbearably conceited; if they should grant to any others a superiority over themselves and yet not believe that

[e] In which the *paterfamilias* exercises his jurisdiction. See Mommsen, pp. 16 ff.; Wenger, *Institutes of the Roman Law of Civil Procedure*, pp. 9 f.

exempla suis exemplis non putant praestare, non possunt dicere quare sibi illos anteponant.

II. Quid? ipsa auctoritas antiquorum non cum res probabiliores tum hominum studia ad imitandum alacriora reddit? Immo erigit omnium cupiditates et acuit industriam cum spes iniecta est posse imitando Gracci aut Crassi consequi facultatem.

3 Postremo, hoc ipsum summum est artificium—res varias et dispares in tot poëmatis et orationibus sparsas et vage disiectas ita diligenter eligere ut unum quodque genus exemplorum sub singulos artis locos subicere possis. Hoc si industria solum fieri posset, tamen essemus laudandi cum talem laborem non fugissemus; nunc sine summo artificio non potest fieri. Quis est enim qui, non summe cum tenet artem, possit ea quae iubeat ars de tanta et tam diffusa scriptura notare et separare? Ceteri, cum legunt orationes bonas aut poëmata, probant oratores et poëtas, neque intellegunt qua re commoti probent, quod scire non possunt ubi sit nec quid sit nec quo modo factum sit id quod eos maxime delectet; at is qui et haec omnia intellegit et idonea maxime eligit et omnia in arte maxime scribenda redigit in singulas rationes praeceptionis, necesse est eius rei summus artifex sit. Hoc igitur ipsum maximum

---

a *Cf.* the place of Imitation in our author's theory, as set forth in 1. ii. 3 above, with the position taken in this Preface (see esp. 4. iv. 7 and 4. vi. 9 below) against borrowing examples which should serve as models for imitation.

b The like point, with respect to rhythm, is made by Cicero, *Orator* 51. 173.

c τεχνίτης, τεχνογράφος. On expertness in criticism see Cicero, *Brutus* 47. 183, 51. 190, 54. 199 ff., 93. 320, *Orator*

the examples of these others excel their own, they cannot explain why they concede this superiority.

II. And furthermore, does not the very prestige of the ancients not only lend greater authority to their doctrine but also sharpen in men the desire to imitate them? Yes, it excites the ambitions and whets the zeal of all men when the hope is implanted in them of being able by imitation [a] to attain to the skill of a Gracchus or a Crassus.

3 Finally, they say, the highest art resides in this: in your selecting a great diversity of passages widely scattered and interspersed among so many poems and speeches, and doing this with such painstaking care that you can list examples, each according to its kind, under the respective topics of the art. If this could be accomplished by industry alone, we should yet deserve praise for not having avoided such a task; but actually, without the highest art it cannot be done. For who, unless he has a consummate grasp of the art of rhetoric, could in so vast and diffuse a literature mark and distinguish the demands of the art? Laymen, reading good orations and poems, approve the orators and poets, but without comprehending what has called forth their approval, because they cannot know where that which especially delights them resides,[b] or what it is, or how it was produced. But he who understands all this, and selects examples that are most appropriate, and reduces to individual principles of instruction everything that especially merits inclusion in his treatise, must needs be a master artist [c] in this field. This, then, is the height of

11. 36, *De Opt. Gen. Dic.* 4. 11, *De Offic.* 3. 3. 15; Dionysius Halic., *De Thuc.* 4.

artificium est—in arte sua posse et alienis exemplis uti.

4 Haec illi cum dicunt, magis nos auctoritate sua commovent quam veritate disputationis. Illud enim veremur, ne cui satis sit ad contrariam rationem probandam quod ab ea steterint ii et qui inventores huius artificii fuerint et vetustate iam satis omnibus probati sint. Quodsi, illorum auctoritate remota, res omnes volent cum re conparare, intellegent non omnia concedenda esse antiquitati.

III. Primum igitur, quod ab eis[1] de modestia dicitur videamus ne nimium pueriliter proferatur. Nam si tacere aut nil scribere modestia est, cur quicquam scribunt aut loquuntur? Sin aliquid suum scribunt, cur quo setius omnia scribant inpediuntur modestia? Quasi si quis ad[2] Olympia cum venerit cursum et steterit ut mittatur, inpudentes dicat esse illos qui currere coeperint, ipse intra carcerem stet et narret aliis quomodo Ladas aut Boiscus Isthmiis[3] cursitarint; sic isti, cum in artis curriculum descenderunt, illos qui in eo quod est artificii elaborent aiunt facere immodeste, ipsi aliquem antiquum oratorem aut poëtam laudant aut scripturam, sic uti in

[1] quod ab eis M Mx ed. mai. : ab eis quod blMx.
[2] ad P²B²Cbld : HPBΠ Mx omit.
[3] Boiscus Isthmiis conj. Mx : bovis cum sisonius (sisoniis C) M : boiscum sisoniis d : boyscū sisonis l : loris cū sisonis b : Boiscus Sicyonius Turnebus : Boeotus Sicyonius Kayser : Boius cum Sicyoniis Gronovius.

[a] Of Sparta, a celebrated long-distance runner (c. 450 B.C.), winner in the Olympic games, whose speed is often referred to by Roman authors; see P.-W. 12. 380–1.
[b] Text corrupt. The runner " Boiscus " (if that reading is correct) is elsewhere unknown. The name (of a Thessalian

technical skill—in one's own treatise to succeed also in using borrowed examples!

4 When the Greeks make such assertions, they influence us more by their prestige than by the truth of their argument. For what I really fear is that some one may consider the view contrary to mine adequately recommended because its supporters are the very men who invented this art and are now by reason of their antiquity quite universally esteemed. If, however, leaving the prestige of the ancients out of consideration, they are willing to compare all the arguments, point for point, they will understand that we need not yield to antiquity in everything.

III. First, then, let us beware lest the Greeks offer us too childish an argument in their talk about modesty. For if modesty consists in saying nothing or writing nothing, why do they write or speak at all? But if they do write something of their own, then why does modesty keep them from composing, themselves, everything they write? It is as if some one should come to the Olympic games to run, and having taken a position for the start, should accuse of impudence those who have begun the race— should himself stand within the barrier and recount to others how Ladas [a] used to run, or Boïscus [b] in the Isthmian games. These Greek rhetoricians do likewise. When they have descended into the race-course of our art, they accuse of immodesty those who put in practice the essence of the art; they praise some ancient orator, poet, or literary work, but without themselves daring to come forth into the stadium of

boxer) occurs in Xenophon, *Anab.* 5. 8, and (of a Samian) in W. Dittenberger, *Syll. Inscript. Graec.*, 3rd ed., Leipzig, 1915, No. 420.

5 stadium rhetoricae prodire non audeant.   Non ausim
dicere, sed tamen vereor ne qua in re laudem modestiae venentur, in ea ipsa re sint inpudentes.   " Quid
enim tibi vis? " aliquis inquiat.   " Artem tuam
scribis;   gignis novas nobis praeceptiones;   eas
ipse confirmare non potes;   ab aliis exempla sumis.
Vide ne facias inpudenter qui tuo nomini velis ex
aliorum laboribus libare laudem."   Nam si eorum
volumina prenderint antiqui oratores et poëtae et
suum quisque de libris sustulerit,[1] nihil istis quod
suum velint relinquatur.

   " At exempla, quoniam testimoniorum similia sunt,
item convenit ut testimonia ab hominibus probatissimis sumi."   Primum omnium, exempla ponuntur nec confirmandi neque testificandi causa, sed

---

[1] sustulerit *Turnebus:* suis tulerit C^2EMx : suus tulerit
C : tuis tulerit M.

---

[a] Cf. *Corpus Fabularum Aesopicarum*, ed. Hausrath, *Fab.*
33 (1), about the man who, boasting when away from Rhodes
that he had " beaten the Olympic record " in a jump he had
made at Rhodes, and promising to produce witnesses of his
exploit if his hearers would come to Rhodes, was challenged
to repeat the leap where he was.
   [b] In Horace, *Epist.* 1. 3. 15 ff., Celsus is advised to be self-
reliant, and not to draw upon writers whose works he has used
in the library of the temple of Apollo—" lest, if by chance
some day the flock of birds come to reclaim their feathers,
the wretched crow stripped of his stolen colours excite
laughter."   Cf. the jackdaw in Phaedrus, *Fab. Aesop.* 1. 3
and Babrius, *Mythiamb. Aesop.* 72. Philodemus, *Rhet.*, ed.
Sudhaus, 2. 67–8, says that in drawing certain technical
principles from other arts, such as dialectic, the rhetoricians
have " decked themselves out with borrowed plumage."   Cf.
also in Lucian, *Pseudolog.* 5, the sophist's speech, " like Aesop's
jackdaw patched together with borrowed plumes of many
colours."

5 rhetoric.[a] I should not venture to say so, yet I
fear that in their very pursuit of praise for modesty
they are impudent. Some one may say to them:
" Now what do you mean? You are writing a
treatise of your own; you are creating new precepts
for us; you cannot confirm these yourself; so you
borrow examples from others. Beware of acting
impudently in seeking to extract from the labour of
others praise for your own name." Indeed, if the
ancient orators and poets should take the books of
these rhetoricians and each remove therefrom what
belongs to himself, the rhetoricians would have
nothing left to claim as their own.[b]

" But," they say, " since examples correspond to
testimony, it is proper that, like testimony, they
should be taken from men of the highest reputation."[c]
First and foremost, examples are set forth, not to
confirm[d] or to bear witness, but to clarify.[e] When I

---

[c] Cf. the rule in Theon 8 (Spengel 2. 110. 25) that in epideictic the judgements must be taken from reputable men.

[d] But cf., just above, eas confirmare, and 4. xliv. 57, end,
exemplo conprobatum.

[e] Cf. Aristotle, Problem. 18. 3 (916 b) : " We more readily
believe in facts to which many bear witness, and examples
and tales are like witnesses; furthermore, belief through
witnesses is easy; " Rhet. 2. 20 (1394 a) : " If we lack enthymemes, we must use examples as logical proofs . . . If we
have enthymemes, we must use examples as witnesses,
subsequent and supplementary to the enthymemes. . . .
When they follow the enthymemes examples function like
witnesses." Cf. also the definition and functions of the
figure exemplum, 4. xlix. 62 below, and note. On Example
as rhetorical induction see Aristotle, Rhet. 1. 2 (1356 b,
1357 b), and cf. Anal. Pr. 2. 24 (68 b ff.); for its place in
Cicero's theory of argumentation, De Inv. 1. xxix. 44 ff., esp.
49, and De Oratore 2. 40. 169. See further Quintilian, 5. 11. 1 ff.,
and on the exemplum in deliberative speaking 3. v. 9 above.

demonstrandi. Non enim, cum dicimus esse exornationem quae verbi causa constet ex similiter desinentibus verbis, et sumimus hoc exemplum a Crasso: " quibus possumus et debemus," testimonium conlocamus, sed exemplum. Hoc interest igitur inter testimonium et exemplum : exemplo demonstratur id quod dicimus cuiusmodi sit; testimonio esse illud 6 ita ut nos dicimus confirmatur. Praeterea oportet testimonium cum re convenire; aliter enim rem non potest confirmare. At id quod illi faciunt cum re non convenit. Quid ita? Quia pollicentur artem se [1] scribere, exempla proferunt ab iis plerumque qui artem nescierunt. Tum quis est qui possit id quod de arte scripserit conprobare, nisi aliquid scribat ex arte? Contraque faciunt quam polliceri videntur. Nam cum scribere artem instituunt, videntur dicere se excogitasse quod alios doceant; cum scribunt, ostendunt nobis alii quid excogitarint.

IV. " At hoc ipsum difficile est," inquiunt, " eligere de multis." Quid dicitis difficile, utrum laboriosum an artificiosum? Laboriosum non statim praeclarum. Sunt enim multa laboriosa, quae si faciatis, non con-

---

[1] artem se E : se artem se PB Π : se artem HCd : artem Mx.

---

[a] From the celebrated speech delivered before an Assembly of the people in B.C. 106 by L. Licinius Crassus in support of the law by which Q. Servilius Caepio sought, on behalf of the Senate, to wrest the judicial powers from the equites. In Cicero, De Oratore 1. 52. 225, the passage is fuller : " Deliver us from our miseries, deliver us from the jaws of those whose cruelty cannot have enough of our blood: suffer us not not to be slaves to any but yourselves as a whole, *whom we both can and ought* to serve." See also Cicero, *Paradoxa Stoic.* 5. 41. The figure of speech is Homoeoteleuton; see 4. xx. 28 below.

say there is a figure of speech which, for instance, consists of like-ending words, and take this example from Crassus: *quibus possumus et debemus*,[a] I am setting up, not testimony, but an example. The difference between testimony and example is this: by example we clarify the nature of our statement, while by testimony we establish its truth. Furthermore, the testimony must accord with the proposition, for otherwise it cannot confirm the proposition. But the rhetoricians' performance does not accord with what they propose. How so? In that they promise to write a treatise of the art, and then mostly bring forward examples from authors who were ignorant of the art. Now who can give authority to his writings on the art unless he writes something in conformity with the art?[b] Their performance is at variance with what they seem to promise; for when they undertake to write the rules of their art, they appear to say that they have themselves invented what they are teaching to others, but when they actually write, they show us what others have invented.

IV. " But," say they, " this very choice from among many is difficult." What do you mean by difficult? That it requires labour? Or that it requires art? The laborious is not necessarily the excellent. There are many things requiring labour which you would not necessarily boast of having done—unless, to be sure, you thought it a glorious

---

[b] *Cf.* Cicero, *De Inv.* 1. vi. 8: " But for a speaker it is a very unimportant thing to speak concerning his art—that Hermagoras has done; by far the most important thing is to speak in conformity with his art—and this, as we all see, Hermagoras was altogether incapable of doing."

tinuo gloriemini; nisi etiam si vestra manu fabulas
aut orationes totas transscripsissetis gloriosum puta-
retis. Sin istud artificiosum egregium dicitis, videte
ne insueti rerum maiorum videamini, si vos parva res
sicuti magna delectabit. Nam isto modo seligere
rudis quidem nemo potest, sed sine summo artificio
7 multi. Quisquis enim audivit de arte paulo plus, in
elocutione praesertim, omnia videre poterit quae ex
arte dicentur; facere nemo poterit nisi eruditus. Ita
ut si Ennii de tragoediis velis sententias eligere aut
de Pacuvianis nuntios, sed quia plane rudis id facere
nemo poterit, cum feceris te litteratissimum putes,
ineptus sis, propterea quod id facile faciat quivis
mediocriter litteratus; item si, cum de orationibus
aut poëmatis elegeris exempla quae certis signis
artificii notata sunt, quia rudis id nemo facere possit,
artificiosissime te fecisse putes, erres, propterea quod
isto signo videmus te nonnihil scire, aliis signis multa
scire intellegemus. Quod si artificiosum est intellegere quae sint ex arte scripta, multo est artificiosius
ipsum scribere ex arte. Qui enim scribit artificiose
ab aliis commode scripta facile intellegere poterit;
qui eliget facile non continuo commode ipse scribet.
Et si est maxime artificiosum, alio tempore utantur

---

a δράματα. Cf. *fabula* in 1. viii. 13, 1. vi. 10, and 2. viii.
12 above. The task of copying was usually entrusted to
slaves.

b Cf. Isocrates, *Ad Nicocl.* 44, on the selection of maxims
from the outstanding poets.

feat to have transcribed by your own hand whole dramas *a* or speeches! Or do you say that that kind of thing requires exceptional art? Then beware of appearing inexperienced in greater matters, if you are going to find the same delight in a petty thing as in a great. Doubtless no one quite uncultivated can select in this way; yet many who lack the highest art can. For any one at all who has heard more than a little about the art, especially in the field of style, will be able to discern all the passages composed in accordance with the rules; but the ability to compose them only the trained man will possess. It is as if you should wish to choose maxims from the tragedies of Ennius,*b* or messengers' reports from the tragedies of Pacuvius; if, however, just because no one who is quite illiterate can do this, you should suppose that having done it, you are most highly cultivated, you would be foolish, because any person moderately well-read could do it easily. In the same fashion if, having chosen from orations or poems examples marked by definite tokens of art, you should suppose that your performance gives proof of superlative art on the ground that no ignoramus is capable of it, you would be in error, because by this token that you offer we see only that you have some knowledge, but we shall need still other tokens to convince us that you know a great deal. Now if to discern what is written artistically proves your mastery of the art, then a far better proof of this mastery is to write artistically yourself. For though the artistic writer will find it easy to discern what has been skilfully written by others, the facile chooser of examples will not necessarily write with skill himself. And even if it is an especial mark of artistic skill, let them

ea facultate, non tum cum parere et ipsi gignere et proferre debent. Postremo in eo vim artificii consumant, ut ipsi ab aliis potius eligendi quam aliorum boni selectores existimentur.

Contra ea quae ab iis dicuntur qui dicunt alienis exemplis uti oportere satis est dictum. Nunc quae separatim dici possint consideremus.

V. Dicimus igitur eos cum ideo[1] quod alienis utantur peccare, tum magis[2] etiam delinquere quod a multis exempla sumant. Et de eo quod postea diximus antea videamus. Si concederem aliena oportere adsumere exempla, vincerem unius oportere, primum quod contra hoc[3] nulla staret illorum ratio, licet enim eligerent et probarent quemlibet qui sibi in omnes res suppeditaret exempla, vel poëtam vel oratorem, cuius auctoritate niterentur. Deinde interest magni eius qui discere vult utrum omnes

[1] cum ideo B^2Cbl^2 : tum ideo P^2l : cum eo d : id HPB Π Mx.

[2] tum magis P^2B^2CΠE : cum magis HPB Mx.

[3] contra hoc Mx ed. mai., all MSS. but H : hoc contra H^1 Mx : hoc H^2.

[a] Cf. the Preface to the Rhet. ad Alex. (1421 a) : " For the so-called Parian sophists, because they did not themselves give birth to what they teach, have no love for it, in their tasteless indifference, and peddle it about for money."

[b] After the Greek writers have had their say, and have been refuted, our author takes up his own " constructive " case; see 4. i. 1.

[c] The theory and practice of presenting examples from a variety of sources were doubtless Peripatetic ; the rhetoricians criticized belong perhaps to the second century B.C. The use

employ this faculty at another time, and not when they themselves should be conceiving, creating, and bringing forth.[a] In short, let them devote their artistic power to this purpose—to win esteem as worthy themselves to be chosen as models by others, rather than as good choosers of others who should serve as models for them.

Against the contentions of those who maintain that we should use borrowed examples I have said enough. Now let us see what can be said from my own particular point of view.[b]

V. Accordingly I say that they are not only at fault in borrowing examples, but make an even greater mistake in borrowing examples from a great number of sources.[c] And let us first look at my second point. Were I granting that we should borrow examples, I should establish that we ought to select from one author alone. In the first place, my opponents would then have no ground[d] for opposing this procedure, for they might choose and approve whom they would, poet or orator, to supply them with examples for all cases, one on whose authority they could rely.[e] Secondly, it is a matter of great concern to the

of one's own examples, on the other hand, goes back to Corax (see Paul Wendland, *Anaximenes von Lampsakos*, Berlin, 1905, pp. 31 ff.) and was characteristic of the sophists and of the author of the *Rhet. ad Alex.* Note that neither point of view can be regarded as characteristically Greek.

[d] Their theory is set forth in 4. i. 1–ii. 3 above.

[e] In Cicero, *De Oratore* 2. 22. 90–3, Antonius discusses the imitation of some one good model; Quintilian, in 10. 5. 19, urges the student to follow this " custom of our ancestors," but in 10. 2. 23 advises him not to devote himself entirely to imitating one particular style. Seneca, *Contr.* 1, *Praef.* 6, takes a stand against the adoption of a single model, however eminent.

[CICERO]

omnia, an omnia neminem,[1] an aliud alium [2] putet
consequi posse. Si enim putabit posse omnia penes
unum consistere, ipse quoque ad omnium nitetur
facultatem.   Si id desperarit, in paucis se exercebit;
ipsis enim contentus erit, nec mirum, cum ipse praeceptor artis omnia penes unum reperire non potuerit.
Allatis igitur exemplis a Catone, a Graccis, a Laelio,
a Scipione, Galba, Porcina, Crasso, Antonio, ceteris,
item sumptis aliis a poëtis et historiarum scriptoribus,
necesse erit eum qui discet putare ab omnibus omnia,
8 ab uno pauca vix potuisse sumi.   Quare unius alicuius esse similem satis habebit, omnia quae omnes
habuerint solum habere se posse diffidet. Ergo
inutilest ei qui discere vult non putare unum omnia
posse.   Igitur nemo in hanc incideret opinionem si
ab uno exempla sumpsissent. Nunc hoc signi est
ipsos artis scriptores non putasse unum potuisse in
omnibus elocutionis partibus enitere, quoniam neque
sua protulerunt neque unius alicuius aut denique
duorum, sed ab omnibus oratoribus et poëtis exempla

[1] omnes omnia an omnia neminem *l* : omnes omnia an
omnia a nemine $P^2B^2C^2$: aliquem omnia an unum omnia
neminem *d* : omnia nomina an neminem *H* : omnia unum
neminem *b* : omnium omnia an omnia a nemine *PBC* II *Mx*.
[2] an aliud alium P^2C : sed aliud alium *E* : aliud alium
(*M*) *Mx brackets.*

---

[a] On the eloquence of these orators see the following
sections in Cicero, *Brutus* : M. Porcius Cato (*cos.* 195 B.C.)
63 ff., 293 ff.; Ti. Sempronius Gracchus (*tr. pl.* 133 B.C.)
103–4, 296; C. Sempronius Gracchus (*tr. pl.* 123 B.C.) 125–6,
296; C. Laelius (*cos.* 140 B.C.), P. Cornelius Scipio Aemilianus
(Africanus Minor, *cos.* 147, 134 B.C.), and Ser. Sulpicius Galba
(*cos.* 144 B.C.) 82 ff.; M. Aemilius Lepidus Porcina (*cos.*
137 B.C.) 95–6; M. Antonius (*cos.* 99 B.C.) and L. Licinius
Crassus (*cos.* 95 B.C.) 139 ff.

student whether he should believe that every one can
attain the sum total of qualities, or that no one can,
or that one individual can attain one quality and
another individual another quality. For if the
student believes that all qualities can exist in one
man, he himself will strive for a mastery of them
all. But if he despairs of this achievement, he will
occupy himself in acquiring a few qualities, and with
these be content. Nor is this surprising, since the
teacher of the art himself has been unable to find all
the qualities in one author. Thus, when examples
have been drawn from Cato, the Gracchi, Laelius,
Scipio, Galba, Porcina, Crassus, Antonius,[a] and the
rest, and some as well from the poets and historians,
the learner will necessarily believe that the totality
could have been taken only from them all, and that
barely a few examples could have been taken from
8 only one. He will therefore be content with emulat-
ing some one author [b] and distrust his own single
power to possess the sum total of qualities possessed
by all the authors. Now it is disadvantageous for the
student to believe that one person cannot possess
all qualities; [c] and so I say, no one would fall into
this opinion if the rhetoricians had drawn examples
from one author alone. Actually, the fact that the
writers on rhetoric have presented neither their own
examples nor those of some single author, or even
two, but have borrowed from all the orators and
poets, is a sign that they themselves have not believed
that any one individual can be brilliant in all the

[b] Who exemplifies only a few virtues.
[c] On the popularity of this maxim in different forms see
Otto, s.v. " omnis " 1 and 2, pp. 254-5.

sumpserunt. Deinde, si quis velit artem demonstrare nihil prodesse ad dicendum, non male utatur
hoc adiumento, quod unus [1] omnes artis partes consequi nemo potuerit. Quod igitur iuvat eorum
rationem qui omnino non probent artem, id non
ridiculum est ipsum artis scriptorem suo iudicio
conprobare ?

Ergo ab uno sumenda fuisse docuimus exempla, si
9 semper aliunde sumerentur. VI. Nunc omnino
aliunde sumenda non fuisse sic intellegemus.

Primum omnium, quod ab artis scriptore adfertur
exemplum id eius artificii debet esse. Ut si quis
purpuram aut aliud quippiam vendens dicat : " Sume
a me, sed huius exemplum aliunde rogabo tibi quod
ostendam," sic mercem ipsi qui venditant aliunde
exemplum quaeritant aliquod mercis, acervos se
dicunt tritici habere, eorum exemplum pugno non
habent quod ostendant. Si Triptolemus, cum hominibus [2] semen largiretur,[3] ipse ab aliis id hominibus
mutuaretur, aut si Prometheus, cum mortalibus
ignem dividere vellet, ipse a vicinis cum testo
ambulans carbunculos corrogaret, ridiculus videretur.

[1] unus *CE Mx ed. mai.* : unius *M Mx.*
[2] hominibus *E* : se hominibus *M* : a se hominibus *Mx.*
[3] largiretur $P^2B^2\Pi E$: gigneretur *M Mx.*

---

[a] Here is reflected the quarrel, in the second century,
between philosophers and rhetoricians concerning education ;
see Hans von Arnim, *Leben und Werke des Dio von Prusa*,
Berlin, 1898, ch. 1, Hubbell, *The Rhetorica of Philodemus*,
pp. 364–382, Kroll in P.-W., " Rhetorik," coll. 1080–90. For
example, the three Greek philosophers who came as am-
bassadors from Athens to Rome in 155 B.C. (and wielded
considerable influence there) were all opposed to rhetoric—

branches of style. Moreover, should any one wish to show that the art of rhetoric is of no benefit for speaking, he might well in support employ the argument that no one man has been able to master all the branches of rhetoric. Is it not ridiculous for a rhetorician himself to approve by his own judgement what thus supports the theory of those who utterly condemn the art of rhetoric? [a]

I have, then, shown that if examples were always to be borrowed, the borrowing should have been from 9 one author. VI. Now we shall learn from the following that they should not have been borrowed at all.

Above all, an example which is cited by a writer on an art should be proof of his own skill in that art. It is as if a merchant selling purple or some other commodity should say: "Buy of me, but I shall borrow from some one else a sample of this to show you." So do these very people who offer merchandise for sale go in search of a sample of it elsewhere; they say: "We have piles of wheat," but have not a handful of grain to show as a sample.[b] If Triptolemus, when dispensing seed to mankind, had himself borrowed it from other men, or if Prometheus, wishing to distribute fire amongst mortals, had himself gone about with an urn begging a few coals of his neighbours, he would have appeared ridiculous.

the Academic Carneades, the Peripatetic Critolaüs, and the Stoic Diogenes the Babylonian.

[b] Cf. Plutarch, Demosth. 23: "Further, [when Alexander demanded the surrender of the Athenian leaders,] Demosthenes said: 'Just as we see merchants selling their stock of wheat by means of a few grains which they carry about with them in a bowl as a sample, so by giving us up, you, without knowing it, give yourselves up too, all of you.'"

[CICERO]

Isti magistri, omnium dicendi praeceptores, non
videntur sibi ridicule facere cum id quod aliis pollicentur ab aliis quaerunt? Si qui se fontes maximos
penitus absconditos aperuisse dicat, et haec sitiens
cum maxime loquatur neque habeat qui sitim sedet,
non rideatur? Isti cum non modo dominos se
fontium, sed se ipsos fontes esse dicant, et omnium
rigare debeant ingenia, non putant fore ridiculum si,
cum id polliceantur, arescant ipsi siccitate? Chares
ab Lysippo statuas facere non isto modo didicit, ut
Lysippus caput ostenderet Myronium, brachia
Praxitelis,[1] pectus Polycletium, sed omnia coram
magistrum facientem videbat; ceterorum opera vel
sua sponte poterat considerare. Isti credunt eos qui
haec velint discere alia ratione doceri posse commodius.

10 VII. Praeterea ne possunt quidem ea quae sumuntur ab aliis exempla tam esse ad [2] artem adcommo-

---

[1] Praxitelae MSS. Mx.
[2] ad P²CE : HPB II Mx omit.

---

[a] Cf. Longinus, De Sublim. 13. 3 : " Plato, who from that
great Homeric spring drew to himself countless side streams; "
Quintilian, 10. l. 46, and Dionysius Halic., De Composit. Verb.
24, on Homer, as source of inspiration, representing his own
conception of Ocean (Il. 21. 196–7).

[b] In the eyes of Rhodians, Chares, who produced the
Colossus in 280 B.C., would belong in this list of celebrated
sculptors of Greece. Lysippus, his teacher, was a con-
temporary of Alexander the Great; Myron fl. 460 B.C.;
Praxiteles was born c. 390 B.C.; Polycleitus fl. 450–420 B.C.
Rhetoricians liked to use the graphic arts for comparison in
their theory. Cf., for example, Cicero, De Inv. 2. i. 1 ff.,
Brutus 18. 70, Orator 2. 8 ff.; Horace, Ars Poet., init. (poem
and painting, as in 4. xxviii. 39 below); Quintilian, 12. 10. 1 ff.;
Dionysius Halic., De Imit. 6 (ed. Usener-Radermacher,

Do not these schoolmasters, teachers of public speaking to all the world, see that they are acting absurdly when they seek to borrow the very thing they offer to bestow? If any one should say that he has discovered the richest of deeply hidden springs, and tell of the discovery while suffering extreme thirst and lacking the wherewithal to slake his thirst, would he not be a laughingstock? When these writers declare that they are not only the masters of the springs, but are themselves the wellsprings [a] of eloquence, and when it is their duty to water the talents of all, do they not think it will be laughable if, whilst making the offer to do so, they are themselves parched with drought? Not thus did Chares learn from Lysippus how to make statues.[b] Lysippus did not show him a head by Myron,[c] arms by Praxiteles, a chest by Polycleitus. Rather with his own eyes would Chares see the master fashioning all the parts; the works of the other sculptors he could if he wished study on his own initiative. These writers believe that students of this subject can be better taught by another method.

10 VII. Furthermore, borrowed examples simply cannot be so well adapted to the rules of the art because

2 [1]. 203, and for the method contrary to that in our author's analogy, fragm. 6a, p. 214); Theon 1, in Spengel 2. 62. 1 ff. *Cf.* also 4. xi. 16 below: " set the style in relief, as with colours "; Cousin, *Études sur Quintilien,* 1. 658 ff.; Friedrich Blass, *Die griechische Beredsamkeit in dem Zeitraum von Alexander bis auf Augustus,* Berlin, 1865, pp. 222 ff.; E. Bertrand, *De pictura et sculptura apud veteres rhetores,* Paris, 1881; Julius Brzoska, *De canone decem oratorum Atticorum quaestiones,* Breslau, 1883, pp. 69 ff., 81 ff.; Lessing, *Laokoon.*

c Cicero, *Brutus* 19. 75, likens the pleasurable effect of Naevius' *Bellum Punicum* to that yielded by a work of Myron; *cf.* also Dionysius Halic., *De Thuc.* 4.

[CICERO]

data, propterea quod in dicendo leviter unus quisque
locus plerumque tangitur, ne ars appareat, in praecipiendo expresse conscripta ponere oportet exempla
uti in artis formam convenire possint, et post in
dicendo, ne possit ars eminere et ab omnibus videri,
facultate oratoris occultatur. Ergo etiam ut magis
ars cognoscatur suis exemplis melius est uti.

Postremo haec quoque res nos duxit ad hanc
rationem, quod nomina rerum Graeca quae conver-
timus, ea remota sunt a consuetudine. Quae enim
res apud nostros non erant, earum rerum nomina non
poterant esse usitata. Ergo haec asperiora primo
videantur necesse est, id quod fiet rei, non nostra
difficultate. Reliquum scripturae consumetur in
exemplis; haec tamen aliena si posuissemus, factum
esset ut quod commodi esset in hoc libro id nostrum
non esset, quod asperius et inusitatum id proprie
nobis adtribueretur. Ergo hanc quoque incommodi-
tatem fugimus.

His de causis, cum artis inventionem Graecorum
probassemus, exemplorum rationem secuti non

---

a Cf. 1. x. 17, 2. xxx. 47, and 4. xxiii. 32. The idea is
widespread in ancient rhetoric; cf. Aristotle, Rhet. 3. 2 (1404
b) : " Hence may be inferred the need to disguise the art we
employ, so that we give the impression of speaking naturally,
not artificially. Naturalness is persuasive, artifice is the
contrary. People take offence at a speaker who employs
artifice, and think he has designs on them—as if he were
mixing drinks for them;" also 3. 7 (1408 b). See further
Philodemus, Rhet., ed. Sudhaus, 1. 200; Dionysius Halic.,
De Lys. 8; Dionysius, Ars Rhet. 8. 16 (ed. Usener-Radermacher, 2 [1]. 322); Longinus, De Sublim. 22. 1 : " For art
is perfect when it seems to be nature, and nature is effective
when she contains art hidden within her," 17. 1–2, 38. 3;
Anon. Seg. 94, in Spengel-Hammer 1 (2). 369; Hermogenes,
De Meth. Gravit. 17 (ed. Rabe, p. 433); Philostratus, Vita

in speaking each single topic is in general touched
lightly, so that the art may not be obvious. In
instructing, on the other hand, one must cite examples
that are draughted expressly to conform to the pattern
of the art. It is afterwards, in speaking, that the
orator's skill conceals his art,[a] so that it may not
obtrude and be apparent to all. Thus also to the end
that the art may be better understood is it preferable
to use examples of one's own creation.

Finally, I have been led to this method by another
consideration also [b]—the remoteness from our own
usage of the technical terms [c] I have translated from
the Greek. For concepts non-existent among us
could not have familiar appellations. The translated
terms, therefore, must seem rather harsh at first—
that will be a fault of the subject, not mine. The
rest of my treatise will be devoted to examples. If,
however, these which I have here set down had been
borrowed from other sources, the result would have
been that anything apt in this book would not be
mine, but whatever is a little rough or strange would
be assigned to me as my own particular contribution.
So I have escaped this disadvantage also.

On these grounds, although esteeming the Greeks
as the inventors of the art, I have not followed their

Apollon. 8. 6; Longinus, in Spengel-Hammer 1 (2). 195. 4;
Cicero, *De Inv.* 1. xviii. 25, 1. lii. 98, *Brutus* 37. 139, *De
Oratore* 2. 37. 156, 2. 41. 177, *Orator* 12. 38, *Part. Orat.* 6. 19;
Ovid, *Metam.* 10. 252; Quintilian, 1. 11. 3, 2. 5. 7, 4. 1. 8–9,
4. 1. 54, 4. 1. 56–58, 4. 2. 59, 4. 2. 126–7, 9. 4. 144, 11. 2. 47.

[b] *Postremo . . . rationem* form a hexameter.

[c] ὀνόματα τεχνικά. Cf. Varro in Cicero, *Academ.* 1. 6. 24:
" Since we are treating unusual subjects you will no doubt
allow me on occasion to use words unheard-of before, as the
Greeks themselves do, and they have now been treating these
subjects for a long time "; Cicero, *Orator* 57. 211.

sumus. Nunc tempus postulat ut ad elocutionis praecepta transeamus.

Bipertita igitur erit nobis elocutionis praeceptio. Primum dicemus quibus in generibus semper [1] omnis oratoria elocutio debeat esse; deinde ostendemus quas res semper habere debeat.

11   VIII. Sunt igitur tria genera, quae genera nos figuras appellamus, in quibus omnis oratio non vitiosa consumitur: unam gravem, alteram mediocrem, tertiam extenuatam vocamus. Gravis est quae constat ex verborum gravium levi et ornata constructione. Mediocris est quae constat ex humiliore neque tamen ex infima et pervulgatissima verborum dignitate. Adtenuata est quae demissa est usque ad usitatissimam puri consuetudinem sermonis.

[1] semper *E Mx ed. mai.* : eorum semper *M* : ferme semper *Mx*.

---

[a] The three kinds do not occur in every correct discourse, but the kinds of correct discourse are limited to these three.

[b] χαρακτῆρες, πλάσματα. Notice the word *figura*. Our author's term corresponding to English "figure of speech" is *exornatio* (σχῆμα), as in 4. xiii. 18 below (Cicero's term, *lumen*, is used only in 4. xxiii. 32 below); *figura* as "figure of speech" appears first in Quintilian.

[c] ἁδρόν (μεγαλοπρεπές, περιττόν), μέσον (μικτόν), ἰσχνόν (λιτόν), and for other terms see W. Schmid, *Rhein. Mus.* 49 (1894). 136 ff. Here is the first extant division of the styles into three. *Cf.* especially Cicero, *De Oratore* 3. 45. 177, 52. 199, 55. 212, *Orator* 5. 20 ff., 23. 75 ff.; Dionys. Halic., *De Demosth.* 1 ff., and for the doctrine as transferred to Composition (σύνθεσις), *De Composit. Verb.*, chaps. 21 ff.; Quintilian, 12. 10. 58 ff.; also Varro in Gellius 6. 14. To Cicero (*Orator* 21. 69 ff.), following a Hellenistic (and doubtless Peripatetic) concept, each of the styles represents a function of the orator, the plain (*subtile*) serving for proof (*probare*), the middle (*modicum*) for delight (*delectare*), and the vigorous (*vehemens*)

theory of examples. Now it is time to turn to the principles of Style.

I shall divide the teaching of Style into two parts. First I shall state the kinds to which oratorical style should always confine itself,[a] then I shall show what qualities style should always have.

11 VIII. There are, then, three kinds of style, called types,[b] to which discourse, if faultless, confines itself: the first we call the Grand; the second, the Middle; the third, the Simple.[c] The Grand type consists of a smooth and ornate arrangement of impressive words.[d] The Middle type consists of words of a lower, yet not of the lowest and most colloquial, class of words. The Simple type is brought down even to the most current idiom of standard speech.

for swaying the hearers (*flectere*). Scholars are not in agreement on the ultimate origin of the fixed categories; some assign the doctrine to Theophrastus (see A. Körte, *Hermes* 64 [1929]. 80, and Wilhelm Kroll, *Rhein. Mus.* 62 [1907]. 86 ff., Introd. to ed. of Cicero, *Orator* [Berlin, 1913], p. 4, note 1, and " Rhetorik," coll. 1074 f.), while others deny this attribution (see G. L. Hendrickson, *Amer. Journ. Philol.* 25 [1904]. 125–46 and 26 [1905]. 249–290, and Stroux, *De Theophrasti virt. dic.*, Leipzig, 1912, chaps. 1, 7, and 8). On varying views of the part played by the Peripatetic ethical idea of the mean (μεσότης) in the development of the doctrine see especially the articles by Hendrickson and Kroll, and S. F. Bonner in *Class. Philol.* 33 (1938). 257–266. *Cf.* the four types of style in Demetrius, *De Elocut.* 36, the twofold division in Cicero, *Brutus* 55. 201; and see Fritz Wehrli, " Der erhabene und der schlichte Stil in der poetisch-rhetorischen Theorie der Antike," *Phyllobolia für Peter von der Mühll*, Basel, 1946, p. 29. Quintilian, 12. 10. 66 ff., considers the limitation to three styles arbitrary.

[d] Echoed below in connection with Epanaphora (xiii. 19), Antithesis (xv. 21), Interrogation (xv. 22), Paronomasia (xxiii. 32), Surrender (xxix. 39—provoking pity), and Asyndeton (xxx. 41—animation).

In gravi consumetur oratio figura [1] si quae cuiusque
rei poterunt ornatissima verba reperiri, sive propria
sive extranea, ad [2] unam quamque rem adcommoda-
buntur, et si graves sententiae quae in amplificatione
et commiseratione tractantur eligentur, et si exornationes sententiarum aut verborum quae gravitatem
habebunt, de quibus post dicemus, adhibebuntur.   In
hoc genere figurae erit hoc exemplum:

12   " Nam quis est vestrum, iudices, qui satis idoneam
possit in eum poenam excogitare qui prodere hostibus
patriam cogitarit?   Quod maleficium cum hoc scelere
conparari, quod huic maleficio dignum supplicium
potest inveniri?   In iis qui violassent ingenuum,
matremfamilias constuprassent, vulnerassent aliquem
aut postremo necassent, maxima supplicia maiores
consumpserunt;   huic truculentissimo ac nefario
facinori singularem poenam non reliquerunt.   Atque
in aliis maleficiis ad singulos aut ad paucos ex alieno
peccato iniuria pervenit;   huius sceleris qui sunt
adfines uno consilio universis civibus atrocissimas
calamitates machinantur.   O feros animos!   O
crudeles cogitationes!   O derelictos homines ab
humanitate!   Quid agere ausi sunt, aut cogitare
possunt?   Quo pacto hostes, revulsis maiorum sepul-
cris, diiectis moenibus, ovantes inruerent in civitatem;
quo modo deum templis spoliatis, optimatibus truci-

[1] consumetur oratio figura $B^2 C \Pi b$:   consumetur oratio
figurae M: consumetur oratio figurae genere Mx: figura
consumetur oratio ld.
[2] ad $C\Pi$:   *other MSS. Mx omit.*

---

[a] 4. xiii. 19 ff.
[b] *Cf.* Cicero, *Verr.* 2. 2. 16. 40:   " How shall one deal with
this man?   What punishment can be found commensurate
with his lawlessness?"

A discourse will be composed in the Grand style if to each idea are applied the most ornate words that can be found for it, whether literal or figurative; if impressive thoughts are chosen, such as are used in Amplification and Appeal to Pity; and if we employ figures of thought and figures of diction which have grandeur—these I shall discuss later.[a] The following will be an example of this type of style:

12 " Who of you, pray, men of the jury, could devise a punishment drastic enough for him who has plotted to betray the fatherland to our enemies? What offence can compare with this crime, what punishment can be found commensurate with this offence?[b] Upon those who had done violence to a freeborn youth, outraged the mother of a family, wounded,[c] or—basest crime of all—slain a man, our ancestors exhausted the catalogue of extreme punishments; while for this most savage and impious villainy they bequeathed no specific penalty.[d] In other wrongs, indeed, injury arising from another's crime extends to one individual, or only to a few; but the participants in this crime are plotting, with one stroke, the most horrible catastrophes for the whole body of citizens. O such men of savage hearts! O such cruel designs! O such human beings bereft of human feeling! What have they dared to do, what can they now be planning? They are planning how our enemies, after uprooting our fathers' graves, and throwing down our walls, shall with triumphant cry rush into the city; how when they have despoiled the temples

---

[c] On the criminal law in respect to wounding with intent to kill, see Mommsen, p. 627.

[d] Cf. the ninth commonplace in 2. xxx. 49 above, the comparison of crimes.

datis, aliis abreptis in servitutem, matribusfamilias et ingenuis sub hostilem libidinem subiectis, urbs acerbissimo concidat incendio conflagrata; qui se non putant id quod voluerint ad exitum perduxisse nisi sanctissimae patriae miserandum scelerati viderint cinerem. Nequeo verbis consequi, iudices, indignitatem rei; sed neglegentius id fero, quia vos mei non egetis. Vester enim vos animus amantissimus rei publicae facile edocet ut eum qui fortunas omnium voluerit prodere praecipitem proturbetis ex ea civitate, quam iste hostium spurcissimorum dominatu nefario voluerit obruere."

ᵃ This passage (see also 4. xxxvi. 48 and 4. xxxix. 51 below, and 2. xxviii. 45 above) is not to be taken (with Mommsen, p. 972, note 1) as evidence that interdiction was the legal punishment for treason exacted of a citizen. Note " bequeathed no specific penalty " above in this example, and see Ernst Levy, *Die röm. Kapitalstrafe*, Sitzungsber. Heidelberg. Akad. (philos.-hist. Klasse) 21, 5 (1930–31). 20 ff.
ᵇ The example is of an *amplificatio criminis*, belonging to the Conclusion of a speech. For an analysis of this passage, see Jules Marouzeau, *Rev. de Philol.* 45 (1921). 155–6, and *Traité de stylistique appliqué au Latin*, Paris, 1935, p. 181 : The diction is grandiloquent, but not artificial as in the passage below illustrating the swollen style. Note the elegant and learned abstract in *-tus* (*dominatu*) for *-tio*, the archaic genitive *deum*, the far-fetched *hostilem libidinem* (adj. serving for genitive of noun), the artificial disjunctions (*e.g.*, *idoneam . . . poenam*), the periods, the tripartite interjections, the chiasmus in *violassent ingenuum, matremfamilias constuprassent*, the play on words (*hominem humanitate, excogitare cogitarit*), the accumulation of epithets and of superlatives, the contrasts as in *uno consilio, universis civibus*, the variety in the echoes (*quo pacto, quo modo*), the peri-

of the gods, slaughtered the Conservatives and
dragged all others off into slavery, and when they
have subjected matrons and freeborn youths to a
foeman's lust, the city, put to the torch, shall collapse
in the most violent of conflagrations! They do not
think, these scoundrels, that they have fulfilled their
desires to the utmost, unless they have gazed upon
the piteous ashes of our most holy fatherland. Men
of the jury, I cannot in words do justice to the shame-
fulness of their act; yet that disquiets me but little,
for you have no need of me. Indeed your own
hearts, overflowing with patriotism, readily tell you
to drive this man, who would have betrayed the
fortunes of all, headlong from this commonwealth,[a]
which he would have buried under the impious
domination of the foulest of enemies." [b]

---

phrasis in *huius sceleris qui sunt adfines*, the expressive verbs
(*excogitare, constuprassent, machinantur, conflagrata, trucidatis*),
and the poetic words (e.g., *moenibus*). Figures of speech are
Paronomasia (see 4. xxi. 29 below) in *excogitare . . . cogitarit*,
Isocolon (see 4. xx. 27 below) in *Quod maleficium . . . conparari, quod huic . . . inveniri*, Apostrophe (see 4. xv. 22
below) in *O feros animos . . . humanitate*, Reasoning by
Question and Answer (see 4. xvi. 23 below) in *Quid agere, etc.*,
and Surrender (see 4. xxix. 39 below) in the last two sentences
of the passage. The passage contains no periods ending with
monosyllables; the example of the middle style below
contains a few. It contains sixteen dichorees ($- \cup - \cup$) in
the clausulae; the example of the middle style contains
eight, and that of the simple style only one. See Friedrich
Blass, *Die Rhythmen der asianischen und römischen Kunstprosa*, Leipzig, 1905, pp. 107–9; Konrad Burdach, *Schlesisch-
böhmische Briefmuster aus der Wende des vierzehnten Jahr-
hunderts* (Vom Mittelalter zur Reformation 5), Berlin, 1926,
pp. 106 ff.; and the notes on 4. xix. 26 and 4. xxxii. 44 below.
Dionysius Halic., *De Demosth.*, ch. 1, chooses Gorgias and
Thucydides as representatives of the grand style.

13   IX. In mediocri figura versabitur oratio si haec,
ut ante dixi, aliquantum demiserimus neque tamen
ad infimum descenderimus, sic:

"Quibuscum bellum gerimus, iudices, videtis—
cum sociis qui pro nobis pugnare et imperium nostrum
nobiscum simul virtute et industria conservare soliti
sunt. Hi[1] cum se et opes suas et copiam necessario
norunt, tum vero nihilominus propter propinquitatem
et omnium rerum societatem quid omnibus rebus
populus Romanus posset scire et existimare poterant.
Hi[2] cum deliberassent nobiscum bellum gerere,
quaeso, quae res erat qua freti bellum suscipere conarentur, cum multo maximam partem sociorum in
officio manere intellegerent; cum sibi non multitudinem militum, non idoneos imperatores, non pecuniam
publicam praesto esse viderent, non denique ullam
rem quae res pertinet ad bellum administrandum?
Si cum finitimis de finibus bellum gererent, si totum
certamen in uno proelio positum putarent, tamen
omnibus rebus instructiores et apparatiores venirent;
nedum illi imperium orbis terrae, cui imperio omnes
gentes, reges, nationes partim vi, partim voluntate
consenserunt, cum aut armis aut liberalitate a populo
Romano superati essent, ad se transferre tantulis
viribus conarentur.. Quaeret aliquis: 'Quid? Fre-
gellani non sua sponte conati sunt?' Eo quidem
isti minus facile conarentur, quod illi quemadmodum

---

[1] Hi *all MSS. but PB*: hii *PB*: Ii *Mx*.
[2] Hi *all MSS. but l*: Hii *l*: Ii *Mx*.

---

[a] 4. viii. 11.

13   IX. Our discourse will belong to the Middle type if,
as I have said above,[a] we have somewhat relaxed our
style, and yet have not descended to the most
ordinary prose, as follows :

" Men of the jury, you see against whom we are
waging war—against allies who have been wont to
fight in our defence, and together with us to preserve
our empire by their valour and zeal.   Not only must
they have known themselves, their resources, and
their manpower, but their nearness to us and their
alliance with us in all affairs enabled them no less to
learn and appraise the power of the Roman people in
every sphere.   When they had resolved to fight
against us, on what, I ask you, did they rely in pre-
suming to undertake the war, since they understood
that much the greater part of our allies remained
faithful to duty, and since they saw that they had at
hand no great supply of soldiers, no competent com-
manders, and no public money—in short, none of the
things needful for carrying on the war?   Even if
they were waging war with neighbours on a question
of boundaries, even if in their opinion one battle
would decide the contest, they would yet come to the
task in every way better prepared and equipped than
they are now.   It is still less credible that with such
meagre forces they would attempt to usurp that
sovereignty over the whole world which all the
civilized peoples, kings, and barbarous nations have
accepted, in part compelled by force, in part of their
own will, when conquered either by the arms of
Rome or by her generosity.   Some one will ask :
' What of the Fregellans?   Did they not make the
attempt on their own initiative ? '   Yes, but these
allies would be less ready to make the attempt

[CICERO]

discessent [1] videbant. Nam rerum inperiti, qui unius cuiusque rei de rebus ante gestis exempla petere non possunt, ii per inprudentiam facillime deducuntur in fraudem; at ii qui sciunt quid aliis acciderit facile ex aliorum eventis suis rationibus possunt providere. Nulla igitur re inducti, nulla spe freti arma sustulerunt? Quis hoc credet, tantam amentiam quemquam tenuisse ut imperium populi Romani temptare auderet nullis copiis fretus? Ergo aliquid fuisse necessum est. Quid aliud nisi id quod dico potest esse?"

14   X. In adtenuato figurae genere, id quod ad infimum et cotidianum sermonem demissum est, hoc erit exemplum:

"Nam ut forte hic in balneas [2] venit, coepit, postquam perfusus est, defricari; deinde, ubi visum est ut in alveum descenderet, ecce tibi iste de traverso: 'Heus,' inquit, 'adolescens, pueri tui modo me pulsarunt; satis facias oportet.' Hic, qui id aetatis ab ignoto praeter consuetudinem appellatus esset, erubuit. Iste clarius eadem et alia dicere coepit. Hic vix: 'Tamen,' inquit, 'sine me considerare.'

[1] discessent *Mx*: discessissent *Ernesti*: descissent *MSS*.
[2] balneas *Mx ed. mai.*, *all MSS. but p* : balineas *p Mx*.

---

[a] By destroying Fregellae when, after a long history of loyalty, she rebelled in 125 B.C., Rome kept her Italian confederacy intact. See 4. xv. 22 and 4. xxvii. 37 below. The figure here is Hypophora; see 4. xxiii. 33 below.

[b] For the maxim (see 4. xvii. 24 below) *cf.* Terence, *Heaut. Tim.* 221; Publilius Syrus 177 (ed. J. Wight Duff and A. M. Duff): "From another's fault a wise man corrects his own," 60: "In another's misfortune it is good to descry what to avoid," and 133; Livy, 22. 39. 10; Tacitus, *Annals* 4. 33.

[c] Whether the example is an excerpt from a speech actually delivered, or our author's own creation, is uncertain. The sentiments are such as Q. Varius Hybrida might have uttered

precisely because they saw how the Fregellans fared.[a] For inexperienced peoples, unable to find in history a precedent for every circumstance, are through imprudence easily led into error; whilst those who know what has befallen others can easily from the fortunes of these others draw profit for their own policies.[b] Have they, then, in taking up arms, been impelled by no motive? Have they relied on no hope? Who will believe that any one has been so mad as to dare, with no forces to depend on, to challenge the sovereignty of the Roman people? They must, therefore, have had some motive, and what else can this be but what I say?" [c]

14 X. Of the Simple type of style, which is brought down to the most ordinary speech of every day, the following will serve as an example:

"Now our friend happened to enter the baths, and, after washing, was beginning to be rubbed down. Then, just as he decided to go down into the pool, suddenly this fellow turned up. 'Say, young chap,' said he, ' your slaveboys have just beat me; you must make it good.' The young man grew red, for at his age he was not used to being hailed by a stranger. This creature started to shout the same words, and more, in a louder voice. With difficulty the youth replied: 'Well, but let me look into the matter.'

in support of his law (90 B.C.) prosecuting those who by malicious fraud compelled the allies to war against Rome; confederates at Rome are referred to in the example of the slack style, 4. xi. 16 below. The present example belongs to the *rationis confirmatio* of an argument (see 2. xviii. 28 above), and is not so impassioned as the example of the grand style above. Dionysius Halic., *De Demosth.*, ch. 3 ff., chooses Thrasymachus, Isocrates, and Plato as representatives of the middle style.

[CICERO]

Tum vero iste clamare voce ista quae perfacile cuivis
rubores eicere potest; ita petulans est atque acerba :
ne ad solarium quidem, ut mihi videtur, sed pone
scaenam et in eiusmodi locis exercitata. Con-
turbatus est adolescens; nec mirum, cui etiam nunc
pedagogi lites ad oriculas versarentur inperito huiusmodi conviciorum. Ubi enim iste vidisset scurram
exhausto rubore, qui se putaret nihil habere quod de
existimatione perderet, ut omnia sine famae detrimento facere posset ? "

15 Igitur genera figurarum ex ipsis exemplis intellegi
poterant. Erant enim et adtenuata verborum constructio quaedam et item alia in gravitate, alia posita
in mediocritate.

Est autem cavendum ne, dum haec genera con-
sectemur, in finitima et propinqua vitia veniamus.
Nam gravi figurae, quae laudanda est, propinqua est

---

^a The Sundial, in the Forum, was a much frequented meeting-
place for gossip; *cf.* Cicero, *Pro Quinctio* 18. 59. The Roman
citizen ordinarily looked down upon actors as beneath his
dignity; they were usually freedmen or slaves. For the
connection between the stage and vice see, *e.g.*, Cicero, *In Cat.*
2. 5. 9.

^b Analysing this example of the *adtenuatum genus* (the
" thinness " refers to lack of adornment and fineness of
texture), Marouzeau, *Traité*, pp. 181–2 and *art. cit.*, pp. 156–7,
points to the forms of colloquial usage (*pedagogi*, the diminu-
tive *oriculas*), idioms like *de traverso*, *coepit* with the passive,
the vulgar use of the archaism *pone* for *post*, and of the
indicative *potest* in a characterizing clause, the expletive use
as in conversation of the ethical dative *tibi* with *ecce*, the
frequent use of the demonstrative *iste* for *hic* or *is*, the

Right then the fellow cries out in that tone of his that might well force blushes from any one; this is how aggressive and harsh it is—a tone certainly not practised in the neighbourhood of the Sundial, I would say, but backstage, and in places of that kind.[a] The young man was embarrassed. And no wonder, for his ears still rang with the scoldings of his tutor, and he was not used to abusive language of this kind. For where would he have seen a buffoon, with not a blush left, who thought of himself as having no good name to lose, so that he could do anything he liked without damage to his reputation?"[b]

15 Thus the examples themselves are enough to make clear the types of style. For one arrangement of words is of the simple type, another again belongs to the grand, and another belongs to the middle.

But in striving to attain these styles, we must avoid falling into faulty styles closely akin to them.[c] For instance, bordering on the Grand style, which is in itself praiseworthy, there is a style to be avoided.

accusative of quality in *id aetatis*, the asyndeton in *satisfacias oportet*, and the type of parataxis characteristic of comedy in *ita petulans est . . . exercitata.* See also J. B. Hofmann, *Lat. Umgangssprache*, Heidelberg, 1936, p. 207. For *heus* see *ibid.*, sect. 17; for *eicere* (= *efferre*), sect. 138. For *quod de existimatione perderet* see Schmalz-Hofmann, pp. 526 f. Note also the brevity of *Hic vix.* The example is a factual, not primarily emotional, *narratio*, which is a division of *sermo*; see 3. xiii. 23 above. Dionysius Halic., *De Demosth.*, ch. 2, chooses Lysias as representative of the simple style.

[c] παρακείμενα ἁμαρτήματα. *Cf.* Longinus, *De Sublim.*, ch. 3, and Horace, *Ars Poet.* 24-8. These deviations (παρεκβάσεις) are Peripatetic in concept; excess in style is judged in relation to the mean. The faulty styles were known to Marcus Varro (Gellius 6. 14); *cf.* also Demetrius, *De Elocut.* 114, 186, 236, 302.

ea quae fugienda; quae recte videbitur appellari si sufflata nominabitur. Nam ita ut corporis bonam habitudinem tumor imitatur saepe, item gravis oratio saepe inperitis videtur ea quae turget et inflata est, cum aut novis aut priscis verbis aut duriter aliunde translatis aut gravioribus quam res postulat aliquid dicitur, hoc modo: " Nam qui perduellionibus venditat patriam non satis subplicii dederit si praeceps in Neptunias depultus erit lacunas. Poenite igitur istum qui montis belli fabricatus est, campos sustulit pacis." In hoc genus plerique cum declinantur et ab eo quo profecti sunt aberrarunt, specie gravitatis falluntur nec perspicere possunt orationis tumorem.

16   XI. Qui in mediocre genus orationis profecti sunt, si pervenire eo non potuerunt, errantes perveniunt ad confine genus[1] eius generis, quod appellamus dissolutum, quod est sine nervis et articulis; ut hoc modo appellem fluctuans, eo quod fluctuat huc et

---

[1] confine *E* : confinii genus *HPB* Π *Mx* : confinium *C*.

---

[a] οἰδοῦν, ἐπηρμένον, ὑπερβάλλον, φυσῶδες. *Cf.* Longinus, *De Sublim.* 3. 4 : " Evil are the swellings (ὄγκοι), both in the body and in diction, which are inflated and unreal, and threaten us with the reverse of our aim " (tr. W. Rhys Roberts); Horace, *Ars Poet.* 27.

[b] Thus violating propriety (τὸ πρέπον). See notes on 3. xv. 26, 4. xi. 16, 4. xii. 17, and 4. xv. 22, and Introduction, p. xx. For a study of the history of this principle, see Max Pohlenz, *Nachrichten von der Gesellsch. der Wissensch. zu Göttingen (Philol.-histor. Klasse)*, 1933, pp. 53–92.

[c] Marouzeau, *art. cit.*, pp. 157–8, and *Traité*, p. 181, analyses the learned affectations in spelling, forms, and construction, all embraced by a *tour de force* in four lines. Note the archaic forms *subplicii, poenite*, and the Lucretian *montis*; the curious *depultus*, representing the primitive form

To call this the Swollen[a] style will prove correct. For just as a swelling often resembles a healthy condition of the body, so, to those who are inexperienced, turgid and inflated language often seems majestic—when a thought is expressed either in new or in archaic words, or in clumsy metaphors, or in diction more impressive than the theme demands,[b] as follows: " For he who by high treason betrays his native land will not have paid a condign penalty albeit hurtl'd into gulfs Neptunian. So punish ye this man, who hath builded mounts of war, destroyed the plains of peace." [c] Most of those who fall into this type, straying from the type they began with, are misled by the appearance of grandeur and cannot perceive the tumidity of the style.

16   XI. Those setting out to attain the Middle style, if unsuccessful, stray from the course and arrive at an adjacent type, which we call the Slack[d] because it is without sinews[e] and joints; accordingly I may call it the Drifting, since it drifts to and fro, and cannot

of the participle; the ancient deponent *fabricari*; the emphatic *venditare*; *perduellionibus*, rare example of an abstract in the plural (the author elsewhere uses *maiestas*; for the difference between the two crimes see H. F. Jolowicz, *Historical Introd. to the Study of Roman Law*, 2nd ed., Cambridge, 1952, p. 327); the highly poetic *lacunas*; the disjunction of *Neptunias* and *lacunas*; the adjective *Neptunias* for the genitive of the noun; the learned double metaphor in *montis* and *campos*. These passages illustrating the faulty styles were doubtless made up by our author, with the examples of the faultless styles in view.

[d] ἐκλελυμένον, διαλελυμένον. *Cf.* Cicero, *Orator* 68. 228.
[e] For the analogy *cf.* Fortunatianus 3. 9 (Halm, p. 126): " What style is the reverse of the middle style ? The lukewarm, slack, and, as I may call it, sinewless style "; and Horace, *Ars Poet.* 26–7.

illuc nec potest confirmate neque viriliter sese expedire. Id est eiusmodi: " Socii nostri cum belligerare nobiscum vellent profecto ratiocinati essent etiam atque etiam quid possent[1] facere, si quidem sua sponte facerent et non haberent hinc adiutores multos, malos homines et audaces. Solent enim diu cogitare omnes qui magna negotia volunt agere." Non potest huiusmodi sermo tenere adtentum auditorem; diffluit enim totus neque quicquam conprehendens perfectis verbis amplectitur.

Qui non possunt in illa facetissima verborum adtenuatione commode versari veniunt ad aridum et exsangue genus orationis, quod non alienum est exile nominari, cuiusmodi est hoc: " Nam istic in balineis accessit ad hunc. Postea dicit: ' Hic tuus servus me pulsavit.' Postea dicit hic illi: ' Considerabo.' Post ille convicium fecit et magis magisque praesente multis clamavit." Frivolus hic quidem iam et inliberalis est sermo; non enim est adeptus id quod habet adtenuata figura, puris et electis verbis conpositam orationem.

Omne genus orationis, et grave et mediocre et adtenuatum, dignitate adficiunt exornationes, de quibus

---

[1] possent *d editors* : possint *the other MSS. Mx.*

---

[a] The phrase *malos et audaces* is used by Sisenna, fragm. 110, *Hist. Rom. Reliquiae*, ed. Hermann Peter, Leipzig, 1914, 1. 291. " Here " refers to Rome.

[b] *Cf.* Sophocles, *Electra* 320 : " Yes, a man entering upon a great enterprise likes to pause."

[c] ταπεινόν, ξηρόν.

[d] Analysing this example of the *sermo inliberalis*, Marouzeau, *Traité*, pp. 103 and 182, and *art. cit.*, p. 157, calls attention to the unsyncopated *balineis* (*cf.* 4. x. 14 and

get under way with resolution and virility. The following is an example: " Our allies, when they wished to wage war with us, certainly would have deliberated again and again on what they could do, if they were really acting of their own accord and did not have many confederates from here, evil men and bold.[a] For they are used to reflecting long, all who wish to enter upon great enterprises." [b] Speech of this kind cannot hold the hearer's attention, for it is altogether loose, and does not lay hold of a thought and encompass it in a well-rounded period.

Those who cannot skilfully employ that elegant simplicity of diction discussed above, arrive at a dry and bloodless kind of style which may aptly be called the Meagre.[c] The following is an example: " Now this fellow came up to this lad in the baths. After that he says: ' Your slaveboy here has beat me.' After that the lad says to him: ' I'll think about it.' Afterwards this fellow called the lad names and shouted louder and louder, while a lot of people were there." [d] This language, to be sure, is mean and trifling, having missed the goal of the Simple type, which is speech composed of correct and well-chosen words.

Each type of style, the grand, the middle, and the simple, gains distinction from rhetorical figures,

4. l. 63), the reinforced *istic* (cf. *iste* in the example of the simple style above), the violation of the concord of number in the Old Latin expression *praesente multis* (see Schmalz-Hofmann, p. 638; W. M. Lindsay, *Syntax of Plautus*, Oxford, 1907, p. 4), the adverbial *post*, the vulgar locution *convicium facere*, the abuse of the demonstrative in *istic, hunc, hic, hic, illi, ille*, the monotonous transitions, the awkward parataxis and short sentences, the employment thrice of *post* or *postea*, and the direct style for the short and insignificant reply.

post loquemur; quae si rarae disponentur, distinctam
sicuti coloribus, si crebrae conlocabuntur, obliquam [1]
reddunt orationem. Sed figuram in dicendo commutare oportet, ut gravem mediocris, mediocrem
excipiat adtenuata, deinde identidem commutentur,
ut facile satietas varietate vitetur.

17   XII. Quoniam quibus in generibus elocutio versari
debeat dictum est, videamus nunc quas res debeat
habere elocutio commoda et perfecta. Quae maxime
admodum oratori adcommodata est tres res in se
debet habere: elegantiam, conpositionem, dignitatem.

Elegantia est quae facit ut locus unus quisque
pure et aperte dici videatur. Haec tribuitur in
Latinitatem et [2] explanationem.

Latinitas est quae sermonem purum conservat, ab
omni vitio remotum. Vitia in sermone quo minus is

---

[1] obliquam *MSS. Mx* : oblitam *Lambinus.*
[2] et *PB²CΠE* : *B Mx* omit.

---

[a] 4. xiii. 18 below.
[b] Thus violating propriety; see note on 4. x. 15 above. If
oblitam be the correct reading, then " they produce an over-
loaded, or overdaubed, style."
[c] *Tractatio*; see note to 2. xviii. 27 above. Dionysius
Halic., *De Demosth.*, chaps. 8 ff., thinks that Demosthenes best
blended all three types of style.
[d] σύνθεσις ὀνομάτων, ἁρμονία. The scanty treatment of
Artistic Composition in 4. xii. 18 below is confined to the
avoidance of faults rather than to constructive theory.
[e] The qualities were chiefly treated by the Peripatetics and
Stoics. The Theophrastan scheme is here modified. The four
qualities in Theophrastus' system were Purity (Ἑλληνισμός),
Clarity (σαφήνεια), Appropriateness (τὸ πρέπον), and Ornamentation (κατασκευή), this last embracing Correct Choice
of Words (ἐκλογὴ ὀνομάτων), Artistic Composition (ἁρμονία),
and the Figures (σχήματα). Thus for our author, *elegantia*

which I shall discuss later.[a] Distributed sparingly, these figures set the style in relief, as with colours; if packed in close succession, they set the style awry.[b] But in speaking we should vary the type of style, so that the middle succeeds the grand and the simple the middle, and then again interchange them, and yet again. Thus, by means of the variation,[c] satiety is easily avoided.

XII. Since I have discussed the types to which style should confine itself, let us now see what qualities should characterize an appropriate and finished style. To be in fullest measure suitable to the speaker's purpose such a style should have three qualities: Taste, Artistic Composition,[d] and Distinction.[e]

Taste makes each and every topic seem to be expressed with purity and perspicuity. The subheads under Taste are Correct Latinity and Clarity.

It is Correct Latinity[f] which keeps the language pure, and free of any fault. The faults in language

comprises two primary qualities of Theophrastus' scheme; Appropriateness (see note on 4. x. 15 above) is here missing; the ornamentation residing in the choice of words is left unconsidered (except for what he says under *explanatio*, and his treatment of Metaphor among the figures; see 4. xxxiv. 45 below); Artistic Composition is a primary quality, and is not treated as a branch of Ornamentation; finally, Ornamentation, represented by *dignitas*, is limited to the Figures. See Stroux, *De Theophrasti virt. dic.*, pp. 22–3, 64–7.

[f] Corresponds to Ἑλληνισμός among the Greek rhetoricians. Solecism and barbarism were studied chiefly by the Stoics. *Cf.* Quintilian, 1. 5. 5 ff., 1. 5. 34 ff.; C. N. Smiley, *Latinitas and* ΕΛΛΗΝΙΣΜΟΣ, Madison, 1906; Hubbell, *The Rhetorica of Philodemus*, p. 295, note 4; Volkmann, p. 396, note 1; Alexander Numenii, *De Schemat.*, in Spengel 3. 9. 25: "Barbarism involves correction of a word, solecism of the syntax."

Latinus sit duo possunt esse: soloecismus et barbarismus. Soloecismus est cum in verbis pluribus consequens verbum superiori [1] non adcommodatur. Barbarismus est cum verbis aliquid vitiose effertur.[2] Haec qua ratione vitare possimus [3] in arte grammatica dilucide dicemus.[a]

Explanatio est quae reddit apertam et dilucidam orationem.[b] Ea conparatur duabus rebus, usitatis verbis et propriis.[c] Usitata sunt ea quae versantur in consuetudine cotidiana; propria,[d] quae eius rei verba sunt aut esse possunt qua de loquemur.[e]

18 Conpositio est verborum constructio quae facit omnes partes orationis aequabiliter perpolitas. Ea conservabitur si fugiemus crebras vocalium concursiones,[f] quae vastam atque hiantem orationem reddunt, ut haec est: "Bacae aeneae amoenissime inpendebant;" et si vitabimus eiusdem litterae

[1] superiori P^2B^2E : superius M Mx.
[2] effertur CE : efferatur $HP B \Pi$ Mx.
[3] possimus $C \Pi E$: possumus $HPBMx$.

---

[a] At this juncture in the discussion of Style rhetoricians would refer to grammatical studies; cf. Quintilian, 8. l. 2; Martianus Capella, 5. 508. Whether our author ever wrote a tract on Grammar we do not know; see notes on 3. ii. 3 and 3. xvi. 28 above. This is the earliest mention in extant literature of a specific Latin ars grammatica. The close connection between grammatical and rhetorical studies is characteristic of Rhodian education.

[b] σαφήνεια.

[c] κοινὰ ἔπη.

[d] οἰκεῖα ἔπη, κύρια ἔπη.

[e] The regular designations of things, literal as against metaphorical, the designations " which were so to speak born with the things themselves " (Cicero, De Oratore 3. 37. 149).

[f] Hiatus, σύγκρουσις φωνηέντων. On this subject cf. Dionysius Halic., De Composit. Verb., ch. 23, and especially

which can mar its Latinity are two: the Solecism and the Barbarism. A solecism occurs if the concord between a word and one before it in a group of words is faulty. A barbarism occurs if the verbal expression is incorrect. How to avoid these faults I shall clearly explain in my tract on Grammar.[a]

Clarity [b] renders language plain and intelligible. It is achieved by two means, the use of current terms [c] and of proper terms.[d] Current terms are such as are habitually used in everyday speech. Proper terms are such as are, or can be, the designations specially characteristic of the subject of our discourse.[e]

18 Artistic Composition consists in an arrangement of words which gives uniform finish to the discourse in every part. To ensure this virtue we shall avoid the frequent collision of vowels,[f] which makes the style harsh and gaping, as the following: " Bacae aeneae amoenissime inpendebant." [g] We shall also avoid the excessive recurrence of the same letter,[h]

Demetrius, *De Elocut.* 2. 68 ff., 5. 299, who, while warning against a jerky style, yet points to the force, music, and harmony of speech that hiatus can bring. Isocrates and his followers, and Demosthenes, avoided hiatus, Thucydides and Plato [in his earlier dialogues] did not; see Cicero, *Orator* 44. 150 ff. Philodemus, *Rhet.*, ed. Sudhaus, 1. 163, thinks hiatus rather frigid, but sometimes convenient.

[g] " The copper-coloured berries hung most invitingly "; Asian in style.

[h] Alliteration; most often Paromoeon to the grammarians; Homoeoprophoron to Martianus Capella (5. 514). Alliteration (as it has been called since early modern times) played a larger rôle in Latin than in Greek style; see Schmalz-Hofmann, pp. 801–3, Marouzeau, *Traité*, pp. 42–7, and Eduard Wölfflin, "Zur Allitteration," *Mélanges Boissier*, Paris, 1903, pp. 461–4.

[CICERO]

nimiam adsiduitatem, cui vitio versus hic erit exemplo
—nam hic nihil prohibet in vitiis alienis exemplis
uti :

O Tite, tute, Tati, tibi tanta, tyranne, tulisti ;

et hic eiusdem poëtae :

quoiquam quicquam quemquam, quemque quisque
conveniat, neget ;

et si eiusdem verbi adsiduitatem nimiam fugiemus,
eiusmodi :

Nam cuius rationis ratio non extet, ei
rationi ratio non est fidem habere admodum ; [1]

et si non utemur continenter similiter cadentibus
verbis, hoc modo :

Flentes, plorantes, lacrimantes, obtestantes ;

et si verborum transiectionem vitabimus, nisi
quae erit concinna, qua de re posterius loquemur ;
quo in vitio est Coelius [2] adsiduus, ut haec est : " In
priore libro has res ad te scriptas, Luci, misimus,

---

[1] *lac.* ; admodum *sugg. Mx.*
[2] Caelius *MSS. Mx.*

---

[a] " Thyself to thyself, Titus Tatius the tyrant, thou tookest
those terrible troubles " (fragm. 108, tr. Warmington); from
Ennius' *Annals*, Bk. I. See Vahlen p. 18. *Cf.* Charisius, ed.
Barwick, p. 370, and Donatus, in Keil, *Gramm. Lat.* 4. 398.
20.

[b] Marx suggests that in the original play this verse might
have been preceded by something like *cum debere carnufex*.
"[Since the rascal] denies that anyone [owes] anything to

272

and this blemish the following verse will illustrate—
for at this juncture, in considering faults, nothing
forbids me to use examples from others:

O Tite, tute, Tati, tibi tanta, tyranne, tulisti.[a]

And this verse of the same poet:

quoiquam quicquam quemquam, quemque quisque
   conveniat, neget.[b]

And again, we shall avoid the excessive repetition of
the same word,[c] as follows:

Nam cuius rationis ratio non extet, ei
rationi ratio non est fidem habere admodum;[d]

Again, we shall not use a continuous series of words
with like case endings,[e] as follows:

Flentes, plorantes, lacrimantes, obtestantes.[f]

Again, we shall avoid the dislocation of words,[g] unless
it is neatly effected—and this I shall discuss later.
Coelius persists in this fault, as the following
illustrates: " In priore libro has res ad te scriptas,

---

anyone, whoever sues whomever." We do not know from
which play (comedy) of Ennius the verse comes.

[e] Transplacement. See 4. xiv. 20 below.

[d] " For when the reasonableness of a reason is not evident,
in that reason it is not reasonable to put any faith at all."
These iambic senarii are by Marx, *Proleg.*, p. 118, thought to
be in the style of Ennius.

[e] Homoeoptoton. See 4. xx. 28 below.

[f] " Bewailing, imploring, weeping, protesting." Spondaic
hexameter, assigned without certitude to Ennius; see Vahlen,
p. 16, Warmington 1. 462. *Cf.* Charisius, ed. Barwick, p. 371;
Diomedes, in Keil, *Gramm. Lat.* 1. 447. 16; and Donatus,
in Keil 4. 398. 23.

[g] Hyperbaton. See 4. xxxii. 44 below.

[CICERO]

Aeli."[a] Item fugere oportet longam verborum continuationem, quae et auditoris aures et oratoris spiritum laedit.

His vitiis in conpositione vitatis reliquum operae consumendum est in dignitate. XIII. Dignitas est quae reddit ornatam orationem varietate distinguens.[b] Haec in verborum et in sententiarum exornationes dividitur.[c] Verborum exornatio est quae ipsius sermonis insignita continetur perpolitione. Sententiarum exornatio est quae non in verbis, sed in ipsis rebus quandam habet dignitatem.

*   *   *[1]

19 Repetitio est cum continenter ab uno atque eodem verbo in rebus similibus et diversis principia sumun-

---

¹ *Transition missing.*

---

[a] L. Coelius Antipater, after 121 B.C., dedicated his *Punic War* (in seven books) to L. Aelius Stilo. In the Preface to Book I he promised that he would use Hyperbaton only when necessary (Cicero, *Orator* 69. 230), but he violated this principle, as here in the Preface to Book II : " In the previous Book, Lucius Aelius, I dedicated to you the account of these events." Following a normal word order the sentence would read : *In priore libro, Luci Aeli, has res scriptas ad te misimus.* Note also that beginning with the fourth word we have a complete dactylic hexameter—an example of epic influence.

[b] κατασκευή (sometimes κόσμος), which includes also *gravitas* (μεγαλοπρέπεια) and *suavitas* (τὸ ἡδύ), as is made clear in 4. lvi. 69 below; see also Cicero, *De Inv.* 2. xv. 49. Ornamentation, worked out exclusively by Figures, dominates our author's theory of Style. The Atticists opposed this kind of domination; see Cicero, *Orator* 23. 78–24. 79.

[c] σχήματα (see note on 4. viii. 11 above) λέξεως and σχήματα διανοίας. The distinction, here met for the first time, is best discussed by Quintilian, 9. 1. 10 ff. Fortunatianus, 3. 10 (Halm, pp. 126–7), divides figures of diction into the grammatical (λέξεως) and the rhetorical (λόγου), probably following

274

Luci, misimus, Aeli." [a]   One should likewise avoid a
long period, which does violence both to the ear of
the listener and to the breathing of the speaker.

These vices of composition avoided, we must
devote the rest of our efforts to conferring Distinction
upon the style.   XIII. To confer distinction upon
style is to render it ornate,[b] embellishing it by
variety.   The divisions under Distinction are Figures
of Diction and the Figures of Thought.[c]   It is a
figure of diction if the adornment is comprised in the
fine polish of the language itself.   A figure of thought
derives a certain distinction from the idea, not from
the words.

*   *   *

19   Epanaphora [d] occurs when one and the same word
forms successive beginnings for phrases expressing

---

a Stoic author.   The ancients regarded Gorgias of Leontini
(fifth century B.C.) as the inventor of σχήματα.   Our author's
treatment is the oldest extant formal one, yet represents a
period preceding that of complete systematization (that of
Quintilian and Phoebammon).   Tropes are considered at
4. xxxi. 42 below; the figures of thought begin at 4. xxxv. 47.
The ancient rhetoricians differ sometimes greatly, sometimes
slightly, in their definitions of figures, which became excessively
numerous as refinements were made in distinguishing them.
The line of demarcation between tropes and figures, and that
between figures of thought and figures of diction were often
vague.   See Quintilian, Bks. 8 and 9, especially 9. 1. 1 ff.;
Julius Rufinianus, *De Schem. Dian.* 1, in Halm, pp. 59–60;
Willy Barczat, *De figurarum disciplina atque auctoribus*, diss.
Göttingen, 1904;   Hermann Schrader in *Hermes* 39 (1904).
563–603;   Kroll, " Rhetorik," coll. 1108–12;   Volkmann, pp.
415 ff., 456 ff.;   Cousin, *Études sur Quintilien*, 1. 437–517,
and vol. 2.

[d] ἐπαναφορά.   ἐπιβολή in Rutilius Lupus, 1. 7 (Halm, p. 6), is
the same figure but also allows the use of synonyms instead of
repeating the precise word.

tur, hoc modo : " Vobis istuc adtribuendum est, vobis
gratia est habenda, vobis ista res erit honori.'' Item :
" Scipio Numantiam sustulit, Scipio Kartaginem
delevit, Scipio pacem peperit, Scipio civitatem serva-
vit." Item : " Tu in forum prodire, tu lucem con-
spicere, tu in horum conspectum venire conaris ?
Audes verbum facere ? audes quicquam ab istis
petere ? audes supplicium deprecari ? Quid est
quod possis defendere ? quid est quod audeas postulare ? quid est quod tibi concedi putes oportere ? Non
ius iurandum reliquisti ? non amicos prodidisti ? non
parenti manus adtulisti ? non denique in omni dedecore volutatus es ? " Haec exornatio cum multum
venustatis habet tum gravitatis et acrimoniae
plurimum ; quare videtur esse adhibenda et ad
ornandam et ad exaugendam orationem.

Conversio est per quam non, ut ante, primum repe-
timus verbum, sed ad postremum continenter rever-
timur, hoc modo : " Poenos populus Romanus
iustitia vicit, armis vicit, liberalitate vicit." Item :
" Ex quo tempore concordia de civitate sublata est,
libertas sublata est, fides sublata est, amicitia sublata
est, res publica sublata est." Item : " C. Laelius
homo novus erat, ingeniosus erat, doctus erat, bonis

ª Cf. the epanaphora of *tu* in the passage from the speech
(Cicero, *De Oratore* 2. 55. 226) delivered by L. Licinius Crassus
pro Planc(i)o against M. Junius Brutus *c.* 91 B.C. : " You dare
behold the light of day ? You dare look these people in the
face ? You dare present yourself in the forum, within the
City, in the plain view of the citizens ? You do not tremble

like and different ideas, as follows: " To you must
go the credit for this, to you are thanks due, to you
will this act of yours bring glory." Again: " Scipio
razed Numantia, Scipio destroyed Carthage, Scipio
brought peace, Scipio saved the state." Again:
" You venture to enter the Forum? You venture to
face the light? You venture to come into the sight
of these men? Dare you say a word? Dare you
make a request of them? Dare you beg off punishment?[a] What can you say in your defence? What
do you dare to demand? What do you think should
be granted to you? Have you not violated your oath?
Have you not betrayed your friends? Have you
not raised your hand against your father? Have you
not, I ask, wallowed in every shame?" This figure
has not only much charm, but also impressiveness and
vigour in highest degree; I therefore believe that it
ought to be used for both the embellishment and the
amplification of style.

In Antistrophe[b] we repeat, not the first word in
successive phrases, as in Epanaphora, but the last,
as follows: " It was by the justice of the Roman
people that the Carthaginians were conquered, by its
force of arms that they were conquered, by its
generosity that they were conquered." Again:
Since the time when from our state concord disappeared, liberty disappeared, good faith disappeared, friendship disappeared, the common weal
disappeared." Again: " Gaius Laelius was a self-
made man, a talented man, a learned man, to good

in fear of that corpse, you do not tremble in fear of the very
images [of your ancestors]? "

[b] ἀντιστροφή. ἐπιφορά in Rutilius Lupus 1. 8 (Halm, pp.
6–7). *Cf.* Disjunction, 4. xxvii. 37 below.

[CICERO]

viris et studiis amicus erat; ergo in civitate primus
erat." Item: "Nam cum istos ut absolvant te
rogas, ut peierent rogas, ut existimationem neglegant
rogas, ut leges populi Romani tuae libidini largiantur
rogas."

20   XIV. Conplexio est quae utramque conplectitur
exornationem, ut et conversione et repetitione [1]
utamur, quam ante exposuimus, et ut repetatur idem
verbum saepius et crebro ad idem postremum rever-
tamur, hoc modo: "Qui sunt qui foedera saepe
ruperunt? Kartaginienses. Qui sunt qui crudelissime bellum gesserunt? Kartaginienses. Qui sunt
qui Italiam deformaverunt? Kartaginienses. Qui
sunt qui sibi postulant [2] ignosci? Kartaginienses.
Videte ergo quam conveniat eos impetrare." Item:
" Quem senatus damnarit, quem populus damnarit,
quem omnium existimatio damnarit, eum vos
sententiis vestris absolvatis? "

Traductio est quae facit uti, cum idem verbum
crebrius ponatur, non modo non offendat animum,
sed etiam concinniorem orationem reddat, hoc pacto:
" Qui nihil habet in vita iucundius vita, is cum

---

[1] lac.; ut et conversione et repetitione *sugg. Mx.*
[2] qui postulant *E* : qui sibi postulent *M Mx.*

---

[a] A free paraphrase of Aeschines, *Adv. Ctes.* 198 : " Whoever, then, on the question of the penalty asks for your vote,
is asking for the remission of your anger; but whoever in the
first speech asks for your vote, is asking for the surrender of
your oath, is asking for the surrender of the law, is asking for
the surrender of the democratic constitution." The Greek
original likewise illustrates Antistrophe.

[b] συμπλοκή. *Cf.* Aeschines, *Adv. Ctes.* 202 : " Against
yourself you are calling him, against the laws you are calling
him, against the democratic constitution you are calling

men and good endeavour a friendly man; and so in the state he was the first man." Again: " Is it acquittal by these men that you are demanding? Then it is their perjury that you are demanding, it is their neglect of their reputation that you are demanding, it is the surrender of the laws of the Roman people to your caprice that you are demanding." [a]

20   XIV. Interlacement [b] is the union of both figures, the combined use of Antistrophe and Epanaphora, which are explained above; we repeat both the first word and the last in a succession of phrases, as follows: " Who are they who have often broken treaties? The Carthaginians. Who are they who have waged war with severest cruelty? The Carthaginians. Who are they who have marred the face of Italy? The Carthaginians. Who are they who now ask for pardon? The Carthaginians.[c] See then how appropriate it is for them to gain their request." Again: " One whom the Senate has condemned, one whom the Roman people has condemned, one whom universal public opinion has condemned, would you by your votes acquit such a one? "

Transplacement [d] makes it possible for the same word to be frequently reintroduced, not only without offence to good taste, but even so as to render the style more elegant, as follows: " One who has nothing in life more desirable than life cannot culti-

him." *Cf.* also the *complexio* (Résumé of an argument) of 2. xviii. 28 above.
    [c] Quintilian, 9. 3. 31, also cites the example, but without naming the figure. The passage might have come from a debate of the sort engaged in by Cato the Elder and Publius Scipio Nasica; see note on 3. ii. 2 above.
    [d] πλοκή, ἀντιμετάθεσις, σύγκρισις.

virtute vitam non potest colere." Item : " Eum
hominem appellas, qui si fuisset homo, numquam tam
crudeliter hominis vitam petisset. At erat inimicus.
Ergo inimicum sic ulcisci voluit, ut ipse sibi reperire-
tur inimicus ? " Item : " Divitias sine divitis esse.
Tu vero virtutem praefer divitiis ; nam si voles divitias
cum virtute conparare, vix satis idoneae tibi videbuntur divitiae quae virtutis pedisequae sint."

21 Ex eodem genere est exornationis cum idem verbum ponitur in hac, modo in altera re, hoc
modo : " Cur eam rem tam studiose curas, quae tibi
multas dabit curas ? " Item : " Nam amari iucundum sit,[1] si curetur ne quid insit amari." Item :
" Veniam ad vos, si mihi senatus det veniam."

In his quattuor generibus exornationum quae adhuc
propositae sunt non inopia verborum fit ut ad idem
verbum redeatur saepius ; sed inest festivitas, quae
facilius auribus diiudicari quam verbis demonstrari
potest.

[1] iucundum sit *M Mx ed. mai.* : iocundum est *E* : iucund-
umst *Mx.*

---

[a] *Cf.* Alexander Numenii (first half of second Christian
century), *De Schemat.*, in Spengel 3. 37 : " It is noble to live
if one but learns how one ought to live."
[b] This passage may belong to the *controversia* concerning
the murder of Sulpicius, l. xv. 25 above. *Cf.* Euripides,
Androm. 590–1 : " *You* a *man*, most cowardly even of
cowards ? Where have *you* any claim to consideration as a
man ? " ; Philemon, fragm. 119, in Kock, *Com. Att. Fragm.* 2.
515 : " Tell me, have *you* any right to speak ? *You* go prattling
among *men* as though you were a *man* ? "
[c] ἀντανάκλασις. διαφορά in Rutilius Lupus 1. 12 (Halm,
p. 8). Akin to Paronomasia, 4. xxi. 29 below.
[d] Lit., " To be loved would be pleasant, if only we should
take care that there is no bitterness in that love." Quin-

vate a virtuous life." [a] Again: "You call him a man, who, had he been a man, would never so cruelly have sought another man's life.[b] But he was his enemy. Did he therefore wish thus to avenge himself upon his enemy, only to prove himself his own enemy?" Again: "Leave riches to the rich man, but as for you, to riches prefer virtue, for if you will but compare riches with virtue, riches will in your eyes prove scarcely worthy to be the lackeys of virtue."

21 To the same type of figure belongs that which occurs when the same word is used first in one function, and then in another,[c] as follows: "Why do you so zealously concern yourself with this matter, which will cause you much concern?" Again: "To be dear to you would bring me joy—if only I take care it shall not in anguish cost me dear."[d] Again: "I would leave this place, should the Senate give me leave."[e]

In the four kinds of figures which I have thus far set forth,[f] the frequent recourse to the same word is not dictated by verbal poverty; rather there inheres in the repetition an elegance which the ear can distinguish more easily than words can explain.

tilian, 9. 3. 69–70, considers this a flat pun even when used in jest, and quotes the example as something to be avoided, not imitated. *Cf.* Lucretius 4. 1133 ff.

[e] Lit., "I would come to you if the Senate should grant me permission." *Cf.* the Pompeian distich, *Corp. Inscr. Lat.* 4. 4971:

Sei quid Amor valeat nostei, sei te hominem scis,
Commiseresce mei, da veniam ut veniam.

"If you have learned the power of Love, if you know that you are human, pity me; give me leave to come."

[f] 4. xiii. 19–xiv. 21.

[CICERO]

XV. Contentio est cum ex contrariis rebus oratio conficitur, hoc pacto: " Habet adsentatio iucunda principia, eadem exitus amarissimos adfert." Item: " Inimicis te placabilem, amicis inexorabilem praebes." Item: " In otio tumultuaris, in tumultu es otiosus; in re frigidissima cales, in ferventissima friges; tacito cum opus est, clamas; ubi loqui convenit, obmutescis; ades, abesse vis; abes, reverti cupis; in pace bellum quaeritas, in bello pacem desideras; in contione de virtute loqueris, in proelio prae ignavia tubae sonitum perferre non potes." Hoc genere si distinguemus orationem, et graves et ornati poterimus esse.

22   Exclamatio est quae conficit significationem doloris aut indignationis alicuius per hominis aut urbis aut loci aut rei cuiuspiam conpellationem, hoc modo: " Te nunc adloquor, Africane, cuius mortui quoque nomen splendori ac decori est civitati. Tui clarissimi nepotes suo sanguine aluerunt inimicorum crudeli-

---

a ἀντίθεσις, ἀντίθετον, *contrapositum* (Quintilian, 9. 3. 81). In Cicero, *Part. Orat.* 6. 21, a feature of the agreeable (*suave*) style. See 4. xlv. 58 below, and cf. *contrarium*, 4. xviii. 25 below.

b Cf. the saying assigned to Critias (leading spirit of the Thirty Tyrants) in Stobaeus, 3. 14. 2: " He who so bears himself towards his friends that he does everything to oblige them, renders hateful for the future that which is a pleasure for the nonce "; also Alexis, fragm. 295, in Kock, *Com. Att. Fragm.* 2. 402: " Avoid a pleasure which brings harm in its wake."

c Cf. Sophocles, *Antig.* 88: " You have a hot spirit for cold business "; Horace, *Ars Poet.* 465: " Empedocles . . . coolly leapt into burning Aetna "; Alexander Numenii, *De Schemat.*, in Spengel 3. 36–7: " They bathe the chilled men in hot springs."

XV. Antithesis[a] occurs when the style is built upon contraries, as follows: "Flattery has pleasant beginnings, but also brings on bitterest endings."[b] Again: "To enemies you show yourself conciliatory, to friends inexorable." Again: "When all is calm, you are confused; when all is in confusion, you are calm. In a situation requiring all your coolness, you are on fire; in one requiring all your ardour, you are cool.[c] When there is need for you to be silent, you are uproarious; when you should speak, you grow mute. Present, you wish to be absent; absent, you are eager to return.[d] In peace, you keep demanding war; in war, you yearn for peace. In the Assembly, you talk of valour; in battle, you cannot for cowardice endure the trumpet's sound." Embellishing our style by means of this figure we shall be able to give it impressiveness and distinction.

22 Apostrophe[e] is the figure which expresses grief or indignation by means of an address to some man or city or place or object, as follows: "It is you I now address, Africanus, whose name even in death means splendour and glory to the stâte! It is your famous grandsons[f] who by their own blood have fed the

Cf. with our author's last example of Antithesis *Anth. Pal.* 11. 305: "Among grammarians you are a Platonist; but if asked about the doctrines of Plato, you are again a grammarian."

[d] *Cf.* Horace, *Serm.* 2. 7. 28: "At home you long for the country; in the country, fickle man, you extol to heaven the distant city."

[e] ἀποστροφή, ἐκφώνησις. Quintilian, 9. 2. 27, considers as a figure only that kind of *exclamatio* which is simulated and artfully composed, and in 9. 3. 97 assigns *exclamatio* to the figures of thought; *cf.* also 9. 2. 38, 9. 3. 24–6, and 4. 1. 63.

[f] Cornelia, daughter of the elder Scipio Africanus, was the mother of the Gracchi.

tatem." Item: " Perfidiosae Fregellae, quam facile
scelere vestro contabuistis, ut, cuius nitor urbis
Italiam nuper inlustravit, eius nunc vix funda-
mentorum reliquiae maneant." Item: " Bonorum
insidiatores, latrocinia, vitam innocentissimi cuiusque
petistis; tantamne ex iniquitate iudiciorum vestris
calumniis adsumpsistis facultatem? " Hac exclama-
tione si loco utemur, raro, et cum rei magnitudo
postulare videbitur, ad quam volemus indignationem
animum auditoris adducemus.

Interrogatio non omnis gravis est neque concinna,
sed haec quae, cum enumerata sunt ea quae obsunt
causae adversariorum, confirmat superiorem orationem, hoc pacto: " Cum igitur haec omnia faceres,
diceres, administrares, utrum animos sociorum ab re
publica removebas et abalienabas, an non? et utrum
aliquem exornari oportuit qui istaec prohiberet ac
fieri non sineret, an non? "

23   XVI. Ratiocinatio est per quam ipsi a nobis
rationem poscimus quare quidque dicamus, et crebro

---

^a Cf. the passage, often used by rhetoricians, in Aeschines,
Adv. Ctes. 133: " But Thebes, Thebes our neighbour-state,
has in one day been swept from the midst of Hellas." After
M. Fulvius Flaccus' bill granting Roman franchise to the
Italian allies failed to pass, Fregellae revolted and was
destroyed in 125 B.C. See 4. ix. 13 and 4. xxvii. 37.

^b Probably addressed to the public informers (quadrup-
latores).

^c A consideration of propriety, τὸ πρέπον. See note on
4. x. 15 above.

^d ἐρώτημα. Rogatio in Cicero, De Oratore 3. 53. 203.
Assigned by Quintilian, 9. 3. 98, to the figures of thought;
see also 9. 2. 7 on the " rhetorical question."

^e Cf. Demosthenes, De Corona 71, on Philip: " By these
acts was he, or was he not, committing wrong, breaking treaty,
and violating the terms of peace? And was it, or was it not,

cruelty of their enemies." Again: " Perfidious Fregellae, how quickly, because of your crime, you have wasted away![a] As a result, of the city whose brilliance but yesterday irradiated Italy, scarce the debris of the foundations now remains." Again: " Plotters against good citizens,[b] villains, you have sought the life of every decent man! Have you assumed such power for your slanders thanks to the perversions of justice? " If we use Apostrophe in its proper place, sparingly, and when the importance of the subject seems to demand it,[c] we shall instil in the hearer as much indignation as we desire.

Not all Interrogation[d] is impressive or elegant, but that Interrogation is, which, when the points against the adversaries' cause have been summed up, reinforces the argument that has just been delivered, as follows: " So when you were doing and saying and managing all this, were you, or were you not, alienating and estranging from the republic the sentiments of our allies? And was it, or was it not, needful to employ some one to thwart these designs of yours and prevent their fulfilment? "[e]

XVI. Through the figure, Reasoning by Question and Answer,[f] we ask ourselves the reason for every

---

right that some man of the Hellenes should come forth to stop these incursions? " This passage was a favourite of the rhetoricians. It may well be that our author has in mind Q. Varius Hybrida, speaking on behalf of his law *de maiestate* (90 B.C.); see 4. ix. 13 above, and note.

[f] αἰτιολογία, ἐξετασμός. Assigned by Quintilian, 9. 3. 98, to the figures of thought. Cf. *sibi ipsi responsio* in Cicero, *De Oratore* 3. 54. 207 and Quintilian, 9. 3. 90, and 4. xxiv. 34 below, with note; also ἀπόφασις in Julius Rufinianus 8 (Halm, p. 40; *cf.* ἀπόφασις [*infitiatio*] in 1. xvii. 27 above). To be distinguished from *ratiocinatio*, the Type of Issue (Reasoning from Analogy), 1. xi. 19 above.

nosmet a nobis petimus unius cuiusque propositionis explanationem. Ea est huiusmodi: " Maiores nostri si quam unius peccati mulierem damnabant, simplici iudicio multorum maleficiorum convictam putabant. Quo pacto? Quam inpudicam iudicarant, ea veneficii quoque damnata existimabatur. Quid ita? Quia necesse est eam, quae suum corpus addixerit turpissimae cupiditati, timere multos. Quos istos? Virum, parentes, ceteros ad quos videt sui dedecoris infamiam pertinere. Quid postea? Quos tantopere timeat, eos necesse est optet necare.[1] Quare necesse est? Quia nulla potest honesta ratio retinere eam quam magnitudo peccati facit timidam, intemperantia audacem, natura mulieris inconsideratam. Quid? veneficii damnatam quid putabant? Inpudicam quoque necessario. Quare? Quia nulla facilius ad id maleficium causa quam turpis amor et intemperans libido commovere potuit; tum cuius mulieris animus esset corruptus, eius corpus castum esse non putaverunt. Quid? in viris idemne hoc observabant? Minime. Quid ita? Quia viros ad unum quodque maleficium singulae cupiditates impellunt, mulieris ad omnia maleficia cupiditas una ducit."[a] Item: " Bene maiores hoc conparaverunt, ut neminem regem quem armis cepissent vita privarent. Quid ita? Quia quam nobis fortuna facultatem dedisset iniquum erat in eorum supplicium consumere quos eadem fortuna paulo ante in amplissimo statu

_____

[1] *lac.*; optet necare *sugg. Brakman* (*Mnemos.* 52 [1924]. 335).

[a] The same argument is used in Seneca, *Contr.* 7. 3 (18). 6.
[b] *Cf.* Quintilian, 5. 11. 39 : " Would not an adulteress on trial for poisoning be regarded as condemned by the judgement of Marcus Cato, who said that every adulteress was the same as a poisoner ? "

statement we make, and seek the meaning of each successive affirmation, as follows: " When our ancestors condemned a woman for one crime, they considered that by this single judgement she was convicted of many transgressions. How so? Judged unchaste, she was also deemed guilty of poisoning.*a* Why? Because, having sold her body to the basest passion, she had to live in fear of many persons. Who are these? Her husband, her parents, and the others involved, as she sees, in the infamy of her dishonour. And what then? Those whom she fears so much she would inevitably wish to destroy. Why inevitably? Because no honourable motive can restrain a woman who is terrified by the enormity of her crime, emboldened by her lawlessness, and made heedless by the nature of her sex. Well now, what did they think of a woman found guilty of poisoning? That she was necessarily also unchaste. Why? Because no motive could more easily have led her to this crime than base love and unbridled lust. Furthermore, if a woman's soul had been corrupted, they did not consider her body chaste. Now then, did they observe this same principle with respect to men? Not at all. And why? Because men are driven to each separate crime by a different passion, whereas a woman is led into all crimes by one sole passion."*b* Again: " It is a good principle which our ancestors established, of not putting to death any king captured by force of arms.*c* Why is this so? Because it were unfair to use the advantage vouchsafed to us by fortune to punish those whom the same fortune had but recently placed in the highest station. But what

c This was true, *e.g.*, of Perseus and Syphax, but not strictly of Jugurtha.

conlocarat. Quid quod exercitum contra duxit?
Desino meminisse. Quid ita? Quia viri fortis est
qui de victoria contendant, eos hostes putare; qui
victi sunt, eos homines iudicare, ut possit bellum
fortitudo minuere, pacem humanitas augere. Et ille
si vicisset, non idem fecisset? Non profecto tam
sapiens fuisset. Cur igitur ei parcis? Quia talem
24 stultitiam contemnere, non imitari consuevi." Haec
exornatio ad[1] sermonem vehementer adcommodata
est, et animum auditoris retinet[2] adtentum cum
venustate sermonis tum rationum expectatione.

XVII. Sententia est oratio sumpta de vita quae aut
quid sit aut quid esse oporteat in vita breviter
ostendit, hoc pacto: " Difficile est primum quidque."
Item: " Non solet is potissimum[3] virtutes revereri
qui semper secunda fortuna sit usus." Item: " Liber
is est existimandus qui nulli turpitudini servit."
Item: " Egens aeque est is qui non satis habet, et is
cui satis nihil potest esse." Item: " Optima vivendi
ratio est eligenda; eam iucundam consuetudo
reddet." Huiusmodi sententiae simplices non sunt
inprobandae, propterea quod habet brevis expositio,
si rationis nullius indiget, magnam delectationem.

---

[1] ad *all MSS. but H* : *HMx omit.*
[2] retinet *CΠE* : retineat *HPB Mx.*
[3] *lac.*; quidque. Item : Non solet is potissimum *sugg. Mx.*

---

[a] For the sentiment *cf.* Cicero, *De Offic.* 1. 11. 35 ff. ;
Horace, *Carm. Saec.* 51 f.; Virgil, *Aeneid* 6. 853.
[b] γνώμη. Aristotle, *Rhet.* 2. 21 (1394 a–1395 b), offers the
classic treatment of maxims. On the virtue of brevity in
maxims, see Demetrius, *De Elocut.* 9. *Sententia* is excluded
from the figures by Quintilian (9. 3. 98).

of the fact that he has led an army against us? I
refuse to recall it. Why? Because it is characteristic
of a brave man to regard rivals for victory as enemies,
but when they have been vanquished to consider them
as fellow men,[a] in order that his bravery may
avail to put an end to the war, and his humanity to
advance peace. But had that king prevailed, he
would not, would he, have done the same? No, no
doubt he would have been less wise. Why, then, do
you spare him? Because it is my habit to scorn, not
emulate, such folly." This figure is exceedingly well
adapted to a conversational style, and both by its
stylistic grace and the anticipation of the reasons,
holds the hearer's attention.

XVII. A Maxim [b] is a saying drawn from life,
which shows concisely either what happens or ought
to happen in life, for example: "Every beginning is
difficult." Again: "Least in the habit of giving
reverence to the virtues is he who has always enjoyed
the favours of fortune." Again: "A free man is
that man to be judged who is a slave to no base
habit." [c] Again: "As poor as the man who has not
enough is the man who cannot have enough." [d]
Again: "Choose the noblest way of living; habit will
make it enjoyable." [e] Simple maxims of this sort
are not to be rejected, because, if no reason is needed,
the brevity of the statement has great charm. But

[c] Cf. Cicero, Paradoxa Stoic. 5. 35: "All wicked men are
therefore slaves—slaves, I say!"; Diogenes Laertius 7. 21;
Philo, Quod Omnis Probus Liber Sit.

[d] A saying of Epicurus: "Nothing is 'enough' to him
who deems 'enough' to be 'too little'" (C. Wotke in
Wiener Studien 10 [1888]. 197, No. 68).

[e] Attributed to Pythagoras (Stobaeus, 3. 1. 29, and Plutarch,
De exilio 8, 602 C).

[CICERO]

Sed illud quoque probandum est genus sententiae quod confirmatur subiectione rationis, hoc pacto: "Omnes bene vivendi rationes in virtute sunt conlocandae, propterea quod sola virtus in sua potestate est, omnia praeterea subiecta sunt sub fortunae dominationem." Item: "Qui fortunis alicuius inducti amicitiam eius secuti sunt, hi, simul ac fortuna dilapsa est, devolant omnes. Cum enim recessit ea res quae fuit consuetudinis causa, nihil superest quare possint in amicitia teneri."

Sunt item sententiae quae dupliciter efferuntur. Hoc modo sine ratione: "Errant qui in prosperis rebus omnes impetus fortunae se putant fugisse; sapienter cogitant qui temporibus secundis casus adversos reformidant." Cum ratione, hoc pacto:

25 "Qui adulescentium peccatis ignosci putant oportere falluntur, propterea quod aetas illa non est inpedimento bonis studiis. At ii sapienter faciunt qui adulescentes maxime castigant, ut quibus virtutibus omnem tueri vitam possint eas in aetate maturissima velint conparare." Sententias interponi raro convenit, ut rei actores, non vivendi praeceptores videamur esse. Cum ita interponentur, multum adferent ornamenti. Et[1] necesse est animi conprobet eam

---

[1] Et *Bornecque*: *lac. Mx.*

---

[a] *Cf.* the Stoic principle assigned to Pythagoras in Stobaeus, 3. 1. 29: "This is God's law: Virtue is the strong and stable thing; all else is nonsense." *Cf.* also 4. xix. 27 below.

[b] The experience, for example, of Timon of Athens (the Misanthrope). For the sentiment see Otto, *s.v.* "amicus," p. 22, and Caesar, *Bellum Civ.* 3. 104. 1.

[c] ἄνευ αἰτίας or ἐπιλόγου.

[d] For the topic of anticipating evil, see Posidonius in Galen, *De plac. Hipp. et Plat.* 4. 7 (Diels, 6th ed., 2. 13–14),

we must also favour that kind of maxim which is
supported by an accompanying reason, as follows:
" All the rules for noble living should be based on
virtue, because virtue alone is within her own control,
whereas all else is subject to the sway of fortune." [a]
Again: " Those who have cultivated a man's friendship for his wealth one and all fly from him as soon as
his wealth has slipped away. For when the motive
of their intercourse has disappeared, there is nothing
left which can maintain that friendship." [b]
There are also maxims which are presented in
double form. Without a reason,[c] as follows: " They
who in prosperity think to have escaped all the on-
slaughts of fortune are mistaken; they who in
favourable times fear a reversal are wise in their fore-
thought." [d] With a reason,[e] as follows: " They who
think that the sins of youth deserve indulgence are
deceived, because that time of life does not constitute
a hindrance to sound studious activities. But they
act wisely who chastise the young with especial
severity in order to inculcate at the age most opportune for it the desire to attain those virtues by
which they can order their whole lives."[f] We
should insert maxims only rarely, that we may be
looked upon as pleading the case, not preaching
morals. When so interspersed, they will add much
distinction. Furthermore, the hearer, when he

Cicero, *Tusc. Disp.* 3. 14. 29, and Plutarch, *Ad Apollon.* 21
(112 D), together with the lines of Euripides (fragm. 964 D)
they cite.

[e] μετ' αἰτίας or ἐπιλόγου. Perhaps a Stoic development of
sententia.

[f] *Cf.* the *Adelphoe* of Terence, in which both theories of
education, in extreme form, are applied with equally bad
results.

tacitus auditor cum ad causam videat adcommodari rem certam ex vita et moribus sumptam.

XVIII. Contrarium est quod ex rebus diversis duabus alteram breviter et facile contraria[1] confirmat, hoc pacto: " Nam qui suis rationibus inimicus fuerit semper, eum quomodo alienis rebus amicum fore speres? " Item: " Nam quem in amicitia perfidiosum cognoveris, eum quare putes inimicitias cum fide gerere posse? Aut qui privatus intolerabili superbia fuerit, eum commodum et cognoscentem sui fore in potestate qui speres, et qui in sermonibus et conventu amicorum verum dixerit numquam, eum sibi in contionibus a mendacio temperaturum? " Item: " Quos ex collibus deiecimus, cum his in campo metuimus dimicare? Qui cum plures erant, pares nobis esse non poterant, hi, postquam pauciores sunt, metuimus ne sint superiores? " Hoc exornationis genus breviter et continuatis verbis perfectum debet esse; et[2] cum commodum est auditu propter brevem et absolutam conclusionem, tum vero vehementer id quod opus est oratori conprobat contraria re, et ex eo quod dubium non est expedit illud

---

[1] *lac.*; contraria *sugg. Mx.*
[2] et *d edd.* : ut *followed by a lacuna Mx.*

---

[a] *Cf.* Aristotle, *Rhet.* 2. 21 (1395 b): "Hearers are delighted when a speaker succeeds in expressing as a universal truth the opinions they hold about particular cases."

[b] ἐνθύμημα, σχῆμα ἐκ τοῦ ἐναντίου. See Quintilian, 5. 10. 2: " There are some who call a conclusion from consequents an epicheireme, while you would find that a majority are of opinion that an enthymeme is a conclusion from incompatibles. And that is why Cornificius calls it Reasoning by Contraries; " 9. 3. 99: " I shall pass by those authors who

perceives that an indisputable principle drawn from practical life is being applied to a cause, must give it his tacit approval.[a]

XVIII. Reasoning by Contraries[b] is the figure which, of two opposite statements, uses one so as neatly and directly to prove the other, as follows: " Now how should you expect one who has ever been hostile to his own interests to be friendly to another's? "[c] Again: " Now why should you think that one who is, as you have learned, a faithless friend, can be an honourable enemy? Or how should you expect a person whose arrogance has been insufferable in private life, to be agreeable and not forget himself when in power, and one who in ordinary conversation and among friends has never spoken the truth, to refrain from lies before public assemblies? " Again: " Do we fear to fight them on the level plain when we have hurled them down from the hills? When they outnumbered us, they were no match for us; now that we outnumber them, do we fear that they will conquer us? " This figure ought to be brief, and completed in an unbroken period. Furthermore, it is not only agreeable to the ear on account of its brief and complete rounding-off, but by means of the contrary statement it also forcibly proves what the speaker needs to prove; and from a statement which is not open to question it draws a

have set almost no limit to the invention of technical terms, and have even assigned to figures what really belongs under arguments." Cf. the topos a fortiori in Aristotle, Rhet. 2. 23 (1397 b); contentio (ἀντίθετον) in 4. xv. 21 above and 4. xlv. 58 below.

[c] Cf. Isocrates, Ad Callim. 56: "One who is so base where the interests of others are concerned—what would he not dare where his own are concerned? "

quod est dubium,[1] ut dilui non possit aut multo difficillime possit.

XIX. Membrum orationis appellatur res breviter absoluta sine totius sententiae demonstratione, quae denuo alio membro orationis excipitur, hoc pacto: " Et inimico proderas." Id est unum quod appellamus membrum; deinde hoc excipiatur oportet altero: " Et amicum laedebas." Ex duobus membris haec [2] exornatio potest constare, sed commodissima et absolutissima est quae ex tribus constat, hoc pacto: " Et inimico proderas et amicum laedebas et tibi non consulebas." Item: " Nec rei publicae consuluisti nec amicis profuisti nec inimicis restitisti."

Articulus dicitur cum singula verba intervallis distinguuntur [3] caesa oratione, hoc modo: " Acrimonia, voce, vultu adversarios perterruisti." Item: " Inimicos invidia, iniuriis, potentia, perfidia sustu-

[1] dubium *CE Mx ed. mai.* : dubio *M* : in dubio *Mx*.
[2] haec *d Rufinus* : suis haec *other MSS. Mx* : solis haec *Lambinus*.
[3] distinguuntur *d edd.* : distinguentur *other MSS. Mx*.

---

[a] κῶλον. The concept originated in comparison with the human body; it came into rhetoric from the art of music. The doctrine of Colon, Comma, and Period is Peripatetic; *cf.* Aristotle, *Rhet.* 3. 9 (1409 a ff.). Quintilian, 9. 3. 98, excludes Colon and Comma from the list of figures. See A. du Mesnil, *Begriff der drei Kunstformen der Rede : Komma, Kolon, Periode, nach der Lehre der Alten,* in *Zum zweihundert-jährigen Jubiläum des königl. Friedrichs-Gymnas.,* Frankfurt on O., 1894, pp. 32–121.
[b] τρίκωλον. Note the dichorees (– ∪ – ⏑) : *consulebas,* and below, *restitisti, per)terruisti, sustulisti, conlocavit, ob)esse possit, contulerunt, domi)nationem* (as also those in the example of Isocolon [*compar*], 4. xx. 27 below). This cadence was a favourite of the Asian orators. Cicero, *Orator* 63. 215,

thought which is in question, in such a way that the inference cannot be refuted, or can be refuted only with much the greatest difficulty.

XIX. Colon or Clause [a] is the name given to a sentence member, brief and complete, which does not express the entire thought, but is in turn supplemented by another colon, as follows: " On the one hand you were helping your enemy." That is one so-called colon; it ought then to be supplemented by a second: " And on the other you were hurting your friend." This figure can consist of two cola, but it is neatest and most complete when composed of three, as follows: " You were helping your enemy, you were hurting your friend, and you were not consulting your own best interests." [b] Again: " You have not consulted the welfare of the republic, nor have you helped your friends, nor have you resisted your enemies."

It is called a Comma or Phrase [c] when single words are set apart by pauses in staccato speech, as follows: " By your vigour, voice, looks you have terrified your adversaries." Again: " You have destroyed your enemies by jealousy, injuries, influence, perfidy."

discusses the dangers resulting from its use: " First it is recognized as rhythm, next it cloys, and then when it is seen to be an easy device it is despised." Longinus, *De Sublim.* 41, disapproves of the agitated movement dichorees give to language: " For all overrhythmical writing is at once felt to be affected and finical and wholly lacking in passion owing to the monotony of its superficial polish " (tr. W. Rhys Roberts). See notes on 4. viii. 12 and 4. xxxii. 44.

[c] κόμμα. Cicero, *Orator* 62. 211, translates the word literally by *incisum*; note *caesa oratione* in our author's definition. Lit., *articulus* = " part jointed on." Commata, rather than cola, are required in the forcible style (χαρακτὴρ δεινός), according to Demetrius, *De Elocut.* 5. 241.

listi." Inter huius generis et illius superioris vehe-
mentiam hoc interest: illud tardius et rarius venit,
hoc crebrius et celerius pervenit. Itaque in illo
genere ex remotione brachii et contortione dexterae
gladius ad corpus adferri, in hoc autem crebro et
celeri corpus vulnere consauciari videtur.

27 Continuatio est densa et continens[1] frequentatio
verborum cum absolutione sententiarum. Ea utemur
commodissime tripertito: in sententia, in contrario,
in conclusione. In sententia hoc pacto: " Ei non
multum potest obesse fortuna qui sibi firmius in
virtute quam in casu praesidium conlocavit." In
contrario hoc modo: " Nam si qui spei non multum
conlocarit in casu, quid est quod ei magnopere casus
obesse possit? " In conclusione hoc pacto: " Quodsi
in eos plurimum fortuna potest qui suas rationes
omnes in casum contulerunt, non sunt omnia com-
mittenda fortunae, ne magnam nimis in nos habeat
dominationem." In his tribus generibus ad continua-
tionis vim adeo frequentatio necessaria est, ut infirma
facultas oratoris videatur nisi sententiam et contrarium et conclusionem frequentibus efferat verbis;
sed alias quoque nonnumquam non alienum est,
tametsi necesse non est, eloqui res aliquas per
huiusmodi continuationes.

[1] densa et continens *E* : et densa *HPB* : densa *B²CΠ* : et
densa et continens *Mx*.

---

[a] περίοδος. For other Latin equivalents of this term see
Cicero, *Orator* 61. 204, *De Oratore* 3. 48. 186; Quintilian, 9. 4. 22.
[b] ἐνθύμημα. See 4. xviii. 25 above.
[c] For the theme *cf.* 4. xvii. 24 above. Our author, unlike
other post-Aristotelian rhetoricians, does not say that the
Period is comprised of *membra*, yet this example seems to
contain four—the upper limit usually allowed; see, *e.g.*,

There is this difference in onset between the last figure and the one preceding: the former moves upon its object more slowly and less often, the latter strikes more quickly and frequently. Accordingly in the first figure it seems that the arm draws back and the hand whirls about to bring the sword to the adversary's body, while in the second his body is as it were pierced with quick and repeated thrusts.

27 A Period [a] is a close-packed and uninterrupted group of words embracing a complete thought. We shall best use it in three places: in a Maxim, in a Contrast,[b] and in a Conclusion. In a Maxim as follows: " Fortune cannot much harm him who has built his support more firmly upon virtue than upon chance." In a Contrast, as follows: " For if a person has not placed much hope in chance, what great harm can chance do him?" In a Conclusion, as follows: " But if Fortune has her greatest power over those who have committed all their plans to chance, we should not entrust our all with her, lest she gain too great a domination over us." [c] In these three types a compact style is so necessary for the force of the period that the orator's power seems inadequate if he fails to present the Maxim, Contrast, or Conclusion in a press of words. But in other cases as well it is often proper, although not imperative, to express certain thoughts by means of periods of this sort.

Cicero, *Orator* 66. 222, and Demetrius, *De Elocut.* 1. 16, but also Quintilian, 9. 4. 125. On the theory of the Period see esp. Aristotle, *Rhet.* 3. 9 (1409 a ff.); Demetrius, *op. cit.*, 1. 10 ff., 5. 244, 303; Cicero, *Orator* 62. 211 ff.; and Josef Zehetmeier, " Die Periodenlehre des Aristoteles," *Philologus* 85 (1930). 192–208, 255–284, 414–436. Aristotle recognized only periods of either one or two cola, and in fact the division into cola was not of primary importance in his theory.

[CICERO]

XX. Conpar appellatur quod habet in se membra orationis, de quibus ante diximus, quae constent ex pari fere numero syllabarum.ᵃ Hoc non denumeratione nostra fiet—nam id quidem puerile est—sed tantum adferet usus et exercitatio facultatis, ut animi quodam sensu par membrum superiori referre possimus, hoc modo: " In proelio mortem parens oppetebat, domi filius nuptias conparabat; haec omina¹ gravis casus administrabant." Item: " Alii fortuna dedit felicitatem, huic industria virtutem conparavit." In hoc genere saepe fieri potest ut non plane par numerus sit syllabarum et tamen esse videatur, si una aut etiam altera syllaba est alterum brevius, aut si, cum in altero plures sunt, in altero longior aut longiores, plenior aut pleniores syllabae erunt, ut longitudo aut plenitudo harum multitudinem alterius adsequatur et exaequet.

Similiter cadens exornatio appellatur cum in eadem constructione verborum duo aut plura sunt verba quae similiter isdem casibus efferantur, hoc modo: " Hominem laudem egentem virtutis, abundantem felicitatis?" Item: " Huic omnis in pecunia spes est, a sapientia est animus remotus; diligentia conparat divitias, neglegentia corrumpit animum,

---

¹ omina *sugg. Mx* : omnia *MSS.*

ᵃ ἰσόκωλον. Sometimes classed as a variety of πάρισον, παρίσωσις, parallelism in structure. The next three figures (*cf.* also Alliteration, 4. xii. 18 above) represent παρόμοιον, παρομοίωσις, parallelism in sound. Together with Antithesis (4. xv. 21 above) this and the next three figures comprise the so-called Gorgianic figures. Isocrates exemplifies the extensive and effective use of Isocolon.

ᵇ 4. xix. 26.

XX. We call Isocolon *a* the figure comprised of cola (discussed above) *b* which consist of a virtually equal number of syllables. To effect the isocolon we shall not count the syllables—for that is surely childish—but experience and practice will bring such a facility that by a sort of instinct we can produce again a colon of equal length to the one before it, as follows: "The father was meeting death in battle; the son was planning marriage at his home. These omens wrought grievous disasters." Again: "Another man's prosperity is the gift of fortune, but this man's good character has been won by hard work." In this figure it may often happen that the number of syllables seems equal without being precisely so *c*—as when one colon is shorter than the other by one or even two syllables, or when one colon contains more syllables, and the other contains one or more longer or fuller-sounding syllables, so that the length or fullness of sound of these matches and counterbalances the greater number of syllables in the other.

The figure called Homoeoptoton *d* occurs when in the same period two or more words appear in the same case, and with like terminations, as follows: "Hominem laudem egentem virtutis, abundantem felicitatis?" *e* Again: "Huic omnis in pecunia spes est, a sapientia est animus remotus; diligentia conparat divitias, neglegentia corrumpit animum,

c Note the phrase and metrical clausula, *esse videatur*, favoured by Cicero. See Tacitus, *Dial. de Orator.* 23 (ed. Gudeman, pp. 29 and 247 f.); Quintilian, 10. 2. 18 and 9. 4. 73; Rufinus, in Halm, pp. 575 and (citing Probus) 583.

d ὁμοιόπτωτον. *Cf.* 4. xii. 18 above.

e "Am I to praise a man abounding in good luck, but lacking in virtue?"

et tamen, cum ita vivit, neminem prae se ducit
hominem."

Similiter desinens est cum, tametsi casus non
insunt in verbis, tamen similes exitus sunt, hoc pacto:
" Turpiter audes facere, nequiter studes dicere;
vivis invidiose, delinquis studiose, loqueris odiose."
Item: " Audaciter territas, humiliter placas."

Haec duo genera, quorum alterum in exituum,
alterum in casus similitudine versatur, inter se
vehementer conveniunt; et ea re qui his bene utuntur
plerumque simul ea conlocant in isdem partibus
orationis. Id hoc modo facere oportet: " Perditissima ratio est amorem petere, pudorem fugere,
diligere formam, neglegere famam." Hic et ea
verba quae casus habent ad casus similes, et illa quae
non habent ad similes exitus veniunt.

29   XXI. Adnominatio est cum ad idem verbum et
nomen acceditur commutatione vocum aut litterarum,

---

 ^a " This man places all his hope in money; from
wisdom is his soul withdrawn. Through diligence he
acquires riches, but through negligence he corrupts his
soul. And yet, living so, he counts no one any one
before himself." Cf. *neclegentiam . . . diligentiam* in
Terence, *Andria* 20 f.
 ^b ὁμοιοτέλευτον. For a study of our author's theory of
Homoeoptoton and Homoeoteleuton see Karl Polheim, *Die
lateinische Reimprosa*, Berlin, 1925, pp. 161 ff.; on the
influence of the theory, see pp. 463 ff.
 ^c Note in the Latin examples of this figure the correspondences in the endings of the verb forms as well as in those
of the adverbs.
 ^d " A most depraved principle it is—to seek love and to
shun self-respect, to esteem beauty and to slight one's
own good name."
 ^e πτωτικά.

et tamen, cum ita vivit, neminem prae se ducit hominem." [a]

Homoeoteleuton [b] occurs when the word endings are similar, although the words are indeclinable, as follows: " You dare to act dishonourably, you strive to talk despicably; you live hatefully, you sin zealously, you speak offensively." Again: " Blusteringly you threaten; cringingly you appease." [c]

These two figures, of which one depends on like word endings and the other on like case endings, are very much of a piece. And that is why those who use them well generally set them together in the same passage of a discourse. One should effect this in the following way: " Perditissima ratio est amorem petere, pudorem fugere, diligere formam, neglegere famam." [d] Here the declinable words [e] close with like case endings, and those lacking cases [f] close with like terminations.[g]

29   XXI. Paronomasia [h] is the figure in which, by means of a modification of sound, or change of letters, a close resemblance to a given verb or noun [i] is pro-

---

[f] ἄπτωτα.

[g] καταλήξεις.

[h] παρονομασία. Cicero, *Orator* 25. 84, warns the speaker of the Attic plain style against the kind of Paronomasia which is produced by the change of a letter; yet cf. *De Oratore* 2. 63. 256 on Paronomasia in verbal witticisms. See Eduard Wölfflin, " Das Wortspiel im Lateinischen," *Sitzungsb. Bayer. Akad. der Wiss. (philos.-philol. und histor. Classe),* 1887 (2), pp. 187–208.

[i] Our author knows four parts of speech : proper name, or noun (*nomen,* ὄνομα), verb (*verbum,* ῥῆμα), common noun, or appellative (*vocabulum,* προσηγορία), conjunction (*coniunctio,* σύνδεσμος); " noun " would include " adjective," as in No. 7 below.

[CICERO]

ut ad res dissimiles similia verba adcommodentur. Ea
multis et variis rationibus conficitur. Adtenuatione
aut conplexione eiusdem litterae, sic: " Hic qui se
magnifice iactat atque ostentat, venit ante quam
Romam venit." Et ex contrario: " Hic quos
homines alea vincit, eos ferro statim vincit." Productione eiusdem litterae, hoc modo: " Hinc avium
dulcedo ducit ad avium." Brevitate eiusdem litterae: " Hic, tametsi videtur esse honoris cupidus,
tantum tamen curiam diligit quantum Curiam? "
Addendis litteris, hoc pacto: " Hic sibi posset temperare, nisi amori mallet obtemperare." Demendis
nunc litteris, sic: " Si lenones vitasset tamquam
leones, vitae tradidisset se." Transferendis litteris,
sic: " Videte, iudices, utrum homini navo an vano

***

^a συστολή. *Cf.* the figure *complexio*, 4. 14. 20 above.
^b " That man who carries himself with a lofty bearing and
makes a display of himself was sold as a slave before coming
to Rome; " *venīt* is a contraction of *veniit*, and precedes
the *tenue* (*venĭt*).
^c " Those men from whom he wins in dice he straightway
binds in chains; " *tenue* precedes *plenius* (*vincĭt* = *vinciit*).
^d " The sweet song of the birds draws us from here into
pathless places." Quintilian, 9. 3. 69–71, quotes this pun,
and the play upon *amari* in 4. xiv. 21 above, as examples to
be avoided, not imitated, being flat even when used in jest;
he marvels that this artifice is included in the textbooks.
Virgil, *Georg.* 2. 328, puns on the same words. Note in connection with the problem of authorship of our treatise that
the example here used for *adnominatio* is, according to
Quintilian, called an example of *traductio* by Cornificius;
cf. 4. xiv. 20 above.

302

duced, so that similar words express dissimilar things. This is accomplished by many different methods: (1) by thinning or contracting [a] the same letter, as follows: " Hic qui se magnifice iactat atque ostentat, venīt antequam Romam venĭt;" [b] (2) and by the reverse: " Hic quos homines alea vincĭt, eos ferro statim vincīt;" [c] (3) by lengthening the same letter, as follows: " Hinc ăvium dulcedo ducit ad āvium;" [d] (4) by shortening the same letter: " Hic, tametsi videtur esse honoris cupidus, tantum tamen cūriam diligit quantum Cŭriam?"; [e] (5) by adding letters, as follows: " Hic sibi posset temperare, nisi amori mallet obtemperare"; [f] (6) and now by omitting letters, as follows: " Si lenones vitasset tamquam leones, vitae tradidisset se"; [g] (7) by transposing letters, as follows: " Videte, iudices, utrum homini

[e] " Does this man, although he seems desirous of public honour, yet love the Curia [the Senate-house] as much as he loves Curia?" The M group of MSS. reads *Curiam mere-tricem*. On this and the next three types of Paronomasia cf. in Phoebammon (Spengel 3. 45 ff.) the four principles governing the formation of all figures: lack, superabundance, transposition, interchange (ἔνδεια, πλεονασμός, μετάθεσις, ἐναλλαγή); in Quintilian, 1. 5. 6 and 1. 5. 38 ff., the four ways of committing barbarisms and solecisms, and, in 6. 3. 53, the poor jests formed by punning in these ways; in Philo, *De aetern. mundi* 22. 113, the four ways (Peripatetic doctrine) in which corruption occurs: addition (πρόσθεσις), subtraction (ἀφαίρεσις), transposition (μετάθεσις), and transmutation (ἀλλοίωσις); and H. Usener, *Sitzungsb. Bayer. Akad. der Wiss.* (*philos.-philol.-hist. Cl.*), 1892, pp. 628–631. *Cf.* also Cicero, *Part. Orat.* 6. 19, on the causes of obscurity in words and periods.

[f] " This man could rule himself, if only he did not prefer to submit to love."

[g] " If he had avoided panders as though they were lions, he would have devoted himself to life;" the text is corrupt. Tertullian, *Apol.* 50. 12, puns on the same words.

[CICERO]

credere malitis." Commutandis, hoc modo: " Deligere oportet quem velis diligere."

Hae sunt adnominationes quae in litterarum brevi commutatione aut productione aut transiectione aut 30 aliquo huiusmodi genere versantur. XXII. Sunt autem aliae quae non habent tam propinquam in verbis similitudinem et tamen dissimiles non sunt; quibus de generibus unum est huiusmodi: " Quid veniam, qui sim, quem [1] insimulem, cui prosim, quae postulem, brevi cognoscetis." Nam hic est in quibusdam verbis quaedam similitudo non tam perfecta quam illae superiores, sed tamen adhibenda nonnumquam. Alterum genus huiusmodi: " Demus operam, Quirites, ne omnino patres conscripti circumscripti putentur." Haec adnominatio magis accedit ad similitudinem quam superior, sed minus quam illae superiores, propterea quod non solum additae, sed uno tempore demptae quoque litterae sunt.

[1] quem *Haase*: quare veniam quem *MSS. Mx.*

---

[a] " See, men of the jury, whether you prefer to trust an industrious man or a vainglorious one."

[b] " You ought to choose such a one as you would wish to love." A form of the saying attributed to Theophrastus, that one must not first love and then judge, but first judge and then love (οὐ φιλοῦντα δεῖ κρίνειν ἀλλὰ κρίναντα φιλεῖν); see Plutarch, *De fraterno amore* 8 (482 B); Rutilius Lupus 1. 6 (Halm, p. 6); Seneca, *Epist.* 3. 2, *De Moribus* 48; Cicero, *De Amic.* 22. 85; Publilius Syrus 134 (ed. J. Wight Duff and A. M. Duff); Stobaeus, 4. 27. 14; Sidonius Apollinaris, *Epist.*

navo an vano credere malitis "; [a] (8) by changing
letters, as follows: " Deligere oportet quem velis
diligere." [b]

These are word-plays which depend on a slight
change or lengthening or transposition of letters, and
30 the like. XXII. There are others also in which the
words lack so close a resemblance, and yet are not
dissimilar. Here is an example of one kind of such
word-plays: " Quid veniam, qui sim, quem insimulem, cui prosim, quae postulem, brevi cognoscetis." [c]
For in this example there is a sort of resemblance
among certain words, not so complete, to be sure, as
in the instances above, yet sometimes serviceable.
An example of another kind: " Demus operam,
Quirites, ne omnino patres conscripti circumscripti
putentur." [d] In this paronomasia the resemblance
is closer than in the preceding, yet is not so close as
in those above, because some letters are added and
some at the same time removed.

5. 11. 1. In modern form : " If you suspect a man, do not
employ him; if you employ a man, do not suspect him."

[c] " Why I come, who I am, whom I accuse, whom I am
helping, what I ask for you will soon know." Cf. Plautus,
Poen. 992 :

> adei atque appella quid velit, quid venerit,
> qui sit, quoiatis, unde sit.

" Go up to him and ask him what he wants, why he has
come, who he is, of what country, and whence he comes."

[d] " Let us see to it, fellow-citizens, that the Conscript
Fathers be not thought to have been utterly duped." Quintilian, 9. 3. 72, considers this kind of paronomasia as pro-
ducing the very worst of trivial effects. Seneca, *Suas.* 7. 11,
reproves for bad taste a speaker who punned on *scripsit* and
proscripsit. It has been conjectured (see Kroehnert, p. 31)
that Crassus may have uttered these words when speaking
on behalf of the Servilian law; see note on 4. iii. 5.

[CICERO]

Tertium genus est quod versatur in casuum com-
31 mutatione aut unius aut plurium nominum. Unius
nominis, hoc modo: " Alexander Macedo summo
labore animum ad virtutem a pueritia confirmavit.
Alexandri virtutes per orbem terrae cum laude et
gloria vulgatae sunt. Alexandrum omnes maxime
metuerunt,[1] idem plurimum dilexerunt. Alexandro
si vita data longior esset, trans Oceanum Macedonum
transvolassent sarisae." Hic unum nomen in commutatione casuum volutatum est. Plura nomina
casibus commutatis hoc modo facient adnomina-
tionem: " Tiberium Gracccum rem publicam admin-
strantem prohibuit indigna nex diutius in eo commorari. Gaio Gracco similis occisio est oblata, quae
virum rei publicae amantissimum subito de sinu
civitatis eripuit. Saturninum fide captum malorum
perfidia per scelus vita privavit. Tuus, o Druse,
sanguis domesticos parietes et vultum parentis asper-
sit. Sulpicio, cui paulo ante omnia concedebant, eum

---

[1] metuerunt *d* : metuerant *other MSS. Mx.*

---

[a] Polyptoton (πολύπτωτον).
[b] Unlike a normal English word order, the Latin permits
the proper noun in each of its cases to be placed at the
beginning of the sentence.
[c] Note that in the two examples the cases are Greek,
lacking the Latin ablative, and that, unlike the disposition in
the second, Roman, example, the cases in the first example
come in a definite order (the accusative preceding the dative).
Alexander's career was favourite material with the

There is a third form of paronomasia, depending on
31 a change of case in one or more proper nouns.[a]   In
one noun, as follows: " Alexander of Macedon with
consummate toil from boyhood trained his mind to
virtue.   Alexander's virtues have been broadcast
with fame and glory throughout the world.   All men
greatly feared Alexander, yet deeply loved him.
Had longer life been granted Alexander, the Mace-
donian lances would have flown across the ocean." [b]
Here a single noun has been inflected, undergoing
changes of case.   Several different nouns, with
change of case, will produce a paronomasia, as
follows: [c] " An undeserved death by violence prevented Tiberius Gracchus, while guiding the republic,
from abiding longer therein.   There befell Gaius
Gracchus a like fate, which of a sudden tore from the
bosom of the state a hero and staunch patriot.
Saturninus, victim of his faith in wicked men, a
treacherous crime deprived of life.   O Drusus,
your blood bespattered the walls of your home,
and your mother's face.[d]   They were only now
granting to Sulpicius every concession,[e] yet soon

rhetoricians.   The common *suasoria* concerned his deliberation whether, having conquered Asia and India, he should
navigate the ocean (when he had heard the voice say:
" *Quousque invicte ?* "); *cf. e.g.*, Seneca, *Suas.* 1. 1, *Contr.*
7. 7. 19, Quintilian, 3. 8. 16.

[d] Irmentraud Haug, *Würzburger Jahrb. für die Altertumswissenschaft* 2 (1947). 113, argues that the reference is to the
bust of Drusus' father.

[e] When in 88 B.C. the quarrel between *populares* and
optimates grew serious, Sulla suspended the *iustitium*, and
fled to his army.   Then Sulpicius, in control, put through
his measures granting the new Italian citizens a fuller share
in political power, and transferring the command in the East
to Marius.

brevi spatio non modo vivere, sed etiam sepeliri
prohibuerunt."

32 Haec tria proxima genera exornationum, quorum
unum in similiter cadentibus, alterum in similiter
desinentibus verbis, tertium in adnominationibus
positum est, perraro sumenda sunt cum in veritate
dicimus, propterea quod non haec videntur reperiri
posse sine elaboratione et sumptione operae; XXIII.
eiusmodi autem studia ad delectationem quam ad
veritatem videntur adcommodatiora. Quare fides et
gravitas et severitas oratoria minuitur his exornationibus frequenter conlocatis, et non modo tollitur
auctoritas dicendi, sed offenditur quoque in eiusmodi
oratione, propterea quod est in his lepos et festivitas,
non dignitas neque pulcritudo. Quare quae sunt
ampla atque pulcra diu placere possunt; quae lepida
et concinna cito satietate adficiunt aurium sensum
fastidiosissimum. Quomodo igitur, si crebro his
generibus utemur, puerili videmur elocutione delec-
tari; item, si raro interseremus has exornationes et in
causa tota varie dispergemus, commode luminibus
distinctis inlustrabimus orationem.

ᵃ The sentiments are those of the Marian party. Ti.
Sempronius Gracchus was clubbed to death by Scipio Nasica
and his followers in 133 B.C. (see 4. lv. 68 below); C. Sempronius Gracchus was killed in flight after the consul Opimius
and his band had stormed the Aventine, in 121 B.C.; L.
Appuleius Saturninus was stoned and torn to pieces by a
mob in the Senate-house, in 100 B.C.; M. Livius Drusus was,
according to Velleius Paterculus, 2. 14, stabbed by an assassin
in the area before his house, in 91 B.C.; on the death, in 88
B.C., of P. Sulpicius Rufus see note on 1. xv. 25 above. Cicero,
De Harusp. Resp. 19. 41 and 20. 43, in which all the above
except Drusus are used as *exempla*, and Seneca, *Octavia*
882–9, in which the fates of the Gracchi and Drusus are

they suffered him not to live, nor even to be buried." [a]

32   These last three figures—the first based on like case inflections, the second on like word endings, and the third on paronomasia—are to be used very sparingly when we speak in an actual cause, because their invention seems impossible without labour and pains. XXIII. Such endeavours, indeed, seem more suitable for a speech of entertainment than for use in an actual cause.[b] Hence the speaker's credibility, impressiveness, and seriousness are lessened by crowding these figures together. Furthermore, apart from destroying the speaker's authority, such a style gives offence because these figures have grace and elegance, but not impressiveness and beauty. Thus the grand and beautiful can give pleasure for a long time, but the neat and graceful quickly sate the hearing, the most fastidious of the senses.[c] If, then, we crowd these figures together, we shall seem to be taking delight in a childish style; [d] but if we insert them infrequently and scatter them with variations throughout the whole discourse, we shall brighten our style agreeably with striking ornaments.

joined, may have used the same source as did our author; *cf.* also Seneca, *Ad Marc. de Cons.* 16. 3 f.

  [b] These figures serve epideictic better than judicial or deliberative oratory. Cicero warns the speaker of the Attic plain style against the use of these three figures (and of Isocolon, *Orator* 25. 84), but allows them in epideictic discourse (*Orator* 12. 38, *Part. Orat.* 21. 72); Quintilian, 8. 3. 12, also justifies the full use of ornamentation in epideictic.

  [c] *Cf.* Cicero, *Orator* 44. 150, and *De Oratore* 3. 25. 97 ff.; also Longinus, *De Sublim.*, ch. 7, and Plutarch, *De recta ratione audiendi* 7 (41 E).

  [d] μειρακιώδης λέξις.

33   Subiectio est cum interrogamus adversarios aut
quaerimus ipsi quid ab illis aut quid contra nos dici
possit; dein subicimus id quod oportet dici aut non
oportet, aut nobis adiumento futurum sit aut offuturum
sit idem contrario, hoc modo: " Quaero igitur unde
iste tam pecuniosus factus sit.   Amplum patrimonium
relictum est?   At patris bona venierunt.   Hereditas
aliqua venit?   Non potest dici, sed etiam a necessariis
omnibus exhereditatus est.   Praemium aliquod ex
lite aut iudicio cepit?   Non modo id non fecit, sed
etiam insuper ipse grandi sponsione victus est.
Ergo, si his rationibus locupletatus non est, sicut
omnes videtis, aut isti domi nascitur aurum aut unde
non est licitum pecunias cepit."

XXIV. Item: " Saepe, iudices, animum adverti
multos aliqua ex honesta re quam ne inimici quidem
criminari possint sibi praesidium petere.   Quorum
nihil potest adversarius facere.   Nam utrum ad
patris sui[1] virtutem confugiet?   At eum vos iurati
capite damnastis.   An ad suam vitam revertetur?
Quam vitam aut ubi honeste tractatam?   Nam hic
quidem ante oculos vestros quomodo vixerit scitis
omnes.   At cognatos suos enumerabit, quibus vos
conveniat commoveri?   At hi quidem nulli sunt.

---

[1] sui *d* : eius *other MSS. Mx.*

---

[a] ὑποφορά, ἀνθυποφορά.   Assigned by Quintilian, 9. 3. 98,
to the figures of thought.   The figure *subiectio* is to be distinguished from the *subiectio* of 2. xviii. 28 and 4. xvii. 24.

[b] Whether by *legis actio* or by the *formula* procedure.   See
Wenger, *Institutes of the Roman Law of Civil Procedure*,
pp. 22 f., 123 ff., 132 ff.

33   Hypophora[a] occurs when we enquire of our adversaries, or ask ourselves, what the adversaries can say in their favour, or what can be said against us; then we subjoin what ought or ought not to be said—that which will be favourable to us or, by the same token, be prejudicial to the opposition, as follows: " I ask, therefore, from what source has the defendant become so wealthy? Has an ample patrimony been left to him? But his father's goods were sold. Has some bequest come to him? That cannot be urged; on the contrary he has even been disinherited by all his kin. Has he received some award from a civil action, whether in the older or the more recent form of procedure?[b] Not only is that not the case, but recently he himself lost a huge sum on a wager at law.[c] Therefore, if, as you all see, he has not grown rich by these means, either he has a gold mine in his home, or he has acquired monies from an illicit source."

XXIV. Another example: " Time and time again, men of the jury, have I observed that numerous defendants look for support in some honourable deed which not even their enemies can impeach. My adversary can do no such thing. Will he take refuge in his father's virtue? On the contrary, you have taken your oath and condemned him to death. Or will he turn to his own life? What life, and wherein lived honourably? Why, the life that this man has lived before your eyes is known to all of you. Or will he enumerate his kinsmen, by whom you should be moved? But he has not any. He will produce

   [c] The *sponsio* in a civil suit was an agreement by the litigants that the loser of the case would pay a certain sum of money.

[CICERO]

Amicos proferet? At nemo est qui sibi non turpe
putet istius amicum nominari." Item: "Credo
inimicum, quem nocentem putabas, in iudicium
adduxisti? Non, nam indemnatum necasti. Leges
quae id facere prohibent veritus? At ne scriptas
quidem iudicasti. Cum ipse te veteris amicitiae
commonefaceret, commotus es? At nihilominus, sed
etiam studiosius occidisti. Quid? cum tibi pueri ad
pedes volutarentur, misericordia motus es? At
eorum patrem crudelissime sepultura quoque prohi-
34 buisti." Multum inest acrimoniae et gravitatis in
hac exornatione, propterea quod cum quaesitum est
quid oporteat, subicitur id non esse factum. Quare
facillime fit ut exaugeatur indignitas negotii.

Ex eodem genere, ut ad nostram quoque personam
referamus subiectionem, sic: "Nam quid me facere
convenit cum a tanta Gallorum multitudine circum-
sederer? Dimicarem? At cum parva manu tum
prodiremus; locum quoque inimicissimum habebamus. Sederem in castris? At neque subsidium
quod expectarem habebamus, neque erat qui vitam
produceremus. Castra relinquerem? At obside-
bamur. Vitam militum neglegerem? At eos vide-
bar ea accepisse condicione ut eos, quoad possem,
incolumis patriae et parentibus conservarem. Hostium condicionem repudiarem? At salus antiquior

---

^a This example bears a very close resemblance to Demos-
thenes, *Adv. Aristogeit.* 1. 76 ff.

^b This passage may perhaps belong to the *controversia* on
the murder of Sulpicius in 1. xv. 25 above.

^c Cf., in Quintilian, 9. 2. 106, προέκθεσις, "which means
telling what ought to have been done and then what has been
done"; also προέκθεσις (*divisio*), 1. x. 17 above.

friends? But there is no one who does not consider
it disgraceful to be called that fellow's friend." [a]
Again: "Your enemy, whom you consider to be
guilty, you doubtless summoned him to trial? No,
for you slew him while he was yet unconvicted. Did
you respect the laws which forbid this act? On the
contrary, you decided that they did not even exist in
the books. When he reminded you of your old
friendship, were you moved? No, you killed him
nevertheless, and with even greater eagerness. And
then when his children grovelled at your feet, were you
moved to pity? No, in your extreme cruelty you
34 even prevented their father's burial." [b] There is
much vigour and impressiveness in this figure
because, after having posed the question, "What
ought to have been done?", we subjoin that that
was not done.[c] Thus it becomes very easy to amplify
the baseness of the act.

In another form of the same figure we refer the
hypophora to our own person,[d] as follows: "Now
what should I have done when I was surrounded
by so great a force of Gauls? Fight? But then our
advance would have been with a small band. Furthermore, we held a most unfavourable position. Remain
in camp? But we neither had reinforcements to look
for, nor the wherewithal to keep alive. Abandon the
camp? But we were blocked. Sacrifice the lives of
the soldiers? But I thought I had accepted them on
the stipulation that so far as possible I should preserve
them unharmed for their fatherland and their
parents. Reject the enemy's terms? But the safety

---

[d] Cf. *sibi ipsi responsio* in Quintilian, 9. 3. 90, there
adjudged a figure of thought rather than of diction; *ratiocinatio*, 4. xvi. 23 above.

[CICERO]

est militum quam inpedimentorum." Eiusmodi consequuntur identidem subiectiones ut ex omnibus ostendi videatur nihil potius quam quod factum sit[1] faciendum fuisse.

XXV. Gradatio est in qua non ante ad consequens verbum descenditur quam ad superius ascensum[2] est, hoc modo: " Nam quae reliqua spes manet libertatis, si illis et quod libet licet, et quod licet possunt, et quod possunt audent, et quod audent faciunt, et quod faciunt vobis molestum non est?" Item: " Non sensi hoc et non suasi; neque suasi et non ipse facere statim[3] coepi; neque facere coepi et non perfeci; neque perfeci et non probavi." Item: Africano virtutem industria, virtus gloriam, gloria aemulos conparavit." Item: " Imperium Graeciae fuit penes Athenienses; Atheniensium potiti sunt Spartiatae; Spartiatas superavere Thebani; Thebanos Macedones vicerunt, qui ad imperium Graeciae brevi tempore adiunxerunt Asiam bello subactam."

[1] factum sit *MMx ed. mai.* : factum est *E* : factumst *Mx.*
[2] ascensum *E* : escensum *Mx* : conscensum *P²CΠd* : consensum *HPB.*
[3] facere statim *H* : statim facere *PΠBC* : facere *E Mx.*

---

[a] Popilius is speaking; see 1. xv. 25 above.
[b] κλῖμαξ. Also ἐπιπλοκή, *ascensus*, and *catena*. This figure joins with Epanaphora, Antistrophe, Interlacement, Transplacement, and Antanaklasis (4. xiii. 19–xiv. 21 above) to form a complete theory of Repetition.
[c] For a like word-play on *libet* and *licet* cf. Aquila Romanus 27 (Halm, pp. 30–31) under Paronomasia (see 4. xxi. 29 above); Cicero, *Pro Quinctio* 30. 94; Calpurnius Flaccus 16.
[d] Quintilian, 9. 3. 55, and others cite, and our author in this example imitates, Demosthenes, *De Corona* 179 : " I did not say this and then fail to make the motion; I did not make the motion and then fail to act as an ambassador; I did not act

314

of the soldiers has priority over that of the baggage." [a]
The result of an accumulation of this kind of hypophora is to make it seem obvious that of all the
possibilities nothing preferable to the thing done
could have been done.

XXV. Climax [b] is the figure in which the speaker
passes to the following word only after advancing by
steps to the preceding one, as follows: " Now what
remnant of the hope of liberty survives, if those men
may do what they *please*,[c] if they *can* do what they
may, if they *dare* do what they *can*, if they *do* what
they *dare*, and if you *approve* what they *do*? " Again:
" I did not conceive this without counselling it;
I did not counsel it without myself at once undertaking
it; I did not undertake it without completing it; nor
did I complete it without winning approval of it." [d]
Again: " The industry of Africanus brought him
excellence, his excellence glory, his glory rivals." [e]
Again: " The empire of Greece belonged to the
Athenians; the Athenians were overpowered by the
Spartans; the Spartans were overcome by the
Thebans; the Thebans were conquered by the
Macedonians; and the Macedonians in a short time
subdued Asia in war and joined her to the empire

as an ambassador and then fail to persuade the Thebans."
Cf. *Rom.* 10. 14; Rosalind in Shakespeare, *As You Like It*
5. 2: " For your brother and my sister no sooner met but
they looked; no sooner looked but they loved; no sooner
loved but they sighed; no sooner sighed but they asked one
another the reason; no sooner knew the reason but they
sought the remedy; and in these degrees have they made a
pair of stairs to marriage "; St. Augustine, *Confessions* 7. 10:
O aeterna veritas et vera caritas et cara aeternitas!; also
Lane Cooper, *Sewanee Rev.* 32 (1924). 32–43.
 [e] Quintilian, 9. 3. 56, uses the same example, representing
it as from a Latin author.

[CICERO]

35 Habet in se quendam leporem superioris cuiusque crebra repetitio verbi, quae propria est huius exornationis.

Definitio est quae rei alicuius proprias amplectitur potestates breviter et absolute, hoc modo : " Maiestas rei publicae est in qua continetur dignitas et amplitudo civitatis." Item : " Iniuriae sunt quae aut pulsatione corpus aut convicio auris aut aliqua turpitudine vitam cuiuspiam violant." Item : " Non est ista diligentia, sed avaritia, ideo quod diligentia est adcurata conservatio suorum, avaritia iniuriosa appetitio alienorum." Item : " Non est ista fortitudo, sed temeritas, propterea quod fortitudo est contemptio laboris et periculi cum ratione utilitatis et conpensatione commodorum, temeritas est cum inconsiderata dolorum perpessione gladiatoria periculorum susceptio." Haec ideo commoda putatur exornatio quod omnem rei cuiuspiam vim et potestatem ita dilucide proponit et breviter,[1] ut neque pluribus verbis oportuisse dici videatur neque brevius potuisse dici putetur.

XXVI. Transitio vocatur quae cum ostendit breviter quid dictum sit, proponit item brevi quid con-

---

[1] breviter *PBCΠd* : explicat breviter *bl Mx*.

---

[a] ὁρισμός. *Cf.* Definition, the subtype of Legal Issue, 1. xi. 19, 1. xii. 21, and 2. xii. 17 above. Quintilian, 9. 3. 91, unlike " Cornificius and Rutilius," excludes *finitio* from the figures of diction. The figure goes back to Prodicus' Correct Use of Terms (ὀρθότης ὀνομάτων) ; see Radermacher, *Artium Scriptores*, pp. 67 ff.

[b] See note on 1. xii. 21 above.

[c] For *iniuria* in Roman law, see Mommsen, pp. 784–808 ; P. F. Girard, *Mélanges de droit romain* (Paris, 1923), 2. 385–411.

AD HERENNIUM, IV. xxv. 34–xxvi. 35

35 of Greece." The constant repetition of the preceding word, characteristic of this figure, carries a
certain charm.

Definition [a] in brief and clear-cut fashion grasps
the characteristic qualities of a thing, as follows:
" The sovereign majesty of the republic is that which
comprises the dignity and grandeur of the state." [b]
Again: " By an injury is meant doing violence to
some one, to his person by assault, or to his sensi-
bilities by insulting language, or to his reputation by
some scandal." [c] Again: " That is not economy on
your part, but greed, because economy is careful
conservation of one's own goods, and greed is wrongful covetousness of the goods of others." Again:
" That act of yours is not bravery, but recklessness,
because to be brave is to disdain toil and peril, for a
useful purpose and after weighing the advantages,
while to be reckless is to undertake perils like a
gladiator, suffering pain without taking thought." [d]
Definition is accounted useful for this reason: it sets
forth the full meaning and character of a thing so
lucidly and briefly that to express it in more words
seems superfluous, and to express it in fewer is
considered impossible.

XXVI. Transition [e] is the name given to the figure
which briefly recalls what has been said, and likewise

---

[d] The last two examples may also illustrate *distinctio*
(παραδιαστολή); see Quintilian, 9. 3. 65 : " But this depends
wholly on definition, and so I doubt whether it is a figure,"
and 9. 3. 82.

[e] A figure combining the functions of the *enumeratio* of
2. xxx. 47 above (ἀνάμνησις, ἀνακεφαλαίωσις, παλιλλογία) and
propositio (προέκθεσις = *propositio quid sis dicturus* in Cicero,
De Oratore 3. 53. 203 and *Orator* 40. 137; *cf.* the *expositio*
[ἔκθεσις] of 1. x. 17 above). *Cf.* in Anon. Seg. 12 (Spengel-

317

sequatur, hoc pacto: " Modo in patriam cuiusmodi
fuerit habetis; nunc in parentes qualis extiterit
considerate." Item: " Mea in istum beneficia
cognoscitis; nunc quomodo iste mihi gratiam ret-
tulerit accipite." Proficit haec aliquantum exornatio
ad duas res: nam et quid dixerit commonet, et ad
reliquum conparat auditorem.

36   Correctio est quae tollit id quod dictum est, et pro
eo id quod magis idoneum videtur reponit, hoc pacto:
" Quodsi iste suos hospites rogasset, immo innuisset
modo, facile hoc perfici posset." Item: " Nam postquam isti vicerunt atque adeo victi sunt—eam
quomodo victoriam appellem, quae victoribus plus
calamitatis quam boni dederit?" Item: " O virtutis comes, invidia, quae bonos sequeris plerumque
atque adeo insectaris!" Commovetur hoc genere
animus auditoris. Res enim communi verbo elata
levius[1] tantummodo dicta videtur; ea post ipsius
oratoris correctionem insignior[2] magis idonea fit
pronuntiatione. " Non igitur satius esset," dicet
aliquis, " ab initio, praesertim cum scribas, ad
optimum et lectissimum verbum devenire?" Est
cum non est satius, si commutatio verbi id erit
demonstratura, eiusmodi rem esse ut, cum eam

---

[1] *Insertion of* levius *suggested by Mx.*
[2] *Insertion of* insignior *suggested by Mx.*

Hammer 1 [2]. 354) ἀνανέωσις, a means used in the Proem
to induce receptiveness—" we recall the points previously
made, and mark out those we intend to discuss," and the
second type of the figure μετάβασις in Rutilius Lupus 2. 1
(Halm, pp. 12 f.). Quintilian, 9. 3. 98, without defining
transitio, classes it as a figure of thought; *transitus* in 9. 2. 61
is rejected as a figure.

briefly sets forth what is to follow next, thus: " You
know how he has just been conducting himself towards
his fatherland; now consider what kind of son he has
been to his parents." [a]   Again: " My benefactions to
this defendant you know; now learn how he has
requited me." This figure is not without value for
two ends: it reminds the hearer of what the speaker
has said, and also prepares him for what is to come.

36   Correction [b] retracts what has been said and replaces it with what seems more suitable, as follows:
" But if the defendant had asked his hosts, or rather
had only hinted, this could easily have been accomplished." Again: " After the men in question had
conquered, or rather had been conquered—for how
shall I call that a conquest which has brought more
disaster than benefit to the conquerors?" Again:
" O Virtue's companion, Envy, who art wont to
pursue good men, yes, even to persecute them." [c]
This figure makes an impression upon the hearer,
for the idea when expressed by an ordinary word
seems rather feebly stated, but after the speaker's
own amendment it is made more striking by means
of the more appropriate expression. " Then would
it not be preferable," some one will say, " especially
in writing, to resort to the best and choicest word at
the beginning?" Sometimes this is not preferable,
when, as the change of word will serve to show, the
thought is such that in rendering it by an ordinary

---

[a] Cf. Demosthenes, De Corona 268, and (cited by Anon.
Seg. 12, in illustration of ἀνανέωσις) Aeschines, Adv. Timarch.
116.

[b] ἐπιδιόρθωσις, ἐπανόρθωσις, related to μετάνοια.

[c] Cf. Horace, Serm. 2. 3. 13: " Are you preparing to
appease envy by forsaking virtue?" Insector is the fre-
quentative form of insequor.

communi verbo appellaris, levius dixisse videaris, cum ad electius verbum accedas, insigniorem rem facias. Quodsi continuo venisses ad id verbum, nec rei nec verbi gratia animadversa esset.

37   XXVII. Occultatio est cum dicimus nos praeterire aut non scire aut nolle dicere id quod nunc maxime dicimus, hoc modo: " Nam de pueritia quidem tua, quam tu omnium intemperantiae addixisti, dicerem, si hoc tempus idoneum putarem; nunc consulto relinquo. Et illud praetereo, quod te tribuni rei militaris infrequentem tradiderunt. Deinde quod iniuriarum satis fecisti L. Labeoni nihil ad hanc rem pertinere puto. Horum nihil dico; revertor ad illud de quo iudicium est." Item: " Non dico te ab sociis pecunias cepisse; non sum in eo occupatus quod civitates, regna, domos omnium depeculatus es; furta, rapinas omnes tuas omitto." Haec utilis est exornatio si aut ad rem quam non pertineat aliis ostendere, quod occulte admonuisse prodest, aut longum est aut ignobile, aut planum non potest fieri, aut facile potest reprehendi; ut utilius sit occulte fecisse suspicionem quam eiusmodi intendisse orationem quae redarguatur.

ᵃ παράλευψις, ἀντίφρασις, *praeteritio,* and sometimes παρα-σιώπησις, which Quintilian, 9. 3. 99, excludes from the figures. *Occultatio* is assigned by Quintilian in 9. 3. 98 to the figures of thought. Cf. *praecisio,* 4. xxx. 41 below, and Cicero's *reticentia* (*De Oratore* 3. 53. 205, and *Orator* 40. 138).

320

word you seem to have expressed it rather feebly, but having come to a choicer word you make the thought more striking. But if you had at once arrived at this word, the grace neither of the thought nor of the word would have been noticed.

37   XXVII. Paralipsis *a* occurs when we say that we are passing by, or do not know, or refuse to say that which precisely now we are saying, as follows: "Your boyhood, indeed, which you dedicated to intemperance of all kinds, I would discuss, if I thought this the right time. But at present I advisedly leave that aside. This too I pass by, that the tribunes have reported you as irregular in military service. Also that you have given satisfaction to Lucius Labeo for injuries done him I regard as irrelevant to the present matter. Of these things I say nothing, but return to the issue in this trial." *b*   Again: " I do not mention that you have taken monies from our allies; I do not concern myself with your having despoiled the cities, kingdoms, and homes of them all. I pass by your thieveries and robberies, all of them." This figure is useful if employed in a matter which it is not pertinent to call specifically to the attention of others, because there is advantage in making only an indirect reference to it, or because the direct reference would be tedious or undignified, or cannot be made clear, or can easily be refuted. As a result, it is of greater advantage to create a suspicion by Paralipsis than to insist directly on a statement that is refutable.*c*

b Speaker, opponent, and Labeo all are unknown. The date may perhaps be assigned to the time of the Marsic war, about 90 B.C.; see Friedrich Muenzer, P.-W. 12. 245.
c Cf. Quintilian, 9. 2. 75.

Disiunctum est cum eorum de quibus dicimus aut utrumque aut unum quodque certo concluditur verbo, sic: " Populus Romanus Numantiam delevit, Kartaginem sustulit, Corinthum disiecit, Fregellas evertit. Nihil Numantinis vires corporis auxiliatae sunt, nihil Kartaginiensibus scientia rei militaris adiumento fuit, nihil Corinthiis erudita calliditas praesidii tulit, nihil Fregellanis morum et sermonis societas opitulata est." Item: " Formae dignitas aut morbo deflorescit aut vetustate extinguitur." Hic utrumque, in superiore exemplo unam quamque rem certo verbo concludi videmus.

38 Coniunctio est cum interpositione verbi et superiores partes orationis conprehenduntur et in feriores, hoc modo: " Formae dignitas aut morbo deflorescit aut vetustate."

Adiunctio est cum verbum quo res conprehenditur non interponimus, sed aut primum aut postremum conlocamus. Primum, hoc pacto: " Deflorescit formae dignitas aut morbo aut vetustate." Postremum, sic: " Aut morbo aut vetustate formae dignitas deflorescit."

Ad festivitatem disiunctio est apposita, quare rarius utemur, ne satietatem pariat; ad brevitatem coniunctio, quare saepius adhibenda est. Hae tres exornationes de simplici genere manant.

---

a διεζευγμένον. Quintilian, 9. 3. 64, says that devices like this and the two following are so common that they cannot lay claim to the art which figures involve.
b Only the first sentence of this translation preserves the Disjunction, which cannot be rendered throughout without violating normal English word order.

AD HERENNIUM, IV. xxvii. 37-38

Disjunction *a* is used when each of two or more clauses ends with a special verb, as follows: " By the Roman people Numantia was destroyed, Carthage razed, Corinth demolished, Fregellae overthrown. Of no aid to the Numantines was bodily strength; of no assistance to the Carthaginians was military science; of no help to the Corinthians was polished cleverness; of no avail to the Fregellans was fellowship with us in customs and in language." *b* Again: " With disease physical beauty fades, with age it dies." *c* In this example we see both clauses, and in the preceding each several clause ending with a special verb.

38 Conjunction *d* occurs when both the previous and the succeeding phrases are held together by placing the verb between them, as follows: " Either with disease physical beauty fades, or with age."

It is Adjunction *e* when the verb holding the sentence together is placed not in the middle, but at the beginning or the end. At the beginning, as follows: " Fades physical beauty with disease or age." At the end, as follows: " Either with disease or age physical beauty fades."

Disjunction is suited to elegant display, and so we shall use it moderately, that it may not cloy; Conjunction is suited to brevity, and hence is to be used more frequently. These three figures spring from a single type.

c Cf. Isocrates, *Ad Demonicum* 6: " For beauty is spent by time or wasted by disease." The saying was popular among Greek Patristic writers; see Engelbert Drerup, *Isocratis Opera Omnia*, Leipzig, 1906, 1. 95.

d συνεζευγμένον. To be distinguished, of course, from *coniunctio* (σύνδεσμος), the part of speech (4. xxx. 41).

e ἐπεζευγμένον.

323

XXVIII. Conduplicatio est cum ratione amplifica-
tionis aut commiserationis eiusdem unius aut plurium
verborum iteratio, hoc modo: " Tumultus, Gai
Gracce, tumultus domesticos et intestinos conparas ! "
Item: " Commotus non es, cum tibi pedes mater
amplexaretur, non es commotus ? " Item: " Nunc
audes etiam venire in horum conspectum, proditor
patriae ? Proditor, inquam, patriae, venire audes in
horum conspectum ? " Vehementer auditorem com-
movet eiusdem redintegratio verbi et vulnus maius
efficit in contrario causae, quasi aliquod telum saepius
perveniat in eandem corporis partem.[1]

Interpretatio est quae non iterans idem redintegrat
verbum, sed id commutat quod positum est alio
verbo quod idem valeat, hoc modo: " Rem publicam
radicitus evertisti, civitatem funditus deiecisti." [2]
Item: " Patrem nefarie verberasti, parenti manus
scelerate attulisti." Necessum est eius qui audit
animum commoveri cum gravitas prioris dicti re-
novatur interpretatione verborum.

39 Commutatio est cum duae sententiae inter se
discrepantes ex transiectione ita efferuntur ut a
priore posterior contraria priori proficiscatur, hoc
modo: " Esse oportet ut vivas, non vivere ut edas." [3]

[1] corporis partem H : partem corporis other MSS. Mx.
[2] deiecisti MSS. Mx ed. mai. : diiecisti Mx.
[3] edas Mx ed. mai., all MSS. but H : edis H Mx.

---

[a] ἀναδίπλωσις. In Quintilian, 9. 3. 28, adiectio. For the
first example cf. Demosthenes, De Corona 143, a favourite
passage with the rhetoricians : " War it is that you are bringing into Attica, Aeschines, an Amphictyonic war."

XXVIII. Reduplication [a] is the repetition of one or more words for the purpose of Amplification or Appeal to Pity, as follows: " You are promoting riots, Gaius Gracchus, yes, civil and internal riots." Again: " You were not moved when his mother embraced your knees? You were not moved?" [b] Again: " You now even dare to come into the sight of these citizens, traitor to the fatherland? Traitor, I say, to the fatherland, you dare come into the sight of these citizens?" The reiteration of the same word makes a deep impression upon the hearer and inflicts a major wound upon the opposition—as if a weapon should repeatedly pierce the same part of the body.

Synonymy or Interpretation [c] is the figure which does not duplicate the same word by repeating it, but replaces the word that has been used by another of the same meaning, as follows: " You have overturned the republic from its roots; you have demolished the state from its foundations." Again: " You have impiously beaten your father; you have criminally laid hands upon your parent." The hearer cannot but be impressed when the force of the first expression is renewed by the explanatory synonym.

39 Reciprocal Change [d] occurs when two discrepant thoughts are so expressed by transposition that the latter follows from the former although contradictory to it, as follows: " You must eat to live, not live to

---

[b] This passage may perhaps belong to the *controversia* on the murder of Sulpicius in 1. xv. 25 above.

[c] συνωνυμία. Quintilian, 9. 3. 98, denies that this is a figure.

[d] ἀντιμεταβολή.

Item: "Ea re poëmata non facio, quia cuiusmodi volo non possum, cuiusmodi possum nolo." Item: "Quae de illo dici possunt non dicuntur, quae dicuntur dici non possunt." Item: "Poëma loquens pictura, pictura tacitum poëma debet esse." Item: "Si stultus es, ea re taceas; non tamen si taceas, ea re stultus es." Non potest dici quin commode fiat cum contrariae sententiae relatione verba quoque convertantur. Plura subiecimus exempla, ut, quoniam difficile est hoc genus exornationis inventu, dilucidum esset, ut, cum bene esset intellectum, facilius in dicendo inveniretur.

XXIX. Permissio est cum ostendemus in dicendo nos aliquam rem totam tradere et concedere alicuius voluntati, sic: "Quoniam omnibus rebus ereptis solum mihi superest animus et corpus, haec ipsa, quae mihi de multis sola relicta sunt, vobis et vestrae condono potestati. Vos me vestro quo pacto vobis videbitur utamini atque abutamini licebit; inpunite in me quidlibet statuite; dicite atque innuite:

---

[a] Ascribed to Socrates. See the Stoic C. Musonius Rufus (first Christian century) in Stobaeus, 3. 18. 37; Plutarch, *Quomodo adulesc. poet. aud. deb.* 4 (21 E); Gellius 19. 2; Athenaeus 4. 158 F.; Diogenes Laertius 2. 34; Stobaeus, 3. 17. 21 ("Socrates, when asked in what respect he differed from the rest of men, replied: ' Whereas they live in order to eat, I eat in order to live.'"); Macrobius, *Sat.* 2. 8. 16. *Cf.* also Quintilian, 9. 3. 85; Clement of Alexandria, *Paed.* 2. 1, and *Strom.* 7. 14; Isidore, *Etym.* 2. 21. 11.

[b] Porphyrio on Horace, *Epist.* 2. 1. 257, attributes this saying to Aristarchus of Samothrace (first half, second century B.C.), the editor and critic of Homer. *Cf. Anth. Pal.* 6. 1 : " For I [Lais] do not wish to see myself as I am, and cannot see myself as I used to be."

eat." [a]   Again: " I do not write poems, because I
cannot write the sort I wish, and I do not wish to
write the sort I can." [b]   Again: " What can be told
of that man is not being told; what is being told of
him cannot be told."   Again: " A poem ought to be
a painting that speaks; a painting ought to be a silent
poem." [c]   Again: " If you are a fool, for that reason
you should be silent; and yet, although you should be
silent, you are not for that reason a fool."   One cannot deny that the effect is neat when in juxtaposing
contrasted ideas the words also are transposed.   In
order to make this figure, which is hard to invent, quite
clear, I have subjoined several examples—so that,
well understood, it may be easier for the speaker to
invent.

XXIX. Surrender [d] is used when we indicate in
speaking that we yield and submit the whole matter
to another's will, as follows: " Since only soul and
body remain to me, now that I am deprived of everything else, even these, which alone of many goods are
left me, I deliver up to you and to your power.   You
may use and even abuse me [e] in your own way as
you think best; with impunity make your decision
upon me, whatever it may be; speak and give a sign

   [c] The saying is ascribed to Simonides (sixth century B.C.)
in Plutarch, *De glor. Athen.* 3 (346 F); see also *Quaest. Conviv.*
9. 15 (748 A), *Quomodo adulesc. poet. aud. deb.* 3 (17 F),
Quomodo adulat. ab amic. internosc. 15 (58 B), *De vita et
poes. Hom.* 216 (ed. Bernardakis, 7. 460). Cf. Cicero,
De Leg. 3. 1. 2 : " It can truly be said that the magistrate is a
speaking law, the law on the other hand a silent magistrate ";
Horace, *Ars Poet.* 361 : " A poem is like a painting ";
Anth. Pal. 11. 145 ; and Lessing, *Laokoon,* Preface.
   [d] ἐπιτροπή.
   [e] Varro in Priscian (Keil, *Gramm. Lat.* 2. 381) makes a
similar play upon *utamur* and *abutamur.*

parebo." Hoc genus tametsi alias quoque nonnumquam tractandum est, tamen ad misericordiam
commovendam vehementissime est adcommodatum.

40   Dubitatio est cum quaerere videatur orator utrum
de duobus potius aut quid de pluribus potissimum
dicat, hoc modo: " Offuit eo tempore plurimum rei
publicae consulum—sive stultitiam sive malitiam
dicere oportet, sive utrumque." Item: " Tu istuc
ausus es dicere, homo omnium mortalium—quonam
te digno moribus tuis appellem nomine?"

Expeditio est cum, rationibus conpluribus enumer-
atis quibus aliqua res confieri[1] potuerit, ceterae
tolluntur, una relinquitur quam nos intendimus, hoc
modo: " Necesse est, cum constet istum fundum
nostrum fuisse, ostendas te aut vacuum possedisse,
aut usu tuum fecisse, aut emisse, aut hereditati tibi
venisse. Vacuum, cum ego adessem, possidere non
potuisti; usu tuum etiam nunc fecisse non potes;
emptio nulla profertur; hereditati tibi me vivo mea
pecunia venire non potuit. Relinquitur ergo ut me
41   vi de meo fundo deieceris." Haec exornatio plurimum iuvabit coniecturales argumentationes. Sed
non erit, tamquam in plerisque, ut cum velimus ea

---

[1] confieri *Stroebel*: non *M*: fieri non *B*: aut fieri aut fieri
non *C*: aut fieri aut non fieri *C²E*: confici *Mx*.

---

[a] ἀπορία, διαπόρησις. Quintilian, 9. 3. 88, uses virtually
the same example, after making the point that Indecision can
belong to either the figures of thought or the figures of diction.
Cf. Demosthenes, *De Corona* 20: " Now what helped him
. . .? The cowardice, ought I to say, or the stupidity, or
both, of the other Greek states."
[b] *Cf.* Demosthenes, *De Corona* 22: " Why, you—what
would be the correct name for one to call you?"

—I shall obey." Although this figure is often to be
used also in other circumstances, it is especially suited
to provoking pity.

40   Indecision occurs when the speaker seems to ask
which of two or more words he had better use, as
follows: " At that time the republic suffered
exceedingly from—ought I to say—the folly of the
consuls, or their wickedness, or both." *a* Again:
" You have dared to say that, you of all men the—
by what name worthy of your character shall I call
you ? " *b*

Elimination *c* occurs when we have enumerated the
several ways by which something could have been
brought about, and all are then discarded except
the one on which we are insisting, as follows: " Since
it is established that the estate you claim as yours was
mine, you must show that you took possession of it as
vacant land, or made it your property by right of
prescription, or bought it, or that it came to you by
inheritance.   Since I was on the premises, you could
not have taken possession of it as vacant land.   Even
by now you cannot have made it your property by
right of prescription.   No sale is disclosed.   Since I
am alive, my property could not have come to you by
inheritance.   It remains, then, that you have ex-
41   pelled me by force from my estate."   This figure will
furnish the strongest support to conjectural arguments, but unlike most other figures, it is not one

----

c Now called the Method of Residues when used in Refutation.   Quintilian, 5. 10. 66 ff. and 7. 1. 31 ff., considers this
argumentorum genus ex remotione under Proof and Refutation,
not under the Figures; see also Cicero, *De Inv.* 1. xxix. 45
(*enumeratio*), and Quintilian, 9. 3. 99, in note on 4. xviii. 25
above.   *Cf.* in Aristotle, *Rhet.* 2. 23 (1398 a), the *topos* from
logical division (ἐκ διαιρέσεως).

[CICERO]

possimus uti; nam fere non poterimus, nisi nobis ipsa negotii natura dabit facultatem.

XXX. Dissolutum est quod, coniunctionibus verborum e medio sublatis, separatis partibus effertur, hoc modo: " Gere morem parenti, pare cognatis, obsequere amicis, obtempera legibus." Item: " Descende in integram defensionem, noli quicquam recusare, da servos in quaestionem, stude verum invenire." Hoc genus et acrimoniam habet in se et vehementissimum est et ad brevitatem adcommodatum.

Praecisio est cum dictis quibus reliquum quod coeptum est dici relinquitur inchoatum, sic: " Mihi tecum par certatio non est, ideo quod populus Romanus me—nolo dicere, ne cui forte adrogans videar; te autem saepe ignominia dignum putavit." Item: " Tu istuc audes dicere, qui nuper alienae domi—non ausim dicere, ne, cum te digna dicerem, me indignum quippiam dixisse videar." Hic atrocior tacita suspicio quam diserta explanatio facta est.

Conclusio est quae brevi argumentatione ex iis quae ante dicta sunt aut facta conficit quid necessario

---

a ἀσύνδετον. Variously also διάλυσις, *solutum, dissolutio.* Aristotle, *Rhet.* 3. 12 (1413 b): " Asyndeta . . . are rightly condemned in the literary style, but in the controversial style speakers do indeed use them because of their dramatic effect." Cf. *dissolutum*, the slack style (4. xi. 16 above).

b The quality of σφοδρότης. Plutarch, *De vita et poes. Hom.* 40 (ed. Bernardakis, 7. 355), assigns to Asyndeton the qualities of rapidity and emotional emphasis.

c ἀποσιώπησις. Sometimes ἀποκοπή, *obticentia, interruptio* (Quintilian, 9. 2. 54, who here also identifies Cicero's *reticentia* with Aposiopesis; see note on *occultatio*, 4. xxvii. 37 above). With the first example cf. Demosthenes, *De Corona* 3, a close parallel.

'which we can use at will, for in general we can use it only when the very nature of the business gives us the opportunity.

XXX. Asyndeton[a] is a presentation in separate parts, conjunctions being suppressed, as follows: " Indulge your father, obey your relatives, gratify your friends, submit to the laws." Again: " Enter into a complete defence, make no objection, give your slaves to be examined, be eager to find the truth." This figure has animation and great force,[b] and is suited to concision.

Aposiopesis[c] occurs when something is said and then the rest of what the speaker had begun to say is left unfinished, as follows: " The contest between you and me is unequal[d] because, so far as concerns me, the Roman people—I am unwilling to say it, lest by chance some one think me proud. But you the Roman people has often considered worthy of disgrace." Again: " You dare to say that, who recently at another's home—I shouldn't dare tell, lest in saying things becoming to you, I should seem to say something unbecoming to me."[e] Here a suspicion, unexpressed, becomes more telling than a detailed explanation would have been.[f]

Conclusion,[g] by means of a brief argument, deduces the necessary consequences of what has been said or

---

[d] For the commonplace cf. Aeschylus in Aristophanes, *Frogs* 867; Lysias, *Adv. Eratosth.* 81; Fronto, ed. Naber, p. 42.

[e] Cf. Demosthenes, *De Corona* 129: "I hesitate, lest in saying things becoming to you, I may be thought to have chosen things to say that are unbecoming to me."

[f] Demetrius, *De Elocut.* 253, makes a like observation.

[g] Like συμπέρασμα in logic. Quintilian, 9. 3. 98, denies that *conclusio* is a figure. Cf. the *conclusio* of 1. iii. 4 and the *duplex conclusio* of 2. xxiv. 38 above.

consequatur, hoc modo : " Quodsi Danais datum erat oraculum non posse capi Troiam sine Philoctetae sagittis, hae[1] autem nihil aliud[2] fecerunt nisi Alexandrum perculerunt, hunc extinguere id nimirum capi fuit Troiam."

42 XXXI. Restant etiam decem exornationes verborum, quas idcirco non vage dispersimus, sed a superioribus separavimus, quod omnes in uno genere sunt positae. Nam earum omnium hoc proprium est, ut ab usitata verborum potestate recedatur atque in aliam rationem cum quadam venustate oratio conferatur.

De quibus exornationibus nominatio est prima, quae nos admonet ut cuius rei nomen aut non sit aut satis idoneum non sit, eam nosmet idoneo verbo nominemus aut imitationis aut significationis causa : imitationis, hoc modo, ut maiores " rudere " et " mugire " et " murmurari " et " sibilare " appellarunt ; significandae rei causa, sic : " Postquam iste

---

[1] hae ΠE : haec MMx.
[2] autem nihil aliud CE : nihil aliud autem P²BΠMx : nihil aliquod autem HP.

---

[a] Philoctetes killed Paris with the bow and arrows of Heracles, and thus fulfilled the oracle revealed by the Trojan seer Helenus that only by means of those weapons could Troy be taken.

[b] These ten figures of diction are *tropi* (τρόποι, tropes), a term our author does not use ; *cf.* Quintilian, 8. 6. 1 : " A trope is an artistic change of a word or phrase from its proper signification to another." Tropes were at first, as here, not separated from figures of thought and diction (σχήματα). Cicero, *Brutus* 18. 69, tells us that the division was of Greek origin. Even in the time of Quintilian (see 9. 1. 1–9) the line of demarcation was not always clear.

[c] ὀνοματοποιία. *Cf.* Julius Caesar in Gellius, 1. 10. 4 : " Avoid, as you would a rock, an unheard-of and unfamiliar

done before, as follows: " But if the oracle had pre-
dicted to the Danaans that Troy could not be taken
without the arrows of Philoctetes, and these arrows
moreover served only to smite Alexander, then
certainly killing Alexander was the same as taking
Troy." [a]

42   XXXI. There remain also ten Figures of Diction,
which I have intentionally not scattered at random,
but have separated from those above, because they
all belong in one class.   They indeed all have this in
common, that the language departs from the ordinary
meaning of the words [b] and is, with a certain grace,
applied in another sense.

Of these figures the first is Onomatopoeia,[c] which
suggests to us that we should ourselves designate
with a suitable word, whether for the sake of
imitation or of expressiveness, a thing which either
lacks a name [d] or has an inappropriate name.   For
the sake of imitation, as follows: our ancestors, for
example, said " roar," " bellow," " murmur,"
" hiss; " for the sake of expressiveness, as follows:

word." Cicero admits unusual (old-fashioned), new, and
metaphorical words, although recognizing that these are
allowed more freely in poetry than in oratory; see *De Oratore*
3. 38. 152 ff., *Orator* 20. 68 and 24. 81, and also the advice
which Horace, *Ars Poet.* 46 ff. and *Epist.* 2. 2. 119–121, gives
to poets to use neologisms, but with restraint. Quintilian
likewise tolerates neologisms despite the danger in their use,
but does not allow Roman speakers the imitative type of
Onomatopoeia, although this was " held as one of the highest
virtues by the Greeks; " see 1. 5. 71 f., 8. 6. 31 f., 8. 3. 35–37.
Cf. also Gellius, 11. 7. 1 : "But as for me I think it more
objectionable and censurable to use words that are new,
unknown, and unheard-of than to use those that are hackneyed
and mean."

    [d] See note on Metaphor, 4. xxxiv. 45 below.

333

in rem publicam fecit impetum, fragor civitatis in primis." Hoc genere raro est utendum, sic ut ne novi verbi adsiduitas odium pariat; sed si commode quis eo utatur et raro, non modo non offendet novitate, sed etiam exornat orationem.

Pronominatio[a] est quae sicuti cognomine quodam extraneo demonstrat id quod suo nomine non potest appellari; ut si quis cum loquatur de Graccis, " At non Africani nepotes," inquiet, " istiusmodi fuerunt." Item si quis de adversario cum dicat, " Videte nunc," inquit, " iudices, quemadmodum me Plagioxiphus[b] iste tractarit." Hoc pacto non inornate poterimus, et in laudando et in laedendo, in corpore aut animo aut extraneis rebus dicere sic uti cognomen quod pro[c] certo nomine[d] collocemus.

43 XXXII. Denominatio[e] est quae ab rebus propinquis et finitimis trahit orationem qua possit intellegi res quae non suo vocabulo sit appellata. Id aut a superiore re conficitur,[1] ut si quis de Tarpeio loquens eum Capitolinum nominet; . . . .[2]; aut invento, ut si quis pro Libero vinum, pro Cerere frugem appellet; . . .;[3] aut instrumento dominum, ut si quis Mace-

---

[1] Text corrupt. Id [aut] a superiore re conficitur *sugg. Mx*: ita ut ventorum (inventor *H*) conficitur *M* : Id aut ab inventore conficitur *C* : id aut ab invento colligitur aut ab inventore conficitur *E*.

[2] *A treatment of the substitution of* inferior res *for* superior res *is missing.*

[3] *A treatment of the substitution of* inventor *for* inventum *is missing.*

---

[a] ἀντονομασία.
[b] Lit., " flat of the blade."
[c] *Cf.* 3. vi. 10 above.
[d] *Pro nomine*, hence the name for the figure, *Pronominatio.*
[e] μετωνυμία.

" After this creature attacked the republic, there was a hullabaloo among the first men of the state." This figure is to be used rarely, lest the frequent recurrence of the neologism breed aversion; but if it is used appropriately and sparingly, then the novelty, far from offending, even gives distinction to the style.

Antonomasia [a] or Pronomination designates by a kind of adventitious epithet a thing that cannot be called by its proper name; for example, if some one speaking of the Gracchi should say: " Surely the grandsons of Africanus did not behave like this! "; or again, if some one speaking of his adversary should say: " See now, men of the jury, how your Sir Swash-buckler [b] there has treated me." In this way we shall be able, not without elegance, in praise and in censure, concerning physical attributes, qualities of character, or external circumstances,[c] to express ourselves by using a kind of epithet in place of the precise name.[d]

43   XXXII. Metonymy [e] is the figure which draws from an object closely akin or associated an expression suggesting the object meant, but not called by its own name. This is accomplished by substituting the name of the greater thing for that of the lesser, as if one speaking of the Tarpeian Rock should term it " the Capitoline "; . . .; or by substituting the name of the thing invented for that of the inventor, as if one should say " wine " for " Liber," " wheat " for " Ceres ";[f] " . . .; " or the instrument for the possessor, as if one should refer to the Macedonians

---

[f] Liber and Ceres are common metonyms; see Cicero, *De Oratore* 3. 42. 167, advising the frequent use of this kind of figure, and *De Natura Deorum* 2. 23. 60, citing Terence, *Eunuch.* 732; Quintilian, 8. 6. 24: " It would be too bold for the severe style of the forum to tolerate our saying ' Liber ' for ' wine ' and ' Ceres ' for ' bread.' "

dones appellarit hoc modo: " Non tam cito sarisae
Graeciae potitae sunt," aut idem Gallos significans:
" nec tam facile ex Italia materis Transalpina depulsa
est "; aut id quod fit ab eo qui facit, ut si quis, cum
bello velit ostendere aliquid quempiam fecisse,
dicat: " Mars istuc te facere necessario coëgit "; aut
si quod facit ab eo quod fit, ut cum desidiosam artem
dicimus quia desidiosos facit, et frigus pigrum quia
pigros efficit. Ab eo quod continet id quod continetur hoc modo denominabitur: " Armis Italia non
potest vinci nec Graecia disciplinis "—nam hic, pro
Graecis et Italis, quae continent notata sunt; ab eo
quod continetur id quod continet, ut si quis aurum
aut argentum aut ebur nominet cum divitias velit
nominare. Harum omnium denominationum magis
in praecipiendo divisio quam in quaerendo difficilis
inventio est, ideo quod plena consuetudo est non
modo poëtarum et oratorum sed etiam cotidiani
sermonis huiusmodi denominationum.

Circumitio est oratio rem simplicem adsumpta
circumscribens elocutione, hoc pacto: " Scipionis
providentia Kartaginis opes fregit." Nam hic, nisi
ornandi ratio quaedam esset habita, Scipio potuit et
Kartago simpliciter appellari.

44   Transgressio est quae verborum perturbat ordinem
perversione aut transiectione. Perversione, sic:

ᵃ This last illustration is used also by the grammarians
Charisius (ed. Barwick, p. 360) and Diomedes (Keil, *Gramm.
Lat.* 1. 458).
    ᵇ Quintilian, 8. 6. 24–5, approves the substitution of container
for content, but allows the converse only to poetic practice.

as follows: " Not so quickly did the Lances get possession of Greece," and likewise, meaning the Gauls: " nor was the Transalpine Pike so easily driven from Italy "; the cause for the effect, as if a speaker, wishing to show that some one has done something in war, should say: " Mars forced you to do that "; or effect for cause, as when we call an art idle because it produces idleness in people, or speak of numb cold because cold produces numbness.[a] Content will be designated by means of container as follows: " Italy cannot be vanquished in warfare nor Greece in studies "; for here instead of Greeks and Italians the lands that comprise them are designated. Container will be designated by means of content:[b] as if one wishing to give a name to wealth should call it gold or silver or ivory. It is harder to distinguish all these metonymies in teaching the principle than to find them when searching for them, for the use of metonymies of this kind is abundant not only amongst the poets and orators but also in everyday speech.

Periphrasis[c] is a manner of speech used to express a simple idea by means of a circumlocution, as follows: " The foresight of Scipio crushed the power of Carthage." For here, if the speaker had not designed to embellish the style, he might simply have said " Scipio " and " Carthage."

44   Hyperbaton[d] upsets the word order by means either of Anastrophe[e] or Transposition. By Anas-

---

[c] περίφρασις. When faulty, it is περισσολογία (Quintilian, 8. 6. 61).

[d] ὑπερβατόν. See 4. xii. 18 above.

[e] ἀναστροφή, Reversal of order. Quintilian, 8. 6. 65, defines ἀναστροφή as a transposition confined to two words.

" Hoc vobis deos immortales arbitror dedisse virtute
pro vestra." Transiectione, hoc modo: " Instabilis
in istum plurimum fortuna valuit. Omnes invidiose
eripuit bene vivendi casus facultates." Huiusmodi
transiectio, quae rem non reddit obscuram, multum
proderit ad continuationes, de quibus ante dictum est;
in quibus oportet verba sicuti ad poëticum quendam
extruere numerum, ut perfecte et perpolitissime
possint esse absolutae.

XXXIII. Superlatio est oratio superans veritatem
alicuius augendi minuendive causa. Haec sumitur
separatim aut cum conparatione. Separatim, sic:
" Quodsi concordiam retinebimus in civitate, imperii
magnitudinem solis ortu atque occasu metiemur."

---

[a] " This I deem the immortal gods have vouchsafed to you
in reward for your virtue." The strictly correct order would
have been *pro vestra virtute*; *virtūtĕ prŏ vēstrā* gives the most
favoured clausula.

[b] " Unstable Fortune has exercised her greatest power on
this creature. All the means of living well Chance has
jealously taken from him." Here the adjectives are separated
from the nouns they modify; *fortūnă vălŭĭt* and especially
casūs făcūltātēs were favoured clausulae (see note next above).
Our author employs the dichoree (– ◡ – ◡́) most. See the
study of the cadences in A. W. de Groot, *Der antike Pro-
sarhythmus*, Groningen and The Hague, 1921, pp. 106–7; in
Henri Bornecque, *Les Clausules Métriques Latines*, Lille, 1907,
pp. 542 ff., 579 f.; and in Burdach, *Schlesisch-böhmische Briefmuster*, pp. 110 ff.; also the notes on 4. viii. 12 and 4. xix. 26,
and the next note here below.

[c] 4. xix. 27. The doctrines of rhythm were not taught as
part of the regular curriculum by the Atticizing rhetoricians
(Cicero, *De Oratore* 3. 49. 188); our author does not mention
Rhythm under Composition in 4. xii. 18 above, save indirectly
in his reference to concinnity in Hyperbaton. Here, however,
he is under Asian influence. *Cf.* Cicero, *Orator* 69. 229 : " We
must not transpose words in an obvious manner for the sake

trophe, as follows: " Hoc vobis deos immortales arbitror dedisse virtute pro vestra." *a* By Transposition, as follows: " Instabilis in istum plurimum fortuna valuit. Omnes invidiose eripuit bene vivendi casus facultates." *b* A transposition of this kind, that does not render the thought obscure, will be very useful for periods, which I have discussed above; *c* in these periods we ought to arrange the words in such a way as to approximate a poetic rhythm,*d* so that the periods can achieve perfect fullness and the highest finish.

XXXIII. Hyperbole *e* is a manner of speech exaggerating the truth, whether for the sake of magnifying or minifying something. This is used independently, or with comparison. Independently, as follows: " But if we maintain concord in the state, we shall measure the empire's vastness by the rising and the setting of the sun." Hyperbole with com-

of achieving a better cadence or a more flowing rhythm ";
Dionysius Halic., *De Composit. Verb.*, ch. 4; and Blass, *Die Rhythmen der asian. und röm. Kunstprosa*, pp. 33 ff. Our author in his rhythms represents the transition between Asian rules and those followed by Cicero; see Bornecque, *op. cit.*, p. 546. On our author's generally ambivalent position with respect to Asianism, see Burdach, *op. cit.*, pp. 96 ff.

d Cicero, *Orator* 56. 187 f.: " It is, then, quite clear that prose should be tightened up by rhythm, but be free of metre . . . There are, to be sure, no rhythms other than those used in poetry "; Crassus in *De Oratore* 1. 33. 151: " Good collocation and good arrangement of words are perfected in writing by means of a certain rhythm and measure not poetical, but oratorical." Thrasymachus of Chalcedon (fifth century B.C.) was the inventor of prose rhythm, and Isocrates excelled in its use (Cicero, *Orator* 52. 175).

e ὑπερβολή. Aristotle, *Rhet.* 3. 11 (1413 a), says that the use of Hyperbole is a juvenile characteristic, betraying vehemence. *Cf.* Quintilian, 8. 6. 67 ff.

[CICERO]

Cum conparatione aut a similitudine aut a praestantia
superlatio sumitur. A similitudine, sic : " Corpore
niveum candorem, aspectu igneum ardorem ad-
sequebatur." A praestantia, hoc modo : " Cuius ore
sermo melle dulcior profluebat." Ex eodem genere
est hoc : " Tantus erat in armis splendor ut solis
fulgor obscurior [1] videretur."

Intellectio est cum res tota parva de parte cognos-
citur aut de toto pars. De parte totum sic intellegitur : " Non illae te nuptiales tibiae eius matrimonii
commonebant ? " Nam hic omnis sanctimonia nup-
tiarum uno signo tibiarum intellegitur. De toto pars,
ut si quis ei qui vestitum aut ornatum sumptuosum
ostentet dicat : " Ostentas mihi divitias et locupletes
45 copias iactas." Ab uno plura hoc modo intellegentur :
" Poeno fuit Hispanus auxilio, fuit immanis ille
Transalpinus ; in Italia quoque nonnemo sensit idem
togatus." A pluribus unum sic intellegetur : " Atrox
calamitas pectora maerore pulsabat ; itaque anhelans
ex imis pulmonibus prae cura spiritus ducebat." Nam
in superiore [2] plures Hispani et Galli et togati, et hic
unum pectus et unus pulmo intellegitur ; et erit illic
deminutus numerus festivitatis, hic adauctus gravitatis gratia.

---

[1] obscurior P^2B^2 Π $l\,d$: obscurius (Mb) Mx *brackets.*
[2] superiore M : superioribus *other MSS. Mx.*

---

[a] *Cf.*, for example, Homer, *Il.* 1. 104 : Agamemnon's
eyes " were like flashing fire " ; in 10. 437 the horses of Rhesus
are " whiter than snow " (Hyperbole with comparison formed
from superiority).
[b] Homer, *Il.* 1. 249, on Nestor. On the popularity of this
passage in antiquity see Otto, pp. 242, 216 f.
[c] συνεκδοχή.

parison is formed from either equivalence or
superiority. From equivalence, as follows: " His
body was as white as snow, his face burned like fire." [a]
From superiority, as follows: " From his mouth
flowed speech sweeter than honey." [b] Of the same
type is the following: " So great was his splendour in
arms that the sun's brilliance seemed dim by
comparison."

Synecdoche [c] occurs when the whole is known from
a small part or a part from the whole. The whole is
understood from a part in the following: " Were not
those nuptial flutes reminding you of his marriage ? "
Here the entire marriage ceremony is suggested by
one sign, the flutes. A part from the whole, as if one
should say to a person who displays himself in
luxurious garb or adornment: " You display your
45 riches to me and vaunt your ample treasures." The
plural will be understood from the singular, as
follows: " To the Carthaginian came aid from the
Spaniard, and from that fierce Transalpine. In
Italy, too, many a wearer of the toga shared the same
sentiment." In the following the singular will be
understood from the plural: " Dread disaster smote
his breasts with grief; so, panting, from out his lungs'
very depth he sobbed for anguish." In the first
example more than one Spaniard, Gaul, and Roman
citizen are understood, and in this last only one breast
and one lung.[d] In the former the quantity is minified
for the sake of elegance, in the latter exaggerated
for the sake of impressiveness.

[d] In ancient physiology the lungs were considered to be the
right and left halves of a single organ, with the windpipe as
the common outlet; cf., for example, Aristotle, De Part.
Animal. 3. 6–7 (668 b ff.), Hist. Animal. 2. 17 (507 a 19).

[CICERO]

Abusio est quae verbo simili et propinquo pro certo et proprio abutitur, hoc modo: " Vires hominis breves sunt ", aut " parva statura ", aut " longum in homine consilium ", aut " oratio magna ", aut " uti pauco sermone." Nam hic facile est intellectu finitima verba rerum dissimilium ratione abusionis esse traducta.

XXXIV. Translatio est cum verbum in quandam rem transferetur ex alia re, quod propter similitudinem recte videbitur posse transferri. Ea sumitur rei ante oculos ponendae causa, sic: " Hic Italiam tumultus expergefecit terrore subito." Brevitatis causa, sic: " Recens adventus exercitus extinxit subito civitatem." Obscenitatis vitandae causa, sic: " Cuius mater cotidianis nuptiis delectetur." Augendi causa, sic: " Nullius maeror et calamitas istius explere inimicitias et nefariam crudelitatem saturare potuit." Minuendi causa, sic: " Magno se praedicat auxilio fuisse quia paululum in rebus difficillimis aspiravit." Ornandi causa, sic: " Aliquando rei

---

[a] κατάχρησις.

[b] Cf. Aristophanes, *Birds* 465: μέγα καὶ λαρινὸν ἔπος τι (" a stalwart and brawny oration," tr. B. B. Rogers).

[c] μεταφορά. Cf. Aristotle, *Rhet.* 3. 2 (1405 a) ff., *Poet.*, ch. 21; Demetrius, *De Elocut.* 2. 78 ff.; Quintilian, 8. 6. 4 ff. According to Cicero, *Orator* 27. 92, metaphor is used for the sake of charm (*suavitas*) or because of the lack (*inopia*) of a proper word; cf. also *De Oratore* 3. 38. 155. Quintilian, 8. 6. 6, says that we use metaphor from necessity or because it achieves greater expressiveness or beauty. Cf. *translatio criminis*, 2. xv. 22 above, and *translatio*, the subtype of Legal Issue, 1. xii. 22.

[d] Quintilian, 8. 6. 8, terms Metaphor a shorter Simile.

[e] Cf. Plautus, *Cist.* 43: " She is married to a husband every day, indeed she is; " and Demosthenes, *De Corona* 129.

Catachresis [a] is the inexact use of a like and kindred word in place of the precise and proper one, as follows: " The power of man is short," or " small height," or " the long wisdom in the man," or " a mighty speech," [b] or " to engage in a slight conversation." Here it is easy to understand that words of kindred, but not identical, meaning have been transferred on the principle of inexact use.

XXXIV. Metaphor [c] occurs when a word applying to one thing is transferred to another, because the similarity seems to justify this transference. Metaphor is used for the sake of creating a vivid mental picture, as follows: " This insurrection awoke Italy with sudden terror"; for the sake of brevity,[d] as follows: " The recent arrival of an army suddenly blotted out the state"; for the sake of avoiding obscenity, as follows: " Whose mother delights in daily marriages";[e] for the sake of magnifying, as follows: " No one's grief or disaster could have appeased this creature's enmities and glutted his horrible cruelty";[f] for the sake of minifying, as follows: " He boasts that he was of great help because, when we were in difficulties, he lightly breathed a favouring breath";[g] for the sake of embellishment, as follows: " Some day the prosperity of the republic,

addressing Aeschines: " Or how your mother practised nuptials in open daylight in the outhouse."

[f] This may perhaps belong to the *controversia* concerning the murder of Sulpicius, 1. xv. 25 above.

[g] *Cf.* Cicero, *Leg. Agr.* 2. 5. 13, on the unintelligible speech of the once truculent Rullus: " The keener-witted persons standing in the Assembly suspected that he had meant to say something or other about an agrarian law "; Quintilian, 8. 4. 28, quotes this sentence of Cicero in illustration of *ratio minuendi*.

[CICERO]

publicae rationes, quae malitia nocentium exaru-
erunt, virtute optimatium revirescent." Translationem pudentem dicunt esse oportere, ut cum
ratione in consimilem rem transeat, ne sine dilectu
temere et cupide videatur in dissimilem transcurrisse.

46   Permutatio est oratio aliud verbis aliud sententia
demonstrans. Ea dividitur in tres partes: similitudinem, argumentum, contrarium. Per similitudinem sumitur cum translationes plures frequenter
ponuntur a simili oratione ductae, sic: "Nam cum
canes funguntur officiis luporum, cuinam praesidio
pecuaria credemus?" Per argumentum tractatur
cum a persona aut loco aut re aliqua similitudo
augendi aut minuendi causa ducitur, ut si quis
Drusum Graccum nitorem[1] obsoletum dicat. Ex
contrario ducitur sic, ut si quis hominem prodigum
et luxuriosum inludens parcum et diligentem appellet. Et in hoc postremo quod ex contrario sumitur,
et in illo primo quod a similitudine ducitur, per
translationem argumento poterimus uti. Per similitudinem, sic: "Quid ait hic rex atque Agamemnon
noster, sive, ut crudelitas est, potius Atreus?" Ex
contrario, ut si quem impium qui patrem verberarit

---

[1] nitorem *M* : numitoremque *E Mx.*

Cicero, *De Oratore* 3. 41. 165, makes the same point; *cf.*
also Aristotle, *Rhet.* 3. 2 (1405 a), Cicero, *Epist. ad Fam.* 16.
17 (Theophrastus' *verecunda tralatio*), Longinus, *De Sublim.*
32. 3, Quintilian, 8. 3. 37.

ἀλληγορία.

The text is corrupt. With Lindemann (ed. Leipzig, 1828,
p. 343) and others I take *Graccum* as a genitive plural. The
policy of M. Livius Drusus, *tr. pl.* in 91 B.C., finds a parallel
in that of C. Gracchus; see Hugh Last in *Cambr. Anc. History*

which by the malice of wicked men has withered
away, will bloom again by the virtue of the Conservatives." They say that a metaphor ought to be
restrained,[a] so as to be a transition with good reason
to a kindred thing, and not seem an indiscriminate,
reckless, and precipitate leap to an unlike thing.

46   Allegory [b] is a manner of speech denoting one thing
by the letter of the words, but another by their
meaning. It assumes three aspects: comparison,
argument, and contrast. It operates through a comparison when a number of metaphors originating in a
similarity in the mode of expression are set together,
as follows: " For when dogs act the part of wolves,
to what guardian, pray, are we going to entrust our
herds of cattle ? " An Allegory is presented in the
form of argument when a similitude is drawn from
a person or place or object in order to magnify or
minify, as if one should call Drusus a " faded reflection of the Gracchi." [c] An Allegory is drawn from a
contrast [d] if, for example, one should mockingly call a
spendthrift and voluptuary frugal and thrifty. Both
in this last type, based on a contrast, and in the first
above, drawn from a comparison, we can through the
metaphor make use of argument. In an Allegory
operating through a comparison, as follows: " What
says this king—our Agamemnon, or rather, such is
his cruelty, our Atreus ? " In an Allegory drawn
from a contrast: for example, if we should call
some undutiful man who has beaten his father

9. 177-84. With Allegory *per argumentum* cf. Antonomasia,
4. xxxi. 42 above.

[d] *Cf.* Quintilian, 8. 6. 54 ff. (*ironia, illusio*); *Rhet. ad Alex.*
ch. 21, 1434 a (εἰρωνεία); Anon., *De Trop.*, in Walz 8. 722
(ἀντίφρασις).

Aeneam vocemus, intemperantem et adulterum Hippolytum [1] nominemus.

Haec sunt fere quae dicenda videbantur de verborum exornationibus. Nunc res ipsa monet ut deinceps ad sententiarum exornationes transeamus.

47 XXXV. Distributio est cum in plures res aut personas negotia quaedam certa dispertiuntur, hoc modo: " Qui vestrum, iudices, nomen senatus diligit, hunc oderit necesse est; petulantissime enim semper iste oppugnavit senatum. Qui equestrem locum splendidissimum cupit esse in civitate, is oportet istum maximas poenas [2] dedisse velit, ne iste sua turpitudine ordini honestissimo maculae atque dedecori sit. Qui parentes habetis, ostendite istius supplicio vobis homines impios non placere. Quibus liberi sunt, statuite exemplum quantae poenae sint in civitate hominibus istiusmodi conparatae." Item: " Senatus est officium consilio civitatem iuvare; magistratus est officium opera et diligentia consequi senatus voluntatem; populi est officium res optimas et homines idoneos maxime suis sententiis deligere et probare." Et: " Accusatoris officium est inferre crimina; defensoris diluere et propulsare; testis dicere quae

___

[1] Ippolytum *Mx*: yppolitum *PΠBCb*: ypolitum *l*: ipolitum *d*: ippolitum *H*.

[2] maximas poenas *b l Mx ed. mai.*: maximae poenae *M Mx*: maximam poenam *Cd*.

___

[a] Called *pius* for his devotion to Anchises, his father.

[b] Rejected the advances of his stepmother Phaedra.

[c] διαίρεσις, μερισμός. Cf. the *distributio* of 1. x. 17, the *distributio* (Broken Tone of Debate) of 3. xiii. 23, and the figure, *divisio*, in 4. xl. 52.

[d] Of πράγματα or of πρόσωπα. Cf. the distinction in the third kind of *narratio*, 1. viii. 13 above.

" Aeneas," [a] or an intemperate and adulterous man " Hippolytus." [b]

This is substantially all I have thought it necessary to say on the Figures of Diction. Now the subject itself directs me to turn next to the Figures of Thought.

47 XXXV. Distribution [c] occurs when certain specified rôles are assigned among a number of things or persons, [d] as follows: " Whoever of you, men of the jury, loves the good name of the Senate, must hate this man, for his attacks upon that body have always been most insolent. Whoever of you wishes the equestrian order [e] to be most resplendent in the state, must want this person to have paid the severest penalty, so that he may not be, through his personal shame, a stain and disgrace to a most honourable order. You who have parents, must prove by your punishment of this creature that undutiful men do not find favour with you. You who have children, must set forth an example to show how great are the punishments that have been provided in our state for men of that stamp." Again, " The Senate's function is to assist the state with counsel; the magistracy's is to execute, by diligent activity, the Senate's will; the people's to choose and support by its votes the best measures and the most suitable men." Again, " The duty of the prosecutor is to bring the charges; that of the counsel for the defence to explain them away and rebut them; that

[e] In accordance with the *Lex Plautia Iudiciaria* of 90/89 B.C. both senators and knights (and also some of the *plebs*) served as *iudices* in the criminal courts. Sulla restored the senatorial monopoly in 82/81 B.C.

sciat aut audierit; quaesitoris est unum quemque
horum in officio suo continere. Quare, L. Cassi, si
testem praeterquam quod sciat aut audierit argumentari et coniectura prosequi patieris, ius accusatoris cum iure testimonii commiscebis, testis inprobi
cupiditatem confirmabis, reo duplicem defensionem
parabis." Est haec exornatio copiosa, conprehendit
enim brevi multa, et suum cuique tribuens officium
separatim res dividit plures.

48   XXXVI. Licentia est cum apud eos quos aut
vereri aut metuere debemus tamen aliquid pro iure
nostro dicimus, quod eos aut quos ii diligunt aliquo in
errato vere reprehendere videamur, hoc modo:
" Miramini, Quirites, quod ab omnibus vestrae
rationes deserantur? quod causam vestram nemo
suscipiat? quod se nemo vestri defensorem pro-
fiteatur? Adtribuite vestrae culpae, desinite mirari.
Quid est enim quare non omnes istam rem fugere ac
vitare debeant? Recordamini quos habueritis defen-
sores; studia eorum vobis ante oculos proponite;
deinde exitus omnium considerate. Tum vobis
veniat in mentem, ut vere dicam, neglegentia vestra
sive ignavia potius, illos omnes ante oculos vestros

ª On the admission of hearsay evidence in Roman Law see
J. L. Strachan-Davidson, *Problems of the Roman Criminal
Law*, Oxford, 1912, 2. 123 ff.; *cf.* 2. viii. 12 above.

ᵇ From the celebrated speech delivered in 113 B.C. (or at
the end of 114) by L. Licinius Crassus in defence of Licinia,
accused with other Vestals of unchastity and condemned.
L. Cassius Longinus Ravilla (whose rule was to insist on the
question of the motive : *Cui bono?*—" for whose advantage
was the crime ? ") was the examining magistrate.

ᶜ παρρησία, *oratio libera*. Quintilian, 9. 2. 27 and 9. 3. 99,
denies that this is a figure. *Cf.* Isocrates, *De Pace* 72 f. :

of the witness to say what he knows or has heard; [a] that of the presiding justice to hold each of these to his duty. Therefore, Lucius Cassius, if you allow a witness to argue and to attack by means of conjecture, passing beyond what he knows or has heard, you will be confusing the rights of a prosecutor with those of a witness, you will be encouraging the partiality of a dishonest witness, and you will be ordaining for the defendant that he defend himself twice." [b] This figure has richness, for it embraces much in little and, by assigning to each his duty, severally distinguishes a number of entities.

48   XXXVI. It is Frankness of Speech [c] when, talking before those to whom we owe reverence or fear, we yet exercise our right to speak out, because we seem justified in reprehending them, or persons dear to them, for some fault. For example: " You wonder, fellow citizens, that every one abandons your interests? That no one undertakes your cause? That no one declares himself your defender? Blame this upon yourselves; cease to wonder. Why indeed should not every one avoid and shun this situation of your making? Bethink yourselves of those whom you have had for defenders; set their devotion before your eyes, and next consider what has become of them all. Then remember that thanks to your—to speak aright—indifference, or cowardice rather, all these men have been murdered before your eyes, and

" While hating those who revile you to your hurt as bearing malice to the state, you ought to praise those who admonish you for your benefit, and think them the best of your fellow-citizens, and think that best of all is the man who can demonstrate most vividly the defects of your practices and the misfortunes that arise from them."

349

trucidatos esse, inimicos eorum vestris suffragiis in amplissimum locum pervenisse." Item: " Nam quid fuit, iudices, quare in sententiis ferendis dubitaveritis aut istum hominem nefarium ampliaveritis? Non apertissimae res erant crimini datae? non omnes hae testibus conprobatae? non contra tenuiter et nugatorie responsum? Hic vos veriti estis, si primo coetu condemnassetis, ne crudeles existimaremini? Dum eam vitatis vituperationem, quae longe a vobis erat afutura, eam invenistis ut timidi atque ignavi putaremini. Maximis privatis et publicis calamitatibus acceptis, cum etiam maiores inpendere videantur, sedetis et oscitamini. Luci noctem, nocte lucem expectatis. Aliquid cotidie acerbi atque incommodi nuntiatur; et iam eum, cuius opera nobis haec accidunt, vos remoramini diutius et alitis ad rei publicae perniciem, retinetis quoad potestis in civitate?"

49 XXXVII. Eiusmodi licentia si nimium videbitur acrimoniae habere, multis mitigationibus lenietur; nam continuo aliquid huiusmodi licebit inferre: " Hic ego virtutem vestram quaero, sapientiam desidero, veterem consuetudinem requiro," ut quod erit[1] commotum licentia id constituatur laude, ut altera res ab iracundia et molestia removeat, altera res ab errato deterreat. Haec res, sicut in amicitia

---

[1] quod erit *M* : ut quod erat *E Mx.*

---

a Whether this passage derives from a speech actually delivered we do not know. The sentiments are appropriate to a tribune of the time of Marius.

b The renewal (*ampliatio*) of a case followed the verdict *non liquet* by the jury, and the president's pronouncement *amplius* (*cognoscendum*). Renewals had to be repeated until

thanks to your own votes their enemies have reached the highest estate." *a* Again: " Now what was your motive, men of the jury, in hesitating to pass sentence on this abominable man, or in allowing him a new trial? *b* Were not the facts charged plain as day? Were they not all proved by witnesses? Was not the answer, on the other hand, feeble and trifling? Did you at this point fear that in condemning him at the first hearing you would be considered cruel? While avoiding a reproach for cruelty, which you would have been far from incurring, you have incurred another reproach—you are considered timid and cowardly. You have met with very great losses, private and public, and now when even greater losses seem to impend, you sit and yawn. During the day you wait for night, at night you wait for day. Every day some troublesome and unpleasant news is announced—yet even now will you temporize longer with the author of these our ills, and nourish him for the destruction of the republic; will you keep him in the commonwealth as long as you can? "

49   XXXVII. If Frank Speech of this sort seems too pungent, there will be many means of palliation, for one may immediately thereafter add something of this sort: " I here appeal to your virtue, I call on your wisdom, I bespeak your old habit," so that praise may quiet the feelings aroused by the frankness. As a result, the praise frees the hearer from wrath and annoyance, and the frankness deters him from error. This precaution in speaking, as in

the verdict of *fecisse videtur* or *non fecisse videtur* was rendered. The *Lex Acilia Repetundarum* (123/2 B.C.) provided against the abuses of this power by juries; it permitted the jury no more than one renewal in a single case at penalty of a fine.

[CICERO]

item in dicendo, si loco fit, maxime facit ut et illi qui
audient a culpa absint, et nos qui dicimus amici
ipsorum et veritatis esse videamur.

Est autem quoddam genus in dicendo licentiae quod
astutiore ratione conparatur, cum aut ita obiurgamus
eos qui audiunt quomodo ipsi se cupiunt obiurgari, aut
id quod scimus facile omnes audituros dicimus nos
timere quomodo accipiant, sed tamen veritate commoveri ut nihilosetius dicamus. Horum amborum
generum exempla subiciemus; prioris, huiusmodi:
" Nimium, Quirites, animis estis simplicibus et man-
suetis; nimium creditis uni cuique. Existimatis
unum quemque eniti ut perficiat quae vobis pollicitus
sit. Erratis et falsa spe frustra iam diu detinemini
stultitia vestra, qui quod erat in vestra potestate ab
aliis petere quam ipsi sumere maluistis." Posterioris
licentiae hoc erit exemplum: " Mihi cum isto,
iudices, fuit amicitia, sed ista tamen amicitia, tametsi
vereor quomodo accepturi sitis, tamen dicam, vos me
privastis. Quid ita? Quia, ut vobis essem probatus,
eum qui vos oppugnabat inimicum quam amicum
habere malui."

ᵃ *Cf.* Plato, *Phaedo* 91 B : " And I would enjoin upon
you to be giving only little thought to Socrates, but much
more to the truth "; and the saying attributed to Aristotle
by Cervantes : *Amicus Plato, sed magis amica veritas.* (See
James Condamin, *Répertoire Alphabétique des Citations,*
Lyons and Paris, 1926, pp. 26 ff.)

ᵇ It has been suspected (see Friedrich Ellendt in Meyer-
Dübner, *Orator. Rom. Fragm.*, 2nd ed., p. 235, and Kroehnert,
p. 30) that this may be a fragment from the speech *De legibus
promulgatis* delivered (in 122 B.C.) by Gaius Gracchus, the
words here being directed against M. Livius Drusus; but
there is no real evidence to substantiate the conjecture.
Rutilius Lupus, 2. 18 (Halm, pp. 20–21), uses as an example
of this figure the following passage from Demosthenes (*Fragm.*

friendship, if taken at the right place, is especially effective in keeping the hearers from error and in presenting us, the speakers, as friendly both to the hearers and to the truth.

There is also a certain kind of frankness in speaking which is achieved by a craftier device, when we remonstrate with the hearers as they wish us to remonstrate with them, or when we say " we fear how the audience may take " something which we know they all will hear with acceptance, " yet the truth moves us to say it none the less." [a] I shall add examples of both these kinds. Of the former, as follows: " Fellow citizens, you are of too simple and gentle a character; you have too much confidence in every one. You think that every one strives to perform what he has promised you. You are mistaken, and now for a long time you have been kept back by false and groundless hope, in your fatuity choosing to seek from others what lay in your power, rather than take it yourselves." [b] Of the latter kind of Frank Speech the following will be an example: " I enjoyed a friendship with this person, men of the jury, yet of that friendship—although I fear how you are going to receive what I shall say, I will yet say it —you have deprived me. Why? Because, in order to win your approval, I have preferred to consider your assailant as an enemy rather than as a friend."

Orat. Att., ed. Baiter-Sauppe, fragm. 54, p. 257): " But shall I refrain from speaking the truth frankly before you? No, I say. I shall not be silent, because the common welfare demands speech. It is by your own doing, men of Athens, that the state is in such great peril. For you have failed to defend yourselves, by recklessly believing every one and by esteeming as most useful the opinions of those whose counsels are most cowardly."

50 Ergo haec exornatio cui licentiae nomen est, sicuti demonstravimus, duplici ratione tractabitur: acrimonia, quae si nimium fuerit aspera, mitigabitur laude; et adsimulatione, de qua posterius diximus, quae non indiget mitigationis, propterea quod imitatur licentiam et sua spontest ad animum auditoris adcommodata.

XXXVIII. Deminutio est cum aliquid inesse in nobis aut in iis quos defendimus aut natura aut fortuna aut industria dicemus egregium, quod, ne qua significetur adrogans ostentatio, deminuitur et adtenuatur oratione, hoc modo: " Nam hoc pro meo iure, iudices, dico, me labore et industria curasse ut disciplinam militarem non in postremis tenerem." Hic si quis dixisset " ut optime tenerem," tametsi vere dixisset, tamen adrogans visus esset. Nunc et ad invidiam vitandam et laudem conparandam satis dictum est. Item: " Utrum igitur avaritiae an egestatis [1] accessit ad maleficium? Avaritiae? At largissimus fuit in amicos; quod signum liberalitatis est, quae contraria est avaritiae. Egestatis? Huic quidem pater—nolo nimium dicere—non tenuissimum patrimonium reliquit." Hic quoque vitatum est ne " magnum " aut " maximum " diceretur. Hoc igitur in nostris aut eorum quos defendemus egregiis commodis proferendis observabimus. Nam eiusmodi res

[1] *lac. after* egestatis *Mx.*

---

[a] ἀντεναντίωσις. Sometimes also μείωσις, λιτότης.
[b] It has been conjectured (see Ellendt in Meyer-Dübner, *Orator. Rom. Fragm.*, 2nd ed., p. 256, and Kroehnert, p. 31)

50 Thus this figure called Frankness of Speech will, as I have shown, be handled in two ways: with pungency, which, if too severe, will be mitigated by praise; and with pretence, discussed above, which does not require mitigation, because it assumes the guise of Frank Speech and is of itself agreeable to the hearer's frame of mind.

XXXVIII. Understatement [a] occurs when we say that by nature, fortune, or diligence, we or our clients possess some exceptional advantage, and, in order to avoid the impression of arrogant display, we moderate and soften the statement of it, as follows: " This, men of the jury, I have the right to say—that by labour and diligence I have contrived to be no laggard in the mastery of military science." If the speaker had here said " be the best " he might have spoken the truth, but would have seemed arrogant. He has now said quite enough both to avoid envy and to secure praise. Again: " Was it then because of avarice or of need that he entered upon the crime? Avarice? But he was most generous to his friends, and that is a sign of generosity, a virtue opposed to avarice. Need? But his father left him a patrimony that was—I do not wish to exaggerate—not the smallest." [b] Here again, calling the patrimony " large " or " very large " was avoided. This, then, is the precaution we shall take in setting forth the exceptional advantages which we or our clients enjoy. For

that this passage may have its source in the speech delivered by Marcus Antonius, in 98 B.C., in defence of Manius Aquilius, accused of extortion; cf. Cicero, *Pro Flacco* 98 : " Aquilius, who had been convicted of extortion on many charges and by many witnesses." But there is no real evidence for the ascription.

et invidiam contrahunt in vita et odium in oratione si inconsiderate tractes. Quare quemadmodum ratione in vivendo fugitur invidia, sic in dicendo consilio vitatur odium.

51   XXXIX. Descriptio nominatur quae rerum consequentium continet perspicuam et dilucidam cum gravitate expositionem, hoc modo: " Quodsi istum, iudices, vestris sententiis liberaveritis, statim, sicut e cavea leo emissus aut aliqua taeterrima belua soluta ex catenis, volitabit et vagabitur in foro, acuens dentes in unius cuiusque fortunas, in omnes amicos atque inimicos, notos atque ignotos incursitans, aliorum famam depeculans, aliorum caput oppugnans, aliorum domum et omnem familiam perfringens, rem publicam funditus labefactans. Quare, iudices, eicite eum de civitate; liberate omnes formidine; vobis denique ipsis consulite. Nam si istum inpunitum dimiseritis, in vosmet ipsos, mihi credite, feram et truculentam bestiam, iudices, immiseritis."

Item: " Nam si de hoc, iudices, gravem sententiam tuleritis, uno iudicio simul multos iugulaveritis: grandis natu parens, cuius spes senectutis omnis in huius adulescentia posita est, quare velit in vita manere non habebit; filii parvi, privati patris auxilio, ludibrio et despectui paternis inimicis erunt oppositi; tota domus huius indigna concidet calami-

---

ᵃ διατύπωσις. Cf. demonstratio (Ocular Demonstration), 4. lv. 68 below, and consequentium frequentatio in Cicero, Part. Orat. 16. 55. The figure is useful for exciting emotions; cf. the tenth commonplace of Amplification in 2. xxx. 49 above.

ᵇ Cf. the example of Comparison in Aristotle, Rhet. 3. 3 (1406 b): " Androtion said of Idrieus that he was ' like a cur let loose from his chain, that flies at you and bites '; so Idrieus, let loose from his chains, was vicious."

things of this sort, if you handle them indiscreetly, in
life provoke jealousy and in a speech antipathy.
Therefore just as by circumspection we escape
jealousy in life, so by prudence we avoid antipathy
in speaking.

51   XXXIX. Vivid Description [a] is the name for the
figure which contains a clear, lucid, and impressive
exposition of the consequences of an act, as follows :
" But, men of the jury, if by your votes you free this
defendant, immediately, like a lion released from his
cage, or some foul beast loosed from his chains,[b] he
will slink and prowl about in the forum,[c] sharpening
his teeth to attack every one's property, assaulting
every man, friend and enemy, known to him or unknown, now despoiling a good name, now attacking a
life, now bringing ruin upon a house and its entire
household, shaking the republic from its foundations.
Therefore, men of the jury, cast him out from the
state, free every one from fear, and finally, think of
yourselves. For if you release this creature without
punishment, believe me, gentlemen, it is against
yourselves that you will have let loose a wild and
savage beast."
    Again : " For if you inflict a heavy penalty upon
the defendant, men of the jury, you will at once by a
single judgement have taken many lives. His aged
father, who has set the entire hope of his last years on
this young man, will have no reason for wishing to
stay alive. His small children, deprived of their
father's aid, will be exposed as objects of scorn and
contempt to their father's enemies. His entire
household will collapse under this undeserved

[c] *Cf.* the second example of Simile, 4. xlix. 62 below, and
the passage of Demosthenes cited in note.

tate. At inimici, statim sanguinulentam palmam crudelissima victoria potiti, insultabunt in horum miserias, et superbi a re simul et verbis invenientur." [1]

Item: " Nam neminem vestrum fugit, Quirites, urbe capta quae miseriae consequi soleant: arma qui contra tulerunt statim crudelissime trucidantur; ceteri qui possunt per aetatem et vires laborem ferre rapiuntur in servitutem, qui non possunt vita privantur; uno denique atque eodem tempore domus hostili flagrat [2] incendio, et quos natura aut voluntas necessitudine et benivolentia coniunxit distrahuntur; liberi partim e gremiis diripiuntur parentum, partim in sinu [3] iugulantur, partim ante pedes constuprantur. Nemo, iudices, est qui possit satis rem consequi verbis nec efferre oratione magnitudinem calamitatis."

Hoce genere exornationis vel indignatio vel misericordia potest commoveri, cum res consequentes conprehensae universae perspicua breviter exprimuntur oratione.

[1] invenientur B^2C: invenietur Π: invehentur Bbd: inveniuntur $HPMx$: invehebuntur l.
[2] flagrat C: flagrabit P^2B^2EMx: flagrabat $H^2B\Pi$: fragrabat P^1: fragrabat H^1.
[3] sinu $H^1P^2B^2CE$: sinū $H^2PB\Pi$: sinum Mx.

---

[a] The example is Greek in origin; see the similar example (illustrating διάλυσις) in Herodian (Walz 8. 603). Notice that the speaker addresses the hearers as *Quirites* at first, and as *iudices* at the end. For content and diction *cf.* the example of the grand style, 4. viii. 12 above. *Cf.* also in Homer, *Il.* 9. 591 ff., Cleopatra's description of the woes that come to

calamity. But his enemies, when once they have won the bloody palm by this most cruel of victories, will exult over the miseries of these unfortunates, and will be found insolent on the score of deeds as well as of words."

Again: " For none of you, fellow citizens, fails to see what miseries usually follow upon the capture of a city. Those who have borne arms against the victors are forthwith slain with extreme cruelty. Of the rest, those who by reason of youth and strength can endure hard labour are carried off into slavery, and those who cannot are deprived of life. In short, at one and the same time a house blazes up by the enemy's torch, and they whom nature or free choice has joined in the bonds of kinship or of sympathy are dragged apart. Of the children, some are torn from their parents' arms, others murdered on their parents' bosom, still others violated at their parents' feet. No one, men of the jury, can, by words, do justice to the deed, nor reproduce in language the magnitude of the disaster." [a]

With this kind of figure either indignation or pity can be aroused, when the consequences of an act, taken together as a whole, are concisely set forth in a clear style.

---

men whose city is captured : " The warriors are slain, the city is wasted by fire, and strangers lead captive the children and deep-girdled women "; the example of Metathesis from an unknown author in Isidore, *Rhet.* 21. 34 (Halm, p. 521) : " Recall your minds to the spectacle of an unhappy city that has been stormed, and imagine that you see all the burning, the killing, the plundering, the pillaging, the bodily injury done the children, the taking captive of the matrons, the slaying of the old men "; Dio Chrysostom 32. 89; and Caesar in Sallust, *Cat.* 51. 9.

52   XL. Divisio est quae rem semovens ab re utramque absolvit ratione subiecta, hoc modo: " Cur ego
nunc tibi quicquam obiciam? Si probus es, non
meruisti; si inprobus, non commovebere." [1] Item:
" Quid nunc ego de meis promeritis praedicem? Si
meministis, obtundam; si obliti estis, cum re nihil
egerim, quid est quod verbis proficere possim? "
Item: " Duae res sunt quae possunt homines ad
turpe conpendium commovere: inopia atque avaritia.
Te avarum in fraterna divisione cognovimus; inopem
atque egentem nunc videmus. Qui potes igitur
ostendere causam maleficii non fuisse? " Inter hanc
divisionem et illam quae de partibus orationis tertia
est, de qua in primo libro diximus secundum narrationem, hoc interest: illa dividit per enumerationem
aut per expositionem quibus de rebus in totam
orationem disputatio futura sit; haec se statim
explicat, et brevi duabus aut pluribus partibus
subiciens rationes exornat orationem.

Frequentatio est cum res tota causa dispersae
coguntur in unum locum, quo gravior aut acrior aut
criminosior oratio sit, hoc pacto: " A quo tandem
abest iste vitio? Quid est cur iudicio velitis eum
liberare? Suae pudicitiae proditor est, insidiator

---

[1] commovebere *d*: commovere *other MSS. Mx.*

---

a προσαπόδοσις, Distributive Reply. *In distributis sup-
posita ratio* in *De Oratore* 3. 54. 207; Quintilian, 9. 3. 93,
doubts whether *distributis subiecta ratio* is a figure. The
figure is related to Dilemma (*duplex conclusio*), used in
argumentation; see 2. xxiv. 38 above. *Cf. distributio*
(4. xxxv. 47) and *ratiocinatio* (4. xvi. 23). *Cf.* also Trimalchio
on Agamemnon's *controversia* in Petronius 48: " If the
business took place, there is no argument; if it did not, it is
all nonsense."

52 XL. Division *a* separates the alternatives of a question and resolves each by means of a reason subjoined, as follows: " Why should I now reproach you in any way? If you are an upright man, you have not deserved reproach; if a wicked man, you will be unmoved." Again: " Why should I now boast of my deserts? If you remember them, I shall weary you; if you have forgotten them, I have been ineffective in action, and therefore what could I effect by words? " Again: " There are two things which can urge men to illicit gain: poverty and greed. That you were greedy in the division with your brother we know, that you are poor and destitute we now see. How, therefore, can you show that you had no motive for the crime? " There is the following difference between the present kind of Division and that other which forms the third part of a discourse, and which I treated in Book I,*b* next after Statement of Facts: the former Division operates through the Enumeration or Exposition of the topics to be discussed throughout the whole discourse; whereas here the Division at once unfolds itself, and by briefly adding the reasons for the two or more parts, embellishes the style.

Accumulation *c* occurs when the points scattered throughout the whole cause are collected in one place so as to make the speech more impressive or sharp or accusatory, as follows: " From what vice, I ask, is this defendant free? What ground have you for wishing to acquit him of the suit? He is the betrayer of his own self-respect, and the waylayer of

b 1. x. 17.
c συναθροισμός. Cf. *enumeratio* in 2. xxx. 47 above, and *consummatio* in Quintilian, 9. 2. 103.

alienae; cupidus, intemperans, petulans, superbus; impius in parentes, ingratus in amicos, infestus cognatis; in superiores contumax, in aequos et pares fastidiosus, in inferiores crudelis; denique in omnes intolerabilis."

53 Eiusdem generis est illa frequentatio quae plurimum coniecturalibus causis opitulatur, cum suspiciones, quae separatim dictae minutae et infirmae erant, unum in locum coactae rem videntur perspicuam facere, non suspiciosam, hoc pacto : " Nolite igitur, nolite, iudices, ea quae dixi separatim spectare, sed omnia colligite et conferte in unum.

XLI. " Si et commodum ad istum ex illius morte veniebat; et vita hominis est turpissima, animus avarissimus, fortunae familiares adtenuatissimae; et res ista bono nemini praeter istum fuit; neque alius quisquam aeque commode, neque iste aliis commodioribus rationibus facere potuit; neque praeteritum est ab isto quicquam quod opus fuit ad maleficium, neque factum quod opus non fuit; et cum locus idoneus maxime quaesitus, tum occasio adgrediendi commoda, tempus adeundi opportunissimum; spatium conficiendi longissimum sumptum est, non sine maxima occultandi et perficiendi maleficii spe; et praeterea, ante quam occisus homo is est, iste visus est in eo loco in quo est occisio facta, solus; paulo

---

^a For the same idea see Cicero, *Part. Orat.* 11. 40.
^b The example that follows is a summary of a conjectural case (with its dependence on the topics of circumstantial evidence) according to the principles set forth above in 2. ii. 3 ff.

the self-respect of others; covetous, intemperate
irascible, arrogant; disloyal to his parents, ungrate-
ful to his friends, troublesome to his kin; insulting
to his betters, disdainful of his equals and mates,
cruel to his inferiors; in short he is intolerable to every
one."

53 Of the same kind is that other Accumulation,
which is very useful in conjectural causes, when the
implications, which were petty and weak because expressed separately, are collected in one place and so
seem to make the subject evident and not dubious,[a]
as follows:[b] "Do not, therefore, men of the jury,
do not consider singly the things I have said, but join
them all together and combine them into one.

XLI. "If the defendant profited from the victim's
death; if also his life is full of dishonour, his heart
most avaricious, and his family fortune very meagre;
and if that crime benefited no one but him;[c] and if
no one else could have done the deed with equal skill,
or he himself could not have done it by methods more
apt; if he neglected nothing that was necessary for
the crime, and did nothing that was not necessary;
and if he not only sought the most suitable place,
but also a favourable occasion for entering upon the
crime, and the most opportune moment for undertaking it; if he spent the longest period of time
in executing it, and not without the greatest hope
of concealing and completing it; and besides, if,
before the victim was murdered, the defendant was
seen, alone, in the place in which the murder was
committed; if soon afterward, during the very

[c] Cf., in 2. iv. 6 above, the prosecutor's use of Comparison,
and for this whole passage Quintilian, 7. 2. 42–44, on Intention
(consilium).

363

post in ipso maleficio vox illius qui occidebatur audita;
deinde post occisionem istum multa nocte domum
redisse constat; postero die titubanter et inconstanter
de occisione illius locutum; haec partim testimoniis,
partim quaestionibus argumentatis omnia conpro-
bantur, et rumore populi, quem ex argumentis natum
necesse est esse verum—vestrum, iudices, est his [1]
in unum locum [2] conlocatis certam sumere scientiam,
non suspicionem maleficii. Nam unum aliquid aut
alterum potest in istum casu cecidisse suspiciose; ut
omnia inter se a primo ad postremum conveniant,
maleficii adfinem fuisse istum [3] necesse est; casu
non potest fieri." Vehemens haec est exornatio et
in coniecturali constitutione causae ferme semper
necessaria, et in ceteris generibus causarum et in
omni oratione adhibenda nonnumquam.

54 XLII. Expolitio est cum in eodem loco manemus
et aliud atque aliud dicere videmur. Ea dupliciter
fit: si aut eandem plane dicemus rem, aut de eadem
re. Eandem rem dicemus non eodem modo—nam id
quidem obtundere auditorem est, non rem expolire—
sed commutate. Commutabimus tripliciter: verbis,
pronuntiando, tractando.

Verbis commutabimus cum re semel dicta iterum
aut saepius aliis verbis quae idem valeant eadem res

---

[1] his *HP²BE* : ex his *ΠCMx.*
[2] unum locum *H², all other MSS. but H* : uno loco *H Mx.*
[3] a]dfinem fuisse istum *inserted to fill lac.*

---

[a] *Cf.* 2. v. 8 above, on Subsequent Behaviour.
[b] All these considerations are discussed above in 2. vi. 9 ff.

commission of the crime, the voice of the victim was heard; if it is established that then, after the murder, the defendant returned home, at dead of night; that on the next day he spoke of the man's murder haltingly and inconsistently [a]—if all these indications are proved, partly by witnesses, and partly by the confessions upon torture [b] which have been adduced in confirmation, and by public opinion, which, born of evidence, must necessarily be true; then, gentlemen, it is your duty to gather all these indications into one, and arrive at definite knowledge, not suspicion, of the crime. To be sure, some one or two of these things can by chance have happened in such a way as to throw suspicion upon this defendant; but for everything to coincide from first to last, he must have been a participant in the crime. This cannot be the result of chance." This figure has force, and in a conjectural issue is almost always essential; in the other types of causes and indeed in all discourse it is to be used occasionally.

XLII. Refining [c] consists in dwelling on the same topic and yet seeming to say something ever new. It is accomplished in two ways: by merely repeating the same idea, or by descanting upon it. We shall not repeat the same thing precisely—for that, to be sure, would weary the hearer and not refine the idea—but with changes. Our changes will be of three kinds: in the words, in the delivery, and in the treatment.

Our changes will be verbal when, having expressed the idea once, we repeat it once again or oftener in

[c] A χρεία, a thought (usually ethical) developed in detail in accordance with definite rules; a favourite type of *progymnasma*.

proferetur, hoc modo : " Nullum tantum est periculum quod sapiens pro salute patriae vitandum
arbitretur. Cum agetur incolumitas perpetua civitatis, qui bonis erit rationibus praeditus profecto
nullum vitae discrimen sibi pro fortunis rei publicae
fugiendum putabit, et erit in ea sententia semper ut
pro patria studiose quamvis in magnam descendat
vitae dimicationem."

Pronuntiando commutabimus si cum in sermone,
tum in acrimonia, tum in alio atque alio genere vocis
atque gestus eadem verbis commutando pronuntiationem quoque vehementius immutarimus. Hoc
neque commodissime scribi potest neque parum est
apertum ; quare non eget exempli.

55 Tertium genus est commutationis, quod tractando
conficitur, si sententiam traiciemus aut ad sermo-
cinationem aut exsuscitationem.

XLIII. Sermocinatio est—de qua planius paulo
post suo loco dicemus, nunc breviter, quod ad hanc
rem satis sit, adtingemus—in qua constituetur
alicuius personae oratio adcommodata ad dignitatem,
hoc modo, ut, quo facilius res cognosci possit, ne ab
eadem sententia recedamus : " Sapiens omnia rei
publicae causa suscipienda pericula putabit. Saepe
ipse secum loquetur [1] : ' Non mihi soli, sed etiam
atque adeo multo potius natus sum patriae ; vita,

---

[1] loquetur H^2P^2C : loquet H : loquitur $PB\Pi EMx$.

---

[a] 4. lii. 65 below.
[b] A *quaestio infinita* ($\theta\acute{\epsilon}\sigma\iota\varsigma$) ; see Quintilian, 3. 5. 5 ff.
[c] *Cf.* Julius Rufinianus 20 (Halm, pp. 43–4) : " $\delta\iota\alpha\lambda o\gamma\iota\sigma\mu\acute{o}\varsigma$
occurs when someone discusses with himself and ponders
what he is doing or what he thinks ought to be done."
[d] *Cf.* Plato, *Epist.* 9. 358 A : " Yet this, too, you ought to
bear in mind—that none of us was born for self alone, but our

other, equivalent terms, as follows: " No peril is so great that a wise man would think it ought to be avoided when the safety of the fatherland is at stake. When the lasting security of the state is in question, the man endowed with good principles will undoubtedly believe that in defence of the fortunes of the republic he ought to shun no crisis of life, and he will ever persist in the determination eagerly to enter, for the fatherland, any combat, however great the peril to life."

Our changes will reside in the delivery if now in the tone of conversation, now in an energetic tone, and now in variation after variation of voice and gesture, repeating the same ideas in different words, we also change the delivery quite strikingly. This cannot be described with complete effectiveness, and yet it is clear enough. Hence there is no need of illustration.

55   The third kind of change, accomplished in the treatment, will take place if we transfer the thought into the form of Dialogue or into the form of Arousal.

XLIII. Dialogue—which I shall soon more fully discuss in its place *a* and shall now touch upon briefly, as far as may be sufficient for the present purpose—consists in putting in the mouth of some person language in keeping with his character, as follows (for the sake of greater clarity, to continue the same theme as above): " The wise man will think that for the common weal he ought to undergo every peril.*b* Often he will say to himself: *c* ' Not for self alone was I born, but also, and much more, for the fatherland.*d*

existence is shared by our country, our parents, and our friends "; Demosthenes, *De Corona* 205: " Every one of those men considered himself to have been born, not to his father and mother alone, but also to his fatherland."

quae fato debetur, saluti patriae potissimum solvatur.
Aluit haec me; tute atque honeste produxit usque ad
hanc aetatem; munivit meas rationes bonis legibus,
optimis moribus, honestissimis disciplinis. Quid est
quod a me satis ei persolvi possit unde haec accepi? '
Exinde ut haec loquetur secum sapiens saepe, in
periculis rei publicae nullum ipse periculum fugiet."

Item mutatur res tractando si traducitur ad exsuscitationem, cum et nos commoti dicere videamur,
et auditoris animum commovemus, sic: " Quis est
tam tenui cogitatione praeditus, cuius animus tantis
angustiis invidiae continetur, qui non hunc hominem
studiosissime laudet et sapientissimum iudicet, qui
pro salute patriae, pro incolumitate civitatis, pro rei
publicae fortunis quamvis magnum atque atrox
periculum studiose suscipiat et libenter subeat?
56 Equidem hunc hominem magis cupio satis laudare
quam possum, idemque hoc certo scio vobis omnibus
usu venire."

Eadem res igitur his tribus in dicendo commuta-
bitur rebus: verbis, pronuntiando, tractando; tractando [1] dupliciter: sermocinatione et exsuscitatione.

Sed de eadem re cum dicemus, plurimis utemur
commutationibus. Nam cum rem simpliciter pro-
nuntiarimus, rationem poterimus subicere; deinde
dupliciter vel sine rationibus vel cum rationibus
pronuntiare; deinde adferre contrarium—de quibus

---

[1] tractando *ME omit*: sed tractando *Cd*: commutabimus
tractando *Mx*.

---

[a] ἀνάστασις.   [b] *Cf.* 4. xvii. 24.   [c] *Cf.* 4. xviii. 25.

Above all, let me spend my life, which I owe to fate, for the salvation of my country. She has nourished me. She has in safety and honour reared me even to this time of life. She has protected my interests by good laws, the best of customs, and a most honourable training. How can I adequately repay her from whom I have received these blessings?' According as the wise man often says this to himself, when the republic is in danger, he on his part will shun no danger."

Again, the idea is changed in the treatment by means of a transfer to the form of Arousal,[a] when not only we ourselves seem to speak under emotion, but we also stir the hearer, thus: "Who is possessed of reasoning power so feeble, whose soul is bound in such straits of envy, that he would not heap eager praise upon this man and judge him most wise, a man who for the salvation of the fatherland, the security of the state, and the prosperity of the republic eagerly undertakes and gladly undergoes any danger, no matter how great or terrible? For my part, my desire to praise this man adequately is greater than my power to do so, and I am sure that this feeling of inadequacy is shared by all of you."

The theme, then, will be varied in speaking in these three ways: in the words, in the delivery, in the treatment. In the treatment we shall vary the theme by two means: by Dialogue and by Arousal.

But when we descant upon the same theme, we shall use a great many variations. Indeed, after having expressed the theme simply, we can subjoin the Reason, and then express the theme in another form, with or without the Reasons;[b] next we can present the Contrary [c] (all this I have discussed under

omnibus diximus in verborum exornationibus; deinde
simile et exemplum—de quo suo loco plura dicemus;
XLIV. deinde conclusionem—de qua in secundo libro
quae opus fuerunt diximus, demonstrantes argumentationes quemadmodum concludere oporteat;
in hoc libro docuimus cuiusmodi esset exornatio verborum cui conclusioni nomen est. Ergo huiusmodi
vehementer ornata poterit esse expolitio, quae
constabit ex frequentibus exornationibus verborum
et sententiarum.

Hoc modo igitur septem partibus tractabitur—ut
ab eiusdem sententiae non recedamus exemplo, ut
scire possis quam facile praeceptione rhetoricae res
simplex multiplici ratione tractetur[1]:

57 " Sapiens nullum pro re publica periculum vitabit
ideo quod saepe, cum pro re publica perire noluerit,
necesse erit cum re publica pereat; et quoniam omnia
sunt commoda a patria accepta, nullum incommodum
pro patria grave putandum est.

" Ergo qui fugiunt id periculum quod pro re
publica subeundum est stulte faciunt; nam neque
effugere incommoda possunt et ingrati in civitatem
reperiuntur. At qui patriae pericula suo periculo
expetunt,[2] hi sapientes putandi sunt, cum et eum
quem debent honorem rei publicae reddunt, et pro

[1] tractetur E : tractatur other MSS. Mx.
[2] expetunt P²B²CE : expetant M Mx : expectant B.

---

[a] 4. xlv. 59–xlix. 62.
[b] 2. xxx. 47 ff.
[c] 4. xxx. 41.
[d] The tractatio (ἐξεργασία) of the chria is freer than that
of the epicheireme in 2. xix. 28 ff. This is our oldest extant
illustration of a chria. Cf. the tractatio in Hermogenes,
Progymn. 3 (ed. Rabe, pp. 6–8).

Figures of Diction); then a Comparison and an Example (about these I shall say more in their place);[a] XLIV. and finally the Conclusion (the essential details of which were discussed in Book II,[b] when I showed how one should bring arguments to a close; in this Book [c] I have explained the nature of that figure of diction which is called Conclusion). A Refinement of this sort, which will consist of numerous figures of diction and of thought, can therefore be exceedingly ornate.

The following, then, will illustrate a treatment in seven parts—to continue the use of the same theme for my example, in order that you may know how easily, by the precepts of rhetoric, a simple idea is developed in a multiple manner: [d]

57 " The wise man will, on the republic's behalf, shun no peril,[e] because it may often happen that if a man has been loath to perish for his country it will be necessary for him to perish with her. Further, since it is from our country that we receive all our advantages, no disadvantage incurred on her behalf is to be regarded as severe.[f]

" I say, then, that they who flee from the peril to be undergone on behalf of the republic act foolishly,[g] for they cannot avoid the disadvantages, and are found guilty of ingratitude towards the state.[h]

" But on the other hand they who, with peril to themselves, confront the perils of the fatherland, are to be considered wise, since they render to their country the homage due her, and prefer to die for

---

[e] The Theme expressed simply ($\chi\rho\epsilon i\alpha$).

[f] The Reasons ($\alpha i\tau i\alpha\iota$).

[g] Expression of the theme in a new form.

[h] The Reasons.

multis perire malunt quam cum multis. Etenim
vehementer est iniquum vitam, quam a natura
acceptam propter patriam conservaris, naturae cum
cogat reddere, patriae cum roget non dare; et cum
possis cum summa virtute et honore pro patria interire, ·malle per dedecus et ignaviam vivere; et cum
pro amicis et parentibus et ceteris necesariis adire
periculum velis, pro re publica, in qua et haec et illud
sanctissimum patriae nomen continetur, nolle in
discrimen venire.

"Ita uti contemnendus est qui in navigio non
navem quam se mavult incolumem, item vituperandus
qui in rei publicae discrimine suae plus quam communi saluti consulit. Navi enim fracta multi in-
columes evaserunt; ex naufragio patriae salvus nemo
potest enatare.

"Quod mihi bene videtur Decius intellexisse, qui
se devovisse dicitur et pro legionibus in hostes immi-
sisse medios. Amisit vitam, at non perdidit. Re
enim vilissima certam et parva maximam redemit.
Vitam dedit, accepit patriam; amisit animam,
potitus est gloriam, quae cum summa laude prodita
vetustate cotidie magis enitescit.

---

^a *Cf.* Cicero, *Phil.* 10. 10. 20 : " But since through the days
and nights every kind of fate surrounds us on all sides, it is
not a man's part, certainly not a Roman's, to hesitate to give
to his country the life he owes to nature."

^b The argument from the Contrary (ἐκ τοῦ ἐναντίου).

^c The argument by Comparison (ἐκ παραβολῆς).

^d The national hero P. Decius Mus, in 295 B.C. at Sentinum
in the war against the Samnites, flung himself upon the
weapons of the enemy, and by this act of devotion brought
victory to the Romans. The like act was attributed to his

many of their fellow citizens instead of with them. For it is extremely unjust to give back to nature, when she compels, the life you have received from nature, and not to give to your country, when she calls for it, the life you have preserved thanks to your country; [a] and when you can die for fatherland with the greatest manliness and honour, to prefer to live in disgrace and cowardice; and when you are willing to face danger for friends and parents and your other kin, to refuse to run the risk for the republic, which embraces all these and that most holy name of fatherland as well.[b]

" He who in a voyage prefers his own to his vessel's security, deserves contempt. No less blameworthy is he who in a crisis of the republic consults his own in preference to the common safety. For from the wreck of a ship many of those on board escape unharmed, but from the wreck of the fatherland no one can swim to safety.[c]

" It is this that, in my opinion, Decius [d] well understood, who is said to have devoted himself to death, and, in order to save his legions, to have plunged into the midst of the enemy. He gave up his life, but did not throw it away; for at the cost of a very cheap good he redeemed a sure good, of a small good the greatest good. He gave his life, and received his country in exchange. He lost his life, and gained glory, which, transmitted with highest praise, shines more and more every day as time goes on.[e]

father (who bore the same name) in a battle against the Latins in 340 B.C. This story was a favourite historical example (see Exemplification, 4. xlix. 62 below) of patriotism.

[e] The argument from Example (ἐκ παραδειγμάτων), and the testimony of antiquity (μαρτύρια τῶν παλαιῶν).

" Quodsi pro re publica decere accedere periculum et ratione demonstratum est et exemplo conprobatum, ii sapientes sunt existimandi qui nullum pro salute patriae periculum vitant."

58 In his igitur generibus expolitio versatur; de qua producti sumus ut plura diceremus quod non modo cum causam dicimus adiuvat et exornat orationem, sed multo maxime per eam exercemur ad elocutionis facultatem. Quare conveniet extra causam in exercendo rationes adhibere expolitionis, in dicendo uti cum exornabimus argumentationem, qua de re diximus in libro secundo.

XLV. Commoratio est cum in loco firmissimo quo [1] tota causa continetur manetur diutius et eodem saepius reditur. Hac uti maxime convenit, et id est oratoris boni maxime proprium, non enim datur auditori potestas animum de re firmissima demovendi. Huic exemplum satis idoneum subici non potuit, propterea quod hic locus non est a tota causa separatus sicuti membrum aliquod, sed tamquam sanguis perfusus est per totum corpus orationis.

---

[1] quo *Mx ed. mai., all MSS. but H* : aquo *H* : a quo *Mx*.

---

[a] Conclusion (ἐπίλογος).

[b] 2. xviii. 28, 2. xxx. 47 ff.

[c] ἐπιμονή. *Cf.* also διατριβή, as, for example, in Aristotle, *Rhet.* 3. 17 (1418 a).

[d] Anon., *Schemata Dianoeas*, in Halm, p. 72. 7, cites in illustration of this figure the famous beginning of Cicero's first oration against Catiline : " How long, in heaven's name, Catiline, will you abuse our patience ? How much longer yet will that madness of yours make mock of us ? To what limit will your unbridled audacity vaunt itself ? "

[e] The basis is the common comparison of a discourse with the human body. *Cf.* ἁδρόν (4. viii. 11 above), ἰσχνόν (4. x.

" But if reason has shown and illustration con-
firmed that it is fitting to confront danger in defence
of the republic, they are to be esteemed wise who
do not shrink from any peril when the security of
the fatherland is at stake." [a]

58 It is of these types, then, that Refining consists.
I have been led to discuss it at rather great length
because it not only gives force and distinction to the
speech when we plead a cause, but it is by far our
most important means of training for skill in style.
It will be advantageous therefore to practise the
principles of Refining in exercises divorced from a
real cause, and in actual pleading to put them to use
in the Embellishment of an argument, which I
discussed in Book II.[b]

XLV. Dwelling on the Point [c] occurs when one
remains rather long upon, and often returns to, the
strongest topic on which the whole cause rests. Its
use is particularly advantageous, and is especially
characteristic of the good orator, for no opportunity is
given the hearer to remove his attention from this
strongest topic. I have been unable to subjoin a
quite appropriate example [d] of the figure, because
this topic is not isolated from the whole cause like
some limb, but like blood [e] is spread through the whole
body of the discourse.

14 above), and esp. *sufflata* (4. x. 15 above), and *dissolutum*
(*sine nervis et articulis*) and *exile* (4. xi. 16 above); Cicero,
Brutus 9. 36 and 16. 64, and *Orator* 23. 76; Horace, *Serm.*
2. 1. 2; in Plato, *Phaedrus* 264 C, Socrates' principle that
every discourse is constructed like a living creature, with a
body of its own and a head and feet, and Aristotle, *Poet.*,
ch. 7 (1450 b). See also La Rue Van Hook, *The Metaphorical
Terminology of Greek Rhetoric and Literary Criticism*, Chicago
diss., 1905, pp. 18 ff.

Contentio est per quam contraria referentur. Ea
est in verborum exornationibus, ut ante docuimus,
huiusmodi: " Inimicis te placabilem, amicis inexorabilem praebes." In sententiarum, huiusmodi: " Vos
huius incommodis lugetis, iste rei publicae calamitate
laetatur. Vos vestris fortunis diffiditis, iste solus suis
eo magis confidit." Inter haec duo contentionum
genera hoc interest: illud ex verbis celeriter relatis
constat; hic sententiae contrariae ex conparatione
referantur oportet.

59   Similitudo est oratio traducens ad rem quampiam
aliquid ex re dispari simile. Ea sumitur aut ornandi
causa aut probandi aut apertius dicendi aut ante
oculos ponendi. Et quomodo quattuor de causis
sumitur, item quattuor modis dicitur: per contrarium,
per negationem, per conlationem, per brevitatem.
Ad unam quamque sumendae causam similitudinis
adcommodabimus singulos modos pronuntiandi.

XLVI. Ornandi causa sumitur per contrarium sic:
" Non enim, quemadmodum in palaestra qui taedas
candentes accipit celerior est in cursu continuo quam
ille qui tradit, item melior imperator novus qui accipit
exercitum quam ille qui decedit; propterea quod
defatigatus cursor integro facem, hic peritus imperator imperito exercitum tradit." Hoc sine simili satis

---

^a 4. xv. 21. The ancient rhetoricians differed widely, some
regarding Antithesis as a figure of diction, others as a figure
of thought, and still others as belonging to both classes; see
Cousin, *Études sur Quintilien*, 2. 46–8.

^b παραβολή. This figure and the next two form a common
triad in post-Aristotelian rhetoric. In Cicero, *De Inv.*
1. xxx. 49, they are divisions of *comparabile* (= ὁμοίωσις).
Cf. Metaphor and Allegory, 4. xxxiv. 45, 46 above, among

Through Antithesis contraries will meet. As I have explained above, it belongs either among the figures of diction,[a] as in the following example : " You show yourself conciliatory to your enemies, inexorable to your friends "; or among the figures of thought, as in the following example : " While you deplore the troubles besetting him, this knave rejoices in the ruin of the state. While you despair of your fortunes, this knave alone grows all the more confident in his own." Between these two kinds of Antithesis there is this difference : the first consists in a rapid opposition of words; in the other opposing thoughts ought to meet in a comparison.

59 Comparison[b] is a manner of speech that carries over an element of likeness from one thing to a different thing. This is used to embellish or prove or clarify or vivify. Furthermore, corresponding to these four aims, it has four forms of presentation : Contrast, Negation, Detailed Parallel, Abridged Comparison. To each single aim in the use of Comparison we shall adapt the corresponding form of presentation.

XLVI. In the form of a contrast, in order to embellish, Comparison is used as follows : " Unlike what happens in the palaestra, where he who receives the flaming torch is swifter in the relay race than he who hands it on, the new general who receives command of an army is not superior to the general who retires from its command. For in the one case it is an exhausted runner who hands the torch to a fresh athlete, whereas in this it is an experienced commander who hands over the army to an inexperienced." This could have been expressed quite

the figures of diction. Comparisons are invented, but drawn from real life; see note on Exemplification, 4. xlix. 62 below.

plane et perspicue et probabiliter dici potuit, hoc
modo : " Dicitur minus bonos imperatores a melio-
ribus exercitus accipere solere " ; sed ornandi causa
simile sumptum est, ut orationi quaedam dignitas
conparetur. Dictum autem est per contrarium.
Nam tum similitudo sumitur per contrarium cum ei
rei quam nos probamus aliquam rem negamus esse
similem.

Per negationem dicetur probandi causa hoc modo :
" Neque equus indomitus, quamvis bene natura
conpositus sit, idoneus potest esse ad eas utilitates
quae desiderantur ab equo ; neque homo indoctus,
quamvis sit ingeniosus, ad virtutem potest pervenire."
Hoc probabilius factum est quod magis est veri simile
non posse virtutem sine doctrina conparari, quoniam
ne [1] equus quidem indomitus idoneus possit esse.
Ergo sumptum est probandi causa, dictum autem per
negationem ; id enim perspicuum est de primo
similitudinis verbo.

60   XLVII. Sumetur et apertius dicendi causa simile—
dicitur per brevitatem—hoc modo : " In amicitia
gerenda, sicut in certamine currendi, non ita convenit
exerceri ut quoad necesse sit venire possis, sed ut
productus studio et viribus ultra facile procurras."
Nam hoc simile est ut apertius intellegatur mala
ratione facere qui reprehendant eos qui, verbi causa,

----

[1] ne *Md* : quidem ne *b l Mx*.

----

[a] *Cf.* Xenophon, *Memorabilia* 4. 1. 3 : " Such as believed
themselves good by nature and looked down upon learning,
Socrates would teach that the greater the natural endow-
ments, the greater is the need of education, pointing out that
spirited and impetuous thoroughbreds, if they are tamed

simply, clearly, and plausibly without the Comparison, as follows: "They say that usually it is inferior generals who take over the command of armies from superior." But the Comparison is used for embellishment, so as to secure a certain distinction for the style. It is moreover presented in the form of a contrast. For a Comparison in the form of a contrast is used when we deny that something else is like the thing we are asserting to be true.

In the form of a negation and for the purpose of proof, Comparison will be used as follows: "Neither can an untrained horse, however well-built by nature, be fit for the services desired of a horse, nor can an uncultivated man, however well-endowed by nature, attain to virtue." [a] This idea has been rendered more plausible, for it becomes easier to believe that virtue cannot be secured without culture, when we see that not even a horse can be serviceable if untrained. Thus the Comparison is used for the purpose of proof, and moreover is presented in the form of a negation, as is clear from the first word of the Comparison.

60 XLVII. A Comparison will be used also for greater clarity—the presentation being in abridged form—as follows: "In maintaining a friendship, as in a foot-race, you must train yourself not only so that you succeed in running as far as is required, but so that, extending yourself by will and sinew, you easily run beyond that point." Indeed this Comparison serves to make more obvious the poor reasoning evinced by the detractors of those who, for example, are

when young, become useful and excellent horses, but if not broken in, become intractable and worthless;" also Quintilian, 5. 11. 24 f.

post mortem amici liberos eius custodiant; propterea quod in cursore tantum velocitatis esse oporteat ut efferatur ultra finem, in amico tantum benivolentiae ut ultra quam quod amicus sentire possit procurrat amicitiae studio. Dictum autem simile est per brevitatem, non enim ita ut in ceteris rebus res ab re separata est, sed utraeque res coniuncte et confuse pronuntiatae.

Ante oculos ponendi negotii causa sumetur similitudo—dicetur per conlationem—sic: "Uti citharoedus cum prodierit optime vestitus, palla inaurata indutus,[1] cum chlamyde purpurea variis coloribus intexta, et cum corona aurea magnis fulgentibus gemmis inluminata, citharam tenens exornatissimam auro et ebore distinctam, ipse praeterea forma et specie sit et statura adposita ad dignitatem, si, cum magnam populo commorit iis rebus expectationem, repente, silentio facto, vocem mittat acerbissimam cum turpissimo corporis motu, quo melius ornatus et magis fuerit expectatus, eo magis derisus et contemptus eicitur; item si quis in excelso loco et in magnis ac locupletibus copiis conlocatus fortunae muneribus et naturae commodis omnibus abundabit, si virtutis et artium quae virtutis magistrae sunt egebit, quo magis ceteris rebus erit copiosus et inlustris et expectatus, eo vehementius derisus et contemptus ex omni conventu bonorum eicietur." Hoc simile exornatione utriusque rei, alterius inertiae

---

[1] indutus P^2CE : induitur M : inductus Mx.

---

[a] See note on Exemplification, 4. xlix. 62 below.
[b] The story of Evangelus of Tarentum at the Pythian games; see Lucian, *Adv. Indoctum* 8–10. *Cf.* also Socrates in Xenophon, *Memorabilia* 1. 7. 2, on the bad flute-player considered in connection with imposture and the life of virtue.

protectors of a friend's children after his death; for a runner ought to have enough speed to carry him beyond the goal, and a friend so much goodwill that in the devotion of friendship he may reach even beyond what his friend is capable of perceiving. The Comparison is moreover presented in abridged form, for one term is not detached from the other as in the other forms, but the two are conjoined and intermingled in the presentation.

A Comparison will be used for vividness, and be set forth in the form of a detailed parallel,[a] as follows: "Let us imagine a player on the lyre [b] who has presented himself on the stage, magnificently garbed, clothed in a gold-embroidered robe, with purple mantle interlaced in various colours, wearing a golden crown illumined with large gleaming jewels, and holding a lyre covered with golden ornaments and set off with ivory. Further, he has a personal beauty, presence, and stature that impose dignity. If, when by these means he has roused a great expectation in the public, he should in the silence he has created suddenly give utterance to a rasping voice, and this should be accompanied by a repulsive gesture, he is the more forcibly thrust off in derision and scorn, the richer his adornment and the higher the hopes he has raised. In the same way, a man of high station, endowed with great and opulent resources, and abounding in all the gifts of fortune and the emoluments of nature, if he yet lacks virtue and the arts that teach virtue, will so much the more forcibly in derision and scorn be cast from all association with good men, the richer he is in the other advantages, the greater his distinction, and the higher the hopes he has raised." This Comparison, by embellishing both

alterius stultitiae simili ratione conlata, sub aspectus omnium rem subiecit. Dictum autem est per conlationem, propterea quod proposita similitudine paria sunt omnia relata.

61 XLVIII. In similibus observare oportet diligenter ut, cum rem adferamus similem cuius rei causa similitudinem adtulerimus, verba ad similitudinem habeamus adcommodata. Id est huiusmodi : " Ita ut hirundines aestivo tempore praesto sunt, frigore pulsae recedunt, . . ." Ex eadem similitudine nunc per translationem verba sumimus : " item falsi amici sereno vitae tempore praesto sunt; simul atque hiemem fortunae viderunt, devolant omnes." Sed inventio similium facilis erit si quis sibi omnes res, animantes et inanimas, mutas et eloquentes, feras et mansuetas, terrestres, caelestes, maritimas, artificio, casu, natura conparatas, usitatas atque inusitatas, frequenter ponere ante oculos poterit, et ex his aliquam venari similitudinem quae aut ornare aut docere aut apertiorem rem facere aut ponere ante oculos possit. Non enim res tota totae rei necesse est similis sit, sed id ipsum quod conferetur similitudinem habeat oportet.

62 XLIX. Exemplum est alicuius facti aut dicti praeteriti cum certi auctoris nomine propositio. Id

---

ᵃ παράδειγμα. Examples are drawn from history. Aristotle, *Rhet.* 2. 20 (1393 a ff.), divides Examples into this type and also that which is invented (but drawn from real life), and the latter again into the Comparison (see 4. xlv. 59 above) and the Fable. Cf. *Rhet. ad Alex.*, ch. 8 (1429 a– 1430 a), and Quintilian, 5. 11. 1 ff. and 8. 3. 72 ff. Examples are recommended especially in deliberative speaking, 3. v. 9 above; cf. Isocrates, *Ad Demonicum* 34, Aristotle, *Rhet.* 1. 9 (1368 a) and 3. 17 (1418 a). Both embellishment (*cf.* 2. xxix. 46 above) and proof (*cf.* 3. iii. 4 above) are here

terms, bringing into relation by a method of parallel
description the one man's ineptitude and the other's
lack of cultivation, has set the subject vividly before
the eyes of all. Moreover the Comparison is presented in the form of a detailed parallel because,
once the similitude has been set up, all like elements
are related.

61   XLVIII. In Comparisons we must carefully see to
it that when we present the corresponding idea for
the sake of which we have introduced the figure we
use words suited to the likeness. The following is an
example : " Just as the swallows are with us in
summer time, and when driven by the frost retire,
. . ." Keeping the same comparison, and using
Metaphor, we now say : " so false friends are with us in
a peaceful season of our life, and as soon as they have
seen the winter of our fortune, they fly away, one and
all." But the invention of Comparisons will be easy
if one can frequently set before one's eyes everything
animate and inanimate, mute and articulate, wild
and tame, of the earth, sky, and sea, wrought by art,
chance, or nature, ordinary or unusual, and can
amongst these hunt out some likeness which is
capable of embellishing or proving or clarifying or
vivifying. The resemblance between the two things
need not apply throughout, but must hold on the
precise point of comparison.

62   XLIX. Exemplification [a] is the citing of something
done or said in the past, along with the definite
naming of the doer or author. It is used with the

included among the functions of Example by our author.
In 4. iii. 5 above the function is declared to be *demonstratio*,
not *confirmatio* or *testificatio*; see note. For *facti et dicti*
in the definition *cf.* Quintilian's recommendation in 12. 2. 29

sumitur isdem de causis quibus similitudo. Rem
ornatiorem facit cum nullius rei nisi dignitatis causa
sumitur; apertiorem, cum id quod sit obscurius magis
dilucidum reddit; probabiliorem, cum magis veri
similem facit; ante oculos ponit, cum exprimit omnia
perspicue ut res prope dicam manu temptari possit.
Unius cuiusque generis singula subiecissemus exempla, nisi et exemplum quod genus esset[1] in expoli-
tione demonstrassemus et causas sumendi in similitudine aperuissemus. Quare noluimus neque pauca
quominus intellegeretur, neque re intellecta plura
scribere.

Imago est formae cum forma cum quadam similitudine conlatio. Haec sumitur aut laudis aut vituperationis causa. Laudis causa, sic: "Inibat in proelium
corpore tauri validissimi, impetu leonis acerrimi
simili." Vituperationis, ut in odium adducat, hoc
modo: "Iste qui cotidie per forum medium tamquam

[1] esset *M* : est *E Mx.*

---

that the speaker know and ponder the noblest things " said
and done " in the past, and the title of Valerius Maximus'
work, *Factorum et Dictorum Memorabilium Libri IX* ; also
Thucydides' division of his material into λόγοι and ἔργα.
See Karl Alewell, *Über das rhetorische* παράδειγμα, Kiel diss.,
Leipzig, 1913, especially pp. 18 ff. Marius Plotius (Keil,
Gramm. Lat. 6. 469) and Apsines, *Ars Rhet.* 8 (Spengel-
Hammer 1 [2]. 281. 10 ff.) treat four methods of drawing
examples : from the like, the contrary, the greater, the less;
cf. 4. xlv. 59 above.

same motives as a Comparison. It renders a thought more brilliant when used for no other purpose than beauty; clearer, when throwing more light upon what was somewhat obscure; more plausible, when giving the thought greater verisimilitude; more vivid, when expressing everything so lucidly that the matter can, I may almost say, be touched by the hand. I would have added individual specimens of each type had I not under Refining demonstrated the nature of Exemplification,[a] and, under Comparison, made clear the motives for its use.[b] Therefore I have been unwilling to make my discussion of it either too brief for it to be understood, or too long once it is understood.

Simile [c] is the comparison of one figure with another, implying a certain resemblance between them. This is used either for praise or censure. For praise, as follows: " He entered the combat in body like the strongest bull, in impetuosity like the fiercest lion." [d] For censure, so as to excite hatred, as follows: " That wretch who daily glides through

---

[a] 4. xliv. 57 above.

[b] 4. xlv. 59 above.

[c] εἰκών. Puttenham's " Resemblance by Imagerie or Pourtrait." Cf. Aristotle, Rhet. 3. 4 (1406 b ff.). In post-Aristotelian rhetoric this appears as a special figure, separate from similitudo (Comparison), 4. xlv. 59 above, to which it is yet closely akin; Minucianus, De Epich. 2 (Spengel-Hammer 1 [2]. 342) attributes greater vividness to εἰκών. Quintilian, 5. 11. 24, advises that this kind of comparison should be used less often than the kind which helps to prove our point. Cf. Cicero, De Inv. 1. xxx. 49. Polybius Sard. (Spengel 3. 108) gives nine figures related to εἰκών.

[d] Cf. Aristotle, Rhet. 3. 4 (1406 b): " When Homer [cf. Il. 20. 164] says of Achilles, ' Like a lion he rushed to meet his foe,' that is εἰκών."

iubatus draco serpit dentibus aduncis, aspectu
venenato, spiritu rabido, circum inspectans huc et
illuc si quem reperiat cui aliquid mali faucibus
adflare, ore adtingere, dentibus insecare, lingua
aspergere possit." Ut in invidiam adducat, hoc
modo: " Iste qui divitias suas iactat sicut Gallus e
Phrygia aut hariolus quispiam, depressus et oneratus
auro, clamat et delirat." In contemptionem, sic:
" Iste qui tamquam coclea abscondens retentat sese
tacitus, cum domo totus ut comedatur [1] aufertur."

63   Effictio est cum exprimitur atque effingitur verbis
corporis cuiuspiam forma quoad satis sit ad intelle-
gendum, hoc modo: " Hunc, iudices, dico, rubrum,
brevem, incurvum, canum, subcrispum, caesium, cui
sane magna est in mento cicatrix, si quo modo potest
vobis in memoriam redire." Habet haec exornatio
cum utilitatem si quem velis demonstrare, tum
venustatem si breviter et dilucide facta est.

L. Notatio est cum alicuius natura certis describitur signis, quae, sicuti notae quae, naturae sunt

---

[1] totus ut comedatur *E Mx ed. mai.* : ut tutus comeditur
M : totus ut comeditur *Mx.*

---

[a] βάσκανος ὀφθαλμός. For the example *cf.* Demosthenes,
Adv. Aristogeit. 1. 52 : " But he moves through the market-
place like a snake or a scorpion with sting raised, darting here
and there, looking about for someone upon whom to bring
down misfortune or calumny or evil of some kind."

[b] The Galli derived their name from a river Gallus in
Phrygia; who drank of it went mad (Ovid, *Fasti* 4. 366).
The worship of the Phrygian Mother Goddess was charac-
terized by extreme wildness.

[c] χαρακτηρισμός, favoured in comedy; *e.g.,* Terence, *Hecyra*
439–41 : " Well, I'll describe him so that you will recognize
him—he is tall, ruddy, curly-headed, heavy-set, blear-eyed,
and has a face like a corpse." Quintilian, 9. 3. 99, excludes
this from the figures.

the middle of the Forum like a crested serpent, with curved fangs, poisonous glance,[a] and fierce panting, looking about him on this side and that for some one to blast with venom from his throat—to smear it with his lips, to drive it in with his teeth, to spatter it with his tongue." To excite envy, as follows: " That creature who flaunts his riches, loaded and weighed down with gold, shouts and raves like a Phrygian eunuch-priest of Cybele[b] or like a soothsayer." To excite contempt, as follows: " That creature, who like a snail silently hides and keeps himself in his shell, is carried off, he and his house, to be swallowed whole."

63   Portrayal[c] consists in representing and depicting in words clearly enough for recognition the bodily form of some person, as follows: " I mean him, men of the jury, the ruddy, short, bent man, with white and rather curly hair, blue-grey eyes, and a huge scar on his chin, if perhaps you can recall him to memory." This figure is not only serviceable, if you should wish to designate some person, but also graceful, if fashioned with brevity and clarity.

L. Character Delineation[d] consists in describing a person's character by the definite signs which, like distinctive marks, are attributes of that character;

---

[a] ἠθοποιία. *Morum ac vitae imitatio* in Cicero, *De Oratore* 3. 53. 204. *Cf.* Theophrastus, *Characters*, especially xxiii, " Pretentiousness." Theophrastus developed the type; Roman comedy favoured it (*cf.* the narratives in Terence, and, for the theme, the *Miles Gloriosus* of Plautus). Of the orators Lysias employs Ethopoeia with special skill. ἠθοποιία may be connected with the simple style (see 4. x. 14 above), although the example of the figure shows an artificial elegance which *sermo* rarely had. Quintilian, 9. 3. 99, excludes ἠθοποιία from the figures.

adtributa; ut si velis non divitem, sed ostentatorem
pecuniosi describere, " Iste," inquies, " iudices, qui se
dici divitem putat [1] esse praeclarum, primum nunc
videte quo vultu nos intueatur.   Nonne vobis videtur
dicere: ' Darem vobis libenter quae clientibus [2]
dant, si mihi molesti non essetis? '   Cum vero
sinistra mentum sublevavit, existimat se gemmae
nitore et auri splendore aspectus omnium prae-
stringere.   Cum puerum respicit hunc unum, quem
ego novi—vos non arbitror—alio nomine appellat,
deinde alio atque alio. ' At eho tu,' inquit, ' veni,
Sannio, ne quid isti [3] barbari [4] turbent,' ut ignoti qui
audient unum putent seligi de multis. Ei dicit in
aurem aut ut domi lectuli sternantur, aut ab avunculo
rogetur Aethiops qui ad balneas veniat, aut asturconi
locus ante ostium suum detur, aut aliquod fragile
falsae choragium gloriae conparetur.   Deinde ex-
clamat, ut omnes audiant: ' Videto ut diligenter
numeretur, si potest, ante noctem.' Puer, qui iam
bene eri naturam norit, ' Tu illo plures mittas
oportet,' inquit, ' si hodie vis transnumerari.'

[1] putat *CE* : putabat *HPB*Π *Mx.*
[2] *lac.* ; darem vobis libenter quae clientibus *sugg. Mx.*
[3] isti *B²E* : is *M Mx* : hi *C.*
[4] barbari *BC*Π*E* : barbaris *P Mx* : barbaros *H.*

---

[a] This gesture, used by Palaestrio in Plautus, *Miles
Gloriosus* 209, is interpreted by Periplecomenus as indicating
thought. *Cf.* the statue of Polyhymnia, No. 195 in A.
Baumeister, *Bilder aus dem griech. und röm. Altertum,* Munich,
1889.
[b] *Cf.,* in Athenaeus, 6. 230, the bragging beggar who owned
in all only a drachm's weight of silver, and would shout to his
one and only slave—but using names as many as the sands in
number : " Boy ! Strombichides ! Don't set before us the
silver we use in winter, but that which we use in summer ! "

for example, if you should wish to describe a man who
is not actually rich but parades as a moneyed man,
you would say : " That person there, men of the jury,
who thinks it admirable that he is called rich, see now
first with what an air he surveys us. Does he not
seem to you to be saying : ' I'd gladly give you
clients' doles, if you didn't try my patience ! ' Yes,
once he has propped his chin on his left hand *a* he
thinks that he dazzles the eyes of all with the gleam
of his jewelry and the glitter of his gold. When he
turns to his slave boy here, his only one *b*—I know
him, and you do not, I think—he calls him now by
one name, now by another, and now by a third : ' Ho
there, you, Sannio,' says he, ' come here, see that
these barbarians *c* don't turn things upside down,'
so that unknowing hearers may think he is selecting
one slave from among many. Whispering in the
boy's ear he tells him either to arrange the dining-
couches at home, or to ask his uncle for an Ethiop *d*
to attend him to the baths, or to station the Asturian
thoroughbred before his front door, or to make ready
some other flimsy stage property which should set
off his vainglory. Then he shouts, that all may
hear : ' See to it that the money is carefully counted
before nightfall,*e* if possible.' The boy, by this
time well knowing his master's character, says :
' You had better send more slaves over there if you
want the counting done today.' ' Go then,' he

---

c Unlike Sannio, who was doubtless home-born.

d In Theophrastus, *Characters* 21. 4, the Man of Petty
Ambition " sees to it that his attendant shall be an Ethiop."

e *Cf.* Calpurnius Siculus 3. 63 f. : " Let him only vie in
feeding kids in number equal to my bulls as these are counted
at nightfall."

' Age,' inquit, ' duc tecum Libanum et Sosiam.'
' Sane.'

" Deinde casu veniunt hospites homini, quos iste
dum splendide peregrinatur invitarat.[1] Ex ea re homo
hercule sane conturbatur, sed tamen a vitio naturae
non recedit. ' Bene,' inquit, ' facitis cum venitis,
sed rectius fecissetis si ad me domum recta abissetis.'
' Id fecissemus,' inquiunt illi, ' si domum novissemus.'
' At istud quidem facile fuit undelibet invenire.
Verum ite mecum.'

" Sequuntur illi. Sermo interea huius consumitur
omnis in ostentatione: quaerit in agris frumenta
cuiusmodi sint; negat se, quia villae incensae sint,
accedere posse, nec aedificare etiamnunc audere,
'tametsi in Tusculano quidem coepi insanire et in
isdem fundamentis aedificare.'

64   LI. " Dum haec loquitur, venit in aedes quasdam
in quibus sodalicium erat eodem die futurum; quo iste
pro notitia domini aedium [2] ingreditur [3] cum hospitibus. ' Hic,' inquit, ' habito.' Perspicit argentum
quod erat expositum, visit triclinium stratum, probat.
Accedit servulus; dicit homini clare dominum iam
venturum, si velit exire. ' Itane?' inquit. ' Eamus,
hospites; frater venit ex Falerno; ego illi obviam
pergam; vos huc decima venitote.' Hospites
discedunt. Iste se raptim domum suam conicit; illi
decima, quo iusserat, veniunt. Quaerunt hunc,

[1] invitarat *Halm* : invitat *b l Mx* : *M omits.*
[2] domini edium *E* : domnediam *M* : domnaedi iam *Mx.*
[3] ingreditur *P²B²CE* : in integro *HPΠB* : it intro *Mx.*

answers, ' take with you Libanus and Sosia.' ' Very
good, sir.'

" Then by chance come guests, whom the rascal had
invited while travelling abroad in splendour. By
this event the man is, you may be sure, quite embarrassed, but he still does not desist from his natural
fault. ' You do well,' says he, ' to come, but you
would have done better to go straight to me at my
house.' ' That we would have done,' say they, ' had
we known your house.' ' But surely it was easy to
find that out from anyone. Still, come with me.'

" They follow. In the meanwhile all his conversation is spent in boasting. He asks : ' How are the
crops in the fields ? ' He says that because his
villas have been burnt, he cannot go to them, and does
not yet dare rebuild them, ' although on my Tusculan
estate, to be sure, I have commenced an insane
undertaking—to build on the same foundations.'

64   LI. " While saying this he comes to a certain
house in which a banqueting club was to meet on that
very day. As if in fact he knew the owner, the
rascal now enters the house with his guests. ' Here,'
says he, ' is where I live.' He scrutinizes the silver
which had been laid out, inspects the dining-couch
which had been spread, and indicates his approval. A
little slave boy comes up. He says aloud to the man
that the master is about to arrive ; would he wish to
leave ? ' Indeed ? ' says the man. ' Let us be off, my
friends. My brother has arrived from the Falernian
country. I shall go to meet him. Do come here at four
o'clock.' [a] The guests depart. The rascal rushes
posthaste to his own home. They, as he had bidden,
come at four o'clock. They ask for him, discover

---

[a] The dinner hour ; cf. Martial, Epigr. 4. 8. 7, 7. 51. 11.

reperiunt domus cuia sit, in diversorium derisi conferunt sese.

" Vident hominem postero die [1]; narrant, expostulant, accusant. Ait iste eos similitudine loci deceptos angiporto toto deerrasse; se [2] contra valetudinem suam ad noctem multam expectasse. Sannioni puero negotium dederat ut vasa, vestimenta, pueros rogaret; servulus non inurbanus satis strenue et concinne conpararat.[3] Iste hospites domum deducit; ait se aedes maximas cuidam amico ad nuptias commodasse. Nuntiat puer argentum repeti, pertimuerat enim qui commodarat. ' Apage te,' inquit, ' aedes commodavi, familiam dedi; argentum quoque vult? Tametsi hospites habeo, tamen utatur licet; nos Samiis delectabimur.'

" Quid ego quae deinde efficiat narrem? Eiusmodi est hominis natura ut quae singulis diebus efficiat gloria atque ostentatione ea vix annuo sermone enarrare possim."

65 Huiusmodi notationes, quae describunt quod consentaneum sit unius cuiusque naturae, vehementer habent magnam delectationem, totam enim naturam cuiuspiam ponunt ante oculos, aut gloriosi, ut nos exempli causa coeperamus, aut invidi aut

---

[1] postero die $P^2\Pi$: posteri die $PBMx$: postridie H : postera die CE.
[2] se E : *other MSS. Mx omit.*
[3] conpararat *Kayser* : conpararet C : conparat HP Mx, comparat B Π E.

---

[a] *Cf.* the situation in Plautus, *Pseud.* 960-2.
[b] *Cf.* Plautus, *Asin.* 444 ff. : [Leonida :] " The cups I lent Philodamus—has he brought them back?" [Libanus :] " Not yet." " Oh? He hasn't? Give things away, if you wish—accommodate a friend with them."

whose house it is, and, hoodwinked, betake themselves to an inn.

" They see the man the next day, tell him their story, make their complaint and their accusation. He assures them that they had been deceived by the similarity of the place and had missed their way by a whole street; [a] he had, to the prejudice of his health, waited for them late into the night. To his boy Sannio he had given the job of borrowing vessels, coverings, and servants, and the little slave, not wanting in cleverness, had quite energetically and artfully procured all these. The rascal leads his guests to his home. He says he has accommodated one of his friends with the loan of his largest mansion for a wedding. The boy reports that the silver is being recalled; for the lender had misgivings. ' Off with you,' says our man, ' I have obliged him with a mansion, I have given him my household of slaves. Does he want the silver,[b] too? And yet, although I have guests, let him use it; we shall be content with Samian.' [c]

" Why should I tell what he next brings to pass? Such is the character of the man that what he effects by empty boasting and showing-off in one day I could hardly recount if I talked a whole year."

65 Character Delineations of this kind which describe the qualities proper to each man's nature carry very great charm, for they set before our eyes a person's whole character, of the boastful man, as I undertook to illustrate, or the envious or pompous man, or the

---

[c] In this ware metal shapes were imitated. By no means the humblest ware, Samian yet represents the inferiority of earthen vessels as against those of metal. See F. O. Waagé, *Antiquity* 11 (1937). 46–55.

[CICERO]

tumidi aut avari, ambitiosi, amatoris, luxuriosi, furis,
quadruplatoris; denique cuiusvis studium protrahi
potest in medium tali notatione.

LII. Sermocinatio est cum alicui personae sermo
adtribuitur et is exponitur cum ratione dignitatis,
hoc pacto: " Cum militibus urbs redundaret et
omnes timore oppressi domi continerentur, venit
iste cum sago, gladio succinctus, tenens iaculum;
III adulescentes hominem simili ornatu subsequuntur.
Inrupit in aedes subito, deinde magna voce: ' Ubi est
iste beatus,' inquit, ' aedium dominus? Quin mihi
praesto fuit? Quid tacetis? ' Hic alii omnes stupidi
timore obmutuerunt. Uxor illius infelicissimi cum
maximo fletu ad istius pedes abiecit sese. ' Per te,'
inquit, ' ea quae tibi dulcissima sunt in vita, miserere
nostri, noli extinguere extinctos, fer mansuete fortunam; nos quoque fuimus beati; nosce te esse
hominem.' ' Quin illum mihi datis ac vos auribus
meis opplorare desinitis? Non abibit.'

" Illi nuntiatur interea venisse istum et clamore
maximo mortem minari. Quod simul ut audivit,

ᵃ διάλογοι. Quintilian, 9. 2. 29 ff., joins this figure and
Personification (next below) as one. Cf. 4. xliii. 55 above.

ᵇ Cf. Plautus, Rud. 315: "Who had three men with him,
wearing cloaks and swords (chlamydatos cum machaeris)."

ᶜ The style is Greek. Cf., for example, Euripides, Androm.
892–3: πρός σε τῶνδε γουνάτων οἴκτειρον ἡμᾶς (" I implore
you by these knees, take pity on me "), and Medea 324;
Sophocles, Oed. Col. 250, and Philoct. 468.

ᵈ Cf. Euripides, Alc. 1065: " Take me not captive who am
already captive "; Sophocles, Antig. 1030: " What feat is it
to slay the slain anew? "; Ovid, Epist. ex Ponto 4. 16. 51:
" What pleasure do you find, Malice, in driving the steel into
limbs already dead? "

ᵉ Cf. Isocrates, Ad Demonicum 21: " You will achieve
self-control if, when in trouble, you regard the misfortunes of

394

miser, the climber, the lover, the voluptuary, the thief, the public informer—in short, by such delineation any one's ruling passion can be brought into the open.

LII. Dialogue [a] consists in assigning to some person language which as set forth conforms with his character, for example: " When the city overflowed with soldiers, and all the citizens, oppressed by fear, kept themselves at home, this fellow appeared in military cloak, armed with a sword, in his hand a javelin. Three young men, equipped like him, follow behind.[b] Suddenly he bursts into the house, and in a loud voice shouts: ' Where is he, the wealthy owner of this house? Why has he not appeared before me? Why are you silent?' At this all are struck dumb with terror. The wife of the unhappy man, bursting into tears, throws herself at this creature's feet, and says: ' By all that is dearest to you in life, I pray you, pity us.[c] Destroy not anew them that are destroyed.[d] Use your good fortune kindly. We too have enjoyed good fortune. Remember that you are human.' [e] ' Why do you not surrender him to me and cease wailing into my ears? He shall not escape.'

" Meanwhile word of this person's arrival and of his clamorous threats of death is brought to the master of the house. Immediately upon receipt of these

others and remind yourself that you are human "; the verse ascribed in Stobaeus, 3. 22. 25, to the poet Hippothoön (or Hippothoüs): " Since you are human, remember the common lot of humanity " (see Nauck, *Trag. Graec. Fragm.*, 2nd ed. [1889], p. 827); Theseus in Sophocles, *Oed. Col.* 567 f.: " I know well that I am mortal and have no greater share in the morrow than you do."

[CICERO]

'Heus,' inquit, 'Gorgia,' pedisequo [1] puerorum, 'absconde pueros, defende, fac ut incolumis ad adulescentiam perducas.' Vix haec dixerat cum ecce iste praesto: 'Sedes,' inquit, 'audax? Non vox mea tibi vitam ademit? Exple meas inimicitias et iracundiam satura tuo sanguine.' Ille cum magno spiritu: 'Verebar,' [2] inquit, 'ne plane victus essem. Nunc video: iure mecum contendere non vis, ubi superari turpissimum et superare pulcerrimum est; interficere vis. Occidar equidem, sed victus non peribo.' 'Ut in extremo vitae tempore etiam sententias eloqueris! Numquam ei quem vides dominari vis supplicare?'[a] Tum mulier: 'Immo iste quidem rogat et supplicat; sed tu, quaeso, commovere; et tu per deos,' inquit, 'hunc examplexare. Dominus est; vicit hic te, vince tu nunc animum.' 'Quin desinis,' inquit, 'uxor, loqui quae me digna non sint? Tace et quae curanda sunt cura. Tu cessas mihi vitam, tibi omnem bene vivendi spem mea morte eripere?'[b] Iste mulierem propulit ab se lamentantem; illi nescio quid incipienti dicere, quod dignum videlicet illius virtute esset, gladium in latere defixit."

---

[1] pedisequo *Skutsch* (*Kleine Schriften*, Leipzig and Berlin, 1914, p. 119): pendens equo H: pedens aequo *PB* II: pedissequa *Cbl*: pedisseca *d*: pediseque *Lambinus Mx*.

[2] verebar *Orelli from a Zurich MS.*: verba *M*: verba metuebam *E Mx*.

---

[a] γνωμολογεῖς.

[b] *Cf.* in Homer, *Il.* 6. 490, Hector's words to Andromache: "But go thou to thine house and attend to thine own tasks."

tidings, 'Hark, Gorgias,' he says to the attendant of his children, 'hide them, defend them, see that you bring them up safe to young manhood.' Hardly had he uttered these words when, behold, this person appears, and says: 'You are still here, rash fool? Has not my voice frightened you to death? Appease my enmity and sate my wrath with your blood.' The master, with proud spirit, replies: 'I feared I might really be conquered. Now I see: You do not wish to contend with me in a trial at law, where failure brings shame, and success glory. You wish to kill me. True, I shall be killed, but I will die unconquered.' 'Sententious[a] even at the point of death! You do not wish to beg your life of me when you see I have you in my power?' Then the woman: 'Nay, truly he begs and implores you. I plead with you, be moved to pity. And do you, in heaven's name, clasp his knees. He has you in his power. He has prevailed over you, and do you now prevail over your spirit.' 'Why do you not cease, my wife,' says he, 'to utter words unworthy of me? Be silent, and attend to your tasks.[b] And you, why do you not, once for all, rob me of life, and yourself, by my death, of every hope of enjoying life?' The intruder thrust the weeping woman from him, and as the master began to say something or other, worthy, I am sure, of his manliness, buried the sword in his side." [c]

[c] Whereas the example of Character Delineation next above is in the spirit of comedy, this example is tragic in nature. As the notes indicate, it is probably of Greek origin, despite certain of its distinctively Roman features. Marx, *Proleg.*, p. 108, thinks that it may perhaps be referred to the *controversia* concerning the murder of Sulpicius, l. xv. 25 above.

[CICERO]

Puto in hoc exemplo datos esse uni cuique ser-
mones ad dignitatem adcommodatos; id quod oportet in hoc genere conservare.

Sunt item sermocinationes consequentes, hoc genus:
" Nam quid putamus illos dicturos si hoc iudicaritis?
Nonne omnes hac utentur oratione? "—deinde
subicere sermonem.

66   LIII. Conformatio est cum aliqua quae non adest
persona confingitur quasi adsit, aut cum res muta aut
informis fit eloquens, et forma ei et oratio adtribuitur
ad dignitatem adcommodata aut actio quaedam, hoc
pacto: " Quodsi nunc haec urbs invictissima vocem
mittat, non hoc pacto loquatur: ' Ego illa plurimis
tropaeis[1] ornata, triumphis ditata certissimis, claris-
simis locupletata victoriis, nunc vestris seditionibus,
o cives, vexor; quam dolis malitiosa Kartago, viribus
probata Numantia, disciplinis erudita Corinthus
labefactare non potuit, eam patimini nunc ab homun-
culis deterrimis proteri atque conculcari? " Item:
" Quodsi nunc Lucius ille Brutus revivescat et hic
ante pedes vestros adsit, is non hac utatur oratione?
' Ego reges eieci; vos tyrannos introducitis. Ego
libertatem, quae non erat, peperi; vos partam
servare non vultis. Ego capitis mei periculo patriam

---

[1] tropeis *P*Π *Mx* : tropheis *P*²*HBCE*.

---

a προσωποποιία. Representing an absent person as present
would not today be regarded as strictly within the meaning
of Personification. *Cf.* Cicero, *De Oratore* 3. 53. 205 (*personarum ficta inductio*); Quintilian, 9. 2. 29–37. See Georg
Reichel, *Quaestiones Progymnasm.*, diss. Leipzig, 1909, pp.
75–88, on this figure as a *progymnasma*. Making the dead
speak was sometimes called εἰδωλοποιία. *Cf.* Cicero, *Orator*

I think that in this example the language assigned to each person was appropriate to his character— a precaution necessary to maintain in Dialogue.

There are likewise Hypothetical Dialogues, as follows: " Indeed what do we think those people will say if you have passed this judgement? Will not every one say as follows: ——? " And then one must add what they will say.

66   LIII. Personification ^a consists in representing an absent person as present, or in making a mute thing or one lacking form articulate, and attributing to it a definite form and a language or a certain behaviour appropriate to its character, as follows: " But if this invincible city should now give utterance to her voice, would she not speak as follows? ' I, city of renown, who have been adorned with numerous trophies, enriched with unconditional triumphs, and made opulent by famous victories, am now vexed, O citizens, by your dissensions. Her whom Carthage with her wicked guile, Numantia with her tested strength, and Corinth with her polished culture, could not shake, do you now suffer to be trod upon and trampled underfoot by worthless weaklings? ' " Again: " But if that great Lucius Brutus should now come to life again and appear here before you, would he not use this language? ' I banished kings; you bring in tyrants. I created liberty, which did not exist; what I created you do not wish to preserve. I, at peril of my life, freed the fatherland; you, even

25. 85: " [The unaffected Attic speaker] will not represent the commonwealth as speaking, or call the dead from the lower world." Volkmann, p. 490, excludes Personification from the figures of thought; see also pp. 280 and 312 on its uses.

liberavi; vos liberi sine periculo esse non curatis.' "
Haec conformatio licet in plures res, in mutas atque
inanimas transferatur. Proficit plurimum in ampli-
ficationis partibus et commiseratione.

67   Significatio est res quae plus in suspicione relinquit
quam positum est in oratione. Ea fit per exsuperationem, ambiguum, consequentiam, abscisionem,
similitudinem.

Per exsuperationem, cum plus est dictum quam
patitur veritas, augendae suspicionis causa, sic:
" Hic de tanto patrimonio tam cito testam qui sibi
petat ignem non reliquit."

Per ambiguum, cum verbum potest in duas pluresve
sententias accipi, sed accipitur tamen in eam partem
quam vult is qui dixit; ut de eo si dicas qui multas
hereditates adierit: " Prospice tu, qui plurimum
cernis." LIV. Ambigua quemadmodum vitanda
sunt quae obscuram reddunt orationem, item haec
consequenda quae conficiunt huiusmodi significationem. Ea reperientur facile si noverimus et animum adverterimus verborum ancipites aut multiplices
potestates.

---

^a Such sentiments as are expressed in these two passages
might have been uttered by tribunes of the plebs in the time
of Marius; see Kroehnert, p. 32. L. Junius Brutus liberated
Rome from the Tarquins and founded the Roman consulate.

^b See 2. xxx. 48–xxxi. 50.

^c ἔμφασις. Meaning conveyed by implication. Really
more a trope than a figure. Cf. Quintilian, 8. 3. 83 : " There
are two kinds of Emphasis; one means more than it says,
the other often means something it does not say."

^d See 4. xxxiii. 44 above (superlatio).

^e This passage is in the spirit of the excerpts, in Cicero, De
Oratore 2. 55. 223–6, from the speech delivered in probably

without peril, do not care to be free.' " [a] Personification may be applied to a variety of things, mute and inanimate. It is most useful in the divisions under Amplification and in Appeal to Pity.[b]

67 Emphasis [c] is the figure which leaves more to be suspected than has been actually asserted. It is produced through Hyperbole, Ambiguity, Logical Consequence, Aposiopesis, and Analogy.

The emphasis is produced through Hyperbole [d] when more is said than the truth warrants, so as to give greater force to the suspicion, as follows : " Out of so great a patrimony, in so short a time, this man has not laid by even an earthen pitcher wherewith to seek a fire for himself." [e]

The emphasis is produced through Ambiguity [f] when a word can be taken in two or more senses, but yet is taken in that sense which the speaker intends ; for example, if you should say concerning a man who has come into many legacies : " Just look out, you, who look out for yourself so profitably." [g] LIV. Even as we must avoid those ambiguities which render the style obscure, so must we seek those which produce an emphasis of this sort. It will be easy to find them if we know and pay heed to the double and multiple meanings of words.

---

91 B.C. by L. Licinius Crassus on behalf of Cn. Planc(i)us against M. Junius Brutus, who had squandered his patrimony. Kroehnert, p. 31, thinks it may come from this speech, but there is no real evidence for the ascription.

[f] Quintilian, 6. 3. 47 ff., considers the play on double meanings only rarely telling, unless helped out by the facts.

[g] The play is upon the double meaning of *cernere* : to " discern " and, in judicial language, " to enter upon an inheritance ; " thus : " you who know exceedingly well how to enter upon bequests."

[CICERO]

Per consequentiam significatio fit cum res quae sequantur aliquam rem dicuntur, ex quibus tota res relinquitur in suspicione; ut si salsamentarii filio dicas: " Quiesce tu, cuius pater cubito se emungere[1] solebat."

Per abscisionem, si, cum incipimus aliquid dicere, deinde praecidamus, et ex eo quod iam diximus satis relinquitur suspicionis, sic: " Qui ista forma et aetate nuper alienae domi—nolo plura dicere."

Per similitudinem, cum aliqua re simili allata nihil amplius dicimus, sed ex ea significamus quid sentiamus, hoc modo: " Noli, Saturnine, nimium populi frequentia fretus esse; inulti iacent Gracci."

Haec exornatio plurimum festivitatis habet interdum et dignitatis; sinit enim quiddam tacito oratore ipsum auditorem suspicari.

68　Brevitas est res ipsis tantummodo verbis necessariis expedita, hoc modo: " Lemnum praeteriens cepit, inde Thasi praesidium reliquit, post urbem Bithynam

---

[1] cubito se emungere *E* : cubiti semugire *H* : cubitis emungi *CΠMx* : cubiti semugi *P* : cubitis emugi *B*.

---

[a] ἐπακολούθησις.

[b] The saying is common, *e.g.*, with reference to the freedman father of the poet Horace, in Suetonius, *De Viris Illustribus, Vita Horatii*, and to the freedman father of Bion of Borysthenes (first half, third century B.C.), in Diogenes Laertius 4. 46. *Cf.* also Plutarch, *Quaest. Conviv.* 2. 4 (631 D), and, illustrating σκῶμμα (*contumelia celata*), Macrobius, *Sat.* 7. 3. 6.

[c] See 4. xxx. 41 above (*praecisio*).

[d] L. Appuleius Saturninus, of praetorian descent, after being removed from the quaestorship by the Senate, joined the *populares*, and thereafter by demagoguery and violence

Emphasis by Logical Consequence [a] is produced
when one mentions the things that follow from a
given circumstance, thus leaving the whole matter in
distrust; for example, if you should say to the son of
a fishmonger: " Quiet, you, whose father used to
wipe his nose with his forearm." [b]

The emphasis is produced through Aposiopesis [c] if
we begin to say something and then stop short, and
what we have already said leaves enough to arouse
suspicion, as follows: " He who so handsome and so
young, recently at a stranger's house—I am unwilling
to say more."

The emphasis is produced through Analogy, when
we cite some analogue and do not amplify it, but by
its means intimate what we are thinking, as follows:
" Do not, Saturninus, rely too much on the popular
mob—unavenged lie the Gracchi." [d]

This figure sometimes possesses liveliness and
distinction in the highest degree; indeed it permits
the hearer himself to guess what the speaker has not
mentioned.

68 Conciseness [e] is the expressing of an idea by the
very minimum of essential words, as follows: " On
his way he took Lemnus, then left a garrison at
Thasus, after that destroyed the Bithynian city,

fought the Senate until he was, in 100 B.C., declared a public
enemy by that body and slain, the mob participating; see
note on 4. xxii. 31 above. Saturninus was influenced by the
political ideas of C. Gracchus. On his grain-bill see 1. xii. 21
above.

[e] βραχυλογία. Also, from another point of view, ἐπιτροχασμός. Cf. *distincte concisa brevitas* and *percursio* in Cicero, *De
Oratore* 3. 53. 202. Quintilian in 9. 3. 99 denies that βραχυλογία is a figure, yet in 9. 3. 50 treats it as a form of
Asyndeton.

[CICERO]

Cium[1] sustulit, inde reversus[2] in Hellespontum
statim potitur Abydi ". Item: " Modo consul
quondam, is deinde primus erat civitatis ; tum pro-
ficiscitur in Asiam ; deinde hostis et exul est dictus ;
post imperator, et postremo vii[3] factus est consul."
Habet paucis conprehensa brevitas multarum rerum
expeditionem. Quare adhibenda saepe est, cum aut
res non egent longae orationis aut tempus non sinet
commorari.

LV. Demonstratio est cum ita verbis res exprimitur ut geri negotium et res ante oculos esse videatur.
Id fieri poterit si quae ante et post et in ipsa re facta

---

[1] Bithynam Cium *Muenzer* : bithiniā *b* : bithinniā *v* :
bithanā *l* : viminachium *M*, Viminacium *Mx*.
[2] reversus *Baiter-Kayser* : rursus *C* : sulsus *HPB* Π :
pulsus *Mx*.
[3] *Insertion of* vii *suggested by Omnibonus and Mx.*

---

[a] Text and reference are uncertain. Friedrich Muenzer
(*Philologus* 89 [1934]. 215–25) believes that the expedition
made in 202–200 B.C. by Philip V of Macedon (Rome declared
war in 200) is indicated. Cius was the city on the Propontis
in Bithynia. The Rhodians were active against Philip;
this passage may come from an actual oration, perhaps
delivered, Muenzer thinks, by Apollonius Molo or Apollonius
ὁ μαλακός. W. Warde Fowler, *Class. Rev.* 29 (1915). 136–7,
and *Roman Essays and Interpretations*, Oxford, 1920, pp.
95–99, thinks the reference is to Lucullus and his fleet in 84
(85) B.C., when he was clearing the Hellespont and Aegean of
the forces of Mithridates for Sulla. Marx (*Viminacium*),
Rhein. Mus. 47 (1892). 157–9, doubts the possibility of
establishing the reference. For other conjectures, see A.
von Domaszewski, *Jahreshefte der oester. archaeol. Inst. in
Wien* 5 (1902). 147–9 (Lysimachia, in the Thracian Chersonese,
and Lucullus), and H. Jordan, *Hermes* 8 (1874). 75–7 (Lysimachia, and Antiochus III after his defeat in 191 B.C. by the
Romans at Thermopylae).

Alexander Numenii, *De Schemat.* (Spengel 3. 22), cites in

Cius; next, returning to the Hellespont, he forthwith
occupies Abydus." *a* Again: " Just recently consul,
next he was first man of the state; then he sets out for
Asia; next he is declared a public enemy and exiled;
after that he is made general-in-chief and finally
consul for the seventh time." *b* Conciseness expresses
a multitude of things within the limits of but a few
words, and is therefore to be used often, either when
the facts do not require a long discourse or when time
will not permit dwelling upon them.

LV. It is Ocular Demonstration *c* when an event is
so described in words that the business seems to be
enacted and the subject to pass vividly before our
eyes. This we can effect by including what has

illustration of ἐπιτροχασμός Demosthenes, *Phil.* 3. 27:
" He has gone to the Hellespont; formerly he marched
against Ambracia; Elis—that important city in the Pelo-
ponnese—he holds; against the Megarians he plotted lately."
If our author's example does not come from a speech actually
delivered, it may be an imitation of this passage.

b The reference is to Marius; see W. Warde Fowler, *Journ.
of Philol.* 10 (1882). 197–205, and *Roman Essays and Interpretations*, pp. 91–95. Marius was consul for the first time in
107 B.C., and for the fifth in 101; in 100, during his sixth
consulship, spent at Rome, he was in complete control of the
state; he departed for Asia in voluntary exile in 99; when,
after the contest with Sulla in 88, he was declared a public
enemy by the Senate and exiled, he fled to Africa; he returned
to Italy in the middle of 87, and soon thereafter received from
Cinna the proconsular *imperium* and the *fasces*; he held the
consulship for the seventh time in January 86 for a few days
until his death. The career of Marius was a common theme
in the rhetorical schools; *cf.* Seneca, *Contr.* 1. 1. 5, Valerius
Maximus, 6. 9. 14.

c ἐνάργεια. To Quintilian, 8. 3. 61, 9. 2. 40, *evidentia,
repraesentatio, sub oculos subiectio.* Sometimes Hypotyposis
(ὑποτύπωσις). Cf. *descriptio,* 4. xxxix. 51 above; Kroll,
" Rhetorik," coll. 1111 f.

erunt conprehendemus, aut a rebus consequentibus aut circum instantibus non recedemus,[1] hoc modo: " Quod simul atque Graccus prospexit fluctuare populum, verentem ne ipse auctoritate senatus commotus sententia desisteret, iubet advocari contionem. Iste interea scelere et malis cogitationibus redundans evolat e templo Iovis; sudans, oculis ardentibus, erecto capillo, contorta toga, cum pluribus aliis ire celerius coepit. Illi praeco faciebat audientiam; hic, subsellium quoddam excors calce premens, dextera pedem defringit et hoc alios iubet idem facere. Cum Graccus deos inciperet precari, cursim isti impetum faciunt et ex aliis alii partibus convolant, atque e populo unus ' Fuge, fuge,' inquit, ' Tiberi. Non vides? Respice, inquam.' Deinde vaga multitudo, subito timore perterrita, fugere coepit. At iste, spumans ex ore scelus, anhelans ex infimo pectore crudelitatem, contorquet brachium et dubitanti Gracco quid esset neque tamen locum in quo constiterat relinquenti percutit tempus. Ille, nulla voce delibans [2] insitam virtutem, concidit tacitus. Iste viri fortissimi miserando sanguine aspersus, quasi facinus praeclarissimum fecisset circum inspectans,

[1] recedemus $P^2C\Pi bv$: recedimus HPB Mx.
[2] delibans *Victorius* Mx *ed. mai.* : delabans $HP\Pi$ Mx : delabens B : edens E.

---

[a] τὰ παρεπόμενα.
[b] τὰ παρακολουθοῦντα, τὰ συμβαίνοντα.

preceded, followed, and accompanied the event itself, or by keeping steadily to its consequences [a] or the attendant circumstances,[b] as follows: " As soon as Gracchus saw that the people were wavering, in their fear that he might, by the Senate's decree, be moved to change his mind, he ordered a convocation of the Assembly. In the meanwhile, this fellow, filled with wicked and criminal designs, bounds out of the temple of Jupiter. In a sweat, with eyes blazing,[c] hair bristling, toga awry, he begins to quicken his pace, several other men joining him. While the herald is asking attention for Gracchus, this fellow, beside himself, plants his heel on a bench, breaks off a leg of it with his right hand, and orders the others to do likewise. When Gracchus begins a prayer to the gods, these creatures in a rush attack him, coming together from all quarters, and a man in the crowd shouts: ' Fly, Tiberius, fly! Don't you see? Look behind you, I say!' Then the fickle mob, stricken with sudden fear, take to flight. But this fellow, frothing crime from his mouth, breathing forth cruelty from the depth of his lungs, swings his arm, and, while Gracchus wonders what it means, but still does not move from the place where he stood, strikes him on the temple. Gracchus does not impair his inborn manliness by a single cry, but falls without uttering a sound. The assassin, bespattered with the pitiable blood of the bravest of heroes, looks about him as if he had done a most admirable deed, gaily extends his murderous hand to his

---

[c] *Cf.* Cicero, *Verr.* 2. 5. 62. 161 : " He [Verres] came into the Forum burning with criminal fury; his eyes blazed, and cruelty stood out on every feature of his face; " cited by Quintilian, 9. 2. 40, and by Gellius, 10. 3. 9.

et hilare sceleratam gratulantibus manum porrigens,
69 in templum Iovis contulit sese." Haec exornatio
plurimum prodest in amplificanda et commiseranda re
huiusmodi enarrationibus, statuit enim rem totam et
prope ponit ante oculos.

LVI. Omnes rationes honestandae studiose collegimus elocutionis; in quibus, Herenni, si te diligentius exercueris, et gravitatem et dignitatem et
suavitatem habere in dicendo poteris, ut oratorie
plane loquaris, nec[1] nuda atque inornata inventio
vulgari sermone efferatur.

Nunc identidem nosmet ipsi nobis instemus—res
enim communis agetur—ut frequenter et adsidue
consequamur artis rationem studio et exercitatione;
quod alii cum molestia tribus de causis maxime
faciunt: aut si quicum libenter exerceantur non
habent, aut si diffidunt sibi, aut nesciunt quam viam
sequi debeant; quae ab nobis absunt omnes difficul-
tates. Nam et simul libenter exercemur[2] propter
amicitiam, cuius initium cognatio fecit,[3] cetera philo-
sophiae ratio confirmavit;[4] et nobis non diffidimus,
propterea quod aliquantum processimus, et alia sunt
meliora quae multo intentius petimus in vita, ut,
etiamsi non pervenerimus in dicendo quo volumus,

[1] nec *Kroll*: ne *MSS. Mx.*
[2] exercemur Π*E*: exerceamur *H²PBC Mx*: exerceamu *H.*
[3] fecit *C*: facit *other MSS. Mx.*
[4] confirmavit *H*: confirmabat *B*: confirmabit *other MSS. Mx.*

---

[a] This is a partisan narrative, probably from a *controversia,*
of the murder of Ti. Gracchus in 133 B.C. by P. Cornelius
Scipio Nasica Serapio and his followers. On the accounts
that we have in the ancient historians see Friedrich Muenzer,
P.–W. 4. 1503.

followers as they congratulate him, and betakes
69 himself to the temple of Jupiter." [a] Through this
kind of narrative Ocular Demonstration is very useful
in amplifying a matter and basing on it an appeal to
pity, for it sets forth the whole incident and virtually
brings it before our eyes.

LVI. I have here carefully collected all the
principles of embellishing style. If, Herennius, you
exercise yourself diligently in these, your speaking
will possess impressiveness,[b] distinction, and charm.[c]
As a result you will speak like a true orator, and the
product of your invention will not be bare and
inelegant, nor will it be expressed in commonplace
language.

Now let us again and again jointly insist (for the
matter will concern us both) upon our seeking,
constantly and unremittingly, by study and exercise,
to master the theory of the art.[d] Others find this
difficult for three main reasons: they have no one
with whom it is a pleasure to practise, or they lack
self-confidence, or they do not know the right path
to follow. For us none of these difficulties exists.
We practise together gladly because of our friendship, which, originating in blood relationship, has in
addition been strengthened by the study of philosophy. We are not without self-confidence, both
because we have made no little progress, and because
there are other and better studies which we pursue
in life more intently, so that even if, in public speaking, we have not reached our goal, we shall miss but

---

[b] μεγαλοπρέπεια.
[c] τὸ ἡδύ.
[d] Cf. 1. 1. 1 above.

parva pars vitae perfectissimae desideretur; et viam quam sequamur habemus, propterea quod in his libris nihil praeteritum est rhetoricae praeceptionis.

Demonstratum est enim quomodo res in omnibus generibus causarum invenire oporteat; dictum est quo pacto eas disponere conveniat; traditum est qua ratione esset pronuntiandum; praeceptum est qua via meminisse possemus; demonstratum est quibus modis perfecta elocutio conpararetur. Quae[1] si sequimur, acute et cito reperiemus, distincte et ordinate disponemus, graviter et venuste pronuntiabimus, firme et perpetue meminerimus, ornate et suaviter eloquemur. Ergo amplius in arte rhetorica nihil est. Haec omnia adipiscemur, si rationes praeceptionis diligentia consequemur exercitationis.

[1] quae *CE Mx ed. mai.* : qua *M Mx.*

a little of the wholly perfect life.[a]   And finally, we know the path to follow, because from these books no principle of rhetoric has been omitted.

Indeed I have shown how in every type of cause one ought to find ideas.   I have told how it is proper to arrange these.   I have disclosed the method of delivery.   I have taught how we can have a good memory.   I have explained the means by which to secure a finished style.   If we follow these principles, our Invention will be keen and prompt, our Arrangement clear and orderly, our Delivery impressive and graceful, our Memory sure and lasting, our Style brilliant and charming.   In the art of rhetoric, then, there is no more.   All these faculties we shall attain if we supplement the precepts of theory with diligent practice.[b]

[a] Philodemus, *Rhet.*, ed. Sudhaus, 1. 250, says that the art of rhetoric does not conduce to a life of happiness.

[b] *Cf.* Dionysius Halic., *De Composit. Verb.*, ch. 26, Conclusion : " Here, Rufus, is my gift to you.   It will be ' worth many others ' if only you will . . . exercise yourself in its lessons every day.   For the rules in textbooks of rhetoric cannot by themselves make expert those who are eager to dispense with study and practice."

INDEX

Except for the writings of Cicero, references in the Introduction and notes to works later than the *Rhetorica ad Herennium* are not listed in this Index.

413

INDEX

animus. See character, qualities of.
anomaly. See analogy.
antanaklasis, 280 n.
Antiphon, 71 n.
antistrophe, figure of diction, 277-279
antithesis, figure of diction, 283, figure of thought, 377; 293 n.
Antonius, (Marcus), vii, xii, xv, xxviii, 245, and notes pp. 7, 33, 38, 39, 86, 207, 243, 355
antonomasia, trope, 335
Apollonius ὁ μαλακός, 150 n., 153 n., 404 n.
Apollonius Molo, xv n., 404 n.
apologus. See fable.
aposiopesis, figure of diction, 331; emphasis through, 401, 403
apostrophe, figure of diction, 283-285
Argive heroes, 119
Argo, 119
argument, =epicheireme, 61, 77, 97, 105-113, 371, defective kinds of, 113-145; in deliberative speaking, 171-173; in arrangement, 185-189; and elimination, 329; in the figure conclusion, 331; and refining, 371, 375. See also epicheireme, proof.
argumentatio. See argument.
argumentum, =realistic narrative, 22, 24; =presumptive proof, or evidence, 62, 70-72, 74, 76, 78, 8, 108, 132, 364, allegory in form of,344; ad hominem, 137 n.
Aristarchus of Samothrace, 326 n.
Aristophanes, 331 n., 342 n.
Aristotle, xv, xvi, xx, and notes pp. 32, 71, 107, 174, 175, 352
  Rhet., xxxiv, and notes pp. 4, 6, 7, 8, 11, 12, 14, 15, 18, 25, 32, 40, 50, 63, 66, 68, 70, 73, 74, 78, 82, 83, 106, 116, 121, 126, 129, 132, 142-144, 147, 160-163, 173, 191, 196, 237, 250, 288, 292-294, 297, 329, 330, 339, 342, 344, 356, 374, 382, 385
  Anal. Pr., 129 n., 237 n.
  De Part. Animal., 341 n.
  Eth. Nic., notes pp. 100, 163, 174, 197
  Hist. Animal., 341 n.
  Magna Moral., 174 n.
  De Mem. et Recollect., 208 n.
  Meteor., 220 n.
  Physica, 220 n.

Aristotle:
  Poetics, notes pp. 24, 151, 375
  Polit., 117 n.
  Problem., 237 n.
  Protrepticus, 174 n.
  Top., 163 n.
  De mundo (Ps.-Arist.), 220 n.
  See also Peripatetic doctrine, Theophrastus.
armies, subhead of might, 161
arms, subhead of might, 161
arousal, means of refining, 367, 369
arrangement, 7, 157, 185-189, 191, Homeric, 188 n., in deliberative speaking, 169-173, in epideictic, 175-183; of an epicheireme, 107-113; of images in mnemonics, 209, of backgrounds, 215
art, concealing art, 251; and nature, 205, 207, 217, 219, 221; an art called idle, 337. See also theory.
articulus, figure of diction, 294-296
Asia, 315, 405
Asianism, xix, xx, xxxiii, and notes pp. 193, 228, 257, 271, 338. See also Atticism.
assumptive, subtype of juridical issue, 43-49
Asturian thoroughbred, 389 n.
asyndeton, figure of diction, 331, 403 n.
Ateius Praetextatus, L., xv n.
Athenians, 315
Athens, 27
Atreus, 345
attentive hearers, aim of direct opening, 13-15
Atticism, notes pp. 228, 274, 301, 309, 338. See also Asianism.
author, aim of, in present treatise, vi; age, xxi-xxii; attitude to Popular party, xxiii-xxiv, 141 n., to Greeks, xxiv-xxv, 221-225, 229-2o1, 2 n., to philosophical studies, 3, 409-411, 2 n.; philosophical bias, xxv; dependence on schools, xv-xvi; knowledge of grammar, 301 n.; treatment of style, xx-xxi; his teacher, xxiii n., 33; question of authorship, vii-xiv; verses possibly made up by, 127 n., 216 n. See also *Rhetorica ad Herennium.*

INDEX

authority, commonplace from, in amplification, 147, speaker's, 309

avarice defined, 317

Backgrounds, in mnemonics, 209–213, 215, 217, 221, 225

banter, means of provoking laughter in introduction, 19

barbarism, xvi, 271, ix n., 303 n.

beauty, physical attribute, in epideictic, 175; and age, 323; in figures of speech, lasting pleasure from, 309. See also dignitas, festivitas, grace, lepos, suavitas.

benivoli auditores. See well-disposed hearers.

Bion of Borysthenes, 118 n., 402 n.

boastful man, 389–393

Boiscus, 235

brevitas, figure of thought, 402–404; in statement of facts, 24–26; and conjunction, 322; a purpose of metaphor, 342; form of comparison, 376, 378–380

broken tone of debate, 197, 201, in physical movement, 203

Brutus, Lucius (Junius), 399, 400 n.

Brutus, Marcus (Junius), 276 n., 401 n.

Caelius, Gaius, 95

Caepio (Quintus Servilius), 45, 238 n.

Caepio, Quintus (Servilius), son of preceding, 39, 87–89

Cannae, 158 n.

Capitoline Hill, 335

caricature. See fabula veri similis.

Carneades, 247 n.

Carthage, 159 277, 323, 337, 399, 159 n.

Carthaginians, 171, 277, 279, 323, 341, 158 n.

Casilinum, 171 n.

Cassius Longinus, L. (cos. 107 B.C.), 48 n.

Cassius Longinus, L. (trib. pleb. 104 B.C.), 45 n.

Cassius (Longinus Ravilla), L., 348 n.

catachresis, trope, 343

Cato (M. Porcius), vii, 245, and notes pp. xvii, xxxii, 103, 116, 158, 169, 279, 286

causa. See motive.

censure. See praise.

central point of accusation, 51, 53

Ceres, 335

challenging some one. See interpellatio alicuius.

change, in arrangement, 187; in voice, 193, 199, 201; of gestures, 203; of names, raising a controversy, 141; of sound or letters, in paronomasia, 301–307, 19-21; of word, in correction, 319–321; three ways of, in refining, 365–375; principle operating in the formation of figures, 303 n. See also reciprocal change.

character, qualities of, in epideictic, 163–169, 175, 179, 181–183

character delineation, figure of thought, 387–395

Chares, 249

charm. See festivitas, grace, lepos, suavitas, also beauty, dignitas.

Charmadas, 208 n.

chria, 365 n., 369–375, 370 n.

Chrysippus, 72 n., 83 n., 87 n.

Cicero, M. Tullius, viii, ix, xii, xxxiii, xxxvii, xxxviii, and notes pp. 31, 32, 33, 41, 217, 252, 299, 330, 339

De Inv., relation to *Rhet. ad Her.*, xxv–xxx; vii, viii, xxi, xxxv, and notes pp. xiv, xv, xxii, 4–12, 14, 16–18, 21, 22, 24, 25, 27, 28, 30, 32–37, 40–44, 46, 48, 50, 52, 58, 62–64, 66, 70, 72, 73, 80, 90, 92, 96, 98, 100, 102, 104, 106–108, 112–116, 119, 121, 125–131, 135–139, 142–144, 147, 148, 150, 153, 158, 162, 163, 171, 172, 174, 228, 237, 239, 248, 251, 274, 329, 376

De Oratore, viii, xxv, xxxiii, xxxv, and notes pp. xxviii, xxxi, 6, 7, 18, 86, 106, 136, 159, 160, 161, 174, 191, 203, 205–208, 230, 237, 238, 243, 251, 252, 270, 276, 284, 285, 296, 301, 309, 317, 320, 333, 335, 338, 339, 342, 344, 360, 398, 400, 403

Orator, notes pp. 86, 190, 191, 199, 221, 232, 248, 251–253, 265, 271, 274, 294–297, 301, 309, 317, 320, 333, 338, 339, 342, 375, 398

415

INDEX

Cicero:
Brutus, notes pp. xvii, xxviii, 31,
45, 73, 114, 189, 194, 204, 232,
244, 248, 249, 251, 253, 332,
375
Part. Orat., notes pp. 12, 50,
144–146, 151, 161, 173, 174,
208, 251, 282, 303, 309, 356, 362
De Opt. Gen. Dic., 233 n.
Top., 148 n., 174 n.
Pro Archia, 206 n.
Pro Caecina, 82 n.
Pro Caelio, 66 n.
In Cat., 262 n., 374 n.
Pro Flacco, 355 n.
Leg. Agr., 343 n.
Pro Ligario, 102 n.
Pro Murena, 103 n.
Phil., 372 n.
Pro Quinctio, 262 n., 314 n.
Pro S. Rosc. Am., 116 n.
Pro Sulla, 103 n.
In Verr., 254 n., 407 n.
Academ., 251 n.
De Amicitia, 304 n.
De Fin., 87 n., 174 n.
De Harusp. Resp., 308 n.
De Leg., 162 n., 327 n.
De Nat. Deor., 162 n., 335 n.
De Officiis, notes pp. 83, 159, 161,
162, 196, 233, 288
Paradoxa Stoic., 238 n., 289 n.
De Re Publ., 136 n.
Tusc. Disp., 206 n., 291 n.
Epist. ad Fam., 24 n., 344 n.
Cimber, 217
circumitio, trope, 336
citizenship, external circumstance,
in epideictic, 175
Cius, 405
clarity, in statement of facts, 25,
27; subhead of taste, 269–271
clause, figure of diction, 295
Cleon, 204 n.
climax, figure of diction, 315–317
Clytemnestra, 31, 51–53
Coelius (Antipater, Lucius), xvii,
273, 158 n.
cognitor, 94
cohortatio. See hortatory tone of
amplification.
Colchians, 119
collectio. See recapitulation.
colon, figure of diction, 295, 299
color, 268

comedies, plots of, **25**
Comitium, 95 n.
comma, figure of diction, 295–297
commiseratio. See pity, appeal to.
commonplaces. See loci.
commoratio, figure of thought, 374
commutatio. See reciprocal change;
change of sound or letters, in
paronomasia.
comparison, figure of thought, 377–
383, 385; with alternative
course, subtype of assumptive
juridical issue, 45, 49, 97–99; of
crimes, commonplace, 151;
in hyperbole, 339–341; division of conjectural issue, 63,
67; aspect of allegory, 345;
in a chria (refining), 371, 373;
means of provoking laughter
in introduction, 21. See also
analogy, simile, similitudo.
complexio, part of epicheireme,
106, 108, 110, 112, 142–144,
185 n.; figure of diction, 278;
eiusdem litterae, in paronomasia, 302, 304
composition, artistic, quality of
style, 269, 271–275
concessio, subtype of assumptive
juridical issue, 44, 98–104
concinna: transiectio, 272, oratio,
278, interrogatio, 284; quae
lepida et, 308; concinnae:
verborum elocutiones, 190,
sententiae, 194
conciseness, figure of thought, 403–
405
conclusion, part of a discourse, 9,
11, 61, 145, 185, in deliberative
speaking, 173, in epideictic,
183, in arrangement, 185, in
delivery, 195; figure of diction,
331–333; period used in, 297;
in a chria, 371, 375; duplex
conclusio, in proof of reason,
126
conduplicatio. See reduplication.
confirmatio. See proof.
conflicting laws, subtype of legal
issue, 35, 37, treatment, 85
conformatio. See personification.
confutatio. See refutation.
conjectural issue, 35, 53, 61–81, 97,
101, 105, 329, case sum-
marized, 363–365

416

INDEX

INDEX

INDEX

figura vocis, 190–200; figurae simulacrorum, 210; figurae=types of style, 252–268

figures: of diction, 275–347, tropes, 333–347; of thought, 347–409; in author's example of grand style, 257 n.

firmamentum, 50, 52

firmitudo vocis, 190–194

flattery, 283

fleets, subhead of might, 161

fluctuans, type of style, 264–266

fortitudo. See courage.

fortuna, subhead of plea of exculpation, 44, 100–102; commonplace, 104; in definition of external circumstances, 174; Fortuna, Fors, and Temeritas, 122

frankness of speech, figure of thought, 349–355

Fregellae, 285, 323

Fregellans, 259, 261, 323

frequentatio, figure of thought, 360–364

friendships, external circumstance, in epideictic, 165, 175, 181, 379–381, false, 383

full voice, in delivery, 193–195, 199–201

Fulvius Flaccus, M., bill of, 284 n.

functions of Senate, magistracy, and people compared, 347, of prosecutor, counsel for defence, and presiding justice compared, 347–349

Galba (Servius Sulpicius), 245

Gauls, 313, 337, 341

genera causarum, tria, 4; quattuor, 10

gesture, 7, 191, 201–205, in refining, 367. See also countenance.

Gnipho, M. Antonius, xv n.

Gorgias, an attendant, 397

Gorgias of Leontini, notes pp. 73, 146, 257, 275, Gorgianic figures, xx, 298 n.

Gorgias, the younger, xx

Gracchi, the, 245, 335, 345, 403, 283 n.

Gracchus, Gaius, 231, 233, 307, 325, and notes pp. xxxi, 344, 352, 403

Gracchus, Tiberius, 307, 407, 408 n.

grace, in delivery, 7, 411, of gestures, 201–203; in epanaphora, 277, in reasoning by question and answer, 289, in tropes, 333, in portrayal, 387

gradatio, figure of diction, 314–316

Grammar, Art of, projected by author, 271

grand style, 253–257, 263, 267

gravis figura. See grand style, gravitas.

gravitas, of delivery, 410, in dignified tone of conversation, 196, in physical movement, 202; in narrative, 24; in epanaphora, 276, in antithesis, 282, in interrogation, 284, in hypophora, 312, in synecdoche, 340, in vivid description, 356, in accumulation, 360; lacking in three figures, 308. See also grand style.

Greece, 315, 337

Greeks, 3, 11, 41, 53, 61, 145, 221, 229 ff., 235, 251, 337, 147 n.

Hannibal, xvii, 159, 171 n.

health, physical attribute, in epideictic, 175, 181

hearsay evidence, 348 n.

Hellespont, 405

Herennius, Gaius, xv, xxvi, 3, 59, 229, 409

Hermagoras, xv, xvi, xxviii, and notes pp. 4, 5, 10, 32, 33, 35, 50, 52, 70, 108, 228, 239

hiatus, 271

Hippolytus, 347

Hippothoön (Hippothoüs), 395 n.

historia, means of provoking laughter in introduction, 20; in narration, 22, 24; historiarum scriptores, 244

Homer, notes pp. 188, 248, 326, 340, 358, 396

homoeoprophoron, 271 n.

homoeoptoton, figure of diction, 299–301, 309, excessive, 273

homoeoteleuton, figure of diction, 301, 309, 238 n.

honourable, the, subhead of advantage, 85, 161–173, 287, 86 n.; kind of cause, 11, 13

hope of escaping detection, division of sign, 67, 69, 363

INDEX

hope of success, division of sign, 67, 69, 363

hortatory tone of amplification, 197–199, 201, in physical movement, 203

humanitas, 102, 104, 152, 254, 288

humile genus causae, 10, 12

humour, in introduction, 19, 94 n., 197 n. See also laughter, facetious tone of conversation.

hyperbaton, trope, 337–339, excessive, 273–275

hyperbole, trope, 339–341, means of provoking laughter in introduction, 21, emphasis through, 401

hypophora, figure of diction, 311–315

hypothetical dialogues, 399

Ignorance, subhead of plea of exculpation, 45, 101; consideration in investigating hope of success, 69, in investigating manner of life, 65; = lack of premeditation, 149

imago, figure of thought, 384–386; in mnemonics, 208–224. See simile.

imitation, means of acquiring rhetorical faculties, 7, 9, 233, 243 n.; imitatio depravata = caricature, means of provoking laughter in introduction, 19; purpose of onomatopoeia, 333

impressiveness. See grand style, gravitas.

indecision, figure of diction, 19, 329

indignation, purpose of apostrophe, 285, of vivid description, 359, of the hortatory tone of amplification (iracundia), 199, of amplification, 146 n., 143 n., 144 n. See also conquestio.

infitiatio, in conjectural issue, 52

inflata oratio, 264

iniuriae, defined, 316

innuendo, means of provoking laughter in introduction, 19

inprudentia. See ignorance.

inrisio. See banter.

insinuatio. See subtle approach.

intellectio, trope, 340

intentio, in conjectural issue, 52

interdiction of fire and water, 141, 256 n.

interlacement, figure of diction, 279

interpellatio alicuius, means of provoking laughter in introduction, 20

interpretation, figure of diction, 325

interrogation, figure of diction, 285, 253 n.

introduction. See exordium, principium, prooemium.

invective. See indignation.

invention, 3–185; 7, 11, 29, 59, 61, 69, 157, 185, 191; of comparisons, 383, 411, 106 n.

inversion, ironical, of the meaning of a word (means of provoking laughter in introduction), 19

iocatio. See facetious tone of conversation.

Iphigenia, a drama, 217

Isaeus, 12 n.

isocolon, figure of diction, 299, 257 n.

Isocrates, xv, xx, and notes pp. 7, 9, 12, 25, 86, 106, 116, 144, 146, 173, 176, 206, 240, 261, 271, 293, 298, 323, 339, 348, 382, 394

issue, type of. See constitutio.

Isthmian games, 235

Italians, 337

Italy, 159, 279, 285, 337, 341, 343

iudicatio. See point to adjudicate.

iudicatum, source of Law, 92–94, faulty citing of, 140, 142

ius, = the Law, 82, 84, 88, 90–96; in definition of justice, 162, 164; commune, 82; ius civile and ius gentium, 92 n.; and rectum, 162 n.

Judicial cause, 5–153; 47, 59, 157, 169, 173, 183

Julius Caesar, Lucius, 160 n.

Julius (Caesar), Sextus, 93

juridical issue, 35, 43–49, 85, 89, 91–105

justice, subhead of the Right, 163, topics, 165, quality of character, in epideictic, 175, 183

justifying motive, 51, 53

Kinds of causes, 5, 173 n., 175 n., 263 n. (see judicial cause, deliberative cause, epideictic), classified on moral basis, 11

421

INDEX

Labeo, Lucius, 321
Ladas, 235
Laelius, Gaius, 245, 277
Latinity, correct, subhead of taste, 269
laudabile. See the praiseworthy.
laughter, in introduction, 19–21.
  See also humour, facetious tone of conversation.
law, the " common." See ius.
Law, sources or departments of, 85, 89, 91–97
legal issue, 35–43, 81–91
legendary narrative, 23–25
Lemnus, 403
lengthening of the same letter, in paronomasia, 303, 305
lepos, 308, 316
letter and spirit, subtype of legal issue, 35–37, treatment, 81–85, 103
lex. See statute law.
Lex Acilia de repetundis, 351 n.
  Appuleia de maiestate, 38 n., 49 n.
  Domitia de sacerdotiis, 37 n.
  Plautia iudiciaria, 140–141 n., 347 n.
  Plautia Papiria, 160 n.
  Sempronia frumentaria, 38 n.
  Servilia iudiciaria, 238 n., 305 n.
  Servilia de repetundis, 37 n.
  Varia de maiestate, 260 n., 285 n.
  See also pp. 35, 37, 39, 41–43, 141, 159; Twelve Tables.
Libanus, a slave, 391
Liber, 335
licentia, figure of thought, 348–354
life, manner of, subhead of probability, in conjectural issue, 63, 65–67, 363, in epideictic, 179–183
litterarum mutatio, in paronomasia, 300, 304, means of provoking laughter in introduction, 20
loci, in mnemonics, 208–212, 214, 216, 220, 224; communes, 72, 74, 80, 82, 84, 96, 98, 102, 104, 146 ff., 182; of justice, 164; division of, in deliberative speaking, 168; ordering of, in arrangement, 188; locus = place, division of sign, 28, 66–68, 98, 362
love at first sight, 115
Lucilius (Gaius), 95, 37 n.

Lucullus, 404 n.
lumen, 308
Lysias, notes pp. 82, 263, 331, 387
Lysimachia, 404 n.
Lysippus, 249

Macedonians, 307, 315, 335–337
magnitudo vocis, 190–192
majesty of the state, sovereign, defined, 39, 87–89, 317, 265 n.
Malleolus, 43
man power, recruiting of, subhead of might, 161
manuscripts of treatise, xxxvii–xl
Marcius Rex, family of, 217
Marius, (Gaius), notes pp. xv, 307, 308, 350, 400, 405
Mars, 337
Marsic War, 159, and notes pp. 139, 140, 321
maxim, figure of diction, 289–293, period in, 297; 240 n.
meagre style, 267
Medea, notes pp. 119, 129, 131
mediocris argumentatio, 113; mediocris figura: see middle style.
Megara, 27
membrum orationis, figure of diction, 294, 298
memory, 205–225; xix–xx, 6 n., 157, 411; natural, 205, 207, 217, 219, artificial, 207 ff.
Menelatis, 217
mentitio, subhead of craft, 160
mercy, plea for, subhead of acknowledgement of the charge, 45, 101, 103–105, 129, 149
metaphor. See translatio.
metonymy, trope, 335–337
Metrodorus, 208 n.
middle style, 253, 259–261, 263, 265
might, subhead of security, 161, 171
mime, a, 45
misericordia. See pity, appeal to.
Mithridates, 404 n.
mnemonic system, 207–225
modestia. See temperance.
modesty claimed by Greek writers, 231, 235, 237
mollitudo vocis, 190, 192, 196–200
money, consideration in motive, 63, 111, 125, in hope of success, 69; subhead of craft, 161; desire for, among topics of temperance, 167; 311, 321, 300 n.

INDEX

mos, source of Law, 82, 84, 88.
See also custom, legal.
motive, subhead of probability, in
conjectural issue, 63
motus corporis, 190, 200–204
Mucius (Scaevola), Publius, 95
Myron, 249

Naevius, 249 n.
naïvety, means of provoking
laughter in introduction, 19
narratio, part of a discourse, 8;
kinds of, 22–28, 30, 58, 144,
in a conjectural cause, 60, in a
legal cause, 80, in a deliberative
speech, 168, in epideictic, 178;
in arrangement, 184, 186; type
of conversational tone, 196,
198–202, 262 n., in physical
movement, 202; and historiography, 24 n.
nature, source of Law, 83, 87, 91,
93; source of vocal volume,
191. See also memory, natural;
art.
necessity, subhead of plea of exculpation, 45, 47, 101
negation, form of comparison,
377, 379
Neptunian gulfs, 265
Nestor, 188 n., 340 n.
nominatio, trope, 332–334
notatio, figure of thought, 386–
394; of images in mnemonic
system, 214
novel tale, means of provoking
laughter in introduction, 21
Numantia, 277, 323, 399
Numantines, 323

Obscenity, avoided in metaphor,
343
occasion, division of sign, 67, 69,
363
occultatio, figure of diction, 320
ocular demonstration, figure of
thought, 405–409
Olympic games, 235, 234 n.
omitting letters, in paronomasia,
303–305
onomatopoeia, trope, 333–335
opening, direct. See principium.
Orestes, 31, 47, 51, 123
organization of treatise, xviii–
xix, 60 n.

Pactum. See agreement.
Pacuvius, (Marcus), 123–125, 137,
241, 94 n., 131 n., 134 n.
painting and poem, 327
Palamedes, 109
Panaetius, 196 n.
paralipsis, figure of diction, 321
parallelism in structure and sound,
298 n.
paromoeon, 271 n.
paronomasia, figure of diction, 301–
309, 253 n., 257 n.
parts of a discourse, xviii, 6 n., 9,
59
pathetic tone of amplification, 197,
199, 201, in physical movement,
203–205
Pelias, King, 119
Pelion's woods, 119
perduellionibus, 264
Pergamum, 6 n., 133
period, figure of diction, 297, 275,
339, 294 n.
Peripatetic doctrine, xv, xviii, and
notes, pp. 6, 94, 156, 184, 196,
229, 242, 247, 252, 263, 268,
294, 303. See also Aristotle,
Theophrastus.
periphrasis, trope, 337
permissio. See surrender.
permutatio, trope, 344–346
persecutio, 88
personification, figure of thought,
399–401, 198 n.
persuasion, non-technical means of,
74 n.
perversio, means of hyperbaton,
336–338
petitio, 88
petty kind of cause, 11, 13
Philemon, 280 n.
Philip V of Macedon, expedition of,
404 n.
Philoctetes, 333
Philodemus, *Rhetoric*, notes pp.
137, 189, 190, 236, 250, 271,
411
philosophy, 3, 121–123, 137, 409–
411; philosophers as against
rhetoricians on education, 246 n.
phrase, figure of diction, 295–297
Phrygian priest, 387
physical attributes, in epideictic,
175, 181; physical beauty and
age, 323

INDEX

proposition, part of epicheireme (see expositio), 107, 109, 185, defective , 115–121, 135; propositio=affirmation, in reasoning by question and answer, 287

Protagoras, 7 n., 73 n.

prudentia. See wisdom.

pun. See litterarum mutatio, paronomasia.

purgatio. See exculpation.

Pythagoras, 289 n., 290 n.

Quadruplator, 132, 284 n., 394

quaestio: see question for decision, torture; quaestio infinita, 366 n.

question for decision, 51

Ratio, part of epicheireme, 106, 108 n., faults of, 120–124; defensionis, 51, 53

ratiocinatio, figure ot diction, 284–288, 257 n.; subtype of legal issue, 34, 40, 88–90

rationis confirmatio. See proof.

realistic narrative, 23–25

reason, part of epicheireme, 107, 108 n., faults of, 121–125; proof of the : see proof.

reasoning, by contraries, figure of diction, 293–295; by question and answer, figure of diction, 285–289, 257 n.; from analogy, subtype of legal issue, 35, 41, 89–91

recapitulation, means of provoking laughter in introduction, 21. See also conclusion, résumé.

receptive hearers, aim of direct opening, 13–15

reciprocal change, figure of diction, 325–327

recklessness defined, 317; 167–169

rectum. See the Right.

redeeming captives, after Cannae, 159

reduplication, figure of diction, 325, 198 n.

refining, figure of thought, 365–375; of invented matter, 107

refutation, defined, 9–11, 33 ff., 59, 61, of defective arguments, 113 ff.; in deliberative speaking, 171–173, in epideictic, 175; arrangement in, 189; and tone of debate, 197

rejection of responsibility, subtype of assumptive juridical issue, 45, 47–49, 105

remotio criminis. See rejection of responsibility.

repetitio. See epanaphora.

reprehensio, of defective arguments,· 112 ff., 120, 10 n. See also refutation.

residues, method of, 329 n.

résumé, part of epicheireme, 107 113, faulty, 143–145

reversal of order, in hyperbaton, 337 n.

rhetoric, censured, 137; and life of happiness, 409–411; and jurisprudence, 90 n., 92 n.; originally judicial, 5 n.; and graphic arts, 248 n.; and philosophy, 246 n.; and poetry, 229 n.; rhetorical question, 284 n.

Rhetorica ad Alexandrum, xv, and notes pp. 6, 9, 12, 13, 32, 62, 66, 70, 73, 74, 100, 101, 144, 145, 147, 151. 174, 175, 242, 243, 345, 382

Rhetorica ad Herennium, as lecture notes, xxi ff.; dating of, xxv f.; style of, xxxii f.; later history of, xxxiv f.; translations of, xxxv f.; editions of, xxxvii; MSS. of, xxxvii–xl; analysis of contents,xlv–lviii ; called *Rhetorica Nova* and *Rhetorica Secunda*, viii. See also author.

Rhodes, 236 n.

Rhodian rhetoric, xv, and notes pp. 6, 150, 153, 193, 270

Rhodians, 248 n., 404 n.

rhythms, doctrine of, xxxiii, 256 n., 338 n., 339 n.

Right, the, subhead of the honourable, 53, 85, 163–169, 171

Roman people, 139, 259, 261, 277, 279, 323, 331, 341

Rome, 303, 399

rumours, in confirmatory proof, 67, 75, 79, 365

Samian ware, 393

Sannio, a slave, 389, 393

Saturninus, Lucius (Appuleius), 39, 49 n., 88 n., 307, 403

Scipio Aemilianus, P. Cornelius, 159, 245, 277, 337

425

INDEX

Scipio (Africanus maior), P. Cornelius, 158 n., 159 n., 283, 315, 335
Scipio Nasica (Corculum), P. Cornelius, 158 n., 279 n.
Scipio Nasica Serapio, P. Cornelius, 308 n., 408 n.
scriptum et sententia. See letter and spirit.
security, subhead of advantage, 161, 169, 171, 173, 179, 369
sententia, figure of diction, 288-292, period in, 296; scriptum et, 34-36, treatment, 80-84, in issue of ambiguity, 84-86; in allegory, 344; figurae sententiarum, 346-408
serious tone of conversation. See dignitas.
sermo, aspect of vocal flexibility, 192, 194, 196, 198-200, in physical movement, 202; cotidianus, 260, 336; inliberalis, 266; vulgaris, 408; uti pauco sermone, 342. See also cotidiana.
sermocinatio, figure of thought, 394-398, in refining, 366-368
shifting of question of guilt, subtype of assumptive juridical issue, 45, 47, 99
shortening of the same letter, in paronomasia, 303
sign, division of conjectural issue, 63, 67, 69, 77, 79, 363-365
significatio, figure of thought, 400-402; = expressiveness, aim of onomatopoeia, 332
simile, figure of thought, 385-387; faulty, in embellishment, 141, 143. See also comparison, similitudo, analogy.
similiter cadens. See homoeoptoton.
similiter desinens. See homoeoteleuton.
similitudo, figure of thought, 376-382, 384; aspect of allegory, 344; emphasis produced through, 400, 402; justifying metaphor, 342; hyperbole with comparison formed from, 340; means of provoking laughter in introduction, 20; similitudines rerum et verborum, in mnemonics, 214-216, 222. See also analogy, comparison, imago, simile.

Simo, 27
Simonides, 327 n.
simple style, 253, 261, 263, 265, 267
Simylus, 206 n.
Sisenna, 266 n.
slack style, 265-267
slapping the thigh, 205
smile of approbation, means of provoking laughter in introduction, 21
Socrates, notes pp. xi, 107, 208, 326, 375, 378, 380
solecism, xvi, 271, 303 n.
Sophists, xvi, 205 n.; Parian, 242 n. See also Gorgias, Prodicus, Protagoras.
Sophocles, notes pp. 82, 266, 282, 394, 395
Sosia, a slave, 391
sources, doctrinal, of treatise, xv ff.
Spaniards, 341
Spartans, 315
spatium. See time, duration of.
speaker's functions, 5, 9, 11, 33, 59, and notes pp. 6, 184, 190
speed, accelerated, subhead of craft, 161
spes celandi, division of sign, 66, 68, 362
spes perficiendi, division of sign, 66, 68, 362
sponsio, 311 n.
statement of facts. See narratio.
status. See constitutio.
statute law, department of Law, 13, 81, 83, 85, 89, 91, 93, 95, 147
(Stilo), Lucius Aelius, xv n., 275
Stoic doctrine, xv, xvi, and notes pp. 6, 7, 9, 32, 83, 86, 91, 107, 161, 162, 163, 173, 174, 175, 196, 220, 268, 269, 275, 289, 290, 291, 326
strategy, division of security, 171
strength, consideration in hope of success, 69; physical attribute, in epideictic, 175, 181; 323, 343, 399
stultitia. See naïvety.
style, xx, 7, 229-411, 156 n.; qualities of, 269 ff.; kinds of, 253 ff., faulty, 263-267; of treatise, xxxii f.; beauty and impressiveness of, as against grace and elegance, 309

426

INDEX

suasoriae, xvii, 157–159, 171, 8 n., 138 n., 307 n.

suavitas, of delivery, 194, of style, 408, 274 n.

subiectio, figure of diction, 310–314

subsequent behaviour, division of conjectural issue, 63, 73

subtle approach, in introduction, 13, 17–21, 29, 169, 175 n., 187 n.

sufflata, type of style, 262–264

Sulla, notes pp. 37, 48, 307, 347, 404, 405

Sulpicius (Rufus), P., 47, 141, 307, and notes pp. 280, 312, 325, 343, 397

summing up, part of conclusion, 145, 147, in epideictic, 183. See also résumé, recapitulation.

superiority, hyperbole formed from, 341

superlatio, trope, 338–340. See also exsuperatio.

surrender, figure of diction, 327–329, 253 n., 257 n.

suspicio. See innuendo.

sustained tone of debate, 197, 201, in physical movement, 203

swollen style, 263–265

synecdoche, trope, 341

synonymy, figure of diction, 325

Tarpeian Rock, 48 n., 335

taste, quality of style, 269–271

Tatius, Titus, 273

temperance, subhead of the Right, in deliberative speaking, 163, topics, 167; quality of character, in epideictic, 175, 181, 183

tempus, subhead of sign, 66, 68, 98, 362; tria tempora for use of subtle approach, 16; tria tempora considered in presumptive proof, 70–72

Terence, notes pp. 260, 291, 300, 335, 386, 387

terms: current, subhead of clarity, 271, in introduction, 21, in simple style, 253, metonymies and, 337; proper, subhead of clarity, 271, = literal, 255; figurative, 255; in grand and middle styles, 253. See also cotidiana.

testimony, and examples, 231, 237, 239; 365. See also witnesses; torture; proof, presumptive; rumours.

Teucer, 35

Thasus, 403

Thebans, 315

Theodectes, 144 n.

Theophrastus, xvi, and notes pp. 6, 107, 190, 191, 194, 202, 209, 220, 253, 268, 304, 344, 387, 389

theory, means of acquiring rhetorical faculties, 7–9; Greek, of examples, 253; precept and example, 231. See also art; practice and theory.

Thesprotus, 131

thinning the same letter, in paronomasia, 303–305

Thrasymachus, 261 n., 339 n.

Thucydides, notes pp. 71, 168, 259, 271, 384

time, duration of, division of sign, 67, 69, 363; point of, division of sign, 67, 69, 363

Timon of Athens, 290 n.

Tisias, 146 n., 184 n.

title of treatise, xv

tone, of amplification, 197–199, in physical movement, 203–205; of conversation, 193, 195, 197, 199–201, in physical movement, 203; of debate, 197, 201, in physical movement, 203

topics. See loci.

tormenta, torture, 74; engines of war, 160

Torquatus, T. Manlius, 159 n.

torture, testimony given under, 75–77, 365

tractatio, of the three kinds of causes, 5 ff.; of narration, 25 n.; of the types of issue, 49 ff., conjectural, 61–81, 61 n., legal, 81–89, juridical, 91–105; of arguments in judicial causes, 105–153, 106 n., in deliberative, 169–173, in epideictic, 173–185, 175 n.; of a chria, in refining, 365, 367–369, 371–375; of the types of style, 268 n.

traductio. See transplacement.

tragedy, 98 n., uses legendary tale, 23; tragedian's delivery, 199

427

INDEX

transference, subtype of legal issue, 35, 39-41, treatment, 89
transgressio. See hyperbaton.
transiectio. See transposition.
transition, figure of diction, 317-319
translatio, subtype of legal issue, 34, 38-40, treatment, 88; —metaphor, trope, 342-344, in allegory, 344, in comparison, 382; criminis, subtype of assumptive juridical issue, 44, 46, 98
translation of Greek technical terms, xxi, 251
transplacement, figure of diction, 279, excessive, 273
transposition, of words, in hyperbaton, 273, 337, 339, in reciprocal change, 325; of letters, in paronomasia, 303-305
treason. See majesty of the state.
trials, 37, 39, 43, 45, 49, 93-95, and notes pp. 38, 48, 66, 276, 314, 321, 348, 355, 401
Triptolemus, 247
tropes, 333-347, xii n.
Troy, 333
turpe genus causae, 10, 12, 16-18
Tusculan estate, 391
tuta. See security.
Twelve Tables, notes pp. 41, 42, 92, 95

Ulysses, 35, 109, 111, 134 n.
understatement, figure of thought, 355
unexpected turn. See praeter expectationem.
unknown authors possibly drawn upon, notes pp. 26, 127, 129, 134, 216, 306, 308, 315, 405, 408
utilitas, aim in deliberative speaking, 160, 168; communis, in definition of equity, 94; threefold, of the direct opening, 20

Varius Hybrida, Q., 140 n., 260 n., 285 n.
verse, means of provoking laughter in introduction, 21
Vestini, Pinnensian, 139
Viminacium, 404 n.
virtues, in plea for mercy, 103; " the primary ", in deliberative speaking, 163-169, 171-173, in epideictic, 175 n., 177-183; virtue and riches, 279-281, and fortune, 289, 291, and habit, 289, and envy, 319, and culture, 379
vis, subhead of security, 160, 170; 16, 64, 98, 100
vita. See life, manner of.
vocal flexibility, 191, 193, 197-201; stability, 191-195; volume, 191-193
voice, in definition of delivery, 7, quality, 191-201, in paronomasia, 301, in refining, 367

Wealth, external circumstance, in epideictic, 175, 183, means of exciting envy in introduction, 17, and virtue, 281, and friendship, 291. See also money.
well-disposed hearers, aim of direct opening, 13, 15-17
wisdom, subhead of the Right, in deliberative speaking, 163-165, 167, quality of character, in epideictic, 175, 183; wise man and his country's peril, 367-375; 137, 299, 351
witnesses, in confirmatory proof, 75-77, 365; in mnemonic system, 215. See also testimony.
women's motive in committing crime, 287

Xenophon, 235 n., 378 n., 380 n.

Zethus, 137

428

INDEX OF GREEK WORDS

References are to the notes, save for a few items (indicated
by a small p.) in the text of the Introduction.

INDEX OF GREEK WORDS

INDEX OF GREEK WORDS

INDEX OF GREEK WORDS

INDEX OF GREEK WORDS